HONG KONG
The Anthropology of
a Chinese Metropolis

CURZON ANTHROPOLOGY OF ASIA SERIES

Series editor
Grant Evans
University of Hong Kong

Asia today is one of the most dynamic regions of the world. The previously predominant image of 'timeless peasants' has given way to the image of fast-paced business people, mass consumerism and high-rise urban conglomerations. Yet much discourse remains entrenched in the polarities of 'East vs. West', 'Tradition vs Change'. This series hopes to provide a forum for anthropological studies which break with such polarities. It will publish titles dealing with cosmopolitanism, cultural identity, representations, arts and performance. The complexities of urban Asia, its elites, its political rituals, and its families will also be explored.

Dangerous Blood, Refined Souls
Death Rituals among the Chinese in Singapore
Tong Chee Kiong

Anthropology and Colonialism in Asia
Reflections on the Japanese, Dutch, Chinese, and Indian Experiences
Edited by Jan van Bremen and Akitoshi Shimizu

Folk Art Potters of Japan
Beyond an Anthropology of Aesthetics
Brian Moeran

HONG KONG
The Anthropology of
a Chinese Metropolis

Edited by
Grant Evans and Maria Tam

CURZON

First published in 1997
by Curzon Press
15 The Quadrant, Richmond
Surrey, TW9 1BP

© 1997 G. Evans and M. Tam

Typeset in Times by LaserScript, Mitcham, Surrey
Printed in Great Britain by
Biddles Limited, Guildford and Kings Lynn

British Library Cataloguing in Publication Data
A catalogue record for this book is available from the British Library

Library of Congress in Publication Data
A catalogue record for this book has been requested

ISBN 0–7007–0601–1 (hbk)
ISBN 0–7007–0602–X (pbk)

CONTENTS

v

LIST OF ILLUSTRATIONS

Figures

1

INTRODUCTION
THE ANTHROPOLOGY OF
CONTEMPORARY HONG KONG

Grant Evans & Maria Tam

When anthropologist Barbara Ward arrived in Hong Kong in 1950 she remarked that in 'the harbour itself, all the local craft were under sail; in the New Territories every particle of flat or terraced land was under rice . . .'. Indeed, rural rhythms still pulsated faintly through the city: 'Street life was also marked by seasonal changes of colour, for most men wore Chinese suits – black in summer and soft bluish grey with wide white turned back cuffs in autumn and winter' (1985:ix). Ward came to Hong Kong firmly convinced that a central tenet of anthropology is the cross-cultural study of meaning, the attempt to see 'through other eyes'. She herself did this by studying a group marginal to mainstream of Cantonese society, the 'Tanka' or boat people. Like many anthropologists of her day she travelled out of the city to carry out her main fieldwork. In the academic division of labour which had developed in both Europe and America anthropologists were allocated tribal peoples and peasants as well as exotic (to some people 'irrational') belief systems, while sociologists studied industrial societies, cities and 'rationality'.

But world politics also dictated where, when and how anthropological fieldwork was done. Prior to 1950 few anthropological studies had been written about China; the work by Fei Hsiao Tung and Frances Hsu was exceptional. After the communist revolution in China anthropology was vilified as an 'imperialist' discipline and disappeared from the mainland until its recent revival (Guldin 1994). Thus, if anthropologists wished to study 'China' they were confined to Hong Kong and Taiwan, so when anthropologists came to Hong Kong in the 1950s and 1960s they invariably headed off to the still rural villages of the New Territories to study what was left of 'traditional China'. The influential work on

1

Chinese lineages by Maurice Freedman was partly based on fieldwork there, as were many other studies. Anthropologists came to Hong Kong to investigate 'traditional China', not the rapidly growing modern city of Hong Kong.

There were some exceptions to this rule however, including an insightful study of a small factory's organization written by Barbara Ward in the mid-1960s where she tried 'to discern what, if anything, was specifically 'Chinese' about the socio-economic relationships involved' (1985:140). Culture came into play 'only in those areas where the demands of technology itself were not overriding' (1985:140), and she found a sum of 'intangibles' (1985:169) which added up to something like a 'Chinese style for running economic institutions' (1985:169), or at least a perceived difference in style. In the context of recent mythologising about the 'uniqueness' of the Chinese firm (trenchantly critiqued by Greenhalgh 1994), Ward's study stands out as a sober and careful piece of research. Perhaps it is also the first real anthropological study of modern Hong Kong. While others did some research in urban locations what they documented there was the persistence of 'tradition'. Only in the early 1970s did urban anthropological research consciously begin with the work of Fred Blake, Greg Guldin, John Meyers and Eugene Cooper. However, this work soon stalled, and when the 'real China' opened up in the 1980s anthropologists flowed across the borders.

Institutional factors also influenced the anthropological study of Hong Kong. When an anthropology department was established at the Chinese University of Hong Kong in 1980 following a division from the sociology department, the emphasis of its staff was on the study on Chinese minorities and Chinese 'traditional' culture. At the University of Hong Kong anthropology, for various reasons, remained a minor stream within the sociology department. In general, it was sociologists who taught about and studied urban industrial Hong Kong.

Only recently have anthropologists begun to focus on modern Hong Kong society. This corresponds to a global shift in anthropological interest which has broken the straightjacket of the old academic division of labour and allowed the anthropological gaze to roam over the whole of human action. Furthermore, in China itself anthropology has revived and it is no longer confined to the ethnology of minorities, but also focuses on the Han and urban anthropological research (Guldin and Southall 1993). In Hong Kong these re-orientations have also been spurred on throughout the 1980s and 1990s by the prospects of re-unification with China in 1997 and an ever intensifying cultural debate about 'Hong Kong Identity'.

CULTURE & IDENTITY

It was the closure of the border with China following the communist revolution in 1949 that gave Hong Kong a heightened sense of distinctiveness. Prior to then it was primarily seen as a place of transit. The migrants who flooded into Hong Kong after the revolution maintained this mood for a while in the 1950s, but soon it became apparent that most of them were here for good. Indeed, the British Colonial Government initially thought there would be a reflux of refugees when conditions stabilised on the mainland. The realisation that the thousands of refugees in their squatter settlements were here to stay brought into existence the massive public housing programme which has gone on ever since. Many of these migrants were from urban China, and fortuitously combined with migrant capital from Shanghai they provided the essential ingredients for the rapid transformation of Hong Kong into a modern industrial society. By 1984, when the Joint Declaration was signed between London and Beijing for the return of Hong Kong to China, a whole new generation had been born and bred in Hong Kong and a unique cultural formation had established itself in the colony. Writing in the *China Quarterly* in 1984 Hugh Baker declared 'The Emergence of Hong Kong Man':

> He is go-getting and highly competitive, tough for survival, quick-thinking and flexible. He wears western clothes, speaks English or expects his children to do so, drinks western alcohol, has sophisticated tastes in cars and household gadgetry, and expects life to provide a constant stream of excitement and new opening. But he is not British or western (merely Westernized). At the same time he is not Chinese in the same way that citizens of the People's Republic of China are Chinese. . . . Hong Kong Man is *sui generis* and the problems of the territory's future are more difficult to resolve because of it.
>
> (1984:478–9)

One might remark that not only is Baker's 'Hong Kong Man' close to journalistic cliché, but also very middle class and male. A few years later Wong Siu-lun argued: 'The Hong Kong Chinese may be described as Westernized only in a superficial sense. They have adopted a number of western folkways [unspecified], but a substantial number of them still adhere to traditional Chinese mores on various aspects of social living' (Wong 1986:307). In 1988 Lau Siu-Kai and Kuan Hsin-

3

Chi published the most comprehensive exploration of the 'mentality' of Hong Kong in their *The Ethos of the Hong Kong Chinese*. They wrote: 'In our 1985 survey, an astonishingly large proportion of respondents (59.5 percent) identified themselves as 'Hongkongese' (*HPung Góng yàhn*) when they were asked to choose between it and 'Chinese'. This Hong Kong identity, though not implying a rejection of China or the Chinese people, necessarily takes China or the Chinese people as the reference group and marks out the Hong Kong Chinese as a distinctive group of Chinese' (1988:2). The Hong Kong ethos, they say, 'represents a mixture of traditional Chinese culture and modern cultural traits . . .' (1988:2). Since then the debate over Hong Kong 'identity' has sharpened. The following book is a product of that debate and is a concerted attempt by anthropologists and people engaged in cultural studies to examine the nature of contemporary Hong Kong culture and society.

As is immediately apparent from the few statements reproduced above, the discourse on Hong Kong culture among academics often echoes the terms found in tourist brochures: Hong Kong is a place where 'East meets West', but where 'Chinese tradition' still holds sway. The common sense appeal of these categories to both *gwáilóu* (foreigner) and Chinese academics, advertising copywriters, journalists and the person in the street who has been brought up on a diet of this rhetoric is itself intriguing. It is an idea which has both a history and a theory of culture embedded within it.

The history of the idea is intimately bound up with Hong Kong's colonial history which until relatively recently saw a radical social and cultural separation between the British colonial officials and expatriate population and their Chinese subjects. For a long time 'East' met 'West' in a kind of cultural stand-off. Of course all colonial powers need to develop a local elite that respects the achievements of the dominant power and who is able to act as 'cultural translators' between the foreigners and the local population. Such a group of 'Anglophiles' did emerge in Hong Kong. We await a full social history of British Colonialism in Hong Kong which hopefully will tease out the culturally enigmatic lives of this 'Anglophile' elite, for they were in the vanguard of the creation of an identifiably modern Chinese culture in Hong Kong. On the other hand, colonialism everywhere also produces its own experts on the colonised peoples, many of whom engage in an extended romance with the dominated culture. We can see this clearly among the French, for example, in Indochina. In Hong Kong, as a counterpoint to the indigenous 'Anglophiles' a group of expatriate 'Sinophiles' emerged. The speciality of the latter was the documentation of 'Chinese tradition', and anthropologists were often found in their ranks. Indeed, in the recent political row over 'traditional' indigenous land rights in the New Territories and alleged discrimination against women (see the chapters below by Selina Chan and Eliza Chan) 'tradition' found some of its strongest supporters among this expatriate group. This colonial history established a powerful discourse of 'East meets West', and the 'modern world meets Chinese tradition'. There was, of course, for a long time a strong 'racial' discourse as well, with the British seeing themselves as representatives of 'civilisation' and Chinese customs as 'barbarian'; while for their part the Chinese held a mirror image of the gwáilóu (foreigner). But this discourse has not survived, although academic and political debates in Hong Kong often disturbingly echo these faded sentiments.

What are the attractions of this 'East meets West' ideological discourse?

First and foremost, it is extremely simple. Its binary structure allows it to accommodate an infinite variety of situations, and better still, it works for both local Hong Kong Chinese and for expatriates. Hong Kong Chinese, when they encounter mainlanders, are able to explain their differences from them by their 'Westerness', when they encounter expatriates they can explain their differences from them by their 'Chineseness'. Expatriates on the other hand quickly recognise Hong Kong's modernity as a familiar 'Westerness', while all differences can somehow be accounted for perhaps by 'traditional Chineseness'. And so on. What is most bewildering about the situation is the rapid code-switching that goes on within it.

But let's look a bit more closely at the structure of this discourse and at the contradictory valuations of 'Western' on the one hand and 'traditional Chinese/Confucianist' on the other.

Westernisation: positive valuation.
- liberalism, freedom of thought, rationality
- egalitarianism, generally and of gender
- industrialization, affluence, science and modern education
- individualism, choice of values in relation to sexuality
- fashion and popular culture

Westernisation: negative valuation.
- family 'breakdown' and divorce
- sexual immorality

- disrespect for authority and liberalism
- advocacy of change and future orientation
- general problems of the modern world

Chineseness ('Confucianism'): positive valuation
  - familism
  - respect for elders
  - social order
  - scholasticism
  - sexual morality
  - hard work
  - 'China's glorious past'

Chineseness ('Confucianism'): negative evaluation
  - conservative morality
  - chauvinistic attitude to women
  - authoritarianism
  - opposed to change

This list could no doubt be extended and refined, but what is immediately apparent from it is its contradictoriness, how an idea valued in one context is not valued in another. In reality individuals hold a mixture of all of these views and in different proportions, and, depending on context, they rapidly code-switch from one point to the other, often being only vaguely aware of the inconsistency. The coexistence of all these views is partly related to the rapidity of social change in Hong Kong, and the mixture of codes within individuals is different between generations who for obvious reasons have experienced different aspects of this rapid social change – we return to the complexities of cultural change below.

The idea of Westernization as an explanation for social and cultural change is perhaps much stronger in Hong Kong than elsewhere in Asia because of the continuation of colonial rule, the predominance of a foreign language in the education and governmental system, and initially the high profile of rich foreign *hohng* (business houses). The process of modernization of Hong Kong society was, therefore, inevitably conceptualised as alien. People everywhere feel powerless in the face of rapid social change and they feel disoriented. Europe itself ('the West') during the massive transformation from feudalism to capitalism experienced similar disquiet, with massive traditionalist messianic movements (unsuccessfully) mobilised against the change. In

Hong Kong this feeling could be partly managed by conceptualising this as a force from the outside – colonialism, Westernisation, and so on, and indeed all the problems which come with industrialisation can in this way also be blamed on 'the West'. Rapid social change also produces a certain nostalgia for an idealised stable past and the idea of 'Chineseness' is important here. Yet attempts to articulate a 'traditional Chinese' way, or a 'Confucian' way, in a modern industrial society encounters fundamental obstacles – which, of course, does not mean that people will not continue to try.

Barbara Ward in her studies of the 'boat people' here in Hong Kong developed a theory of 'conscious models' in order to understand 'Tanka' ideas of Chineseness. Often when she asked the people in the village of Kau Sai why they follow a particular custom they answered: 'Because we are Chinese'. This she says was their conscious model of the social system which they carried in their minds in order to explain, predict or justify their behaviour as 'Chinese'. The problem begins, however, upon the investigator's realization that people in different locations of China have different ideas about what it means to be 'Chinese'. There are, therefore, a variety of conscious models 'a number of different Chinese ideal patterns varying in time and space with varying historical development and the demands of particular occupations and environments' (1985:42). The overarching model is a rather idealised version of Chineseness promoted by the traditional literati. This ideal, always incompletely known by ordinary Chinese, was what they aspired to but fell short of. Yet each group believed that the way they lived more closely approximated the ideal than any other neighbouring group which they observed. They constructed an observer's model of these other groups as distinct from the model they had of their own way of doing things which Ward called their immediate model. Thus they carried in their minds an ideal or ideological model of Chineseness, their observer models of other Chinese groups, and their immediate model of themselves which may vary considerably from other groups and from the ideal model. 'Strictly speaking,' writes Ward, 'the only people who can observe differences between immediate models are outsiders (or social scientists); what a Chinese layman compares is his own immediate model of his own social arrangements with his own "observer's" model of the other fellow's' (1985:51).

Following from these ideas of Ward what we are suggesting is that the framework elaborated earlier constitutes some of the elements of the conscious model held by people living in modern Hong Kong. It allows them too to construe some people as more Chinese than others, or less (as with 'ABC's', American Born Chinese, as explored in Greg Guldin's chapter below). The important thing to bear in mind about conscious models is that, as Levi-Strauss who stimulated Ward's work remarks: 'conscious models are . . . by definition very poor ones, since they are not intended to explain the phenomena but to perpetuate them' (1968:281).

The coherence of Ward's model hinged on the reality of an ideal Chineseness, one modelled on the literati of the Ching Dynasty. The collapse of the old structure left a hole at the centre of the Chinese system, and so throughout the Twentieth Century Chinese intellectuals and others have endlessly debated what it means to be 'Chinese'. Nationalism has been the main overarching ideology to step into the vacuum, although different nationalists have disagreed on what is 'essentially' Chinese. For example, the victorious communist nationalists for a long time attacked Chinese 'feudal' beliefs and practices, as had the Guomindang in its early days. The latter however became a defender of Chinese tradition from its base in Taiwan after 1949, and only recently has Beijing supported a re-exploration of Confucianism. In other words, the cultural content of Chinese nationalism has been under continuous renegotiation.

In a recent essay on culture and identity in Hong Kong by Chan Hoi-man a recurring theme is Hong Kong's lack of 'a unifying cultural foundation' (1994:447). Thus Hong Kong would appear to epitomise the century long crisis of Chinese identity. He writes, Hong Kong 'identity can only be defined in relation to its vacuous centre' (1994:460). This 'vacuous centre' in Hong Kong is filled by popular culture, which however can only paint over the fragmentary nature of the colony's culture. Nevertheless, it acts as 'the key dynamic' because 'popular culture is decidedly also the primary sphere of consciousness and sentiment where the concerns, anxieties, and foreboding of society as a whole find their expression. In the absence of any hegemonic framework of high culture, national culture, and so forth, popular culture in Hong Kong must play the role – set the agenda – of 'culture' *per se*' (1994:449). While he goes on to give a stimulating discussion of aspects of this popular culture in Hong Kong it is, in the end, for him an ersatz culture. Without a state and its attendant high culture to anchor it in the strong winds of the modern world Hong Kong identity can only be ephemeral. An unacknowledged consequence of this, of course, is the fragility of Hong Kong culture in the face of reintegration into the Chinese state.

Others are more sanguine, and interestingly their observations come from areas usually associated with 'high culture' – painting, literature and architecture. Writing of the evolution of painting in modern Hong Kong David Clarke points to the difficulty painters have always had of elaborating a positive identity. Young artists, therefore, have begun to assert a negative identity, one which breaks with 'the grand narratives of both Modernization and Chinese nationalism.' Earlier artists in Hong Kong had tried to link these two powerful terms, 'their juniors seem to be able to live more easily with their rootlessness, and to produce, within a western modernist formal vocabulary, an art which is in many respects deeply post-modern, and primarily local in its interests' (1994:86). If indeed Hong Kong art epitomises the post-modern then Chan Hoi-man's anxieties about the 'vacuous centre' of the territory's culture would seem misplaced, unless of course he wishes to fill it with the grand narrative of Beijing's version of nationalism. Otherwise, Hong Kong high culture in fact could place itself with the avant garde which has no need to fill the centre. This is certainly one implication of the argument advanced by Rozanna Lilley in her chapter in this book on the performance group, Zuni Icosahedron.

Perhaps this peculiar feature of Hong Kong culture is epitomised by the people's self-description as HPung Góng Yàhn, a term so redolent with local meaning we toyed with it as a title for this book but found it ultimately untranslatable into English. It not only signifies a life-style, but also something more than a resident yet less than a people. And perhaps it is this atmosphere which produced the magical realism of, for example, Xi Xi's *My City: A Hong Kong Story* (1989;1993) with its irreverent literary use of the vernacular.

Much of the debate around Hong Kong identity and culture is dogged by either implicit conceptions of culture, or unclearly defined ones. The most deceptive category is, of course, 'traditional Chinese culture'. To their credit Lau and Kuan acknowledge the problems of deploying such a concept: 'there is always a risk that what is considered traditional in this discourse might turn out to be largely a straw-man, assembled through subjective judgements and with dubious scattered pieces of evidence' (1988:3). They lament the absence of 'systematic empirical data of the traditional values of the common Chinese people in the past' (1988:3), but is the substitution of an ideal, fantasy past an adequate substitute? And why is it needed for an analysis of contemporary Hong Kong culture? There are no answers given by the authors. A concomitant of the construction of a 'traditional Chinese culture' is the construction of an ideal type of a modern 'western' society against which the values

9

in Hong Kong are compared. In this case, however, the authors cannot argue that there is no 'systematic empirical data' available on various 'Western' societies and there is no excuse for constructing a 'straw man'. But this is what the authors in fact do, following a long line of other authors. Thus, in the end Hong Kong is discussed in relation to two ideal types – an ideal West and an ideal East (China) – and the theoretical discussion proceeds by way of listing presences or absences of ideal features, using a framework in which tradition and modernity function as inert causes. Of course, in this way, Hong Kong can never be an ideal typical 'Western' society, nor an ideal 'Chinese' one either, but then no society ever can be. In this way the sociology of Hong Kong has succumbed to a form of idealism in which analysis of the real world is spirited away.

CULTURE: THE CONCEPT

Culture, however, in modern anthropology is not inert but actively negotiated and argued about through time. It is in a continual process of construction, and attention has to be paid to *process* if we are to really develop adequate cultural analyses of modern Hong Kong.

The word culture and the concept attached to it has had a long and complicated history, and its meaning is still changing in response to broader social changes. Anthropologists have been more inclined to research and write about culture than sociologists. For purposes of clarification we can distinguish two main contemporary ideas of culture: 1. *ideological* and 2. *analytical*. By ideological is meant a conception which is only partial and therefore distorting, and often serves to obscure power relations. By analytical we mean an attempt to construct an open scientific discourse on the idea of culture.

1. Ideological

This includes the idea of so-called *high culture* and *low-culture or popular culture*. So-called high culture refers to the 'arts', classical music and so on. Low culture refers to the festivals and songs etc. of the masses. The former is usually considered more refined, the latter crude. The important point to note about this concept of culture is: who defines what is high or low? In other words who has the *power* to make such a definition? Most often this power has been exercised by intellectual elites closely allied to state power, and the differentiation has been one way of legitimating power. For example: The traditional Chinese state's claim to represent a superior high culture legitimised its assertion of dominance over various minority cultures on its periphery. States in most modern societies patronise 'the arts'.

A second ideological idea is one which overlaps with some analytical ideas of culture. This is the idea that a culture is homogenous, and that the world is made up of clearly demarcated, unified cultures. In the modern world this idea is often conflated with, or identified with, a nation. In this regard nationalism and debates associated with it have had an important impact on our attempts to conceptualise culture. There is a strong and widely held belief in the idea of unitary cultures.

2. Analytical

The analytical idea of culture which most easily overlaps with the ideological idea of cultures as homogenous is *functionalism*. This concept of society argues that societies are held together because the individuals and groups within them hold a common set of values and beliefs – i.e. a common culture. This culture, it is argued, is transferred from one generation to the next by the process of socialization, and this ensures cultural and social continuity. Beliefs which hold the society together were therefore 'functional', and it is argued that the particular values or beliefs of any culture exist because they contribute towards cultural stability, i.e. they make the society 'function'. It is easy to see that this reasoning is circular: certain beliefs are found in a culture because they are functional, and by definition they must be functional if they exist. Consequently, this theory is, firstly, unable to explain cultural change over time – i.e. why beliefs and values change over time – and, secondly, it is unable to offer an explanation for the obvious disagreements, different beliefs and views held, and practices followed by different individuals and groups within a society. One consequence is that outside forces (e.g. 'Westernization') are invoked to explain change.

The modern anthropological view of culture tries to conceptualise empirical diversity within a culture, and tries to explain why a culture changes over time.

The idea of 'culture' as a unity, they argue, has been largely a product of the ideology of modern nationalism, and modern states tend to propagate this idea along with their educational apparatuses and mass media.

Anthropologists now argue that the idea of culture is a convenient framework for expressing the ongoing dialogue, debate and negotiation that takes place between different individuals, groups, institutions, genders, ethnicities, and so on which make up a society, concerning the content or meaning of the culture they are in. For example, what it means to be 'Chinese', what it means to be a Chinese woman or a Chinese man, about marriage, divorce, aesthetics, and etiquette, and so on. In their homes, at work, in schools, in the mass media, in speeches by politicians and public figures, people discuss these issues, argue about them, and negotiate them. In short, they *construct* their culture.

They do this, however, often in terms of *culturally identifiable parameters*. For example, Chinese people differ greatly among themselves about the significance and importance and interpretation of 'Confucianism' – most in fact know little of the formal philosophy. But almost everyone agrees that its ideas (however they are identified) are important to discuss and debate. Whereas, for example, Confucius is not central to French cultural debates, but the French philosopher Rousseau is. In other words, different cultures do have *distinct symbolic reference points* in their discourses about culture. So, here we are suggesting that the *idea* of Confucius (as distinct from his actual philosophical writings) functions as a *cultural symbol*. The 'globalisation' of culture means that cultural debates and the parameters of these debates are increasingly shared along with certain global symbols.

Culture is not an identifiable 'thing', it is an ongoing social *process* of debate, dialogue and negotiation, primarily conducted among people who place themselves within the broad parameters of that culture, recognise its symbols, and use its language. But it can also include outsiders who choose to participate in that 'internal' cultural debate.

Culture is the ongoing, never-ending process of construction of human meaning, it is the ongoing process of trying to say who we are and what our lives mean – which includes the many rituals and symbols within a culture. It includes trying to decide what it means to be 'Chinese', 'Japanese', 'Thai' or 'Australian', 'man' or 'woman', etc. These meanings are always changing – sometimes slowly, sometimes fast.

The anthropological analysis of culture is concerned both with these changing meanings within a culture, and with the broader processes which may have stimulated those changes, such as industrialisation, globalisation, war, revolution, and so on.

So, one of the consequences of nationalism in the modern world is that while we all like to think that we live in stable, unified cultures, in fact internal and external forces are changing culture all the time. And perhaps it is in the nature of modernity, with its rapid social changes, to have fantasies of cultural unity – an imaginary stable point in a changing world.

THE STUDY OF HONG KONG CULTURE

This approach to culture gives us a different way of thinking about culture in Hong Kong compared with past studies. If Hong Kong culture is in fact constructed through a process of social argument, a discussion about what is relevant from the Chinese past for the present, about what is relevant from the rest of the world for the constitution of meaningful lives within Hong Kong, then analysis should try to trace the participants in these cultural arguments, to try to understand their reasons for selecting one aspect of culture and discarding another, and for choosing one set of symbols while disregarding others. So the question would become not how an inert tradition continues to affect the present but how people in the present 'choose' or do not 'choose', to keep alive certain cultural beliefs and practices from the past. Or even why they may revive them after having discarded them for some years or decades. Similarly, rather than some blanket concept of 'Westernization' anthropologists of contemporary Hong Kong need to focus their attention on the processes by which ideas and cultural artifacts are borrowed from the global corpus of culture; what things are incorporated into modern Hong Kong culture from among the many possibilities and why – from Japanese comics to white bridal gowns. The social and cultural logics which inform this process of selection and rejection is what defines Hong Kong culture and its uniqueness.

In the following pages we begin this task, but before we introduce our authors we wish to draw the reader's attention to a more political argument around Hong Kong identity and culture which has been made by Mathew Turner in an essay *60's / 90's – Dissolving the People* produced for an exhibition on 1960s popular culture. He writes: 'If, as we are constantly told, Hong Kong's history, economy and society are all 'unique', then so too are its people.' But, he says, despite Britain's attempts to get people to identify with Hong Kong through launching various cultural programmes after the riots of 1967, both the UK government and China have been wary of acknowledging a distinctive Hong Kong culture. He writes: 'in formal documents the People's Republic assumes that there is no such thing as a "people" of Hong Kong, and indeed the *Joint Declaration* describes the population in neutral, neutralizing terms such as "inhabitants" or "residents", while local culture is rendered merely as "life-style"'. What, he asks, does 'life-style' mean in this context, especially when it is guaranteed to remain 'unchanged for 50 years'? He goes on: 'Since no society could "remain unchanged for 50 years", how will social change be legitimized? At the heart of agreements on Hong Kong's future lies a slippery neologism which may be interpreted to mean almost anything.' Most importantly, he suggests that the denial of a distinctive culture is also part of a strategy to deny Hong Kong a distinctive political status. But historian John Young points out, 'there is no historical precedent for the Hong Kong-Chinese to rely on . . . Exactly how much of the Hong Kong identity as we know it will remain after the transfer of sovereignity is an unknown . . .'. Although pessimistic, he concludes, 'one thing is certain, the Hong Kong experience has been a unique one in the history of Modern China, and perhaps in the history of the world, and it deserves, and needs to be, recorded' (Young 1996).

Hong Kong's unique place within a wider Chinese cultural universe further complicate the 'cultural/political' manoeuvres swirling around it. Through films, magazines and Canto-pop, Hong Kong reaches out to the large overseas Chinese population. As Lynn Pan puts it: 'Hong Kong is the world capital of overseas Chinese popular culture, the heart of a whole climate and ambience of thinking' (1991:370). And, part of what it projects is a regionally conscious 'Cantonese' culture. In a special issue of *Daedalus* on Chinese identity, Helen Siu (1993) has attempted to locate Hong Kong within the broader context of the long-standing tension between southern China and the central Chinese state. She draws attention to how the development of Hong Kong, and especially its new middle classes, has added a dynamic new element to the creation of a modern Chinese culture, one which defies 'a standardizing cultural narrative' emanating from Beijing. But perhaps that precisely is the 'threat' felt by Beijing, for a distinctive Hong Kong (or Taiwanese) culture, underlines the possibility, or the fact, that 'Chineseness' is not homologous with the nation-state of China. Indeed it raises the spectre of distinct nation-states which are predominantly Chinese culturally, but not part of a unified China.

Greg Guldin in his chapter takes up the question of Chinese ethnic identity in Hong Kong and attempts to elaborate a model of the different levels and modalities of Han identity in Hong Kong and briefly speculates on the emergence of 'a new Hong Kong ethnicity model' after 1997 as Hong Kong people adjust themselves to being part of a larger China (*daaih luhk*). But in line with current anthropological thinking on ethnicity Guldin emphasises that the category 'Han' contains no invariant content. Inevitably, Guldin also points to the position of foreigners in this ethnic (some still call it racial) schema, in particular gwáilóu, a term reserved for Europeans. Uses of gwáilóu (literally, ghost person) in everyday life in Hong Kong reflects much of the ambivalence in the ongoing, but fading, colonial reality of Hong Kong. Indeed, the letters columns of the English press occasionally burst to life with disputes over the use of this term, some foreigners seeing its use as 'racist', others not. In fact, sometimes it is spoken with bitterness by Chinese, and sometimes it is used playfully, and indeed some foreigners themselves join the play and use it self-referentially. The ambivalence of this word reflects a deeper social and cultural issue. In surveying the sociology and anthropology of Hong Kong what is truly surprising is how little study has been done of this fundamental cross-cultural relationship in Hong Kong society, both historically and in the present. Such a blindspot in the intellectual optic of Hong Kong is perhaps revealing of something more profound about cross-cultural relations here. Earlier we pointed to the need for a social history of the Anglophile elite in Hong Kong who are intriguing precisely because they straddle this divide. Authors working on Macau also signal an important difference between the two colonies when they point to the significance of the 'mestizo' Macanese group there, which only serves to highlight the low profile of the equivalent group of 'mixed-race' people in Hong Kong. In this twilight of the colonial era we can only stress the importance of studying this question if we wish to understand the evolution of Hong Kong's culture and society.

Anthropologists in recent years have, with gusto, turned their attention to food and have demonstrated the many cultural messages communicated by the way we eat and what we eat. Food is an important ethnic marker for Chinese people and therefore it is not surprising that Hong Kong peoples' quest for identity should be partly articulated through the medium of food. The new middle class life-styles here play an important role in this process. In the bright, new, sanitised, herbal tea shops of Hong Kong with their tasteful 'traditional' Chinese decor Cheng Sea-ling sees 'a kind of fantasy world in which Hong Kong people can find an affirmation of their Chinese identity'. But like much else in Hong Kong today the nature of this fantasy is partly dictated by the impending re-unification with China, for it appeals to a fantasy of China rather than the stark reality of the Beijing regime.

In the following chapter Philip Robertson takes the Hong Kong Film unit as a case study in colonial documentary rhetoric. His essay engages with 'post-modernist' and 'post-colonial' theories, which have entered into an intense dialogue with anthropology in recent years, causing some questioning and re-evaluation of ethnographic film. A recent book which reflects this dialogue draws attention to the problematic 'realist' assumptions of documentary. Anthropologist Leslie Devereaux writes:

> documentary film cannot help participating in the codes and conventions of fictional cinema, even as it signals its genre difference. . . . By the devices of narrativity in documentary or ethnographic film, the social reality of others is rendered into an ideal of transparency through which we imagine we understand them. The laws of naturalism in film and the techniques of invisible assemblage work to produce a fullness of meaning that obscures what is left out.
>
> (1995:330)

As Robertson shows, this was also true of the productions of the Film Unit in Hong Kong. From its founding in the early 1960s, he suggests, the Unit was an anachronism and this caused revealing, sometimes almost surreal, slippages in its imperial rhetoric. Ironically, the images left behind by the Unit are now an important part of the memory archive for those seeking to construct a contemporary Hong Kong identity. Depending on how they are used, he suggests, they can continue as sources of mystification or alternatively, of critical awareness in Hong Kong's cultural debate.

The following chapter by Rozanna Lilley on the performance group Zuni Icosahedron provides another case study and continues the debate on the forms of representation around Hong Kong's identity and future. Also drawing on 'post-modern' theorists she sets out to demonstrate how Zuni opens up an alternative 'imaginary' space within which the future can be thought – a space free from the stifling polarities of Capitalism Vs. Communism; West vs. East; Chineseness vs. non-Chineseness, and so on. Hong Kong's 'bi-cultural' reality, the words of one of Zuni's producers, means it is uniquely placed to provide a critique of these meta-categories. It is extremely difficult to estimate in any quantitative sense the impact of a group like Zuni. But within Hong Kong's culture and society it undoubtedly plays the role of a collective intellectual whose 'business', says Ulf Hannerz, is 'to carry on traffic between different levels and fields of meaning within a culture, to translate between abstract and concrete, to make the implicit explicit and the certain questionable, to move ideas between levels of consciousness, to connect ideas which superficially have little in common, to juxtapose ideas which usually thrive on separateness, to seize on inconsistency, and to establish channels between different modes of giving meanings external shape . . .' (1992:139).

In the next chapter Christina Cheng Mui-bing reads Hong Kong's spectacular architecture as a cultural 'text'. Through an intriguing comparison of the controversial receptions of the Bank of China buildings in both Macau and Hong Kong she finds traces of their distinct colonial histories and elaborates on how our built environment, no matter how 'postmodern' the design, provides raw material for cultural and political arguments in these last two fragments of empire on the southern coast of China. These debates demonstrate, she says, the unique and paradoxical nature of de-colonisation in Hong Kong because 'the colonised subaltern citizens do not welcome decolonization and liberation, but they much prefer foreign rule.'

As we saw earlier, when anthropologists started coming to Hong Kong they headed off into the still rural New Territories to study the 'traditional' male-dominated lineages there. But today lineage land which once grew rice now supports massive high rise buildings and many people have grown fat on the proceeds of the sale of this land. Lineages continue to hold real estate in the New Territories, but in conditions radically different from 'traditional China'. Two young women anthropologists, Selina Chan and Eliza Chan, report on their findings in these radically changed conditions, and in the context of a dispute over female rights to inheritance in the New Territories. One of the many paradoxes of colonialism in Hong Kong is that it preserved the rights of lineages in the New Territories long after they were suppressed on the mainland, and indeed, as Selina Chan reports, many people now see what is encoded in colonial law as 'tradition'. Ironically, one of Eliza Chan's female claimants looks forward to the situation after 1997 when 'Qing Law' will finally be abolished by the communists. Both of these articles provide clear examples of the historically contingent and negotiated nature of Chinese culture and kinship in Hong Kong, against a political and ideological backdrop of 'tradition'. Selina Chan writes of how the changing status of women in the wider society and the changing role of land in family and kinship solidarity, in the context of a fossilized legal system, has led to practical modifications of female inheritance while appearing outwardly to conform to 'tradition'. Her chapter is an important warning to those (anthropologists, or others) who reify 'traditional' Chinese kinship. This is also true of Eliza Chan's chapter which provides a fascinating account of how women who are the only surviving members of their natal families try to manipulate sentiments of affection to surmount the formal rules of patrilineality in order to make a claim on their fathers' property.

The following essay by Diana Martin also looks at the position of women in modern Hong Kong, but here the focus is on the entry of these women in massive numbers into the workforce and the consequences of this for childcare. Her contention is 'that the Hong Kong mother's identity as a worker is stronger than her identity as a mother'. Martin claims that these modern choices by Hong Kong women are buttressed by appeals to 'traditional' attitudes towards children and childcare. She is struck by the absence of debate around the status of children in Hong Kong. But as the later chapter by Grant Evans indicates, debates around the place of children in a rapidly changing Hong Kong are to be found not necessarily in the more formal discourses of say, nurses or social workers, but in panics about ghosts which reveal an intense anxiety about children. It is clear that complex changes in attitudes towards children are taking place in Hong Kong as the family structure changes and as the cultural definitions of adulthood and childhood are modified.

Hong Kong's transformation into a modern metropolis has seen the restructuring of its sacred map. Graeme Lang charts the emergence of new nodes of sacred power in the city's high-rise landscape, such as the extraordinarily popular Wong Tai Sin Temple, a 'God Palace'. At the same time older temples have fallen into disuse. Far from seeing a collapse of religious beliefs and practices in the glittering modern white-collar financial world of Hong Kong one in fact sees a religious search for alternative sources of power. Lang writes: 'scattered among the great concrete warrens of the city, and in the surrounding hills, are a large number of shrines and temples where such invisible powers can be tapped.' There may be, he says, some evidence that young people are losing interest in Chinese religious practices, but even if this is true temples and the sacred landscape can also be seen as nodes of 'cultural memory as well as nodes of sacred power'. Janet Scott then explores the ubiquitous world of paper offerings in Hong Kong, so central to funeral rituals. In her detailed examination of paper offerings she finds an area of 'tradition' which is expanding and transforming in accordance with the demands of wider cultural changes, while simultaneously providing a sense of cultural continuity. Grant Evans provides a detailed account of a rumour that swept through Hong Kong based on the assumption that ghosts were part of a TV commercial. Not only does he show how this rumour contained cultural, social and political messages, but he also illustrates how, contrary to the expectations of some streams of sociology, the mysterious and the irrational are not likely to be banished forever from industrial societies.

Finally, the chapter by Kingsley Bolton and Christopher Hutton looks to youth and their 'bad language' as a source of linguistic innovation in Hong Kong Cantonese. The 'official' or proper attitude to *chòu háu* as somehow not part of Hong Kong culture in some respects parallels the general attitude to Cantonese as a language, i.e. that it is some kind of inferior form of Chinese – 'real' Chinese being represented by Mandarin. Some people will even tell the unsuspecting foreigner that Cantonese cannot be written, just as it is also suggested that chòu háu cannot be written. But, of course, it can be and thousands and thousands of young Hong Kong males and females consume this vernacular through the medium of comics everyday. The attitude to Cantonese and to comics reflects very clearly the ideological idea of high culture and low culture referred to earlier in this introduction, buttressed in this case by the claims of the central Chinese state's language policy. Xi Xi's novel *My City* was strongly criticised by 'literary policemen' (Xi Xi's words) for its liberal use of Cantonese vocabulary and syntax, but she rejected these criticisms saying that to have written otherwise would have been to turn the novel into 'someone else's city' or 'some other city'. Increasingly, local Chinese newspapers, in particular the new and spectacularly successful *Apple Daily,* make unprecedented use of Cantonese language, sharpening a sense of linguistic identity at a time when more and more Mandarin can be heard in the streets of Hong Kong, and in the shadow of the almost certain onslaught of 'official' Chinese after 1997. In this book we have chosen to transliterate Cantonese using the Yale system, rather than converting Cantonese into Mandarin Pinyin as is commonly done. Bolton and Hutton's foray into the forbidden territory of bad boys and bad language brings to light (for rarified academics, at least) a vital and vibrant side of Hong Kong's culture which literary and other cultural 'policemen' would like to see ignored or suppressed.

These essays are simply the beginning of an anthropology of urban Hong Kong. The takeover of Hong Kong by China in 1997 which looms so large in the minds of Hong Kong people at present and haunts contemporary cultural debates, will be the next dramatic chapter in the rapid and bewildering transformation of this society. Hopefully this book will stimulate future studies of this modern Chinese metropolis.

REFERENCES CITED

Baker, Hugh
    1984 Life in the Cities: The Emergence of Hong Kong Man. China Quarterly:467–479.
Chan Hoi-man
    1994 Culture and Identity. *In* The Other Hong Kong. Hong Kong: Chinese University Press.
Clarke, David
    1994 Between East and West: Negotiations With Tradition and Modernity in Hong Kong Art. Third Text, Autumn/Winter:71–86.
Devereaux, Leslie and Roger Hillman, Editors
    1995 Fields of Vision. Berkeley, Los Angeles, London: University of California Press.
Greenhalgh, Susan
    1994 De-orientalizing the Chinese Firm. American Ethnologist 21(4): 746–775.
Guldin, Greg and Aidan Southall, Editors
    1993 Urban Anthropology in China. Leiden: E.J. Brill: New York.
Guldin, Gregory Eliyu
    1994 The Saga of Anthropology in China. New York: M.E. Sharpe, Armonk.
Hannerz, Ulf
    1992 Cultural Complexity: Studies in the Social Organization of Meaning. New York: Columbia Press.
Lau Siu-Kai and Kuan Hsin-Chi
    1988 The Ethos of the Hong Kong Chinese. Hong Kong: Chinese University Press.
Levi-Strauss, Claude
    1968 Structural Anthropology. London: The Penguin Press.
Pan, Lynn
    1991 Sons of the Yellow Emperor, The Story of the Overseas Chinese. London: Mandarin Paperbacks, Michelin House.
Siu, Helen
    1993 Cultural Identity and the Politics of Difference in South China. Daedalus 122(2).
Ward, Barbara E.
    1985 Through Other Eyes. An Anthropologist's View of Hong Kong. Hong Kong: The Chinese University Press.
Wong Siu-lun
    1986 Modernization and Chinese Culture in Hong Kong. China Quarterly 106:306–325.

Young, John D.
    1996 Identity in Flux: Nationalism and Chinese Culture in British Hong Kong, 1946–1996. Paper presented to the American Historical Association Annual Meeting, Atlanta, Georgia, USA, January 4–7.

IDENTITY

2

HONG KONG ETHNICITY
OF FOLK MODELS AND CHANGE*

Gregory Eliyu Guldin

Ethnicity as a concept has been much maligned as a conceptual organizing frame over the last decade or so, but it still can serve us adequately if we are clear about its contingent nature and its shifting referents. In the arena of Chinese identities, there has long been a recognition of the prima facie ethnicity of the Overseas Chinese of Southeast Asia and elsewhere,[1] and the rage of the 1980s and early 1990s among foreign researchers has been to focus on the oft-contentious ethnicity of the non-Han 'minority nationalities' which comprise about 7% of China's billion-plus population.[2]

This non-Han focus, however, has obscured the often-problematical ethnicity of the Han majority. In the past, even those studies that concentrated on this aspect of Chinese social organization spoke in conflicting terms of speech-groups (Cohen 1968; Skinner 1957), regional or provincial groups (Eberhard 1965; Huang 1982), ethnic groups (Anderson 1967; Blake 1981; Wang 1975), or even 'sub-ethnic regional groups' (Hamilton 1977). Although these and other studies[3] have begun the task of unmasking the various peoples and cultures that lie behind the common label 'Chinese', (or more precisely, Han Chinese) the subject unfortunately remains enshrouded in a confusing welter of inconsistent labels and inadequate definitions.

Yet conceptual clarity is needed and attainable and researchers like Crissman (1967) and Huang (1980) early on pointed the way with their Evans-Pritchard-like focus on the nesting segmentation of Chinese communities, both those overseas and at home. What is required are

---

*This article first appeared in the *Journal of Chinese Studies*, Vol. 1, June 1984. It has since been revised and updated.

models of Chinese ethnicity which incorporate the many levels of identity that Chinese ethnicity is both actively and potentially organized on and which are sensitive to changes over time. Only by an ethnosemantic mapping out of the multiple levels of Chinese ethnic identities can we follow John Galaty's (1982) admonition to avoid 'finding' ethnic categories and instead discover whether folk ethnosociology itself makes use of the categories which appear relevant to outsiders. In the case of Hong Kong, this model-building process led, in the early 1980s, to the discovery of a level of identity and a complexity of ethnic conceptual organization that had escaped anthropological focus. A return to the process a decade and a half later revealed changes in the ethnic landscape which necessitated a remapping of the ethnicity model.

ONE FOLK MODEL AMONG MANY

Pursuing such a strategy, however, requires persistence and comparison, because the model that emerges from the study of any particular Chinese ethnic locale will not be a 'universal' Chinese ethnic identity levels model but one firmly ensconced in the realities and folk perceptions of that time and place. Just as each Chinese ethnic group has its own 'conscious model' of what it means to be Chinese (Ward 1965), so too will each ethnic group have its own folk model of Chinese ethnicity and will the dynamics of ethnicity vary for each Chinese locale. Each model must be mapped out as faithfully to the local reality as possible; only after several such models have been presented can we envision a more encompassing Chinese ethnic identity model.

The first folk model of Chinese ethnicity presented hereafter is a Hong Kong version. It is a folk view of Chinese ethnicity as seen by the majority *Gwóngdùng yàhn* (Guangdongren, Cantonese)[4] population of the colony during the mid-1970s and as such is bound to reflect the uneven quality of popular knowledge of Chinese ethnicity as well as conditions in Hong Kong at that time. Ambiguous, a-historical, and sometimes even (objectively) 'incorrect' in its judgments or classifications, this folk model conforms not to the preconceptions and scholarly insights of sinologists but to its own logic.[5] By purposely keeping such outside (non-native) insights to a minimum, this paper attempts to come as close as possible to presenting the reader with a Hong Kong native's view of the often complex and bewildering (even to Chinese) world of Chinese ethnic identity.

Before mapping out this complex world of multiple ethnic levels, however, let us first familiarize ourselves with the contours of Hong Kong's ethnic universe. *Seuhnghói yàhn, Chìu Jàu yàhn,* and *Haakgà yàhn* (Shanghairen, Chaozhouren, and Hakka), as well as other groups make their home in the colony, but without doubt Hong Kong is, ethnically and demographically speaking, a 'Cantonese world'. A brief introduction to the mid-1970s ethnic world-view of Hong Kong's Gwóngdùng yàhn is thus imperative.

CANTONESE "CHAUVINISM"

Gwóngdùng yàhn have always had quite a strong sense of their own ethnicity and peoplehood. They have felt proud of the role of their province (and they do consider it *theirs,* no matter that minorities also live there) as a progressive force in Chinese history and of the achievements of Gwóngdùng people at home and abroad. Broad agreement exists among Gwóngdùng yàhn that they are, if not perhaps the originators of Chinese culture, at least its best executors. Other Chinese also feel this to some extent, but perhaps not as strongly as the Gwóngdùng yàhn. Whatever the results of such a cross-ethnic or cross-provincial comparison, it is certainly true that Gwóngdùng yàhn judge non-Gwóngdùng yàhn by Gwóngdùng yàhn standards and as the overwhelming majority in Hong Kong they have no trouble in putting forth the idea that to be Gwóngdùng yàhn is to be the best kind of Chinese one could possibly be.

Gwóngjàu (Guangzhou, Canton), the provincial capital, is also seen as the acme of ethnic Cantonese sophistication and culture. The district in which it is located, Panyu, speaks a dialect that is alleged to be the purest form of *Gwóngfúwá* (Cantonese);[6] it is this tongue that is widely used and understood in the 3/4 of Guangdong and the southern half of Guangxi Province that comprise the breadth of ethnic Cantonese settlement (Lau 1969:3). Knowledge of this Gwóngfúwá, furthermore, is essential for all groups in Hong Kong. Alone amongst all Chinese places, Hong Kong is the only area where *Póutūngwá* (Mandarin, Putonghua) as the national language is not taught as a matter of course;[7] indeed, Gwóngdùng yàhn will only countenance Mandarin from foreigners – all Chinese must speak to Gwóngdùng yàhn in 'Chinese,' and to Hong Kong's Gwóngdùng yàhn this definitely means Gwóngfúwá. Speaking Mandarin or *Chìu Jàu Wá* (Chaozhou) or Haakgà (Hakka) will usually not get you very far if you're speaking to a Cantonese vendor. Even when non-Gwóngdùng yàhn make the attempt to speak *Gwóngdùngwá* and do get served, many Cantonese find it more an occasion for amusement than communication or trade.

Gwóngdùng yàhn view themselves as, first and foremost, fond of good food; secondly, hard-working; and lastly, a friendly and polite people given to the active pursuit of a good life for their family. In Hong Kong during the 1970s those perceived as furthest removed from 'Cantoneseness' were, not surprisingly, the *'gwáilóu'* – the 'white' non-Chinese foreigners[8]. The primarily British colonials were ambivalently viewed both as models of 'progress' and 'Modernity' as well as 'barbarians' who lack the subtleties of Chinese civilization and culture. The small but visible overseas Indian/Pakistani (the 'Ah Cha')[9] community was looked down on with near-universal contempt for their alien ways, although a grudging respect for their hard work and language competencies was also often accorded them.

All Chinese, by contrast, are considered related groups, or a least on the same side of the Chinese/'gwáilóu' boundary line. Their degrees of closeness vary though; oftentimes Gwóngdùng yàhn will not even define the Haakgà or the fishing peoples (*téhnggà yàhn*; the Tanka; the *Hohklóu*) as real Chinese (cf. Ward 1965). Yet even those acknowledged as real Chinese do not find immediate acceptance if they are not Gwóngdùng yàhn. One Shanghai immigrant complained that when people from other areas of China lived in Shanghai they were quickly absorbed, especially when they had learned to speak fluent Shanghainese and had lived there for a number of years,

> But things aren't so pleasant with the Cantonese. A friend of mine speaks perfect or near-perfect Gwóngdùngwá since he came here to Hong Kong when he was very small – and still people constantly point him out as a Seuhnghói yàhn. I myself have lived here for twelve years, have a Cantonese wife and am still viewed as an outsider, a *ngoi sáang yàhn*, (waishengren; 'outside-province' person). The Gwóngdùng yàhn will always treat us non-Cantonese as *ngoi deih yàhn* (outsiders).

The Gwóngdùng yàhn do indeed view Northerners (*Bāk fōng yàhn*) and Seuhnghói yàhn as 'barbarians' to some extent because: 1) they talk loudly and are known to quarrel often because of their bad tempers, 2) they put up a false front and like to show off even when poor, e.g. wear good clothes even when they can't afford it, and 3) in general, just aren't friendly. Furthermore, one should bear in mind that these categories of 'Northerners' or 'Seuhnghói yàhn' themselves have a very Cantonese

28

Hong Kong referent. As we can see in Figure 2.5, the categories encompass a regional grouping, 'Seuhnghói yàhn', which for most of the postwar period has served as a catchall category to include all ngoi sáang yàhn from north of Gwóngdùng, regardless of their provenance north or south of the Yangzi, the traditional Chinese north-south dividing line.

Other groups of 'barbarians' are lumped by Gwóngdùng yàhn into the 'Chìu Jàu lóu' (Chaozhou Guys) category which comprises Fūkgin yàhn, Chìu Jàu yàhn, and Hohklóu (Fujianese, Chaozhou and Hoklo). The characteristics of this group include: 1) Also talking loudly, 2) having bad tempers which cause them to fight and bully people of other groups, 3) 'clannishness', 4) having little good taste, being rough types who work in the lowest status, manual labor jobs, and who, even when they are well-to-do, cannot help mixing themselves in illegal and demeaning activities such as Hong Kong's lucrative drug traffic.

In sum, then, we get a division by Gwóngdùng yàhn of people in Hong Kong into seven separate categories (see Figure 2.1);

(1) Gwóngdùng yàhn, wherein separate counties of origin are acknowl-edged but the primacy of Gwóngjàu is unassailable,
(2) Haakgà yàhn (Hakka), seen as a predominately rural and unsophisticated population,
(3) 'Chìu Jàu lóu', including Fūkgin yàhn, the Hóiluhkfùng (Hai-Lu Feng) Hohklóu and Chìu Jàu yàhn,
(4) the Fisher People, the téhnggà yàhn and the Hohklóu,
(5) Seuhnghói yàhn and the Northerners, distinguishable as non-Southern Chinese,
(6) Gwáilóu and foreigners of every ilk, and
(7) overseas Chinese, betwixt and between gwáilóu, barbarians and a whole slew of Chinese identities.

LANGUAGE GROUPS OR ETHNIC GROUPS?

With our Hong Kong ethnic baptism behind us, let us now step-by-step analyze the various ethnic identity levels that cognitively underlie such a complex ethnic map. Some caution, however, is in order since Chinese group identities are not single-stranded 'ethnic' ones. Shared Chinese social identities can be based on surname, occupation, political faction, language/dialect, or place or origin (Blake 1981; Cohen 1968; Crissman 1967; Hong 1976; Weiss 1974). As Crissman has pointed out (1967:190), the social identity characterized as 'ethnic' is often based

29

on a combination of the above identities, and it is through the combination and re-combination of these principles of identity that a Chinese community achieves its segmented status. Most students of the Overseas Chinese have seen these segments derived primarily from language differences (e.g. Crissman 1967:186,190; Kwong 1958:44; Skinner 1958:4–5) but this emphasis is misplaced if we are seeking to understand *ethnic* communities rather than simply attempting to denote the boundaries of *language* communities. Language differences do not make inviolate ethnic boundaries; as in the USA and elsewhere, ethnic groups can persist without retaining their linguistic idiosyncracies (Cohen 1969, 1974; Gordon 1964; Greeley 1977).

Is there something special then about Chinese ethnic groups which requires linguistic distinctiveness for boundary maintenance? Logic argues against such a conclusion for although language differences are now helping to maintain ethnic boundaries, there is no need to insist that the boundaries are dependent on them. Blake, for one, has pointed out that linguistic boundaries are not solely linguistic constructs, that they tend to be arbitrary, that is, sociological. 'There are gradients and lines rather than language boundaries; and factors influencing mutual intelligibility . . . are not purely linguistic but are also sociological in nature' (Blake 1981:17).

This de-emphasis on linguistic distinctiveness, furthermore, squares well with much anthropological thinking on ethnicity. Ethnicity can be seen as a status ascribed to a group of people who regard themselves and are regarded by others as descended from common ancestors. Common cultural patterns are a prevalent but by no means necessary concomitant element of this status (Charsely 1974:350; Barth 1969:12). Ethnic boundaries can therefore both be drawn to *separate* groups speaking the *same* language (e.g. Irish and English in Great Britain), as well as to *include* groups speaking *differing* languages (witness 'Chinese' ethnicity in Southeast Asia or the emergence of a Native American 'Indian' identity in the USA). Thus freed of the traditional requirement to view Chinese ethnicity solely in terms of language groups, we can immediately embark on an unrestrained exploration of the varying Chinese ethnic identity levels which characterize Hong Kong ethnicity.

PROVINCIAL ETHNICS OR SPEECH-GROUP ETHNICS?

During my mid-1970s fieldwork in Hong Kong, while undertaking a study of the Fūkgin yàhn (Fujianese) community resident there,[10] I was in the habit of asking all informants '*néih haih mātyéh yàhn?*' ('What type of person are you?') and usually got the conventional '*ngóh haih Gwóngdùng yàhn*' (I am a Gwóngdùng yàhn, or Fūkgin yàhn, or Chìu Jàu yàhn, etc.) in return. One day, while visiting the clerks of a large department store, the usual question was asked of a new clerk, Chen, and the usual response, 'I am a Gwóngdùng yàhn', was generated. Yet this time many of the other clerks snickered and smiled as this researcher persisted in asking Chen about his 'Gwóngdùng-ness.' These clerks did not consider Chen *really* a Gwóngdùng yàhn because, they explained, 'he's not a Gwóngdùng yàhn at all, but a Haakgà yàhn!' Chen, unperturbed, insisted on his Gwóngdùng yàhn identity.

Puzzling at first, this was not merely a case of mistaken identity, but instead reflected two sharply varying applications of the label 'Gwóngdùng yàhn'. In Gwóngdùng Province itself three major ethnic peoples are recognized both by the people there and by outsiders: (1) Chìu Jàu yàhn (concentrated along Gwóngdùng's eastern coast), (2) Haakgà yàhn (eastern inland Gwóngdùng), and (3) the rest of the people, the majority, who live in central, northern and western Gwóngdùng.

What to call this last group is something of a problem, a problem which in ethnoscientific terms can be seen as one of overlapping linguistic domains. The people of this last group have traditionally called themselves 'Gwóngdùng yàhn' ('Gwóngdùng People'), although '*Gwóngjàu yàhn*' (derived from the centrally located provincial capital of Gwóngjàu) has also been used to designate this group and the language they speak. The problem with the former referent is simple: if we call this group 'Gwóngdùng yàhn', how are we to distinguish them from the other people who, because they live in Gwóngdùng Province, are also 'Gwóngdùng yàhn' (as the Haakgà clerk Chen stoutly maintained)? Calling the provincial majority 'Gwóngjàu yàhn' solves the problem only in so far as Gwóngjàu is allowed to symbolically represent all the ethnically similar people of the province who speak Gwóngdùngwá (i.e. Gwóngjàuwá) or a closely related dialect.[11] However, a new problem then arises from the reverse perspective when we wish to refer to the residents of Gwóngjàu City: how to distinguish this narrow meaning of 'Gwóngjàu yàhn' from its broader ethno-linguistic referent? Such a solution merely transfers the locus of ambiguity.[12]

Such ambiguity, of course, is what enabled Chen's co-workers to tease him about his identity; they preferred the narrow interpretation of 'Gwóngdùng yàhn', and Chen the broader. More important, however, is the introduction here of a distinctly separate level of identity: the provincial. Figure 2.2 maps out the position that this new level of

31

identity occupies vis-a-vis the other levels of identity we have so far discussed, and helps clarify the above discussion.[13] We can clearly see how 'Gwóngdùng yàhn' is a term with both provincial and ethno-linguistic referents and, likewise, how the use of a county-level term, Gwóngjàu yàhn, to take on these wider meanings of inclusiveness merely shifts our labeling problem.

These tiers of identity – that of ethno-linguism and of province – do not necessarily contradict or work against each other, nor are most Chinese confused by them. Moreover, depending of the circumstances, either membership category may give rise to an identity which circumscribes an ethnic group. Once we acknowledge the potential existence of both speech-group-based ethnicity and province-based ethnicity as well, much of the confusion surrounding the variable meanings of 'Gwóngdùng yàhn' ethnicity is cleared up.

NATION, NATIONALITY, AND RELIGION

'Chinese' identity, of course, also exists on the more inclusive levels of nation-state/society and nationality.[14] On the national level Chinese identity is accorded to all citizens of the Chinese nation-state while at the same time there has long been a recognition of nationality differences between China's Han majority and non-Han minority groups. This nationality level, traditionally, also served as an outer boundary of Chinese identity with 'Chineseness' associated almost exclusively with Han Chinese and their culture. Although the problem of 'Han Chauvinism' is not as acute in today's China as it was in the recent past, this potential level of Chinese identity is still very much an important one, although in Hong Kong an equivalence of 'Chinese' and 'Han' identities is assumed.

Still another level has traditionally been recognized above the provincial plane – the so-called 'regionalism' of Southerners versus Northerners. Although Eberhard (1965:602) does indeed propose just such a North/South dichotomy for China and even though Gwóngdùng yàhn do make a distinction between Southerners and Northerners, we must be leery of assuming, therefore, that *ipso facto* this is a major factor of Chinese ethnicity in all cases. It seems not to be in Hong Kong; people do not discriminate along such lines. The key identity question is not whether or not you are a 'fellow-Southerner' (as against 'those Northerners') but whether or not you are a Gwóngdùng yàhn.[15] Non-Cantonese intuitively sense this basic fact of life in Hong Kong and often feel a sympathy with 'other-province' groups, regardless of the location of their homeland North or South of the Yangzi River.[16]

Regionalism therefore exists only as an abstract conceptual label and does not serve as a basis for formation of 'Southern' or 'Northern' Chinese ethnic groups in Hong Kong.[17] Although these broad regional divisions of North and South China can be used to order one's conceptual framework and data, such an exercise would be largely an academic one. Our Hong Kong Chinese Ethnic Identity Levels Chart (Fig. 2.3) thus retains Regionalism merely in a state of broken-line semi-reality.

FUJIANESE IDENTITY

The concept of regionalism or regional groupings among China's many ethno-linguistic groups is nonetheless still a valid concept since some intermediate level is indeed necessary between nationality and ethno-linguistic group. The provincial is one such level but not all identity structures are mediated through a provincial identity; such is the case, for example, for Hong Kong's Fujianese (Fūkgin yàhn) community, as will be seen below.

We have already seen the difficulties incurred in the use of the label 'Gwóngdùng yàhn', sometimes referring to an ethnolinguistic group, sometimes to all the people in the province. The problem is even greater with Fujian Province, for there no one ethnic group dominates the area as do the ethnic Gwóngdùng yàhn in the province that bears their name. In Fujian, three distinct group areas are recognized – Southern, Northern, and Middle (or Western) – but none of these is acknowledged by the others as *the* most typical or dominant Fujianese group. Two groups do, however, claim preeminence and it is these two groups that are best represented in Hong Kong's Fujianese community: Southern Fujianese ('*Hahmùhn yàhn*') and Northern Fujianese ('*Fūkjàu yàhn*').[18]

This rivalry between the two groups reflects the fact that while wide agreement exists among Gwóngdung yàhn that things as they are done in Gwóngjàu are the most typically Cantonese – in language, customs, and food – these is no such unanimity among Fujianese. Some Fujianese point to their province's more rugged geography and the resultant isolation of many districts as an explanation for the lack of strong persistence of 'feudal' (i.e. traditional or pre-modern) ways and local attachments. This strong sense of county or locality is unusual when one considers that Gwóngdùng yàhn in Hong Kong cannot always identify what district or area of Gwóngdùng Province other ethnic Gwóngdùng yàhn are from or even if the Gwóngdùng yàhn in question is a '*tùhng heùng*', i.e. someone who is also from or traces his descent from one's home county.

Yet at the same time, Fujianese also recognize close links between southern Fujianese and Northern Fujianese (due to similar customs and a common provincial origin), and between Southern Fujianese and the Chìu Jàu population of eastern Gwóngdùng (similar language, some customs the same). At once more parochial (with greater emphasis on the sub-provincial levels of identity), and more universalistic (with feelings of ethnic kinship that cut across provincial boundaries), Fujianese identity (in Hong Kong at least) obviously operates in a manner significantly different from what a province-oriented Identity Levels Chart (such as Fig. 2.3) would lead us to suspect.

THE REGIONAL GROUPING

The folk and anthropological recognition of broad cultural, linguistic and historical similarities among some of China's many ethno-linguistic groups introduces an important new element into our understanding of Chinese ethnicity and identity. Such similarities among the Haakgà of Fujian, Guangdong and Jiangxi (Kiangsi) provinces and among the southern Fujianese, Northern Fujianese and Chaozhou warrant our clustering of these populations into two 'Regional Groupings', labeled the *Haakgà* and the 'Máhn'[19] respectively.[20]

This new level of identity, however, does not fit neatly into our old Hong Kong Ethnic Identity Levels Chart. The borders between these regional groupings are *not* coterminous with provincial borders, so we are forced to view Chinese identity from a different perspective – that of the regional Grouping (see Fig. 2.4). This new domain immediately helps us understand why Southern Fujianese were more adept at ethnic identifications on the ethno-linguistic level while Gwóngdùng yàhn seemed to identify best at the provincial. In reality both are dealing with the same level of identity, the ethno-linguistic. Since Gwóngdùng yàhn comprise a dominant majority of Gwóngdùng Province, there is a close correlation for them between provincial and ethno-linguistic identification. For Fujianese, by contrast, no such ethnic people-provincial equation could possibly exist; the Máhn regional grouping extends over the borders of Fujian Province and Fujian itself is populated by at least three component ethno-linguistic groups.

This new perspective can perhaps also help us to deal with another one of Hong Kong's many ethnic groups, the so-called 'Seunghoiyan'.[21] Had we only the Provincial Domain of Fig. 2.3 to work with we would be forced to place 'Seuhnghói yàhn' in our 'Northerners' box on the Regional level. This would be misleading, as we have seen, because non-Northerners, non-'Seuhnghói yàhn', do not identify or relate in any way as 'Southerners'. Nor would arranging the 'Seuhnghói yàhn' according to province of origin be any more accurate in describing these peoples' Hong Kong ethnic identity. A far better solution would be to place the 'Seuhnghói yàhn' on the regional grouping level since in Hong Kong all Central or Northern Chinese do indeed from a regional grouping similar to that of the Máhn, Gwóngdùng yàhn and Haakgà.

This tendency to discriminate at the regional grouping level is quite strong in Hong Kong. A general homogenizing process has been in operation in Hong Kong during the past few decades whereby county-level differences among the Gwóngdùng yàhn and others and even ethno-linguistic barriers among those from Fujian Province are gradually being overcome. The repeated insistence of Gwóngdùng yàhn on lumping all 'Máhn' together – over the vociferous objections of the Fujianese ethno-linguistic groups[22] – will perhaps even lead one day to the emergence of a common 'Máhn' identity in Hong Kong. This blithe violation of the supposed sacro-sanctity of Chinese 'speech groups' should give pause once again to those who insist on viewing all Chinese ethnic groups as *language* groups.

The regional grouping domain thus adds an important dimension to our understanding of Chinese ethnicity. Existing on a conceptual plane parallel to the provincial, the regional grouping domain offers both an alternative classificatory scheme to social scientists and an increased degree of identity choice to Chinese. Figure 2.5 sums up the potential identity levels as they appeared in the 1970s and includes reference to the cross-cutting non-ethnic identities of occupation, ideology, surname, and specific locality.

HONG KONG MODEL OF ETHNICITY: TAKE TWO

Appearances of such charts and models to the contrary, however, ethnicity is not a static phenomenon. Ethnicity, both as a dimension of human life and as an intellectual construct, changes over time as it reflects changes in society and in intellectual currents. Thus the first model of Chinese ethnicity charted above (and its explication), while a useful guide to the Hong Kong realities of the mid and late 1970s, has become outdated and needs revision. During the intervening two decades since then, Hong Kong has begun to operate in a new macro-reality and this has changed both ethnicity in Hong Kong and our thinking about ethnicity. The 'opening' of China after the death of Mao Zedong and the inauguration of the 'reform era' have combined with the 1984 Sino-British agreement on the return of Hong Kong to Chinese sovereignty to change Hong Kong's ethnic equations and the way we should think about Chinese ethnicity.

One change that seems called for is in our conceptualization of the 'national' level. In an era of three vigorous Chinese entities in the guise of Taiwan and Hong Kong as well as the People's Republic, it seems prudent to make recognition of an even greater level of connectedness between all three legs of this triangle. This new conceptualization has been dubbed 'Greater China' and seeks to focus us on the most inclusive level yet, that of 'Chineseness' as a people. This category has strong cultural referents and, in its most expansive definition, includes Overseas Chinese as well.

There is an ambiguity surrounding this term, however. On the one hand, it supersedes the three political entities that inhabit the Chinese territorial universe. Yet on the other, if it is a culturally-based identity, then the sense of commonality is more accurately described as a *Han* Chinese ethnic identity, exclusive of the non-Han (or non-Chinese) population elements in the three societies' populations. Figure 2.6 charts the former sense of the term, while Figure 2.7, by inverting Levels One and Two, attempts to indicate the term's narrower referents. Given the emergence of new ethnically-based states such as Kazakhstan and Kirgizstan on China's westernmost borders, it behooves us to ponder the possibility that for the non-Han nationalities as well, nationality identification might cross or encompass different societal boundaries.

The previous greater salience of the ethnolinguistic level in Hong Kong also seems to have faded somewhat, with a complementary increase at the societal level. Homogenizing factors at work in Hong Kong include a higher percentage of the population being Hong Kong-born, the continuing acculturative influence of Cantonese both linguistically and socially, and the continuing prosperity of the society as a whole. A richer, more influential, and world-class city has emerged from the refugee entrepot of the 1940s and the second-class manufacturing base of the 1960s, and with it the self-confidence of the Hong Kong population has risen tremendously. The June 4th incident, and the speculation, prospects, and problems surrounding '1997' have all joined to reinforce the feeling of a separate Hong Kong identity, and this has served to decrease the stress on other levels of identity.[23]

1997's creation of the new Hong Kong Special Administrative Region means that Hong Kong will once again revise its sense of self and its constituent identities. Without a doubt, a more integral role in both the Chinese nation and in the Cantonese world of the Pearl River Delta will recast old loyalties, boundaries, and identities. Will, for example, we see a continuation of Hong Kong's ongoing integration into Guangdong, with identity coherence following on the economic, communications, and social linkages already in place? Perhaps the decolonization process will mean that Hong Kong's high profile sense of identity will begin to fade in the next generation as its citizens live their lives as Chinese subjects in a south Chinese province and region. Portuguese Goa followed just such a process or identity reintegration after its sudden absorption by India over thirty years ago; perhaps Hong Kong will too. Or will Hong Kong's ethnicity pattern follow that of the Shenzhen Special Economic Zone, as large numbers of both high and low prestige *daaih luhk yàhn* (mainlanders) converge on the former Crown Colony? In the nearby SEZ, these waishengren are undergoing a rapid process of acculturation to Cantonese culture, all the while reinvigorating the local economy, society and culture.

Given such possibilities, it is safe to say that a new Hong Kong ethnicity model will emerge. Yet even so, it is likely that our seven levels will endure as intertwining guidelines to the possibilities inherent in Hong Kong Chinese identities (see Figure 2.8). Migrant populations have inundated Hong Kong before; if the past is any guide to the future, levels four and five should reassert themselves as continuing axes of Hong Kong ethnicity.

CHINESE ETHNICITY
AND THE SEVEN LEVELS OF IDENTITY

Since ethnic group formation consists of the transformations of a potential category of identification into the actual basis of group interaction in a society (Charsely 1974:359; Cohen 1974:ix),[24] Chinese ethnic groups may emerge at *any* of these seven identity levels. Which *particular* level becomes an ethnically significant one will depend on the peculiar circumstances of a given location. Thus in the Overseas Chinese communities of Southeast Asia levels one and six are often invoked, in Hong Kong first level five and then level two, and in Xiamen

City level seven. Ethnicity is not only a variably used resource (Cohen 1974: xv),[25] it is fundamentally a variable and situational concept itself.

To the lasting vexation of anthropologists and students of Chinese groups, there is no simple and ever-lasting 'Chinese ethnicity.' For every Chinese place a different Chinese ethnic identity levels chart may very well be required. Yet it will only be after many such ethnic mappings have been carried out that we will get a clearer understanding of the totality of Chinese ethnicities in all their subtleties.

NOTES

1 Among the many volumes dealing with Overseas Chinese, see especially Purcell (1965), Skinner (1957), T'ien (1953) and Wickberg (1965) for discussions of Chinese/Southeast Asian ethnic relations.

2 Ethnic differences between the Han majority and the non-Han minority populations of China, like those differences between Overseas Chinese and the natives of Southeast Asia, have long been noted and commented on (Gladney 1991, Harrell 1990, Jankowiak 1993, Mosely 1966, Rin 1975, Wiens 1953; see also Guldin 1991).

3 Such as Ward's (1965) delineation of the 'varieties of the conscious (Chinese) model' and Crissman's (1967) analysis of the 'structural principles' of Overseas Chinese community segmentation.

4 The Yale Cantonese romanization will be used for most Cantonese place names and Hong Kong-based terms; where I feel the Pinyin Mandarin or another rendering may aid identification, I will enclose that word in parentheses the first time the new word is used. Thus Gwóngdùng yàhn (Cantonese); Fūkgin yàhn (Fujianese, Fukienese); and Chìu Jàu yàhn (Chaozhouren, Chìu Jàu, Teochiew). When referring to places or peoples outside of Gwóngdùng Province, however, the Pinyin Mandarin form will be used.

5 Those specifically interested in these very social science and historical insights should consult Eberhard (1965) and Wiens (1953), among others.

6 The term Gwóngfúwá derives from the imperial era's Gwóngfújàu (Guangfu Zhou, Guangfu Prefecture) centered around Gwóngjàu, here it designates the 'Cantonese' language.

7 Since the late 1980s, this has begun to change, as schools and the media have introduced Putonghua in preparation for the post-1997 reintegration of Hong Kong with China.

8 Gwáilóu, lit. Ghost fellow, has continued to carry derogatory valuation in contrast to the more neutral 'sài yàhn' or Westerner.

9 The terms 'Ah Cha' or 'Moluo Cha' are said to be derived from the Indian migrant population's frequent use of 'bohut acha' which means very good in 'Indian'.

10 See Guldin (1977a, 1977b, 1982, 1985) for a description of Hong Kong's Fujianese community.

11 The language tie though can not be pursued too strongly; Toisaanwa (Taishan speech) and some other dialects are often unintelligible to the standard Gwóngdùngwá-speaker. And many Gwóngjàu yàhn (the city variety) vociferously object to including their non- Gwóngjàu City country cousins in any category labeled 'Gwóngjàu yàhn'.

12 Huang Shuping of Zhongshan University suggests we refer to this ethnolinguistic Gwóngdùng group as 'Gwóngfú yàhn'.

13 The reader should be aware that Figures 2.2, 2.3, and 2.4 are simplified. Full mapping would require the addition of boxes on the provincial, ethno-linguistic and county levels.

14 'Nationality' as used here follows current Chinese usage to distinguish among the Han and the 50-odd 'minority nationalities' (síu sok màhn juhk) of the People's Republic. As such it does not carry precisely the same meaning when used by political scientists to denote a people among whom there exists a significant movement toward political, economic or cultural autonomy (K. Deutsch 1966).

15 Crissman reports a parallel discrimination in other Chinese cities between locals and other Chinese who are more or less 'foreign' (1967:201).

16 The Yangzi (Yang Tze) River is the traditional dividing line between North and South China.

17 The case of the 'Northern Chinese' of Hong Kong, the so-called 'Seuhngho i yàhn', will be discussed below.

18 With the cities of Hahmùhn (Xiamen; Amoy) and Fūkjàu (Fuzhou; Foo Chow), symbolically representing the two regions.

19 The word ' Máhn' derives from the largest river in Fujian Province, the Máhn, is also the one-character abbreviation for the province, and thus seems appropriate as a title for this regional grouping (cf. Blake [1981] and his term 'Hokkien').

20 Actually these groupings are even more composite entities than I explain here. The Gwóngdùngwá Hakka, for instance, are composed of distinct populations, of Baoan Hakka, East River Hakka, Southwest Gwóngdùng Hakka, etc. The Máhn grouping, furthermore, should also include a group that although it is not significant in Hong Kong, certainly belongs in any comprehensive Máhn grouping: the ethnolinguistically-related Taiwanese.

21 'Seuhnghói yàhn' is actually a catch-all term in Hong Kong for all Central and sometimes even Northern Chinese.

22 Those from Fujian Province resent being classified with the Chìu Jàu for fear the lower social prestige of the Chìu Jàu will adhere to all the Máhn grouping. A similar process is at work in the USA, where dark-skinned Caribbean migrant populations endeavor to establish identities distinct from that of African-Americans.

23 The non-Chinese population has also changed significantly. Substantially diminished in both numbers and influence, the British in their declining days have seen the Americans and Japanese replace them as the key foreign groups in business and society. Yet even these groups are dwarfed by the far more numerous though lower prestige Filipino population, comprised mostly of female domestic workers.

24 Arnold Strickon (personal communication) postulated just such a develop-ment from the abstract/potential 'national population' category to both

'collectivities' and 'ethnic groups'. For Chinese ethnicity such a transformation is theoretically possibly on seven different identity levels.
25 Bailey (1969), Barth (1967) and others have spoken of how people constantly evaluate the benefits gained by a reallocation of their time and resources into newer or slightly different patterns. Ethnic decisions are likewise often based on the shifting benefits of being 'Chinese' today, 'Fujianese' tomorrow, and 'from Xiamen' the next day (cf. Huang 1982:260).

REFERENCES CITED

Anderson, E.N., Jr.
    1967 Prejudice and Ethnic Stereotypes in Rural Hong Kong. Kroeber Anthropological Society Papers 37:90–107.
Bailey, F.G.
    1969 Strategems and Spoils. New York: Schocken Books.
Barth, Fredrik
    1967 On the Study of Social Change. American Anthropologist 69:661–669.
    1969 Introduction. In Ethnic Groups and Boundaries. F. Barth, ed. Boston: Little, Brown & Co.
Blake, C. Fred
    1981 Ethnic Groups and Social Change in a Chinese Market Town. Asian Studies at Hawaii, No. 27. Hawaii: Hawaii University Press.
Charsley, S.R.
    1974 The Formation of Ethnic Groups. In Urban Anthropology. A. Cohen, ed. Pp. 337–368. London: Tavistock Publications.
Cohen, Abner
    1969 Custom and Politics in Urban Africa: A Study of Hausa Migrants in Yoruba Towns. London: Routledge and Kegan Paul.
    1974 Introduction: The Lesson of Ethnicity. In Urban Ethnicity. A. Cohen, ed.
Cohen, Myron
    1968 The Hakka or 'Guest People': Dialect as a Sociocultural Variable in Southeast Asia. Ethnohistory 15(3):237–292.
Crissman, L.W.
    1967 The Segmentary Structure of Urban Overseas Chinese Communities. Man 2:185–204.
Deutsch, Karl
    1966 Nationalism and Social Communication. Cambridge, Mass: MIT Press.
Eberhard, Wolfram
    1965 Chinese Regional Stereotypes. Asian Survey 5:596–608.
Galaty, John G.
    1982 Being Maasai. American Ethnologist 9:1
Gladney, Dru C
    1991 Muslim Chinese: Ethnic Nationalism in the People's Republic. Cambidge: Harvard University.
Gordon, Milton M.
    1964 Assimilation in American Life. New York: Oxford University Press.

Greeley, Andrew H.
1971 Why Can't They Be Like Us? New York: E.P. Dutton and Co.
Guldin, Gregory E.
1977a 'Little Fujian (Fukien)': Sub-neighborhood and community in North Point, Hong Kong. Journal of the Hong Kong Branch of the Royal Asiatic Society. Pp.112–119.
1977b Overseas at Home: The Fujianese of Hong Kong. Unpublished Ph.D. dissertation, University of Wisconsin-Madison.
1982 Whose Neighborhood is This? Ethnicity and Community in Hong Kong. Urban Anthropology 9(2):243–263.
1985 Measuring Urban Ethnicity. In City and Society: Studies in Urban Ethnicity, Lifestyle and Class. A. Southall, Peter Nas, Ghaus Ansari,eds. Pp. 71–86. Leiden Development Series No. 7. Institute of Cultural and Social Studies, University of Leiden, the Netherlands.
1991 The Organization of Minority Studies in China. China Exchange News 19(2):7–12.
Hamilton, Gary G.
1977 Ethnicity and Regionalism: Some Factors Influencing Chinese Identities in Southeast Asia. Ethnicity 4:347–351.
Harrell, Stevan
1990 Ethnicity, Local Interests and the State: Yi Communities in Southwest China. Comparative Studies in Society and History 32(3):515–548.
Huang Shu-Min
1980 The Development of Regionalism in Ta-Chia, Taiwan: An Non-Kinship View of Chinese Rural Social Organization. Ethnohistory 27(3):243–265.
Jankowiak, William
1993 Urban Mongols: The Search for Dignity and Gain. In Urban Anthropology in China. Gregory Guldin and Aidan Southall, eds. Pp. 316–338. Leiden, the Netherlands. E. J. Brill.
Kwong, Alice Jo
1958 The Chinese in Peru. In Colloquium on Overseas Chinese. M. Fried, ed. New York: International Secretariat, Institute of Pacific Relations.
Lau Chiu Yung
1969 A Geographical Study of the Chiu Chau People of Hong Kong Island. Unpublished B.A. thesis, University of Hong Kong Geography Department.
Long, Lawrence
1976 Recent Immigrants in the Chinese-American Community: Issues of Adaption and Impacts. International Migration Review 10:509–514.
Moseley, George
1966 The Party and the National Question in China. Cambridge, MA: MIT Press.
Purcell, V.
1965 The Chinese in Southeast Asia. London. Oxford University Press.
Rin, Hsien
1975 The Synthesizing Mind in Chinese Ethno-Cultural Adjustment. In Ethnic Identity. G. DeVos and L. Romanucci-Ross, eds. Palo Alto, CA: Mayfield Publishing Co.

Skinner, G. William
  1957   Chinese Society in Thailand. New York: Cornell University Press.
T'ien, Ju-Kang
  1953   The Chinese of Sarawak, A Study of Social Structure. London: London School of Economics, Department of Social Anthropology.
Wang Shih-ch'ing
  1974   Religious Organization in the History of a Chinese Town. *In* Religion and Ritual in Chinese Society. Arthur Wolf, ed. Pp. 71–92. Stanford: Stanford University Press.
Ward, Barbara
  1965   Variations of the Conscious Model: The Fishermen of South China. *In* Relevance of Models of Social Anthropology. M. Banton, ed. Pp. 113–137. London: Tavistock Publications.
Weiss, M.
  1974   Valley City: A Chinese Community in America. Cambridge: Schenkman Publishing Company.
Wickberg, Edgar
  1965   The Chinese in Philippine Life, 1850–1898. New Haven: Yale University Press.
Wiens, Harold J.
  1953   China's March into the Tropics. Washington. Office of U.S. Naval Research.
Wilmott, W.
  1967   The Chinese in Cambodia. Vancouver: University of British Columbia.

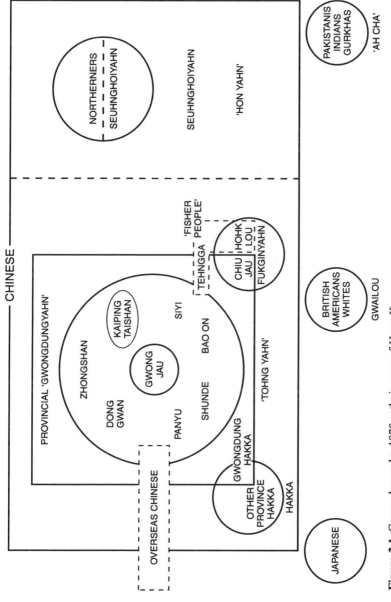

Figure 2.1 Gwongdungyahn 1970s ethnic map of Hong Kong

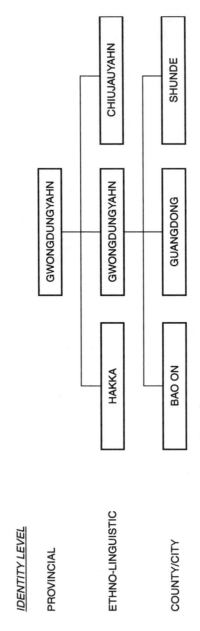

Figure 2.2 'Gwongdungyahn' identity referents

44

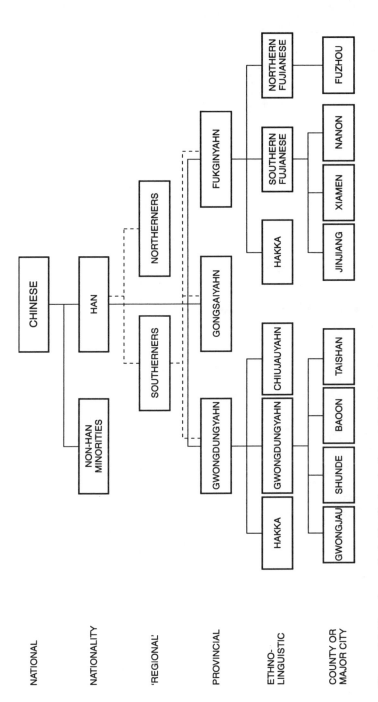

Figure 2.3 Hong kong ethnic identity levels: the provincial domain

NATIONAL

NATIONALITY

'REGIONAL'

PROVINCIAL

ETHNO-LINGUISTIC

COUNTY OR MAJOR CITY

CHINESE

NON-HAN MINORITIES

HAN

SOUTHERNERS

NORTHERNERS

GWONGDUNGYAHN

GONGSAIYAHN

FUKGINYAHN

HAKKA

GWONGDUNGYAHN

CHIUJAUYAHN

HAKKA

SOUTHERN FUJIANESE

NORTHERN FUJIANESE

GWONGJAU

SHUNDE

BAOON

TAISHAN

JINJIANG

XIAMEN

NANON

FUZHOU

45

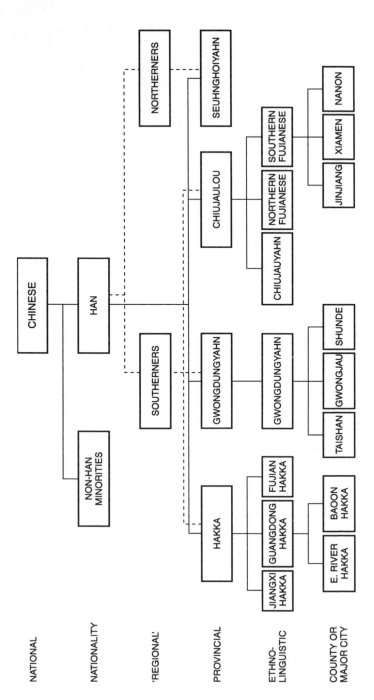

Figure 2.4 Hong Kong ethnic identity levels: The regional grouping

46

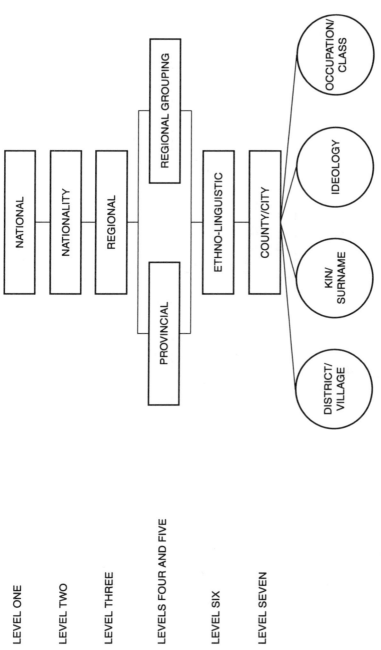

Figure 2.5 1970s Hong Kong-derived Chinese identity model

47

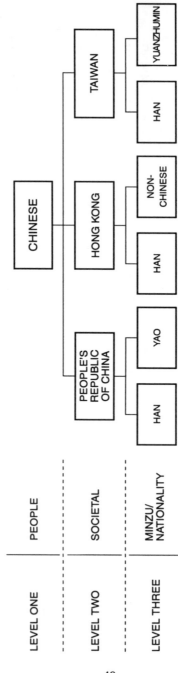

Figure 2.6 Societal-based referent for 'Chinese'

48

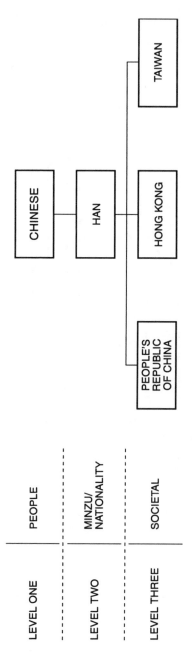

Figure 2.7 Nationality-based referent for 'Chinese'

49

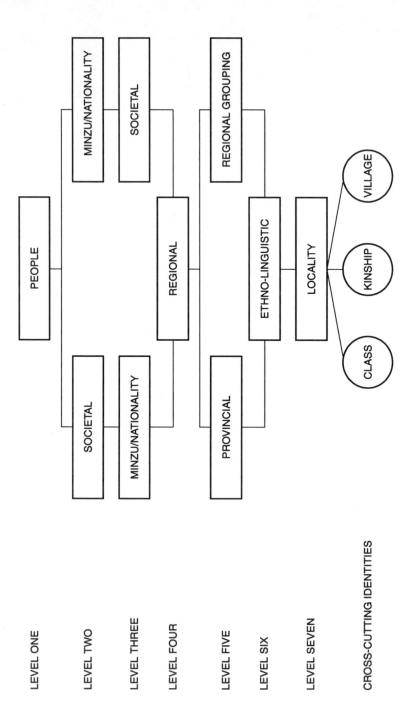

LEVEL ONE

LEVEL TWO

LEVEL THREE

LEVEL FOUR

LEVEL FIVE

LEVEL SIX

LEVEL SEVEN

CROSS-CUTTING IDENTITIES

PEOPLE

SOCIETAL

MINZU/NATIONALITY

MINZU/NATIONALITY

SOCIETAL

REGIONAL

PROVINCIAL

REGIONAL GROUPING

ETHNO-LINGUISTIC

LOCALITY

CLASS

KINSHIP

VILLAGE

Figure 2.8 Revised Chinese ethnic identity levels

3

BACK TO THE FUTURE
HERBAL TEA SHOPS IN HONG KONG

Cheng Sea Ling

My childhood memories of drinking herbal tea are associated with tears and fierce fights with my grandmother. These ended in a bitter defeat every time. Grandma, generally tolerant, would not have me leave a drop of the herbal tea on the pretext that it was 'good for me'. Yet the concoction - the epitome of bitterness in a matching colour of dark brown - that has been brewing in the earthen clay pot for several hours was in no way appealing to a child who had a sweet tooth. The old saying, 'Bitter medicine is good medicine' never worked for me! Herbal tea shops at that time were places where only the aged and the 'old-fashioned' visited. However, herbal tea shops have emerged in the late 1980's as an arena for both 'traditional' and 'modern' health-conscious people. Nowadays, even I occasionally pick up a bowl of the once-horrifying 'twenty-four herbs' concoction to 'curb' my 'heat'.

This article seeks to portray the development of herbal tea shops in Hong Kong in a period of rapid social and economic changes. Herbal tea is an important part of Cantonese folk medicine. Its survival despite the onslaught of scientism and modernism in the 1970's and 1980's is evidence of the strong hold Chinese folk medicine has on peoples' lives in Hong Kong. Now, in the 1990's, it has made a triumphant revival. Consumption of herbal tea and visits to herbal tea shop have become a culturally loaded act, a sign of one's social status, cultural and health beliefs. Herbal tea shops in Hong Kong society have played many a role that contributes to its people's health conditions, social cohesion, and cultural identity. A brief social history of herbal tea shops, their image and functions, reveals a most interesting process of identity negotiation and construction among Hong Kong Chinese. It is my argument that the revival of herbal tea shops, that reached a peak in the 1990's, is part of a nostalgic movement among Hong Kong Chinese. This nostalgia is a reaction to the identity crisis that arises from the prospect of returning to the 'motherland', after 150 years of British rule. To affirm their Chinese identity, a romantic past has emerged to appeal to the population. Herbal tea shops, reconstructed and re-identified, have become part of this nostalgia, a yearning for a secure yesterday to counter-balance an uncertain tomorrow.

HERBAL TEA THAT COOLS

'Herbal tea' is in fact not a literal translation - in Cantonese, it is called *lèuhng chàh* - 'cooling tea'. The name denotes its perceived effects of eliminating too much heat in the body according to the Chinese medical system. Balance is important in the cosmology of Chinese medicine and should be maintained, according to the folk version, between dichotomies of 'hot/cold' and 'wet/dry'. Imbalances would lead to bodily discomforts or illnesses. Consumption of herbal tea is common in the Southern parts of China where hot and humid weather predisposes its inhabitants to 'overheating'.

The multiple uses of herbal tea makes this system easy to use and good to think. Herbal tea is consumed to 'curb heat' - *chìng yiht* when signs of overheating like sore throats, indigestion, and pimples arise, or to prevent imbalances of *hei* (such as after eating large quantities of 'hot' food). Different effects are associated with the various herbal teas - chrysanthemum tea and five-flower tea are assumed to be mildly cooling, while sesame drink, sugarcane juice and sour plum juice are good for promoting digestion, and since their effects are mild they can also be taken simply as a drink. Twenty-four-herb tea is generally perceived as strongly cooling and good for curing 'hot' diseases like flu and fevers. Herbal tea is medicinal as well as thirst-quenching.

Herbal tea shops provide people who have not the time or resources to attend long hours of boiling with a convenient means of self-medication as well as a drink to quench thirst. The shops also operate as a public venue. Set against these basic functions, the social history of herbal tea shops is also closely interwoven with the development of Hong Kong society.

BEGINNINGS (1897-1945): THE LEGEND OF
WONG LO KAT

The importance of herbal tea shops during this period can be attributed to the inaccessibility of other medicines for most inhabitants in the colony, especially the Chinese population who were poor. Traditional Chinese medicines like herbal tea and other herbal medicine, like those distributed by the Taoist temple of *Wong Tai Sin* in its early days, which were either very cheap or free, were welcomed by the needy masses. During these early years, Hong Kong suffered various attacks of the plague which caused thousands of deaths.

The name 'Wong Lo Kat' to Hong Kong people is synonymous with herbal tea. Few know (myself included, before this study) that it is actually a specific concoction of herbal tea. According to Ms. Wong, director of Wong Lo Kat (International) Ltd., Wong Lo Kat was the first herbal tea shop in Hong Kong registered in 1897 with the Hong Kong government. Wong Lo Kat was the man who 'discovered' the prescription for a herbal tea that cured all diseases and won so much acclaim that he was summoned by the Qing Emperor Man Chung (清文宗) who gave him the title of Imperial Doctor. His first shop was set up in Guangzhou in 1853 under his own name. The first shop in Hong Kong was located in Man Mo Temple in Chik Street.

Packaged tea was sold as 'Wong Lo Kat **Medical** Tea locally and overseas to Europe, England, American, Holland and various ports of the South Pacific' (Wong 1987:44). In 1915 the shop was moved to Aberdeen Street. Both locations were in the area now called Central, just a few streets away from the main road where most people lived and where a lot of tea shops and restaurants could be found.

During the Japanese occupation, the shop's business increased as 'ordinary hospitals, both private and public, were fully occupied, and most people could not afford the costs of private doctors, naturally they come for a glass or two and bought some packaged tea home in case of sudden needs'. Wong Lo Kat herbal tea was also used by the 'Japanese soldiers and their families who relied on Wong Lo Kat herbal tea to cure diseases'(Wong 1987:120).

Both before and during the war, health conditions were poor and infectious diseases were rife and epidemics frequent and often fatal. Those who managed to get themselves a space in the common two or three-storey tenements had to put up with increasing overcrowding and pollution. The Hong Kong Annual Report in 1938 describes how the extension of the Sino-Japanese hostilities to South China during the year resulted in a still greater influx of refugees and led to further 'aggravation of the various public health problems such as overcrowding, malnutrition and epidemic disease'(1938:23). The number of residents per floor in the tenements went from twenty to sixty. Overcrowding itself is considered a cause of heat, and coupled with the poor health conditions, the accessibility of herbal tea made it the natural guardian for all who believed in its effects.

It has been suggested by T. W. Chan (personal communication, 1995) that the use of herbal tea was spread among the early migrants through their kinship networks. The early settlers who had benefited from the distribution and effects of herbal medicine introduced their newly arrived kin into these practices and beliefs. The pattern of migration via kinship networks thus facilitated the spread of herbal tea use.

It may be of interest to note that the rise of Wong Tai Sin, the 'Refugee God' (Lang & Ragvald 1988,1993) began in a similar situation: the provision of herbal medicine to the masses of poor people. Lang & Ragvald (1988) found Wong Tai Sin a 'natural, if obscure, choice as a patron god for a Taoist herbal medicine business' (1988:62) as he was said to have successfully created a drug for immortality with cinnabar - immortality being the major preoccupation of Taoists. Wong Tai Sin thus started attracting his first local worshippers in one of the oldest areas on the island - Wanchai. The number of his followers continued to grow when the temple was moved to its present location in Kowloon in 1921. The practice of 'offering herbal medicine prescriptions from the god, along with a limited supply of free medicine, brought a steady growth in visitors, especially among the newer immigrants' during the 1929's and 1930's, thereby adding to the great appeal of Wong Tai Sin (1993:44). The survival of the temple and its herbal medicine business through the Japanese war was explained in terms of the god's intervention. It has been interpreted by the temple historians, as well as those who witnessed how the temple emerged from the destructions of war relatively unscathed, that the god's protective might and blessings have ensured the well-being of the temple and its neighbourhood.

The survival of Wong Tai Sin and Wong Lo Kat are both perceived as miraculous, though the former has a much greater religious aura than the latter. Herbal medicine has been important for these two institutions in gaining popularity both before and after the war, when health conditions were poor and health care facilities lacking. The herbal tea of Wong Lo Kat, a secular establishment with no religious strings attached, must have enjoyed a general appeal, including the followers of Wong Tai Sin.

THE GATHERING PLACES (1946-68)

This was a period of rapid population growth and intensified urbanisation during which herbal tea became a 'social beverage'. Herbal tea shops turned into popular settings for consorting with ones's fellow patrons, similar to the rise of coffeehouses in the 16th-century Near East studied by Hattox (1986).

Wong Lo Kat was quick to seize on the opportunity and expanded its chain of shops in the most densely populated areas - four other branches came into being between 1946-47 in Wanchai, Sai Ying Pun and Queen's Road West on Hong Kong Island, and one in Shanghai Street on Kowloon Peninsula. They also produced a new packaged herbal tea which were convenient to carry, facilitating the spread of herbal tea. Though official statistics are lacking before 1950, the first batch of permits issued by the Urban Services Department in 1951 suggests that many were already in operation before government regulation of these establishments (Fig 1).

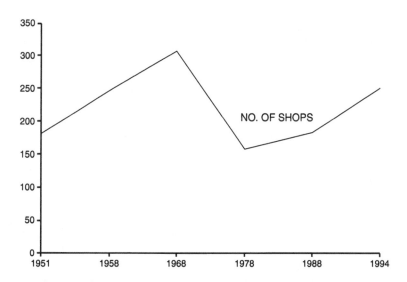

FIGURE 1. Number of Permits in Force for Chinese Herb Tea Issued by the Urban Services Department (Information obtained from the Urban Council and Urban Services Statistical Reports).

The number of herbal tea shops grew throughout the period - their healthy growth being the result of strategic adaptations. To attract business, herbal tea shops diversified their range of drinks and equipped themselves with the newest inventions in the electronic media - the radio in the 1940's, jukeboxes in the 1950's and television sets in the 1960's. These were all beyond most people's reach at the time. By turning themselves into social and entertainment centres, herbal tea shops attracted patrons from different generations and became popular amongst the young. Higher income groups had their own exclusive places.

The well being of the majority of people during the earlier part of the period did not improve significantly - the population of 600,000 during the Japanese occupation suddenly rose to 1,600,000 in 1946, and another wave of refugee influx from the mainland in the early 1950's continued to create tremendous pressure on local resources. Overcrowding and health problems remained prominent issues the Government had to deal with. Housing conditions in the 1950's-1960's described by L. F. Goodstadt (1969) suggest that in spite of increased government control and resettlement, housing standards for most were still unsatisfactory on the tenement floors. Many occupants in the cubicles had 'neither light nor ventilation'; ordinary daily routines like cooking or washing became major problems. 'The cramped space in which most families live restricts the activities of their members...The poor conditions make the home very unattractive, and it is a place in which members of the family spend as little time as possible - especially in the summer'. The lack of reasonable housing drove people out of their 'homes' but recreational facilities were also inadequate. So, for these economically less advantaged people, herbal tea shops provided a channel of escape from their humdrum lives by creating an easily accessible and physically comfortable public place that connected them with each other and the world at large. In this way herbal tea shops played a socially integrating role.

By the 1950's, besides medicinal teas, a variety of health drinks became available at herbal tea shops; five-flower tea, chrysanthemum tea, almond drink, sesame drink were among the more well-known ones. The popular turtle jelly (*gwai lìhng gou*)[1] was first introduced at this time in the Shanghai Street Wong Lo Kat. People visited herbal tea shops not only for the herbal tea, but also for the space, a seat, the electric fan, and the radio. Ms Wong, the Director of Wong Lo Kat (International) Ltd., recalls that journalists would sit in the shop for a whole day with just one drink.

Installations of radios since the late 1940's made herbal tea shops the place to be for the common people for whom overcrowding was a problem and for whom few other entertainments were available. The Rediffusion (Hong Kong) Limited, franchised by the Government in 1948, operated a wired broadcasting system in the Colony. The Chinese radio programmes offered plays, stories, concerts and Cantonese operas. These broadcast programmes were immensely popular and available through the tea shops at a low cost - 10 cents per drink. It was said by one informant that football matches then were a major event, and people at work might get permission to gather at herbal tea shops to listen to live broadcasts of the matches. It was also a popular gathering place everyday at 12 noon for the unemployed, the retired and housewives who were loyal fans of the popular broadcast stories hosted by the famous broadcaster Lee Ngo.

In the 1950's, jukeboxes in some herbal tea shops were a major attraction for the younger generations. Many local Cantonese films produced in this period featured trendy young people (men with a slick-back hairstyle, folded-up shirt collars and women typically in mini-skirts) socialising and dancing to western music from the jukeboxes in herbal tea shops. Two of my informants recalled the herbal tea shops with jukeboxes. One of them remembers, as a kid, following her elder brother to the shop. She would have a drink of sugarcane juice, chrysanthemum tea or almond drink, and insert a 10 cent coin into the jukebox and select her choice. The other informant was unable to spare the money to visit these shops but she vividly remembers these scenes.

Television programmes were pioneered by Rediffusion in 1957, and Wong Lo Kat shops were among the first to install television sets in their shops in 1958-9.[1] Programmes include presentations such as Cantonese operas, dance orchestras, night-club acts, children's features, and interviews'. There were also outside broadcasts of sports and special events, and a local and international newsreels each evening. The rental fee of $55 per month for both service and maintenance of the set was too great for most people[2]. Therefore, herbal tea shops became the natural choice for those who yearned for a glimpse of their own society and the outside world transmitted through television. Ng Ho, lecturer at the Department of Journalism and Communications in Hong Kong Baptist University, recalled his own youthful days in the 1960's, as one of many who were still living in tenement housing: 'We loved watching television. Very few people have their own TV sets, I remember standing outside the room of our landlady's and peeped through the door gap to watch television. She was the only one in the house to have a TV set. Otherwise, I would run to the herbal tea shops and pay 10 cents for a drink of almond tea and watch television there.'

According to Matthew Turner, Hong Kong people in the late 1960's had developed 'an identity of life-style, a shared recognition of similar self-images, real or desired, of existential choices, from food to education, that had to be made now that Hong Kong people could no longer be guided either by Chinese tradition, or Chinese modernity'(1994:4). Hong Kong before the 1960's was a transit lounge for goods as well as of people, not the ultimate place to settle in or to be identified with. Yet the development of a local manufacturing and export economy, the Chinese Manufacturers' Exhibition of Hong Kong Products that was only second in scale to the Chinese New Year, the gradual improvements of both private and public housing, the media productions that increasingly drew on the local way of life, the exposure through trade and media to the international world and western ways of life as models of modernity, all stimulated a complex discourse on Hong Kong identity that people in the Colony began to negotiate. These struggles over a Chinese identity culminated after 1967 in a painful rejection of China when communist virulence was exposed during the Cultural Revolution. For those who could afford to among the first generation of local born, their search for a modern identity thus took off in the 1970's. However, with the gradual realisation of this goal, the popularity of herbal tea shops fell to its lowest ebb as Hong Kong took off in its search for modernity.

A MODERN METROPOLIS WITHOUT HERBAL TEA SHOPS (1969-84)

In 1969, Hong Kong's first satellite earth station enabled direct telecasts between Hong Kong, the United States and other countries (1969 Hong Kong Report). It was a fitting symbol of Hong Kong's entry into the global market. This was a period which saw Hong Kong's rise as an international city and its people were making every effort to be modern. In this context, it is interesting to note how the number of herbal tea shops took a downward turn in 1969 from 306 to 295, not a significant decrease but the beginning of a continuous decline which continued right into the late 1980's. The social functions of herbal tea shops that had been so prominent in the past decades were progressively taken over by the family and other entertainment establishments. More

58

importantly, its 'traditional roots' led to its marginalization in the march towards a metropolitan identity.

The Government committed itself to large scale projects for the improvement of social conditions. Town planning and urban renewal were vigorously carried out. A ten-year housing programme which pledged to provide public housing to half of the population was declared in 1972. The living environment as well as economic conditions rapidly improved for most people.

Television sets evolved from a luxury into a necessity for the household in the burgeoning economy of the 1970's. The first wireless television broadcast station - Hong Kong Television Broadcasts Ltd (HK-TVB) began regular broadcasts in November, 1967. By 1969, 'nine out of ten Hong Kong homes are reached by broadcasting services and approximately one in three has a television set' (Hong Kong Report 1969:240-241). Television gradually became part of everyday life. The times when one had to go to herbal tea shops to watch TV had gone. Entertainment establishments increased in number and variety - bowling centres and dancing parties were more common, discotheques were the 'hippest' place to be after the mid-1970's.

Icons of modernity like McDonald's arrived in 1974, followed by other similar fast food chains like Kentucky Fried Chicken and Burger King. The modern, American decor and immaculately clean environment of these eateries were symbols of the modern world. Those who had benefited from the economic boom were willing to spend more for the better - epitomised by having 'western meals' like steaks on hot grills served at the table.[3] Other eateries found success by resorting to ostentatious decor, and expensive and exotic tastes - the Jumbo Floating Restaurant is a clear illustration, while hotel grill rooms were the place for the 'westernised' and, certainly, well-off. Cuisines from other Asian countries, in particular Vietnam, Thailand and Japan, also found their own niche in the local market in the 1980's. This culinary expansion of the local palate demonstrated the growth of Hong Kong as a metropolitan city.

There was a tendency to believe that 'All that is modern is good', which became the driving force of Hong Kong society during this dramatic period. The good things were increasingly within the reach of those who had attained or believed in the prospects of upward mobility. The eating out culture of HK people embarked on a vigorous path of diversification. The significance of food consumption as a demonstration of wealth, knowledge and status is increasingly seized by those who have benefited from the economic boom. The decline of herbal tea shops was a result of changing perceptions - in this context of immense diversification and modernisation - and its products were something from the past which had not caught up with the times and thus were relegated to the sidelines.

In the 1970's, the formation of a modern Hong Kong identity as distinct from mainland Chinese or Taiwanese, could be discerned in the media. Cantonese pop songs (pioneered by Sam Hui) triumphed over mandarin pop songs and gained popularity with lyrics that marked a local identity and a common aspiration. Television series represented Hong Kong's success as a result of its hardworking, intelligent and virtuous people. A Hong Kong identity distinct from mainland Chinese was clearly visible by 1979 when the television character of a mainland immigrant 'A Can' was ridiculed as a dumb and greedy country-pumpkin. The sense of identification with the mainland before the late 1960's had vanished. It was 'a historical movement between genuine attempts to accommodate political refugees from China following 1949 and later resentment of economic migrants from the Mainland who became objects of mirth.' The pejorative stereotyping of Mainlanders evident in the 'A Can syndrome' arose out of a new local consciousness (Cheng Yu 1985 & 1990 in Lilley 1993:278).

The period was a time of rationality and scienticism, of economic expansion and the accumulation of wealth, of conspicuous consumption and consumerism - these were the dominant discourses on modern life that were fundamentally opposed to the folk traditions as represented by herbal tea shops. It was also a time when the boundary between the public and the private was strengthened - increased self-sufficiency of the household in terms of space and resources made public space less necessary and attractive. Herbal tea shops as public spaces and herbal tea as a symbol of the traditional suffered serious setbacks in the course of Hong Kong's search for a modern identity.

IN SEARCH OF CHINESENESS: 1985-PRESENT

In this period, we can see a return of herbal tea shops in a conspicuously 'Chinese' image, particularly strong in the 1990's. Their revival could be seen in the light of rising health consciousness, a yearning for enchantment in the metropolis, the rise of an eating-out culture that interacts with a changing family meal pattern, and surrounding all of these, a search for Chinese cultural identity.

Revival and reformation of herbal tea shops

Concerns for health have been swarming into the local scene from various directions and cumulated in a call for the return to the natural from 1980's onwards, increasing in scale and influence ever since. A denunciation of MSG gave rise to some restaurants and products marketing themselves as 'MSG-free'. Calls for a diet with more fibre, less sugar and less fat were found in all kinds of media and daily talk about food. Healthy eating has become part of the modern Hong Kong lifestyle.

Clever entrepreneurs have made use of these new concerns for the body and created a whole new image for herbal tea shops. A modern, hygienic image was designed for Wong Lo Kat's first shop in the 1980's. In 1987, Wong Lo Kat (Ltd) Co. aimed at building an image 'like an ordinary place serving drinks', explains its current director, Ms Wong. It deliberately de-emphasized the medicinal effects of herbal tea. Ms Wong points out, 'People might think, 'why should I drink herbal tea, I'm not sick!' When I first started the shop business, I was not so sure about the market. Even though people accept Chinese medicine, maybe they are very specific about the prescription, they might not just come in for a drink.' It may be for the same reason that the term 'medical tea' has been replaced by 'herbal tea' on the package of Wong Lo Kat's products. Moreover, Ms Wong also admits that since their brand is very well-known, it is not necessary to be emphatic about the medicinal qualities of the drink. To retain its 'traditional' image, Wong Lo Kat continues with its old practice of giving sweet preserved plums to those who have had the bitter taste twenty-four herb tea.

Popularisation of herbal tea started in 1985 with Wong Lo Kat herbal tea *chìng lèuhng chàh* as ready-to-drink box drinks, available in supermarkets and convenience stores. This further buttressed the role of herbal tea as soft drinks, originally composed only of chrysanthemum tea in the packaged drinks business, bringing in a Chinese element onto the shelves filled with carbonated beverages. Furthermore, Wong Lo Kat, followed by others such as Sung Mau Tai (生茂泰), produced a variety of instant herbal tea with different medicinal effects, often specified on the packages or elaborated with a separate sheet, the latter frequently emphasising the historical pedigree of the prescription. Honey herbal (川貝枇杷蜜), Cane and Carrot Juice (甘火竹蔗汁) etc. are some of the versions available, as a modern counterpart to those from the mainland with quality packaging as guarantee of hygiene and modernity, thus more appealing to the urban middle class who pay for both the effects and image.

Contrary to the older brand, the new wave of herbal tea shops in the 1990's has tried in various ways - naming, decor and product diversification - to establish themselves as part of Chinese cultural heritage while maximising business. These new players in the game do not have the long-established reputation of Wong Lo Kat or Kung Wo Tong to guarantee success, and it is necessary to make their name by accommodating the changing health, cultural and social needs of the people.

Naming

Names reminiscent of a traditional world are used - 'Hui Lau Shan', which was a famous herbal tea shop in Yuen Long before the 1970's, or Hung Fook Tong (鴻福堂), Tung Chi Tong (同治堂)[4] , or a famous charitable Chinese clinic Po Chi Lam (寶芝林) situated in Fo Shan (佛山).

Curiously, the last is a chain started by a famous film star Kwan Tak Hing (關德興) well known for his role as Wong Fei Hung (黃飛鴻), the Chinese kung-fu expert as well as medical practitioner who ran the clinic Po Chi Lam. The character is well-known for his expertise in martial arts as much as his virtues as a righteous, disciplined, humble master of charity. Ms Lee, one of the directors of Po Chi Lam, says that the shops are intended to carry on the charitable nature of the original Po Chi Lam by providing Chinese medicine to people. Suffice to note that the names of herbal tea shops are designed to remind us of their Chinese origins.

Decor

There are chiefly two styles which herbal tea shops adopt: the dominant one assumes the look of a family main hall. Motifs of Chineseness, like golden dragons, are frequently used. The names of the shops are often golden-plated on a wooden tablet and hung high at the centre of the shop's front. A golden bell-shaped Taoist urn is found in many of them. The Taoist concerns of longevity and alchemy are evoked with these urns known for brewing medicine. This motif, though present in some old herbal tea shops like Kung Wo Tong, has not been a prominent feature in the past.[5] Wood features strongly in the whole makeup of the shop furniture, the walls and the arches. Two rhyming couplets in Chinese calligraphy articulating the 'spirit' of the shop can be seen in a number of shops. Chinese paintings may also be seen in the shop.

The other style foregrounds Nature, suggesting a rustic life of peace and simplicity. The Best Herbal Tea Shop chain displays medicinal herbs in various ways - in glass cabinets or large glass tubes, depending on individual shop size - but the message is that they are faithful to the original use of Chinese medicinal herbs. There is also a running waterwheel at every shop's front, constantly on the move, suggesting a life of harmony with Nature. Together with the dominant green shade, as well as the use of fake tree trunks as seats, a sense of tranquillity and Nature is created as one consumes the drink among the herbs displayed. It is a place where enchantment in a 'disenchanted world' (Weber) can be found.

We should also note that these herbal tea shops have adopted an open design - no doors to push open as people enter. This is so in spite of the fact that air-conditioning is provided in all of them. Unlike the new restaurants of the 1970's with their conspicuous stickers on their doors that read 'Air conditioning -Please close doors!'. This openness is suggestive of a communal life in a friendly neighbourhood. The removal of the physical barrier of doors attempts to symbolise a world without suspicion and few social barriers. It is an attempt to create the old tea-shop kind of atmosphere whereby the customers could sit and watch as life went buzzing by out on the streets. In the actual operation of the shop, however, customers are not as welcome as in the pre-modern era to linger on in the shop. The manager of Po Chi Lam says, 'It's not so good for a customer to sit for half an hour with only one drink, we need more business.' The atmosphere is, thus, an illusion rather than a genuine attempt to induce communality.

Such decor tries to stimulate a leisurely pace of life for its customers by making reference to the lives of the old literati, to a traditional and sophisticated way of life, and to a harmonic coexistence with Nature. It is an appeal to modern urban dwellers who desire a break from the hubbub of everyday life.

Products

Diversity is a must for those who want to survive fierce competition. Diversity and syncretisation govern the expansion of herbal tea shops. Besides the basic types of herbal tea, all new herbal tea shops have added new drinks or snacks to their list - items that would have surprised people who frequented herbal tea shops in the 1950's. Some feature fruit juices and desserts - Hui Lau Shan being the most successful, along with their famous sago fruit mix. They managed to expand between 1992-94, on a franchise basis, to almost 40 branches. Others also try to enhance their repertoire of traditional items with fruit desserts. Variations on a theme can be seen as new drinks and new desserts made with different herbs can be found in every shop. Po Chi Lam introduced a drink of Papaya Milk with *géi jí*. American ginseng with turtle jelly is currently the main marketing item for a number of chains.

Health is the dominant theme in this diversification, and so herbal tea shops are clearly a case of the localisation of the global health trend. Alongside aerobic dance, the bestseller book Fit for Life, diet and slimming programmes, MSG-free cuisine and vegetarianism, herbal tea shops have found their niche in the rising health consciousness by drawing on traditional Chinese medicine and health concepts and placing them side by side with items *perceived* as 'western foods': in this case, the fresh fruit desserts.[6] Epitomised in the advertising slogan of Tung Chi Tong, 'Chinese medicine of Han formula, Fresh Fruit Delicacies', the new herbal tea shops' survival need to cater for the syncretic beliefs and needs of the consumers. The interest in and recognition of Chinese medicine in modern Hong Kong are rapidly on the rise in the run-up to 1997.

Herbal tea shops? The case of Hui Lau Shan

Hui Lau Shan has been the most prominent of all among Chinese herb tea permit holders. Its first shop was founded in Yuen Long before the 1970's, most famous for its turtle jelly. In the 1990's, its arrival in Causeway Bay, one of the busiest business districts on Hong Kong island, as a herbal tea shop was accompanied by the introduction of fresh fruit desserts with sago. The fresh fruit sago business has become synonymous with Hui Lau Shan,which has claimed to be the creator of 'fresh fruit sago mix (首創鮮果西米露)'. Their business has also expanded into selling 'handmade beef balls'. The diversification of its products from turtle jelly and herbal tea to fresh fruit sago mix and related desserts, and now to beefballs, has led to an 'identity crisis' in 1994.

It has established itself more as a fruit and dessert shop than a herbal tea shop. The display of fresh fruits and the counter with blenders filled with different fruit juices in every shop is a far cry from herbal tea shops. Many of those who have visited Hui Lau Shan are not even aware of the availability of twenty-four herb tea and turtle jelly. Others said they would go to other shops for these traditional items for Hui is only good for desserts. Few recognise it as a herbal tea shop and as one of my informants pointed out that the Taoist urn is not present anymore.[7] Hui Lau Shan has marginalized herbal tea to a self-service counter which is obviously designed to discourage people from consuming drinks (HK$5-10) inside the shop, saving seats for those who are paying much more for the fruit desserts (HK$20-35).

Shops like Hui Lau Shan and Po Chi Lam are no longer just places for herbal tea. They have turned into health food halls that combine the provisions of a herbal tea shop, a fruit stall and a dessert shop - businesses that were previously distinct. They are places to visit in between shopping trips, after the movies or after a meal. The peak of business is often after lunch and dinner for most herbal tea shops in business districts, plus afternoon tea time in the shopping districts. The popularity of these new 'snack' shops reflect changes in the meal patterns of Hong Kong people. Between-meal eating activities have become much more popular in Hong Kong, particularly desserts. The spread is also a reflection of changing trends of consumerism. The new herbal tea shops have in fact grown on the fertile grounds laid by chain dessert specialty shops like Daniel (燉奶佬) with simple, practical design and small shop size that serve a mixture of traditional Chinese desserts (almond paste, sesame paste, and other sweet soups) and fresh fruit desserts (mainly sago with fruits, fresh fruit and milk drinks). Hui Lau Shan and others have incorporated these snacks in addition to herbal tea to cater for the consumers' palate, eating patterns (increased consumption of snacks), modern health concerns, as well as demand for stylish decor. The final triumph of these desserts by overshadowing the sale of herbal tea illustrates their greater popularity as well as profitability. This further encourages the shopowners to develop their products in the direction of snacks rather than drinks.

At the same time, Hui Lau Shan is facing a 'crisis of identity' because it has violated the Urban Services Department's regulations on herbal tea shops.[8] However, diversification is, as explained by the director of Po Chi Lam, a necessary survival strategy in view of the high rents. They have to risk breaking regulations in order to sustain business.[9] On the other hand, this 'identity crisis' compels us to look into the revival of herbal tea shops as such. There is more to it than the resilience of beliefs in Chinese folk medicine. People obviously go there for things other than just herbal tea. The statistical growth of herbal tea shops would look very different without Hui Lau Shan, which has deviated from official as well as popular conceptions of herbal tea shops. The case of Hui Lau Shan makes it necessary to look at the popularity of these shops in another light.

NOSTALGIA AND CULTURAL IDENTITY

Herbal tea shops may signify a modern sentimental yearning for the past. We should note that these ethnic 'establishments are designed for local Chinese rather than tourists: the English language and non-Chinese visitors are conspicuous by their absence from these shops. The boundary between Chinese and foreigners in popular eateries is probably strongest in these outlets. Are they part of a 'romantically sanitised version of Chinese history' (Lilley 1993:267) which does not have to be authentic as long as it shows us what a Chinese herbal tea shop should be and what this Chineseness is idealised as? Echoes may be found in Lilley's analysis of television in Hong Kong (1993) about the 'defence of "Chinese culture"' through production of old costume films or serialisation of Chinese novels and stories,

> an idealist preoccupation with authentic origins, stereotypes which endow present reality with, to borrow a phrase from Jameson, 'the spell and distance of a glossy mirage.
>
> (Lilley 1993:267)

Similarly, herbal tea shops are no longer 'old-fashioned' or backward - they have been renewed and transformed through our embracing of nostalgia. And as Robert Nisbet writes: 'Nostalgia tells us more about present moods than about past realities' (cited in Davis 1979:10).

As television productions indicate, herbal tea shops are not alone in this move 'back to the future'. Nostalgic eating has been found in other parts of our food culture since the late 1980's and has become more prominent in the past few years. 'Ah Yee Leng Tong' is one of the first popular Chinese restaurants to have a traditional decor and a detailed account of the medicinal effects of soups in their menus. The upmarket congee restaurant 'Big Bowl' and the dessert and snack shop 'Sweet Dynasty' have decor and advertisements with a distinctively Chinese flavour - shop logos using Chinese calligraphy or in the form of a sculpted name chop, posters with Chinese woman dressed in *chèuhng sàam* complemented by waitresses in similar dress code, not to mention wooden tablets and furniture - that appeal to our nostalgia for 'something Chinese'. Quotations from Chinese classics in their publicity material are used to illustrate their virtues. 'Yat Chau Health Restaurant' - with its own restaurant, its own Chinese herbalist stationed there to consult and prescribe, and its own herbal medicine shop - is an institutionalization of the Chinese concepts of health and diet, proclaiming a legitimate status for Chinese medicine not available at the governmental level. Nostalgic decor is not only found in eateries, a high class department store has adopted the look of an old Shanghai tailor shop and the name of 'Shanghai Tang', using simplified Chinese characters as another means to convey its 'Chineseness'. This in itself is ironic since simplified characters were not in use in those pre-communist days. Furthermore, age-old brands like Two Girls perfume have been revived and are building up their own market in the fierce competition with international labels. Though equipped with a modern logo, the old posters with two Chinese girls in chèuhng sàam are the chief marketing tools. Pulling itself out of obsolescence, Two Girls Brand has found acceptance in modern Hong Kong by bringing in a diversity of new products under its traditional image, selling them in super-malls like the Times Square. The new herbal tea shops are definitely not alone in this return to the 'past'. Significantly, director of Po Chi Lam insists that the decor of their shops is not a return to the past, but part of the 'new trend'.

The 'Chinese' image is more important than the content for these enterprises. In this context, it seems that food has become secondary - whether the tea or dessert in herbal tea shops does have its proclaimed effects are not a matter of central concern; it is the 'Chineseness' of the consumption experience that is cherished. Similarly, the authenticity of the reference to elites drinking tea or having desserts in such a way needs no validation. The important thing is that we are having a taste of an idyllic past and of the 'roots' of our culture, that we are finally coming to terms with our Chinese identity. The full page advertisement of Shanghai Tang, the newly opened department store, succinctly articulates this in their captions:

Grab Hold of The Image-nation of Sino-Centrism,
With a Clear Direction To Have an Auspicious opening.
抓緊大中國主義的形象化傾向，旗幟鮮明地開張大吉。
(Ming Pao 4/3/1995)

Hundred Flowers Bloom, Hundred Fabrics Together,
Hundred Goods and Gifts, Hundred Colour Revolt.
百花齊放，百錦交集。百貨精品，百色起義。

(Ming Pao 5/3/1995)

Juxtaposing Chinese folk ideas of suspiciousness and nationalism, the consumerist ideal and revolutionary slogans, against a background with marching young revolutionaries in a flowery frame is a clever mixture of the competing discourses in contemporary Hong Kong. The appeal is designed specifically to the Chinese population in Hong Kong (and maybe, the relevant authorities), for the English copy has little of this mixture with the caption, *Joyful Shop Now Swollen to Great Size, Put Your Foot in It* (South China Morning Post 4/3/1995) and *Please View Our Honest and Sophistication Products from Very Long Range* (South China Morning Post 5/4/1995). What the press says about Shanghai Tang also applies to herbal tea shops, and other 'nostalgic' enterprises,

traditional Chinese products served up with a modern, funky spin and set in an atmosphere of Old World Chinese elegance.

(South China Morning Post 25/2/1995)

I find in this 'new trend' an active reconstruction of the 'past', a kind of fantasy world in which Hong Kong people could find an affirmation of their Chinese identity.

Why has this nostalgic movement emerged at such a time? What does this nostalgia tell us about 'present moods'? Interestingly, the revival of herbal tea shops started slowly in 1985, a year after the signing of the Joint Declaration, and has been gathering much momentum in the past few years -in the run-up to 1997 and in a time of extreme uncertainty under strained relations between the Chinese and British governments. In the words of Davis (1979), the Hong Kong people are experiencing an 'identity discontinuity'. Chineseness which was identified as an obstacle to modernisation is now being re-evaluated and appreciated in the light of the handover. Hong Kong people are to become Chinese people and not British subjects after more than 150 years of British rule. A Hong Kong metropolitan identity has to be negotiated with its Chinese 'roots'. It is a collective identity crisis and a collective search for identity. Chinese systems of knowledge about the cosmos like geomancy, astrology, *fùng séui*, have sprung up from the depths of popular culture to become dominant discourses in our search for meaning in the present - such as in the ghost train advertisement discussed by Grant Evans in the pages below.

That there is no active discovery of what contemporary China has to offer is a sign of reservation about the impending identity. What is being retrieved from the archives of Chinese culture is the apparently familiar and the folkloric, an indefinable past that all Chinese is expected to recognise because of its apparent familiarity and strong Chinese essence. It is not a nostalgia of a specific past, like that in the United States in the 70's[10] that found the world of the 50's a comforting realm, and an affirmation of their identities. Those who are most affected by the uncertainty of the transition, namely the younger generations whose futures are closely bound up with the political future of Hong Kong, are also the most active participants in the nostalgia. They are also the generations who have been brought up to recognise the 'Chineseness' as represented by herbal tea, the wooden arches, the furniture and Taoist urns. It is a collective nostalgia removed of any political or nationalistic sentiments or content. Decolonisation in Hong Kong has failed to bring about the usual joys in the prospects of rediscovering a national identity. There is little to rejoice over for Hong Kong people who are uncertain and worried about the future. It is an exceptional case in the history of decolonisation in which even the hope of autonomy and self-rule after the colonialists departed is never seriously entertained. When reality has little to offer, it seems, Hong Kong people take the active step to search for the folkloric and idyllic.

I agree with Davis (1979) that 'nostalgic evocation of some past state of affairs occurs in the context of present fears, discontents, anxieties, or uncertainties', and that nostalgia is an attempt 'to abort or, at the very least, deflect' the threat of identity discontinuity (Davis 1979:108). In the attempt to minimise havoc in the transition of sovereignty, the return to Chinese roots is not one without its doubts or suspicion.

CONCLUSION

One can picture the little Wong Lo Kat herbal tea shop, situated near the Man Mo Temple a century ago, standing as the guardian of the masses who had few other means to manage their lives besides the shop's miraculous concoction of herbs. The ecology of the colony made herbal tea a much needed means of self-medication when institutional provisions were seriously inadequate and living conditions deplorable. Bodily balance of 'hot', 'cold', 'wet' and 'dry' were practically the only guidelines along which the Chinese could govern their lives by, and herbal tea was the most convenient and accessible means for maintenance of health.

Having survived the war side by side with their patrons, herbal tea shops pioneered by Wong Lo Kat spread vigorously by opening more shops and producing packaged teas for sale. In order to attract business, herbal tea shops established themselves as social and entertainment centres for the majority who lacked a private space. By bringing people of different origins into the same venue, herbal tea shops contributed to the integration of community who shared a common plight of poor living and working conditions. Yet by exposing them to the modern world through the electronic media, herbal tea shops participated in their own downfall and they were abandoned during the colony's search for modernity in the 1970's to search for modernity, pioneered by the first generation of local born people.

In the construction of a metropolitan Hong Kong identity, traditional Chineseness had to be abandoned in favour of the international and the modern. It was not until the mid-1980's that a revival of herbal tea shops began as part of the search for identity at a time of intense uncertainties. The representation of herbal tea shops as part of traditional Chinese culture explains their popularity among a population eager to mark themselves as Hong Kong Chinese before the handover to the Communist Chinese government.

> Representations of a past before Communism collapse the problem of national identification and objections to the present regime. It is an aesthetic mode which mesmerises with the comfort of continuity, which demands little engagement with the dilemmas of current experience.

> (Lilley 1993:267)

Maybe it is a kind of escapism, but one with good cause at a time of significant transition. Chinese medicine and its related practices like geomancy have re-emerged as 'positive, desirable cultural symbols' (Wu 1979:29) in the decade before 1997 for the Chinese nationals-to-be who have found in a romantic past an ideal to which their identity can lay claim.

Herbal tea is a symbol of the Chinese folk system of beliefs and practices. The uses of herbal tea shops have been engaged in a continuous process of construction, maintenance and negotiation of

Hong Kong identity. Herbal tea shops are a reflection of the increasing prominence traditional Chinese medicine has gained in the few years before the return to China, where Chinese medicine enjoys legitimacy within the state. More importantly, herbal tea shops 'dramatised' for us the vigorous processes of a cultural identity construction at a time of rapid social and political changes, when the impending national identity is regarded with suspicion and uncertainty. Hopes and fantasies about the future are thus displaced to the cultural realm. Nostalgia as manifested in the new herbal tea shops, among other businesses, is a perfect illustration of Davis's argument that: 'nostalgia is a distinctive way...of relating our past to our present and future...nostalgia is deeply implicated in the sense of who we are, what we are about, and...whither we go' (Davis 1979:31).

NOTES

1 Information from the Hong Kong Report 1958 shows that there were 2,500 subscribers at the end of 1958. Information from the Cost of Living Survey 1958-63/4 conducted and published by the Hong Kong Commerce and Industry Department Statistics Branch shows that there were 10,834 television subscribers among 680,000 households in 1961.
2 A semi-skilled worker earned $4-$8 a day in 1958 (Hong Kong Report 1958).
3 In the 1970's, going to a western-style restaurant was an event in itself and children (like myself) regarded it as a treat, and were usually taken there as some sort of reward.
4 The word *tóng* means hall, as used in *chì tóng* - ancestral hall.
5 These Taoist urns could not be found in pictures of Wong Lo Kat in the 1940's and 1950's.
6 Health and fitness advice, chiefly from the American nutritionists and publishers, emphasize the need to gain vitamins and fibre in their most *natural* forms, as in fresh fruits.
7 Actually, I managed to locate the 'original' Hui Lau Shan in Causeway Bay. It has the Taoist urn, but it is obscurely placed behind a rubbish bin of about the same height, next to the side door rather than the shop's front.
8 The Urban Services Department has regulations that specify twelve items that can be sold in licensed Chinese herbal tea shops. Hui Lau Shan and similar shops have violated this regulation by selling things beyond the list, thus turning themselves into a 'restaurant' which would require a range of renovations and expansions in order to comply with the minimum requirements for restaurant size and availability of washrooms.
9 During the interview, the director of Po Chi Lam told me that the two desserts cabinet would be removed the following day to prepare for an Urban Services Department inspection. However, the menus which have a long list of desserts and other non-herbal-tea items would not be removed because, 'they won't be that strict'. So, one can observe that the regulations are not readily invoked to penalise illegitimate businesses of herbal tea shops.
10 The nostalgia in the US in the 1970's takes place when the country is engaged in a period of rapid changes and a crisis of identity.

REFERENCES CITED

Anderson, E. N.
  1980 'Heating' and 'Cooling' Foods in Hong Kong and Taiwan. Social
         Science Information, 19(2):237-268.
  1984 'Heating and Cooling' Foods Re-examined. Social Science
         Information 23(4/5):755-73.
Anderson & Anderson
  1975 Folk Dietetics in Two Chinese Communities, and Its Implications for
         the Study of Chinese Medicine. In Medicine in Chinese Cultures:
         Comparative Studies of Healthcare in Chinese and Other Societies,
         Arthur Kleinman ed. Washington: US Dept of Health, Education, and
         Welfare, Public Health Service, National Institutes of Health.
Davis, Fred
  1979 Yearning for Yesterday: A Sociology of Nostalgia. The Free Press:
         New York
Guldin, G.
  1980 Whose Neighbourhood is This? Ethnicity and Community in Hong
         Kong. UrbanAnthropology 9(2).
Hong Kong Government
  1938 Hong Kong Report.
  1969 Hong Kong Report.
Hong Kong Urban Council & Sanitary Department
  1950-51 Annual Report. Pp.39.
Hong Kong Urban Council & Urban Services Department
  1958 Statistical Report Appendix. p.2.
  1959 Statistical Report Appendix. p.52.
  1962 Statistical Report Appendix. p.62.
  1965 Statistical Report Appendix. Table 21.
  1967 Statistical Report Appendix. p.67.
  1968 Statistical Report Appendix. p.71.
  1969 Statistical Report Appendix. p.105.
  1971 Statistical Report Appendix. p.133.
  1972 Statistical Report Appendix. Table 19.
  1974 Statistical Report Appendix 33.
  1978 Statistical Report Appendix 26.
  1983 Statistical Report Appendix. p.10.
  1985 Statistical Report Appendix. p.29.
  1988 Statistical Report Appendix. p.39.
  1989 Statistical Report Appendix. p.48.
  1990 Statistical Report Appendix. p.58.

Information of 1992, 1993, 1994 from communications with the Urban Services Department

Koo, L. C.
  1984 The Use of Food to Treat and Prevent Disease in Chinese Culture. Soc. Sci. & Med (18)9:757-764.

Lang, G. & Ragvald L.
  1988 Upward Mobility of a Refugee God: Hong Kong's Huang Daxian. The Stockholm Journal of East Asian Studies 1.
  1993 The Rise of a Refugee God: Hong Kong's Wong Tai Sin. Hong Kong: Oxford University Press.

Lilley, R.
  1993 Claiming Identity: Film and Television in Hong Kong. History and Anthropology 6(2-3):261-292.

Tam, S. M.
  1984 Cooling Tea: Past, Present and Future. Unplublished B. Soc. Sci. Thesis, Department of Anthropology, The Chinese University of Hong Kong.

Topley, Majorie
  1975 Chinese and Western Medicine in Hong Kong: Some Socialand Cultural Determinants of Variation, Interaction and Change. In Medicine in Chinese Cultures: Comparative Studies of Healthcare in Chinese and other Societies. Arthur Kleinman ed. Washington: US Dept of Health, Education, and Welfare, Public Health Service, National Institutes of Health.

Turner, Matthew
  1994 60's/90's Dissolving the People. Publication by the Arts Centre.

Wu, D. Y. H.
  1979 Traditional Chinese Concepts of Food and Medicine in Singapore. Institute of SoutheastAsian Studies, Singapore Occasional Paper No.55.

CULTURAL STUDIES

4

OF MIMICRY AND MERMAIDS
HONG KONG AND THE
DOCUMENTARY FILM LEGACY

Philip Robertson

I feel I am a broker conducting the biggest deal between history and the future. Among those who live in Hong Kong at this time, who doesn't?

Popular songwriter Luo Dayou[1]

'Plover Cove Reservoir' (1962) is a typical black and white newsreel from the *Hong Kong Today* series produced on a monthly basis during the 1960s by the film-making arm of colonial Government, the Hong Kong Film Unit. In keeping with the magazine item's prosaic title, for most of its five minute duration the commentary matter-of-factly describes the engineering processes involved in reclaiming a small inlet from the sea to create a freshwater lake, then the film draws to a close with a night sequence of men on board a small fishing trawler hauling in nets. 'After the seawall is built and as the salt water is being pumped out,' the Cantonese voice-over explains, 'Government workers prepare to clean the basin by trawling for small fish and other marine life, working day and night.' Suddenly, out of the darkness, a young woman rises unnoticed from the black water and climbs aboard; she is naked from the waist up, her long hair covering her breasts, and from the waist down she wears a scaly fishtail costume. In the reverse angle shot which follows, a worker turns from handling the nets and catches sight of the mermaid, now reclining on the net-strewn deck; in medium close shot, he registers astonishment and delight. As if unsure whether the worker's amateur acting has made the point of the scene strongly enough, the commentary spells it out: 'Is it a dream or the real thing?' The film then cuts back to a wide shot of the mermaid, who smiles coyly and extends her arms in invitation. As if in response to the question, and affirming an answer in favour of reality, the fisherman jumps into the frame to embrace the mermaid. On this note the sequence and with it the news item itself fades to black.

The audience – Chinese and expatriate, young and old – laugh and applaud. It is November 1994, and this screening takes place at the Hong Kong Arts Centre as part of an exhibition entitled *Hong Kong Sixties: Designing Identity*. A documentary filmmaker by trade, I am presenting a talk on the Hong Kong Film Unit's work which places it within a specific film tradition and reads it in terms of current documentary theory.[2] In this cross-cultural setting, with its own ambiguities of power and knowledge, the mermaid in the newsreel raises a set of related questions about documentary film itself. These are questions about the form's negotiation of power and knowledge at a specific cultural site, and they have to do with the interaction of memory, history and the documentary tradition. This essay is concerned with a particular conjunction of post-colonial subjectivity and its archive. It seeks to theorise the construction, through documentary film, of an earlier Hong Kong as a way into understanding aspects of contemporary cultural production. To my mind, and on many levels, the mermaid is spectacularly out of time, and out of place. As she clambers from the dark South China Sea on board the Hong Kong Government fishing boat, the mermaid rises out of myth into history, surfaces from dreaming into representation and crosses time-honoured borders between fiction and documentary. It is at these blurred boundaries that this essay is situated, a place of dislocation and transition which resonates with to that of the people of Hong Kong.

PROJECTING HONG KONG

The first official public reference to the Hong Kong Film Unit invokes a term with a history: 'there is no doubt that the short film is both an invaluable medium for reaching large sections of Hong Kong's population and an excellent vehicle for 'projecting' Hong Kong overseas' (HKGAR 1960:243). This felicitous metaphor for the promotion of official policies through the screening of films comes from a specific institutional and formal tradition, that of the documentary movement founded by John Grierson, the 'father of British documentary' (Barsam 1973:7). In his history of Australia's Commonwealth Film Unit, Moran notes:

Projection was the preferred term in [the Commonwealth Film Unit] for the generation of national awareness . . . It has been used by Canadians about their documentary films, and indeed it was a favourite term of Grierson's, both in Canada and in Britain. In particular it was the term used in a seminal pamphlet by Grierson's patron, Sir Stephen Tallents at the Empire Marketing Board, for the idea of national ideology, *The Projection of England* (1932).

(Moran 1991:135)

As well as defining both an ideology and an aesthetic which was to dominate documentary for a generation (Barnouw 1993), this movement also created an institutional structure which was readily reproduceable throughout the British Empire, under the guidance of Grierson himself in Canada (1939), New Zealand (1941) and Australia (1945) (Moran 1991). In 1958 it was extended to Hong Kong, when the Public Relations Officer submitted a confidential report to Government on his return from a London conference for British Foreign Service information officers. The Report argued for a greatly expanded and 'modernised' publicity apparatus and for the establishment of a Government film-making capability:

Apart from prestige documentary films in colour, running time 15 to 20 minutes, of which we could with profit use at least one a year, the field for short news and magazine items to be used both in cinema newsreels and television programmes is practically unlimited . . . . [Television's] consumption is so voracious that almost any competently made news "short" with reasonable story value is likely to secure acceptance.

(Murray 1958:7–8)

Behind the Report's argument lay a fear that Hong Kong was falling behind other 'colonial territories' in terms of expenditure on publicity: in fact, lying third from the bottom in a list of 24 that included numerous African, Mediterranean and Carribean possessions as well as others closer to home such as 'Singapore, Malaya, Fiji and Brunei' (Murray 1958:2, and Appendix 'D'). 'Comparisons are notoriously odious and can be misleading, but most colonies are spending much more on their information services' (Murray 1958:2). By late 1959 a film unit comprising four people – an expatriate writer/director/producer, known as the Unit Head or Films Officer, and three locals who managed the photographic and organisational work – was officially in place (HKGAR 1960:242–243) (see Figure 1).

The output of this small film-making team fell into three distinct forms or genres: half-hour documentaries aimed at overseas audiences, monthly newsreels and magazine items for both local and international consumption, and educational material produced on behalf of other Government Departments for purely local use. It is significant that only two of these categories are present in the Report which led to the Unit's founding:

> Suitable subjects for films are – like those for illustrated booklets – abundant. We need initially a good general film dealing with the Colony as a whole, and this should probably be brought up to date and re-angled at least every three years. Our industrial expansion, specific aspects of that expansion, our tourist attractions, our achievements in resettlement and rehousing, the port of Hong Kong, educational programmes and so on, can all be considered either for full length prestige films or as magazine items.
>
> (Murray 1958:8)

The category that has been elided here is informational film intended solely for local audiences. Taken together with its invocation of television, which would not arrive in Hong Kong for another decade, this exclusion suggests that the Report had its eyes fixed firmly overseas. Colonialism structures its audience into a hierarchy of value, placing its metropolitan masters above the demands of local audiences, then maps this hierarchy on to the production process. For the Hong Kong Film Unit, this meant that their flagship, prestige documentaries of the 1960s (and well into the 1970s), were produced by either London corporate film production houses or their local expatriate-staffed off-shoots (HKGAR 1960–70).[3] The Film Unit production schedule became a question of selecting appropriate 'writers' and 'voices' for different audiences. In this regard the Report represents a classic *locus* of colonial discourse (see Spurr 1993), where the brute realities of media and economic power wielded locally is displaced into an 'international' language of markets and outlets deriving from the commercial television and film distribution industries, a jargon of 'story-value' and 'angles' drawn from Western media (Murray was a journalist), and common-sense models of audience and communication theory.[4]

The Unit's first effort at 'projecting Hong Kong overseas' – the 'prestige documentary in colour' of the 1958 Report – was subcontracted out to Cathay Films of Singapore, a European-staffed production house which set up a local arm on the strength of this one job.[5] After final vetting by London, *This is Hong Kong* was 'approved, subject to certain minor modifications' in late 1960 (HKGAR 1960:243). In the same year the expatriate Films Officer and his local team also produced their first films intended for Hong Kong people themselves, 'four short films explaining the aims of the 1961 Census to the community at large' (HKGAR 1960:242). Shot in black and white on silent 35mm cameras, combining actuality shots of Hong Kong street scenes with awkwardly dramatised 'typical family' scenes, featuring standard library music and a patronising Cantonese voice-over translated from an English original, these were low-budget local versions of Grierson's 'educationals' (Grierson 1946:78–80). Like colonialism, the Griersonian aesthetic erects its own scale of production value which runs from 'bread and butter' work at the bottom to more 'prestige' production at the top. In Hong Kong, of course, this hierarchy is coloured by ideas of race.

Fine formal distinctions within this work of the Unit between documentary, propaganda and film journalism are not important for my argument, though they are of course a matter of on-going debate in documentary theory (Paget 1990; Winston 1995), as they were in Grierson's day (Adamson 1993). Grierson himself entered this debate in oft-quoted terms: 'I look on the cinema as a pulpit', and 'it is as a hammer rather than a mirror that I have sought to use the medium' (Grierson 1946:12, 24). Nevertheless, he has difficulty pinning his project down:

> The documentary idea, after all, demands no more than that the affairs of our time shall be brought to the screen in any fashion which strikes the imagination and makes observation a little richer than it was. At one level, the vision may be journalistic; at another, it may rise to poetry and drama. At another level again, its aesthetic quality may lie in the mere lucidity of its exposition.
>
> (Grierson 1946:19)

And elsewhere:

> Beyond the newsmen and the magazine men and the lecturers (comic or interesting or exciting or only rhetorical) one begins to wander into the world of documentary proper, into the only world in which documentary can hope to achieve the ordinary virtues of

an art. Here we pass from the plain (or fancy) descriptions of natural material, to arrangements, re-arrangements, and creative shapings of it.

(Grierson 1946:79)

The film syntax that the British documentary movement developed over the whole body of its work is consistent, however, and readily characterised. Arising as a solution to the limitations of contemporary film technology – unblimped 35mm cameras which made synchronised sound recording impossible, heavy and cumbersome equipment, and slow film speeds – the classic Griersonian documentary typically constructs its argument through a highly-crafted 'montage' set to music of silent, staged actuality material. Its narrative is driven by the aptly-named 'voice-of-God' commentary (see Winston 1995; Nichols 1991; Barnouw 1993). This particular 'jargon of authenticity' in turn authorises meaning and truth (Arthur 1993); the formal conventions become naturalised as transparent reproduction of reality. This specific representational style with its characteristic epistemological under-pinnings is shared by all the work of the movement, including both documentary aspiring to the 'ordinary virtues of art' and their more humble cousins, the 'educationals'. The style becomes 'the classic documentary' (Barnouw 1993).

But somewhere between Government informational film and 'prestige documentary' lies that more ambiguous category of Hong Kong Film Unit production: the 'monthly newsreel or magazine item'. It is here that the mermaid surfaced in 1962. In this 'hybrid' film form the twin hierarchies of colonialism and Griersonian documentary do not appear as stable as theory might wish.

RHETORIC OF EMPIRE

What is startling about the mermaid's appearance is her irruption without warning into a film discourse that operates by other rules entirely. 'Plover Cove Reservoir' is constructed like all the Film Unit's work according to the aesthetics of Griersonian documentary. Indeed, the night fishing sequence may be read as direct homage to one of the tradition's masterpieces, *Drifters* (1929) (Barnouw 1993:87–88).[6] Mermaids do not normally surface in these 'realist documentary' texts, at least not without being marked off in some way from the actuality footage that surrounds them, clearly coded as dream sequence or poetic interlude (Winston 1995). Yet, as the shot by shot description at the beginning of this essay signals, none of the classic conventions for representing ghosts or dreams – for example, double exposure, soft focus, effect lighting, signature music – are brought to bear here: the mermaid exists on the same plane of reality as the fisherman who embraces her. What I want to suggest is that the mermaid sequence hints at the kind of tensions and slippages that may occur when a film form invented to service a metropolitan, national project at a particular moment in history is deployed thirty years later in colonial space. Both the Hong Kong Film Unit and its body of documentary work is – like the figure of the mermaid – out of time, out of place.

Writing in 1988, Teresa Ma characterises Film Unit production during the 60s as follows:

> The documentaries of the day [were] apolitical, devoid of ideology, flavourless. Even then what remained was not exactly objective. For the colonial bureaucrats, events worth chronicling were royal visits, trade fairs, new roads, power plants, dams, housing projects, schools and police crackdowns on drug smugglers and bootlegging rings. The footage is a homage to civil service achievements.
>
> (Ma 1988:77)

This is fair description but an unsatisfactory reading, which overlooks the films' formal manoeuvres and under-estimates the particular force of the Griersonian aesthetic. Far from being devoid of ideology, the work of the Film Unit reads at the level of documentary rhetoric as a sustained, skilfully-crafted argument about progress, modernity and history. Whether as half-hour 'prestige documentary' or newsreel 'magazine item', this rhetoric argues for the maintenance of a particular political system and advances a specific ideology. Viewed in this way, the Hong Kong Film Unit becomes a case-study in the discourse of colonialism. Drawing on thematic structures, tropes and metaphors which are fundamental to this particular Western project of appropriation and control, the Hong Kong Film Unit speaks and writes the argument in a classic 'rhetoric of empire', to borrow the title of Spurr's analysis (Spurr 1993). Edward Said characterises imperialism as a 'structure of attitude and reference' whereby the Western powers looked at 'Others' in terms of a limited and recurring representational repertoire: images, symbols, figures, metaphors. He argues that this cultural production was deployed in turn to justify the actual work of invasion, occupation and exploitation (Said 1978, 1994). The Film Unit was an anachronistic player in this colonial project which shaped Hong Kong in the 60s, and classic Griersonian documentary provided a film form and syntax completely appropriate to it.

Trumpeting new civil engineering projects, home and workplace visits by Governors and Minor Royalty and the wonders of modern technology, the films of the Hong Kong Film Unit claim to 'document' an irresistible movement forward in history and a modernity that is exclusively Western. Chinese culture is rarely part of this dynamic, but functions rather as a kind of exotic curiosity with some potential for the tourism industry. When portrayed, it is an unchanging 'Oriental' backdrop against which the drama of progress takes place. The work of the Film Unit routinely structures itself through this dialectic: thus 'Plover Cove Reservoir' is preceded in its edition of *Hong Kong Today* by an item on the 'up-to-date' nature of the local feature film industry, and followed by a report on the traditional 'bun festival' at Cheung Chau. Real events of public life have been selected, translated from contingency into history and narrative, and the whole then set to an imperial tune.

'Hong Kong Village Lights Up', about the installation of a small diesel electric generator on the island of Peng Chau, is a clearer example from the same monthly newsreel series of how this rhetoric of empire works. The chosen story-line reduces the meaning of electricity for this isolated island – its potential for refrigeration, water pumping, and communication, for example – to a single trope, electric lighting. This manoeuvre enables the structuring of the whole film in terms of an imagery of light and dark. An opening impressionistic *paean* to the lights of Hong Kong at night, edited to a fast city rhythm, is followed by slow-paced, day-time, bucolic scenes on the island: old people in traditional costume meander through fields and unpaved lanes, living icons of a culture that has remained 'unchanged for centuries', as the commentary notes. Into this archetypically static Orient storms the gift-bearing technology of the West and with it the Twentieth Century in a whirlwind of noise and excitement: an army helicopter carrying the new generator. As it descends out of the sun into a welcoming party of curious old people and children, the scene is instantly familiar from travel and exotica film genres going back to missionary lantern slide shows (see Stephen 1993). This clichéd dialectic of light and dark, modern and traditional, recurs throughout the film: inside a gloomy tea house early in the film a 'village elder' demonstrates his old oil lamp for the (expatriate) District Officer; the logic of this earlier scene becomes clear when the elder later places his hand on an electric lightshade in a similarly awkward gesture: in a 'school-room' scene which has been staged at night to emphasise the film's central imagery. Intercut with this sequence which ends the film is a shot of a sign illumined by electric light, with the name of the island painted in Chinese characters. An ironic reference to the traditional practice of carving a rural village's name in stone, this image also provides narrative closure by returning us to the city lights of the film's opening sequence. Bringing light where before there was only darkness is, of course, a classic, indeed Conradian trope of the rhetoric of empire.

For those familiar with the work of the Grierson era these relics from the Hong Kong documentary archive produce what can only be described as a 'shock of recognition'. It is not just that the underlying rhetoric revels in classic 'orientalist' tropes, but that it is embedded in an earlier, historically specific style of representation. The topics, formats, production values, images, sounds, structures, and narratives of a documentary project from the 1930s seem to have been revived or rather, resurrected into a kind of half-life in the 1960s. At the time of the Hong Kong Film Unit's founding the Griersonian documentary was under challenge within its metropolitan heartlands. Deployed in an oppositional rhetoric, 16 mm sync sound was revolutionising the documentary form: *Primary* (1960) in the U.S. and 'direct cinema'; *Lonely Boy* (1961) in Canada and 'challenge for change'; *Chronique D'un Eté* (1960) in France, and *'cinéma verité'*. What united these diverse new formal approaches was a common desire to question the classic documentary's authority and authenticity; to empower on the one hand the individual voice of the film-maker, and on the other hand the film subject, permitted for the first time to speak; and finally, to view with distrust the twin projects of nationalism and imperialism (O'Connell 1992; Loizos 1993; Winston 1995). Elsewhere among the 'Units' seeded by Grierson around the British Empire, film-makers were seeking and experimenting with a 'native voice' for documentary (Evans, Gary 1984; Moran 1991). In Australia, for example, *From the Tropics to the Snow* (1964) – the Commonwealth Film Unit's annual omnibus film directly comparable to the 'prestige documentaries' of the Hong Kong Film Unit – is an irreverent, self-relexive look at the whole genre of sponsored documentary (Moran 1991:18). It is against these developments in documentary theory and practice that the Hong Kong Film Unit's revival of the Griersonian tradition must finally be measured. More to the point, if the Film Unit is a paradigm case in both institutional structure and rhetorical style of the discourse of colonialism, then its work is fundamentally about identity and power. As such, it returns to haunt us in the present as archive and living legacy for contemporary documentary film-makers.

QUESTIONS OF IDENTITY

In both Chinese and Western mythology the anomalous mermaid partly represents ideas and anxieties about identity. She is a hybrid figure, formed in discrete parts half from one world and half from another. 'Hybridity' as a metaphor for the post-colonial experience, of being both *one* and *other* at the same time, is the subject of an extensive debate in cultural studies which there is no need to rehearse here (see Lee 1996). However, it is clear that the mermaid retains a presence in the popular consciousness and culture of Hong Kong. She re-appeared most recently in late 1993, when 'fears and fascination came bubbling to the surface last week with reports that a mermaid had been caught in Hong Kong', as the *Sunday Morning Post* sub-head put it (SCSMP 17/10/93). Anthropologist Grant Evans attempted to unravel the meanings behind this mystery appearance, and among other things, saw shades of contemporary intra- and inter-ethnic debates (Evans 1993). But it is not a question here of tracing the figure back through Chinese myth, local folklore or even her history in Hong Kong's popular imagination. Nor does it matter whether the idea for staging the mermaid sequence in 'Plover Cove Reservoir' came from expatriate or local scriptwriters. Indeed, it is likely that she represents nothing more than a felicitous, sexy high-note on which to end a particularly dull newsreel. My argument is rather, that the idea of the mermaid is made possible by a specific conjunction of history and documentary that obtained in Hong Kong then and continues to act today on cultural production.

Griersonian documentary is staged like fiction, and a scene involving an actress posing semi-nude must have crossed many budgetary and other hurdles within the Film Unit before finally reaching the screen in 1962. The mermaid sequence thus says something about institutional thinking with regard to audience. Particularly in the 'hybrid' newsreel, audience and filmic address posed a problem for the Unit's film-makers: it was always at least a double or split negotiation between domestic and international markets. The newsreels played simultaneously in London and Hong Kong ('shown in some 40 cinemas throughout the Colony') and were also caravanned around community halls and villages in the New Territories by portable projection teams (HKGA 1960:242). In fact, in its first few years the Unit devoted the bulk of its local resources to the production of 'newsreel shorts', and claimed them as its most successful venture in 'projecting' itself both overseas and within the community (HKGAR 1962:272). The uncertain cultural circumstances of the mermaid's origin, then, is matched by ambiguities in her spectatorship. Her usefulness lay in the way she exoticised the Other for metropolitan audiences, while at the same time playing to the local house on different terms.

This kind of doubly-coded, ambiguous textual voice which speaks through Chinese Gods and Goddesses, or magical and mythical figures and other heroes and heroines played by local actors and actresses, becomes a familiar device in Film Unit production as the decade wears on. *Report to the Gods* (1967), for example, structures its diegesis through the character of Tso Kwan, the Chinese Kitchen God, who in the words of the Film Unit catalogue 'comes to life and appears in many guises and reports to the gods on what his family have achieved in the previous year in the fields of education, housing, medicine, science and industry' (GIS Catalogue 1991:97). One approach to exploring this characteristic construction of a protagonist with an 'ambiguous', multi-layered identity is through the idea of copying or imitation, which seems to resonate well with aspects of Hong Kong's economic history and her entrepreneurial reputation. Mathew Turner coins the term 'ersatz design', for example, to characterise what he calls 'an enduring and very successful strategy of Chinese capitalism [which resulted from] the interactions between Chinese and Western design' in Hong Kong: 'Ersatz design is cheap, derivative, opportunistic and culturally defused; yet at the same time it is flexible, creatively adaptive and highly commercial' (Turner 1993:3). If this kind of imitative yet creative process is understood in terms of performance – as in dance, theatre or film – it calls up a range of suggestive tropes: miming the Other, acting a part, playing a role. If not the mermaid-as-hybrid metaphor, then, perhaps that of the mimic provides a more helpful way into understanding Hong Kong's specific coloniality and its construction of identity.

Theorising from an Indian coloniality that is historically both more distant and more brutal than Hong Kong's, Homi Bhabha explores mimicry and mockery as responses to the colonial condition. He views them in a negative light: central to colonial subjectivity, they act as mechanisms for social control which attack the integrity of both coloniser and colonised. Yet he notes: 'The epic intention of the civilising mission . . . often produces a text rich in *trompe-l'oeil*, irony, mimicry and repetition' (Bhabha 1994:85). If, however, the same effects are regarded as a positive response to colonial power, then they provide a suggestive reading for this essay, in terms of what I have playfully alluded to with the question of the mermaid. Bhabha's analysis can be applied, for example, to the Film Unit's 1967 flagship film, *Report to the Gods:*

> The "unthought" across which colonial man is articulated . . . results in the *splitting* of colonial discourse so that two attitudes persist; one takes reality into consideration while the other disavows it and replaces it by a product of desire that repeats, re-articulates "reality" as mimicry.
>
> (Bhabha 1994:91 original emphasis)

REPORTING TO THE GODS

On one level, *Report to the Gods* writes Hong Kong for an overseas audience in the Film Unit's familiar rhetoric of empire. A dialectic is constructed between old and new, Eastern and Western, disordered and ordered space: the 'ugly disease' of hillside squatter huts housing refugees *versus* the more pleasing 'natural' environment of a Western aesthetic, a 'landscape' disfigured by a 'rash'; dark, dirty temporary settlements and inner city slums *versus* the high-rise clarity of modern housing blocks; the disorder of hawker-infested pedestrian ways *versus* the ordered car traffic of the wide boulevards of Central District; old people working with their hands *versus* modern machine-dominated factories; the crowded living space of an extended family *versus* the cosy new flat of a happy, fictional nuclear family. Set up as a model for Hong Kong's aspiring middle-classes, the Kitchen God's host family is portrayed by visiting London filmmaker Brian Salt as well on its way into the ranks of the bourgeois, working happily into the night, children as well, making plastic flowers. Another set of comparisons positions our 'star' family on a global imperial grid: poised somewhere between peasant farmers and 'native' villages in India and Africa on the one hand, and on the other set against an unattainable Western dream world of leisured life-style and carpeted homes where plastic flowers provide a tasteful decorative touch. By this racist sleight-of-hand the family becomes necessarily a second-rate, *oriental* bourgeoisie, and by extension so too does Hong Kong's. The logic is not subtle: the Kitchen God drinks tea in a dark, dirty, traditional tea-house, makes a face and examines his cup, then is seen three shots later sipping beer on a sunlit western-style patio. This is Griersonian documentary at its most scripted and staged.

There are more sophisticated strategies at work as well, one of which might be termed the construction of absence. For example, long sequences dedicated to hospital laundries, personal hygiene and vocational training imply their lack or impossibility before the intervention of colonial Government. Another significant absence is the Chinese voice and its Cantonese language. The local actor who plays the character of the Kitchen God has been dubbed into an aristocratic British voice. As in the vast majority of the Film Unit's work, no other Chinese speak throughout the film; the language has been 'disappeared'.[7] Working class males are also curiously absent, while old people populate the streets or do craftwork and schoolchildren crowd the camera to applaud modernity. By contrast and reinforcing this absence, young women are well-represented: they are especially suited to work in assembly lines because they have uniquely 'deft' fingers, the commentary informs us. As either symbols of modernity (fashion shows) or alternatively ancient arts (embroidery), they also make an appearance to sing and dance, dress and undress (like the mermaid).[8] As recent post-colonial and feminist critique suggests, one consequence of imperial ownership is the figurative emasculation of the colonial male, engineered here as disappearance or absence from representation (Alloula 1986; Martin 1992).

However, the main structuring element of *Report to the Gods* is the conceit of the Kitchen God, who comes to life in the home of this model Chinese family and becomes the film's narrator. Each year, he says, 'I have to report to heaven on how the people are behaving themselves. For many years now I have been able to give a good report.' Uttered in the context of civil unrest in 1966–1967, this statement is disingenuous to say the least, but it accurately describes the film's rhetorical purpose. In the Chinese pantheon, the higher authority to whom the Kitchen God reports is the Emperor. The film's conceit is that this hierarchy exactly replicates the administrative structure of colonial government; the Kitchen God represents the Governor reporting on the people of Hong Kong to London. Indeed, *Report to the Gods* is precisely an annual report in film form from the colonial administration in Hong Kong to its imperial capital. Through this conceit, then, government assumes a mantle of divine authority for the current order; obedience to colonial power shades into an ethic. 'Reading against the grain' like this, as Said puts it, reveals the real project of the Hong Kong Film Unit: these short films and newsreels represent the colonial government talking to itself, and to its sources of authority in the metropolitan centres of the West. They are arguments for a continuing British imperial role in Asia, pleas for understanding and boasts of being needed (Said 1994).

However, this kind of over-determined reading while persuasive does not exclude others, nor address how the film may be viewed locally. Moreover, it tends to discount whatever may be specific to Hong Kong in the text; it totalises both the apparatus of representation and its audience. Leung Sing Bor, the actor playing the Kitchen God in *Report to the Gods*, was a famous comedian of the 60s, well-known to local audiences. His characterisation – as a friendly, chubby fellow, with the all-too-human defects of a liking for good food, strong drink and pretty women – may well work to mask with self-deprecating humour the colonial authority's power, but it also mocks it at the same time. He plays the role of trickster, popping up in unlikely places, gesturing with a nod and a wink to the audience, conducting himself with a knowing pomposity. The dubbed upper-class British voice merely adds to this range of distancing effects: the transformation into caricature of the British civil servant is complete. In fact, the notion of mimicry may be taken a step further: in details of dress and gesture his performance also imitates local businessmen and minor civil servants, those with yellow faces and white masks, to paraphrase Fanon (Fanon 1968). The role becomes a caricature of colonial mimicry, in Bhabha's sense of the term. Viewed through local eyes, then, his performance is always playing against another order of knowledge that the audience brings to it. As *they* 'know', Leung Sing Bor is merely performing a role drafted for him by expatriate scriptwriters, in the service of a false portrayal of contemporary Hong Kong, impersonating a Chinese God for his usual fee; it's all in day's work. Setting the text in this context begins to bring home the full force of the insight into colonial subjectivity that Bhabha's ideas of 'mimicry', 'mockery', and 'sly civility' provide (Bhabha 1994:85):

It is from this area between mimicry and mockery, where the reforming, civilizing mission is threatened by the displacing gaze of its disciplinary double, that my instances of colonial imitation come. What they all share is a discursive process by which excess or slippage produced by the *ambivalence* of mimicry (almost the same, *but not quite*) does not merely rupture the discourse, but becomes transformed into an uncertainty which fixes the colonial subject as a "partial" presence. By "partial" I mean both incomplete and virtual.

(Bhabha 1994:86)

Bhabha is exploring moments when the text falters: genre rules are broken; the rhetoric shows signs of hesitation or self-doubt; there is a lapse that interrupts the smoothness of the performance. I want to suggest that the mermaid represents one such moment, and the Kitchen God another. The descriptive passages above give no feel for the sheer sophistication of *Report to the Gods*: the quality of its *mise-en-scène*, montage, production values, rhetorical skills. This is finely-crafted work, but the surface gloss does not square with its dialectical simplicities. There is an ambivalence in the film: form and content do not quite mesh or gel. Indeed, the film often reads as a caricature of the classic documentary project, with Grierson's 'First Principles of Documentary' become empty circus tricks, the formulae deployed without purpose, integrity or commitment (Grierson 1946:78). Bhabha's 'slippage or excess' lies in this gap between seriousness and playfulness in the film. It is as if the film itself wore a poker-faced attitude of self-mockery. Flaunting its rhetorical flourishes and cleverness, the film exhibits a kind of self-awareness that calls into question its own project. In the same way, I suggest, the mermaid when she surfaces in 'Plover Cove Reservoir', 'playing a role' like Leung Sing Bor as the Kitchen God, points to a knowing complicity between image and spectator, and to a sense of playfulness in negotiating messages within messages: a kind of 'I know that you know that I know that'.

DOCUMENTARY AS ARCHIVE

The *Hong Kong Sixties: Designing Identity* exhibition where my screening takes place is merely the most recent example of an increasingly urgent archaeology of the past that has been underway since the return of Hong Kong to Chinese sovereignty was decided in 1984. The films were last screened publicly a few years earlier, at the 12th Annual Hong Kong Festival, in 1988. Entitled *Changes in Hong Kong Society through Cinema*, the Hong Kong Cinema Retrospective section of the festival for the first time since its founding in 1976 featured 'documentaries, newsreels, [and] home movies', making it 'markedly different from past retrospectives which have, all along, focused on fictional films and genre cinema' (Li Cheuk-to 1988:9). 'There is a need to understand our history because Hong Kong is a city commonly thought of as having no history,' remarks Li Cheuk-to in the Festival catalogue (Li Cheuk-to 1988:9). The establishment of the Hong Kong Film Archive (from which documentary, however, is currently excluded) (Fonoroff 1993), the revival of the Urban Council's

Hong Kong Independent Short Film and Video Awards (1992), the storm of protest in the popular press attending the removal of the Government archives to an outlying district are all indices of the current archiving impulse. The politics of this retrieval of the material past is clear enough: it is a double-movement looking both backwards and forwards, an effort to trace what has been forgotten, repressed or lost over time, and at the same time a working out of current desires and needs in terms of the material culture that survives. In this politics of selection, re-valuation and re-interpretation, the concept of authenticity becomes a central site or trope of the debate, as Chow emphasises (Chow 1991). In the climate of a 'city at the end of time' (Leung 1992), documentary film and photographs occupy an unstable place in this process of negotiating the future in light of the past.

The *Designing Identity* exhibition theorises the birth of a unique Hong Kong culture – an identity that is neither that of other sites in the Chinese diaspora nor reduceable to the metropolitan cultures of either Beijing or London – as it traces the 'competing, contradictory representations of Hong Kong life-style' at play during 'one, turbulent decade', as Guest Curator Mathew Turner puts it:

> An harmonious blend of East and West was presented in school textbooks and trade promotions, public information campaigns and tourist publicity. Yet these "made for export" images survived domestic crises and political conflict, and came to articulate local reflections of identity. By the end of the decade it was plain that a modern Hong Kong people and a Hong Kong life-style were here to stay.
>
> (Turner 1995:xvi)

As the exhibition demonstrates, this identity is being constructed retrospectively across thirty years of history, and out of memory, relic and archive. The Film Unit's importance lies in the fact that it is the primary source of documentary images of the 60s housed in Hong Kong.[9] The survival of the work of the Government's propaganda apparatus is a consequence on the one hand of the propensity within a governing bureaucracy for the archiving of its work, and on the other hand of official indifference to other sources of local film and cultural history. However, what is at stake when official history becomes naturalised through this process is the notion of documentary truth.

Under the heading 'Warning: Eating Bitter Chocolates', Mathew Turner writes in the Preface to the Exhibition Catalogue:

This is a chocolate box exhibition with a bitter centre. For the sixties was also an era of harsh working conditions and grim housing; a raw decade of poverty, exploitation, sacrifice and instability. But if Hong Kong people had to "eat bitterness" during the Sixties, they also chose to consume sugar-coated images of freedom, westernization and affluence, laying the foundations for an ambiguous cultural identity.

(Turner 1995:xv)

This is not the place to argue current theory about documentary's epistemological status (see Nichols 1991,1994; Renov 1993; Winston 1995; Rabinowitz 1994; Solomon-Godeau 1991). Commonsense notions of the photographic process's value as evidence and of its power to witness retain a strong grip on us, although Hong Kong has yet to have them tested in court as they were in the United States during the Rodney King case. These claims to truth mean that the past as constructed by documentary film becomes a key player in the economy of dream, memory, and fact that is contemporary Hong Kong culture's on-going work of self-representation. But it is not enough to simply point out the economic realities of colonialism that are masked in Film Unit films. Turner's notions of 'ambiguous cultural identity' and his chocolate box image with its 'either-or' of appearance *versus* reality does not take us far in exploring the construction of colonial subjectivity. The documentary gaze in coloniality is not so simple. As this essay suggests, it becomes rather a kind of negotiated 'space between' subject and object where their two gazes cross, along the lines of Bhabha's 'displacing gaze'.

In this 'dislocated' gaze we look somewhere between the mermaid and her filmic representation, we see the game being played, we get the joke. In *Report to the Gods*, for example, the spectator is positioned through sophisticated editing of point-of-view shots to look through the eyes of the Kitchen God. The tensions and finally, untenability of this position in turn force the spectator into a kind of indeterminate third place, a site that is neither that of the Kitchen God nor that of his puppeteer. Thus displaced, the spectator's gaze becomes an imaginative construction, a 'pretend' gaze.[10] Even in its own time, I suggest, the anachronistic work of the Hong Kong Film Unit engaged in a performance or unconscious game with its audience, working through a kind of self-mockery which both drew on and played against local knowledges.

Today the aura of authenticity and dignity that documentary acquires over time complicates the game. On the one hand, the Film Unit archive is widely sourced by mainstream productions to 'illustrate' Hong Kong's past, yet as this essay makes clear, there are real dangers in direct quotation.[11] On the other hand however, these images also sometimes play a more knowing, self-aware, ironic role in Hong Kong today. In early 1995, for example, a popular promotional clip for Star TV's *Channel V,* the music video channel which targets teenagers, inserted Film Unit footage into its own discourse. Fast-cut contemporary images and digital video effects are contrasted with these static black and white images which now stand for a nostalgically remembered past: two young women dressed in the styles of the 60s – significantly, one Asian and the other European – enter a changing room to re-emerge immediately, by way of a jump-cut edit, in old-fashioned, one-piece bathing suits; a student formally recites for the teacher in a primitive, roof-top classroom; an elderly woman works on a foot-pedaled sewing machine, in what looks like a home-factory situation. The voice-over urges: 'It's not too late to change! Tune into Channel V! Your grades won't go down and your grandmother won't mind too much! Just make sure you find out what's in it before she does! Keep up or be left out!' The message is clear: Hongkong's lifestyle has changed radically – like a jump-cut edit – since the way of life portrayed in these archaic, ironically-deployed, and faintly ridiculous 'documentary' images. Today's teenagers are the 'now' generation, accustomed to rapid change, looking forward to an exciting, high-tech future, courtesy of satellite television and MTV. These Hong Kong Film Unit fantasies from the 60s, then, have another life in the 90s, deployed by the current generation of film-makers in a new rhetoric of modernity and progress.

For some contemporary Hong Kong documentary film-makers, the need to negotiate their post-coloniality *vis a vis* the Griersonian tradition is expressed more directly. *Cultural Identity of the 60s?* (1994) is described by filmmaker Bacon Cheung as 'combining footage of rare documentaries and popular film of Hong Kong in the 60s, however, the line between these two elements [is] blurred. [There is a] self-reflexive quality as video'(Cheung 1994: programme notes). His film intercuts scenes from popular commercial features of the time with sequences from the Hong Kong Film Unit archive featuring the same actors and actresses performing as 'workers' or 'typical family' members. Poised somewhere between the documentary and experimental film, *Cultural Identity of the 60s?* mounts an attack on both the classic documentary's imperial ideology and the formal aesthetic that is complicit with it. At the same time, Cheung issues a warning about both the photographic archive's and the documentary's claims to truth. We know from Barthes that the truth of photography, and by extension documentary, is truth to presence rather than truth to appearance: 'Every photograph is a certificate of presence' (Barthes 1993:87). What post-colonial film-makers question is, finally, whose presence?

DOCUMENTARY – DREAM OR REALITY?

One of the reason's for declaring my writing position in this essay is to signal the on-going nature of these complicities in Hong Kong documentary. Griersonian documentary, for example, lives on in two places: as corporate and sponsored video within an expatriate-dominated filmmaking community, and in the form of social issue films at Radio Television Hong Kong, the institution that eclipsed the Hong Kong Film Unit as the film-making arm of Government in the early 70s. The first group comprises both some of the 'old China hands' from the 60s and also a new wave of 'blow-ins' from the European diaspora, including myself. The rhetoric of corporate video may be more naked than that of the Film Unit as it makes its argument on behalf of international capital, but it makes identical choices regarding audience and form. RTHK is arguably similarly strait-jacketed by the underlying needs and aesthetics of its own historical project, the invention of a middle-class for Hong Kong.[12]

If documentary is understood in Foucault's terms, as a discourse of knowledge and power, for which the Hong Kong Film Unit provides a case-study, then its centrality to cultural studies becomes clearer. It remains surprising that critical work on Hong Kong cinema virtually ignores documentary. For example, anthropologist Rozanna Lilley's recent survey of 'local critical discourses about television and film' throws up only one documentary, Shu Kei's *Sunless Days* (1990),[13] and is blind not only to the long and influential documentary tradition within say, RTHK, but also to the vast amount of actuality material and locally-produced documentary that *does* somehow make its way on to Hong Kong television (Lilley 1993).

In its own way, Hong Kong is a vital site of much experimentation and dynamic 'creative treatment of actuality', even and perhaps especially within commercial television: news, current affairs, tabloid journalism, and yes, even documentary. Hong Kong crews travel the world in pursuit of their own exotic places and Others; sex and ghost documentaries find ready markets internationally; and 'root searching' is not confined to intellectuals in exile. There is also an active independent film and video underground, comprising political and experimental video art groups such as *Video Power* and *Videotage*. Even in a media environment governed by oligopoly, as *The Other Hong Kong Report* puts it, advances in camera, editing, sound and computing technology provide some room for manoeuvre. A dozen small production houses produce *karaoke* video backgrounders: arguably a new, semi-drama, semi-documentary genre. What all this suggests is that the notion of documentary itself, conceived as a privileged way of knowing to be practised by a professional elite, needs closer interrogation. 'Documentary is a clumsy description, but let it stand', Grierson notoriously remarks (Grierson 1946:78). In post-colonial space, let's not.

NOTES

1 Production Notes, cited in Chow:1991:169, her translation.

2 An early draft of this chapter based on the talk is published in the *Hong Kong Sixties: Designing Identity* catalogue, ed. Mathew Turner and Irene Ngan, under the title 'From the Rhetoric of Empire to the Discreet Charm of the Bourgeois: The Hong Kong Film Unit 1959–1969', Hong Kong Arts Centre, 1995.

3 The GIS archive is extremely disorganised. However, the evidence of the credits on major productions and personal reminiscences by filmmakers active during the Sixties – Michael Gascoyne, Jack Bygraves, Charles Wang, and Elaine Forsgate-Myers – support my argument. However, the point is not crucial to the main thrust of the essay.

4 I mean to suggest here that not only is cross-cultural communication not theorised, but local conditions are not even researched. It is simply assumed that what works in England will work in the Colony; a discourse – in Foucault's sense comprising both texts and their means of delivery – designed for a citizenry in a democracy is mapped on to a very different politics and demographics: a poor, refugee populace in an undemocratic colony.

5 Personal communication, Michael Gascoyne; this manoeuvre also enabled the Government to report that the film was produced by 'Cathay Film Services (Hong Kong) Limited' (HKGAR:1960:243).

6 *Drifters* was one of the few films that Grierson himself made; thereafter he became more of a figurehead, gathering a team of young film-makers around him who came to constitute what history calls the British Documentary Movement. This essay uses 'Grierson' and 'Griersonian' to stand for the formal aesthetics of this movement, and all three terms are interchangeable with that other common description, 'the classic documentary' (Barnouw:1993).

7 The production format of the film – like all the Unit's in-house work, shot

on an unblimped 35mm Arri ST – does not sufficiently explain such radical absence. When the post-1967 political climate demanded a re-invigorated effort at community relations, *Hong Kong Today* began featuring sync sequences such as performances by Teddy Robbins and his band and speeches by, for example, Miss Hong Kong.

8 As the *Hong Kong Sixties: Designing Identity* Exhibition demonstrates, the twin urges to forge both an industry (fashion) and a certain modernity (read 'Western society') resulted in a whole new imagery of women, promulgated in film as in other media at the time.

9 More extensive archives exist in the capitals of the Colony's past and future imperial masters: Beijing, London, Tokyo and Washington.

10 Rey Chow's notion of the 'simulated gaze' strikes a similar chord: 'Contrary to the model of western hegemony in which the coloniser is seen as a primary, active 'gaze' subjugating the native as passive 'object', I want to argue that it is actually the coloniser who feels looked at by the native's gaze. This gaze, which is neither a threat nor a retaliation, makes the coloniser 'conscious' of himself, leading to his need to turn this gaze around and look at himself, henceforth 'reflected' in the native-object . . . In the silence of the native-as-object . . . this simulated gaze is between the image and the gaze of the coloniser' (1993:51–52).

11 The GIS archive is regularly sourced these days by overseas television companies preparing their '1997' documentaries.

12 In time history caught up with the contradictions of the Hong Kong Film Unit's project. The 'disturbances' of 1966–67 are widely regarded as marking fundamental changes in Hong Kong society, a major turning point in the process of forging a distinct identity and inventing the modern 'belonger' of today. They marked the end of 'the unreformed colonial state', provoking a radical change in the Government's thinking about ways of legitimising its presence (Scott:1989). Blaming a failure in communication as the cause of the civil unrest, Government found a new base of political legitimacy in the idea of a bourgeois that would have a stake in society and would assent to government by technocracy. This new strategy demanded a whole new apparatus of representation. The Hong Kong Film Unit was an early casualty as attention and resources shifted to Radio Television Hong Kong in the 1970s.

13 Lilley names *Sunless Days* in the context of a discussion about political censorship, noting that it faced difficulties finding a screen in Hong Kong. It was, however, financed and broadcast by Japanese Television (NHK). Shu Kei struck a 16mm print at his own expense in order to pursue local screenings, but apart from the Arts Centre, where as Lilley notes it *was* screened, there are few cinemas in Hong Kong equipped for 16mm (personal communication).This is not to deny the presence of censorship in Hong Kong nor *Sunless Days'* status and importance as a locally-conceived documentary about local issues. My point rather is to question its status as sole representative of documentary in Lilley's overview of the Hong Kong scene.

REFERENCES CITED

Adamson, Judy
   1993   Changing Times. *In* The Big Picture: Documentary Filmmaking in
          Australia, papers from the Second Australian Documentary Conference,
          Melbourne: National Centre for Australian Studies, Monash University.
Alloula, Malek
   1986   The Colonial Harem. *In* Theory and History of Literature Series,
          Volume 21, Minneapolis: University of Minnesota Press.
Arthur, Paul
   1993   Jargons of Authenticity: (Three American Moments). *In* Theorising
          Documentary. Michael Renov, ed. New York: Routledge.
Bhabha, Homi
   1994   The Location of Culture. London: Routledge.
Barnouw, Erik
   1993   Documentary: A History of the Non-Fiction Film. 2nd Revised
          Edition.Oxford: Oxford University Press.
Barsam, Richard Meran
   1973   Non-Fiction Film: A Critical History. London:George Allen and
          Unwin.
Barthes, Roland
   1993   Camera Lucida. London: Vintage.
Chan, K.
   1994   The Other Hong Kong Report. Hong Kong: Chinese University Press.
Cheung, Bacon
   1994   Programme Notes, Short Film and Video screening at Hong Kong
          Science Museum, March 12,1995. Hong Kong Independent Short
          Film and Video Awards. Hong Kong: Urban Council Publishing.
Chow, Rey
   1991   Between Colonizers: Hong Kong's Postcolonial Self-Writing in the
          1990s. Diaspora 2:2:151–170.
   1993   Writing Diaspora. Bloomington: Indiana University Press.
Evans, Gary
   1984   John Grierson and the National Film Board of Canada. Toronto:
          University of Toronto Press.
Evans, Grant
   1993   Bringing the Mermaid Back to Port. Article in the Sunday Morning
          Post (SMP), October 17, 1993; and letters column, SMP, October 24,
          1993.
Fanon, Frantz
   1968   Black Skin, White Masks. London: MacGibbon and Kee.
   1970   A Dying Colonialism. New York: Grove Press.
Fonoroff, Paul
   1993   Saved Any Movies Lately? Article in South China Morning Post,
          January 3,1993.
Foucault, Michel
   1979   Discipline and Punish:The Birth of the Prison. Alan Sheridan,
          translated.Harmondsworth: Peregrine.

Government Information Service (GIS)
1991   Catalogue, loose mimeographed pages.
Grierson, John
1946   Grierson on Documentary. Forsythe Hardy, ed. London: Collins.
Ho, Oscar
1995   People With No Faces. *In* Hong Kong Sixties: Designing Identity
       Catalogue (An Introduction). Hong Kong: Hong Kong Arts Centre.
Hong Kong Government Annual Report (HKGAR),1960–1970.
Lee, Gregory
1996   Troubadours, Trumpeters, and Troubled Makers: Lyricism, Nation-
       alism and Hybridity in China and Its Others. London: Hurst and
       Company.
Leung Ping-kwan
1992   City at the End of Time. Gordon T. Osing, translated. Twilight Books
       Company and Department of Comparative Literature, University of
       Hong Kong.
Li Cheuk-to
1988   Introduction to Changes in Hong Kong Society Through Cinema
       (Festival Programme). 12th Hong Kong Film Festival, Hong Kong:
       Urban Council.
Lilley, Rozanna
1993   Claiming Identity: Film and Television in Hong Kong. History and
       Anthropology 6:2–3:261–292.
Loizos, Peter
1993   Innovation in Ethnographic Film: From Innocence to Self-Conscious-
       ness. 1955–1985. Chicago: University of Chicago Press.
Ma, Teresa
1988   Chronicles of Change 1960s–1980s. *In* Changes in Hong Kong
       Society Through Cinema (Festival Programme). 12th Hong Kong
       Film Festival, Hong Kong: Urban Council.
Martin, Jeannie
1992   Missionary Positions. Australian Left Review (ALR), May 1992:35–36.
Memmi, Albert
1990   The Colonizer and the Colonized. London: Earthscan Publications.
Moran, Albert
1991   Projecting Australia: Government Film Since 1945. Sydney:
       Currency Press.
Murray, J.L.
1958   Government Publicity in Hong Kong, A Report by the Public
       Relations Officer (J.L.Murray). Confidential Report, Hong Kong
       Collection, University of Hong Kong Libraries.
Nichols, Bill
1991   Representing Reality: Issues and Concepts in Documentary. Bloo-
       mington: Indiana University Press.
1994   Blurred Boundaries: Questions of Meaning in Contemporary Culture.
       Bloomington: Indiana University Press.
O'Connell. P.J.
1992   Robert Drew and the Development of Cinema Verite in America.
       Chicago: Southern Illinois University Press.

Paget, Derek
1990   True Stories?: Documentary Drama on Radio, Screen and Stage. Manchester: Manchester University Press.
Rabinowitz, Paula
1994   They Must Be Represented: The Politics of Documentary. London: Verso.
Said, Edward
1978   Orientalism. London: Routledge Kegan Paul.
1994   Culture and Imperialism, London: Vintage.
Scott, Ian
1989   Political Change and the Crisis of Legitimacy in Hong Kong. Hong Kong: Oxford University Press.
Solomon-Godeau, Abigail
1991   Photography at the Dock: Essays on Photographic History, Institutions, and Practices, Minneapolis: University of Minnesota Press.
South China Morning Post (SCMP).
South China Sunday Morning Post (SCSMP)
Spurr, David
1993   The Rhetoric of Empire: Colonial Discourse in Journalism, Travel Writing and Imperial Administration. Durham, N.C.: Duke University Press.
Stephen, Anne
1993   Pirating the Pacific: Images of Travel, Trade and Tourism. Sydney: Powerhouse Publishing.
Tatlow, Antony
1993   Postcolonialism and Culture. Unpublished paper, Department of Comparative Literature, University of Hong Kong.
Turner, Mathew
1993   Ersatz Design. Unpublished Ph.D. Thesis, London: Royal College of Art.
1995   Introduction. *In* Hong Kong Sixties: Designing Identity Catalogue, Hong Kong: Hong Kong Arts Centre.
Winston, Brian
1995   Claiming the Real: The Documentary Film Revisited. London: BFI Publishing.

FILMOGRAPHY

A Million Lights Shall Glow, Hong Kong, GIS, 1969.
Chronique D'un Eté, France, Jean Rouch and Edgar Morin, 1960.
Cultural Identity of 60s?, Hong Kong, Bacon Cheung, 1994.
Drifters, U.K., John Grierson, 1928.
From the Tropics to the Snow, Australia, Richard Mason, 1965.
Hong Kong Today, Hong Kong, GIS Magazine Series, 1961–74.
Hong Kong Village Lights Up, Hong Kong, GIS Newsreel, 1962.
Lonely Boy, Canada, Wolf Koenig, 1961.
Plover Cove Reservoir, Hong Kong, GIS Newsreel, 1962.

Primary, U.S.A., Richard Leacock and Drew Associates, 1960.
Report to the Gods, Hong Kong, GIS, 1967.
Sunless Days, Hong Kong, Shu Kei, 1990
The Magic Stone, Hong Kong GIS, 1969.
Year of the Ram, Hong Kong, GIS, 1968.

5

RESURGENT CHINESE POWER IN POSTMODERN DISGUISE
THE NEW BANK OF CHINA BUILDINGS IN HONG KONG AND MACAU

Cheng Miu Bing, Christina

INTRODUCTION

Architecture is the science of building raised to a fine art. Like any work of art, it can also be considered 'textual' for broader cultural exegesis. Mikhail Bakhtin says a text is 'any coherent complex of signs' (Bakhtin 1986:103), a definition which encompasses everything from literature to visual and aural works of art, as well as everyday action and communication. Given this pantextual idea, we can approach architecture as a commonplace of contemporary discourse embracing a wide semiotic range and exhibiting the entire spectrum of artistic practices, cultural manifestations and political implications. By engaging with architecture as **text** in a kind of 'threshold encounter' with the vogue of the 'postmodern', this paper attempts to examine the new Bank of China Buildings in Hong Kong and Macau.[1] These two buildings are not merely skyscrapers using high technology and the rhetoric of postmodern design, they also exhibit cultural connotations and political overtones and are expressions of a vicarious ideology of resurgent power in the two colonies. The questions to raise are: what features are considered 'postmodern' in these two buildings? Are there any problems in the creation and interpretation of architectural metaphors between the architect's intention and the general public's reaction? How is political power 'textualized' in architecture and how do these two Bank buildings represent the political power of the Chinese government well in advance of the destined decolonization of Hong Kong and Macau? Through a 'reading' of these two Bank buildings, it is hoped to provide some insights into the relationship between culture and politics, predicated on architecture, in the crucial years leading up to the handover of British Hong Kong and Portuguese Macau to China on 1 July 1997 and 20 December 1999 respectively.

THE POSTMODERN IN ARCHITECTURE

The two new Bank of China Buildings in Hong Kong and Macau have both been described as examples of postmodern architecture. The term 'postmodern' was first used in architecture in 1945 by Joseph Hudnut,[2] and the rubric of 'postmodernism' then emerged in America and Europe in the 1970's as a cultural phenomenon, (or rather, a cultural dominant as Fredric Jameson has called it), which soon manifested itself in other aspects of cultural production – art, literature, photography, film, dance, music, etc. Its deconstructive impulse constitutes a liberative force in the re-definition of cultural endeavours, and a critique of the monotony of universal Modernism's vision of the world. Postmodern architecture has in a sense stood in opposition to the established authority of the Modern Movement (1910–45), but it is not a repudiation of the past.[3] It is also inappropriate to describe postmodern architecture as 'anti-Modern' and 'ultra-Modern' as the former connotes a rejection and the latter refers to an extremism. In postmodern architecture, the past is neither ignored nor completely denied, but previous styles and designs are warmly digested, assimilated and embraced as vital sources for architectural expression; it is a playful eclecticism of architectural gestures. Charles Jencks, one of the best known popularizers of postmodernism, contends that 'the primary dualism concerned élitism and populism, the undeniable conflicting pressures which any good architect must face' (Jencks 1977:6). In his opinion, the major objective of postmodern architecture is to overcome the disjunction between élites (e.g. professional architects) and various publics, in its attempt to communicate with both. In a word, Jencks sees postmodern architecture as a kind of double-coding, pluralistic and hybrid. In addition, Jencks and other postmodern theorists have tended to refer to 'semantic' and 'syntactic' dimensions of architecture in order to focus on aspects of signification and meaning. They endorse a referential notion of meaning, in the hope that forms can be read as words; buildings, they say, can convey messages (McLeod 1985:31–33).

However, it is worth remembering Ferdinard de Saussure's aphorism – in language there can be differences without positive terms (Saussure 1974:120), that is, there is no inherent relationship between the signifier

103

and the signified in the semiotic systems. Perhaps, therefore, architectural meaning can also be interpreted arbitrarily; there is no necessary one-to-one relationship between the professional architect's intention and the public's reception. Architecture, as an expressive medium, is often ambiguous to the general populace. As Robert Venturi aptly points out, 'An architectural element is perceived as form and structure, texture and material. These oscillating relationships, complex and contradictory, are the source of the ambiguity and tension characteristic to the medium of architecture' (Venturi 1977:20). In *Learning from Las Vegas* (1989) Venturi et al insist that architects should abstain from pursuing some abstract, theoretical, and doctrinaire ideals but rather they had better learn from the study of popular and vernacular landscapes, and learn from the rejection of purity in forms, in order to communicate with the general public. Seen in this light, postmodernism in architecture stages itself as a kind of aesthetic populism, as the very title of Venturi's influential manifesto, *Learning from Las Vegas*, suggests.

In a similar vein, Heinrich Klotz argues, 'Whenever present-day architecture observes other laws in addition to functional aptness and maximum simplicity of basic forms, whenever it moves away from abstraction and tends toward representational objectivization, I call it postmodern' (Klotz 1988:4). For Klotz, only after architecture is liberated from the abstraction of pure utility, that is, its functionalism, is there a possibility for the emergence of beauty and for the transcendence of its subservience to mere practical usage. His forthright declaration is that postmodern architecture is not just functional but fictional. In a sense, the artistic fiction can take us beyond reality to a world of fantasy and imagination. Contrary to the univalency of Modern architecture, the multivalency of postmodern architecture seems to invoke what Charles Jencks and Fredric Jameson have characterised as 'schizophrenia' (a sense of dislocation) induced by fragmentation, which is a common feature of the postmodern 'mind-set'. Such a breakdown of the temporal order of things also gives rise to an eclectic treatment of the past. Like postmodern art, postmodern architecture also abandons historical continuity and memory but tries to 'plunder' history and to take bits and pieces from the past for present use. The bricolage of historical elements is reminiscent of the collage paintings of Georges Braque and Pablo Picasso in the 1920's.

Figure 5.1 Bank of China Building in Hong Kong

Figure 5.2 Chinese-style gardens at the base of the Bank

Figure 5.3 The Hongkong Bank Building

Figure 5.4 Two bronze lions outside the Hongkong Bank in Central

Figure 5.5 Governor's residence in the foreground with the China Bank 'blades' in the background

Figure 5.6 Citibank Tower

Figure 5.7 Bank of China Building in Macau

Figure 5.8 (above) Hong Kong's Post-modern skyline: 1. The Entertainment Building; 2. Nine Queens Road central; 3. Ritz-Carlton Hotel

Figure 5.9 (left) The Amaral Equestrian Monument

Figure 5.10 The Amaral statue being removed

Figure 5.11 The Bank of China building without the Amaral statue

I.M. PEI'S BANK OF CHINA BUILDING

Among the monotonous, rigid, and graceless high-rise buildings in Hong Kong, the new Bank of China Building[4] (see Figure 5.1) commands unrivalled attention partly because of its unusual prismatic shape and partly because of its monumentalism. Completed in 1989 and officially opened in May, 1990, the shining grey-green faceted building was designed by the renowned Chinese American architect, I.M. Pei and Partners, winning for it the Grand Award for Engineering Excellence in 1989 from the American Consulting Engineers Council (Chung 1989:96). Pei, who is well-known to the world for his contributions to major museums, often maximises the use of geometric forms of triangles and cubes to produce an aggregation of angular masses. In Washington, D.C., Pei's East Building of the National Gallery of Art (completed in 1978) is a success in creating diamond-shaped towers over a large triangular building on the irregular trapezoidal site.

Again, Pei manipulates the same angular structure in the Louvre, Paris with a steel and glass pyramid in the main courtyard of the Louvre serving as the principal entrance to the museum and welcoming hall for the general public. This transparent, crystal pyramid (completed in 1989) was once a controversial issue because there appeared to be an irreconcilable hiatus between the triumph of high technology and the delicacy of the baroque Palace. Like the National Gallery in Washington and the crystal pyramid in the Louvre in Paris, the Bank building in Hong Kong equally received unfavourable comments although it had won a prestigious prize. The Bank is yet another stunning exercise of Pei's favourite modernist device, the manipulation of abstract geometry.

The 70-storey edifice with a height of 1,209 feet was once the tallest building not only in Hong Kong but in Asia, and ranked the fourth tallest building in the world. However, it was superseded by the Central Plaza[5] (1,228 ft. high), which was completed in 1992. The Bank building is at the same time functional and fictional, and transcends purity of form. Moreover, the architect's peculiar treatment of space and the rebellious motive to create theatrical rigour and fanciful imagination seem to embrace postmodern rhetoric, but the overall design is more like a modernist building. While it is a high-tech edifice, being predominantly based on the expressive qualities of technological procedures and construction, it is also an eclectic mixture of historicising forms and tends to go beyond functionality. In a postmodern attempt to localize with familiar features, the lower part of the building is flanked by two traditional Chinese style gardens (see Figure 5.2), consisting of 'natural' scenes of mountains, flowers, trees and streaming cascades.

These 'scenes' are also typical of traditional Chinese landscape paintings, which immediately add a sense of double-coding to pander to the populace. In view of the ultra-modern top storeys, Pei reserves at least some allegiance to vernacular favour by incorporating, in a less abstract way, a sense of traditional Chinese styles in its base and entrance hall. However, unlike the old Bank of China Building which is guarded by a pair of stone lions for warding off evils spirits, the new headquarters is iconoclastic and discards the Chinese inclination for placing the motif of lions at the entrance. By and large, the Bank building straddles high technology, modernist ideas and postmodern rhetoric, but eschews the Chinese tradition of having guarding lions.

A SYMBOL OF RESURGENT POWER

The Bank's prismatic tower dominates almost every view of Hong Kong harbour and is symbolic of the power of the People's Republic of China, the Bank's owner (Davey 1990:4). It can also be interpreted as a wrestling match with the British, the latter represented by the new Hongkong Bank Building[6] (see Figure 5.3) which was hailed by Michael Sandberg, the Chairman of the Hongkong and Shanghai Banking Corporation, as the most ambitious and innovative of all its previous bank buildings (Lambot & Chambers 1986:Foreword). Completed in 1985 and inaugurated in April, 1986, the 52-level steel-framed high-tech Hongkong Bank Building was designed by the British architect Norman Forster and Associates and is owned by British tycoons. The project costs HK$5.3 billion and was the world's most expensive piece of real estate. Its machine age structure and its massive steel frame are reminiscent of Richard Rogers and Renzo Piano's Georges Pompidou National Centre of Art and Culture, also known as the Beaubourg, opened in 1977 in Paris. Like the Georges Pompidou National Centre, the Hongkong Bank Building's 'transparency' is a central feature of the overall design. Both the Bank of China Building and the Hongkong Bank Building are basically manifestations of high technology in the machine age.

However, Norman Forster is more *fùng séui*-conscious[7] and 'a Chinese geomancer has been consulted on all matters sensitive to local tradition, particularly fùng séui issues' (Architecture and Urbanism 1986:67). The 'up' and 'down' escalators were also carefully positioned on the ground floor in order to maximise the 'dragon's vein' of beneficial *hei* (or flux of energy) to flow in and (presumably) to remain, bringing good fortune. Moreover, a pair of 1930's bronze lions was geomantically and ritually re-positioned at the entrance of the building in order to be 'harmonious with the contour of the hill behind' (Mimar Architecture in Development 1988:40). These two bronze lions (see Figure 5.4) were formerly used to guard the entrance of the Bank's 1935 predecessor.

The postmodern pastiche of the nostalgic motif and the high-tech new building at once forms a continuity in discontinuity, in which the bronze lions assume a renewed aura by resuming their guard duties. In short, the Hongkong Bank Building can be considered postmodern because of its loopback effect which links the historical bronze lions with the new structure, whereas the Bank of China Building is more modernist in conception than postmodern.

The locations of these two bank buildings are not without significance in the power struggle between the two governments. The Hongkong Bank Building is located in the heart of the financial-commercial arena, One Queen's Road Central, whereas the Bank of China Building is marginalized at the far end of Central District at One Garden Road. Moreover, unlike the Hongkong Bank Building which faces the Statue Square and an MTR station, the Bank of China Building is isolated and entwined by flyovers. It is located at what Fredric Jameson would call a 'hyperspace' in postmodernity. A postmodern hyperspace is a problematic space in which the human body is incapable of locating itself, or unable to organise its immediate surroundings perceptually, nor cognitively map its position in a mappable external world (Jameson 1984:83). If one wants to go to the Bank of China Building, one may experience something like a mutation in built space and may also encounter difficulty in physical trajectories, since the building is surrounded by flyovers and is not easily accessible by pedestrian walkway. It could be surmised that the owners of the Bank of China were unable to enjoy the same privilege in Hong Kong for choosing a prime location for its new headquarters as the Chinese authorities in Macau did. In this spirit, power is apparently exercised in the very structure of location and space.

If the new Hongkong Bank Building is seen as a last parade of British power in Hong Kong since the first establishment of the Hongkong Bank in 1864 in Wardley House at One Queen's Road Central, the new Bank of China Building certainly represents the resurgent power of the Chinese government. As Wang Deyan, Chairman and President of the Bank of China, said at the opening ceremony of the new headquarters, 'The construction of this Tower is, in itself, not only an evidence of our confidence in the future of Hong Kong, but also an indication of Bank of China Group's entering into a new historical stage' (Pictorial Album: Bank of China Tower Hong Kong 1991:13). No doubt, under the banner of dubious postmodern fad, the Bank of China Building is an exhibition of power through its spectacular visual dominance and its record-breaking height, even though it is physically marginalized from Central District.

The emergence of these two high-tech bank buildings readily speaks for apparent competition and conflict. As Charles F. Emmons writes:

> When the new 47-storey Hongkong and Shanghai Bank was to be constructed in the early 1980s in Central District on the site of the previous structure, a geomancer was engaged whose advice to alter the proposed structural design resulted in the inversion of triangular elements on the outside. For a couple of years the new bank towered over its competitor from the People's Republic of China, the Bank of China, but in the late 1980s a new Bank of China was built close by up the hill. Over 70 storeys tall, it dwarfed nearby structures and was covered in triangles (sometimes considered unlucky) that might cast evil reflections on the Hongkong and Shanghai Bank. All in all, a bad omen for those worried about China taking over in 1997.
>
> (Emmons 1992:44)

The tallest bank building vying for the lead with the most expensive bank building, in a sense, symbolically disguises political and economic rivalry in fùng séui between the departing British colonial regime and the coming Chinese government.

THE SCHIZOPHRENIC UNDERSTANDING AND THE ISSUE OF FÙNG SÉUI

The Bank of China Building offers an unusual opportunity to examine the correlation between the architect's intention and the populace's reaction to architectural gestures. The design principles at work in this building are modernist. It is conceived as a cube, rising out of the ground, and divided diagonally into quadrants. As the structure moves upward, the mass is diminished one quadrant at a time until it is reduced to a single, triangular prism, and is accentuated further by two 208-feet high twin mast at the apex. It is Pei's intention to create a crystalline

Euclidean vision in reflective glass and aluminium (Architectural Record 1985:137) and the prismatic design is meant to convey goodwill and to add 'new brilliance to the prosperity of Hong Kong' (Pictorial Album: Bank of China Tower Hong Kong 1991:13). Furthermore, the rising quadrants of the structure attempt to incorporate the Chinese traditional symbol of bamboo as an auspicious sign. Bamboo is a popular motif in Chinese culture and often signifies modesty, constancy, refinement and protection from defilement (Olderr 1986:9). According to the Bank's General Fact Sheet:

> The building comprises four triangular glass shafts rising to different heights, the inspiration for this design being derived from a Chinese proverb, using bamboo as a symbol: its sectioned trunk propelled ever higher by each new growth, denoting growth and prosperity.
> (Bank of China Building, Hong Kong: General Fact Sheet 1987:1)

Using bamboo as a metaphor, the inspiration of the design came from the successive and steady growth of bamboo which symbolises liveliness and prosperity. In addition, the four triangular shafts terminating at different levels symbolise the enterprising spirit and future growth of the Bank of China as it shoots skywards section by section, and the mirror glass of the building reflects the lights after nightfall and is made analogous to a diamond embedded in Hong Kong (Profile of the Bank of China Tower). However, contrary to the architect's intention, the angular Bank has been received as an ominous structure by many Hong Kong Chinese. It is believed that the Bank's four triangular prisms are negative symbols in Chinese architectural iconography owing to the fact that they are the opposite of circles which traditionally symbolise money, perfection and prosperity. Moreover, the 'big crosses' on the surface of the Bank building are signs of 'no' and the 'X' motif is perceived as another source in creating disharmonious effects.

Despite the Bank building's beautiful crystalline structure and its auspicious architectural intention, Peter Davey reiterates what local geomancers have put forward that the Bank building is strangely sinister and is bad fùng séui to the public:

> In fact, from a distance, the Bank of China resembles not so much a crystal as a praying mantis, with two aerials at the apex resembling the antennae of the insect and the horizontal slot in the skin below them emphasising the likeness to a sinister mask.
> (Davey 1990:4)

Through different interpretations, 'the growing bamboo' is displaced as 'a harmful praying mantis' and the twin masts are seen as the antennae of the insect. According to a local geomancer, Lee Gūi Ming, the two poles at the top, like two menacing needles, cast bad effects on the Sino-British-Hong Kong relationship (Keih Man 1992:11). In addition, the triangular prisms are also likened to numerous daggers which disrupt the fùng séui of the surrounding skyscrapers because those shining blades seem to be in the process of hacking into the Bank's neighbours. In particular, one 'sharp blade' is said to cut across the colonial governor's mansion (see Figure 5.5) and some have even speculated that the Bank's owners have attempted to disturb British rule through a vicarious use of architectural fùng séui. Completed in 1855, Government House was designed by Charles St George Cleverly and was situated in an once imposingly elevated location in Upper Albert Road looking out over the Victoria Harbour.[8] Many local people believe that when it was built the designer and architect must have been experts in geomancy because around the site there were tall trees at the back and a curving road. The curves are perceived as a fùng séui strategy to keep out bad luck which travels only in straight lines (Emmons 1992:41 & Waring 1993:133). At that time, the colonial governor's mansion was believed to have enjoyed tremendous geomantic prosperity. Over the years, as the city grew around it, its location was gradually undermined. According to a local geomancer, Ah Lohk (pen name), Government House now fails to command good fùng séui, owing to the fact that it is surrounded by skyscrapers, and above all, it is severely disrupted by the Bank of China Building's prismatic shape. Moreover, the ominous geomantic influence of the Bank building was already in force when construction began in April 1985, because later in 1986 Governor Edward Youde (1982–1986) suddenly died of an heart attack during an official visit to Beijing (The Metropolitan Weekly, 23 December 1995). When his successor, David Wilson (1987–1992), came, he was advised by sinologists to modify the rectangular fountain, which was said to resemble a western-style coffin, to a round shape[9] and some willow trees were also planted in the garden in order to counter the malignant hei. However, the juggernaut force of the sharp edges was so strong that the 'dwarfed' Government House could not possibly avert the impact. Consequently, not only was David Wilson 'called back' to Britain, but Chris Patten, the twenty-eighth Governor of Hong Kong, was hospitalised and was personally attacked by the populace of Hong Kong and the Chinese officials in the wake of a number of political quarrels and economic failures (The Metropolitan Weekly, 23 December 1995).[10]

Given the Bank building's sinister image, Peter Wesley-Smith also reveals the unease felt by many Hong Kong citizens:

It is said that the sharp edges of the new Bank of China building in Hong Kong bring bad luck to those at whom they point unless the malevolent influences they project are deflected by the judicious placement of a mirror or eight-sided diagram.

(Wesley-Smith 1992:1)

The Bank building thus has been considered a kind of demonic architecture which arouses great anxiety among its neighbours and the general public concerning the imminent reunification with China.[11]

In this spirit, the Bank building best illustrates that the creation and interpretation of metaphor is not a one-to-one relationship but there may exist a gap in perception. The mode of reception by the general populace in relation to the interpretation of architectural semantics is more dependent on local codes and vernacular characteristics than on the architect's conception and intention. This discrepancy in interpretation leads to a 'schizophrenic' understanding of the auspicious bamboo metaphor. As David Harvey points out, urban design should be 'sensitive to vernacular traditions, local histories, particular wants, needs, and fancies, thus generating specialised, even highly customised architectural forms that may range from intimate, personalised spaces, through traditional monumentality, to the gaiety of spectacle' (Harvey 1989:66). However, Pei seems to be indifferent to vernacular traditions which do not favour angular forms in architecture. Although he is a Chinese American, Pei fails to incorporate circular architectural motifs that traditionally symbolise harmony and prosperity, and instead indulges in a game of geometry. The result is indeed a classic modernist failure.

The arrangement of buildings often involves competition and conflict over the issue of fùng séui. In this respect, Maurice Freedman writes:

It is very important to grasp the idea that in the Chinese view a building is not simply something that sits upon the ground to serve as a convenient site for human activity. It is an intervention in the universe; and that universe is composed of the physical environment and men and the relationships among men. Men are bonded to the physical environment, working good or ill upon it and being done good or ill to by it . . . In principle, every act of construction disturbs a complex balance of forces within a system

made up of nature and society, and it must be made to produce a
new balance of forces lest evil follow.

(Freedman 1979:318)

The Chinese popular system of fùng séui is not merely concerned with
the subtlety of cosmic conformity between architecture and social
relations, it also suggests possible alterations in order to redress an
undesirable environment. Charles F. Emmons considers fùng séui to be a
rather broad, eclectic type of magical system whose major function is to
help people relieve anxieties about the physical and social environment
(Emmons 1992:49). The bad fùng séui of the Bank building, in this
particular context, reflects tension, anxiety, challenge and competition
and the disharmonious ordering of social relations in space. As a
remedial reaction to the eerily 'evil' Bank and its 'malevolent'
influence, its immediate neighbour, the Citibank Tower (see Figure
5.6), completed in 1992, located at 3 Garden Road, cannily employs four
arch-like parallelograms in its architectural structure as 'shields' to
offset the harmful pointed edges, and the Central Plaza also emerges in
the form of 'a triangular file' to blunt its sharpened blades (Keih Man
1992:13 & Ming Pao Daily News 26 March 1995). As such, the
development of these edifices in a Chinese metropolis is willy-nilly
caught in the game of fùng séui and objectifies men's relationship by
means of constructions. Fùng séui, after all, is still an active belief in this
high-tech era, and is not yet overborne by architectural technology.
Rather, it goes hand in hand with (post)modern capitalism as a means of
competition and redress.

THE "SISTER" IN MACAU

While the towering Bank of China Building in Hong Kong has received
an extra-ordinary amount of attention, the new Bank of China Building
in Macau[12] (see Figure 5.7), is no less a spectacle than its 'sister'. But
unlike its marginalized 'sister' in Hong Kong, the Bank building,
completed in 1991, occupies the most prominent spot in the tiny enclave.
Its location at once reveals the different political relationships between
British-ruled Hong Kong and Portuguese-administered Macau and
China. The Bank's owners perhaps were able to have this prime site due
to the amicable Sino-Portuguese relationship after the 1987 Joint
Declaration. But the excellent location also points to different colonial
histories of the two places: Portugal acquired Macau on sufferance from

China,[13] but Britain took Hong Kong by conquest and the imposition of unequal treaties on China. These different histories are now reflected in the events surrounding the return of the two places to China. While Hong Kong is caught in a frustrating tug-of-war between London and Beijing over transition issues, Macau is marching much more smoothly towards its reunification with China, and Portugal is more accommodating to China than Britain. The prominent site of the Bank building in Macau can thus be considered a political statement.

Standing in its unchallenging monumentalism, the 37-storey Bank of China Building in Macau was designed by Remo Riva,[14] and was completed in 1991 by P & T Architects and Engineers. It is said to be 'like its sister in Hong Kong, a statement of corporate success and confidence in the future' (Prescott 1993:75). Moreover, much in the same way as its sister, the Bank of China in Macau is laden with political implications as manifested in its imposing height. The building is approximately 166 metres above the road level and is the tallest structure ever in Macau.[15] It embraces a classical tripartite division of base, shaft, and capital, but is still close to the grave monumental structures among the skyscrapers in Hong Kong. The central octagonal tower is flanked by attached wings on either side and capped by a prismatic triangular capital, a trendy architectural feature considered a 'trademark' in postmodern fad by Patrick Lau Sau Shing, professor of architecture in the University of Hong Kong (Ming Pao Daily News 10 December 1993). However, the penchant for crowning the top of a building with a prismatic triangle is merely a postmodern mannerism and is nowadays perceived as a postmodern cliché by Ho Tao, a renowned Chinese architect and designer. This kitschy feature was often adopted by designers in the so-called postmodern buildings in Hong Kong, such as the Entertainment Building (also designed by Remo Riva), the Nine Queen's Road Central (the name of the building), the Ritz-Carlton Hotel (see Figure 5.8), and the Central Plaza. While the octagonal main tower is expressed by the use of curtain walling, the wings by structural glazing strip windows and Portuguese pink granite, small strips in Barrocal white are employed to modulate the elevation. Unlike its 'sister' in Hong Kong, the Bank building in Macau is flanked by the familiar guarding lions at the entrance. The whole building is a celebration of modern technology, with its glittering silver glass, with the indispensable motif of lions. Like the Entertainment Building, Riva employs the same pastiche idea by capping the top with a triangular prism in order to embellish the building and to have a pretext to call it postmodern architecture. It is in fact a postmodern simulacrum in Macau.

Similar to fashion promotion, architects and developers borrow fashionable names and add trendy elements. Being crowned with an 'imported' foreign label – postmodern, the postmodern buildings in Hong Kong and Macau readily sound different and can meet the consumers' insatiable desire for ever-changing fashion. But most of these buildings' 'postmoderness' is unconvincing when compared with the postmodern tenets in architecture as discussed earlier. They in fact resemble modernist slab blocks rather than postmodernist playful eclecticism.

ANACHRONISTIC DECOLONIZATION AND A "PRE-POSTCOLONIAL" ERA

The Bank of China building in Macau is not merely a skyscraper office building owned by the Chinese government, it is a political landmark in disguise signifying Chinese authority and influence. The architectural gesture reeks with political overtones and is a metonymic representation of the resurgent power after some four hundred years of foreign administration. Let us first turn to examine the relationship between Macau and Portugal since the 1960's.

The 1974 political upheaval in Portugal had a certain impact on Macau. The 'Carnation Revolution' of 25 April 1974 successfully ousted the 46-year totalitarian rule of António de Oliveira Salazar and Portugal eventually evolved into a democratic state. The liberation from fascist dictatorship also led to a belated wave of decolonization and the new government advocated 'a policy of good relations and friendship with all peoples on the basis of mutual interests, non-interference, independence and equality among nations' (Cremer 1991:131–2). However, even before this process of decolonization in other Portuguese colonies, Portugal had already relinquished much of its power in Macau during the climax of China's Cultural Revolution (1966–67). At that time, Macau was in a state of anarchy and the administration was paralysed. The Portuguese settlers would have readily 'evacuated' from Macau had China simply requested them to do so, but Lisbon was informed that China wished Macau to remain as it was, largely because the change in Macau's status might shock the people of Hong Kong. The Portuguese, therefore, retained a militarily and politically indefensible little colonial anachronism in Asia (Hanna 1969:4). It was indeed a uniquely ironic historic inversion of the colonial relationship. In addition, it was an anomaly par excellence because it

114

was the radical Cultural Revolution in China which allowed the colonial era in Macau to continue. Frantz Fanon remarks that 'Decolonization, which sets out to change the order of the world, is, obviously, a programme of complete disorder' (Fanon 1971:27). He is of the opinion that decolonization is always a violent phenomenon, because it is the meeting of two opposed forces. However, China's decision not to put an end to Portuguese colonisation confounds Fanon's paradigm of Manichean enmity between native and coloniser. Fanon's argument fails to apply to Macau's ambiguous historical situation where questions of nationality, sovereignty and government have never been clearly defined.

The new Bank of China Building plays an important, if not peculiar, role in the actualisation of Macau's anachronistic decolonization. It was the pretext for the removal of a colonial icon, the bronze statue of the former colonial governor Amaral, from in front of the Bank building. João Maria Ferreira do Amaral was a wayward governor of Macau (1846–1849). After taking office, he implemented a series of high-handed reforms aimed at lessening Chinese influence in Macau. His strong policies eventually led to his assassination by the Chinese. The Amaral equestrian monument (see Figure 5.9) was inaugurated in 1940 as a celebration of Portugal's 8th centenary as an independent nation in the Iberian Peninsula and as a belated commemoration of his prowess. The bronze sculpture is a representation of a fierce authority depicting the brute strength and overwhelming rage of the commander who is engaged in the climax of the battle to suppress his Chinese attackers.

The Amaral statue can be considered a masterpiece of Portuguese artwork. It breaks the solidity of forms and is charged with an exaggerated tautness and a kind of Baroque theatricality of dramatic, vigorous movement. The human psyche of Amaral's infuriated agony and dauntless resolution to combat the Chinese, the prancing stride and the bulging muscles of the horse are portrayed in a frozen action – a moment being arrested in a snapshot effect. But this monument was seen as the extant icon of Portuguese colonisation in Macau after the destruction of the Mesquita statue.[16] While Amaral was hailed by the Portuguese as one of the most outstanding governors of Macau as well as a hero/martyr, he was regarded as an invader/oppressor by the Chinese. As such, Lu Ping, Director of China's State Council's Hongkong and Macau Affairs Office, said in 1990 that the statue was 'a symbol of colonialism' and must be removed before 1999 (Lee; SCMP 29 Oct 1992).

The newly completed Bank of China Building perhaps hastened the removal of the statue on 28 October 1992 (see Figures 5.10 and 5.11).

115

The final fate of the five-tonne bronze statue was to be shipped back to Portugal from where it had come. The reasons for elimination of the equestrian monument provide a revealing comparison with the Bank of China's reception in Hong Kong. It was believed that the monument created bad fùng séui for the Bank's new headquarters. When looking at the entrance of the Bank building, it seemed that Amaral's whip was flogging the whole building; while from the opposite direction, when looking from the statue, it looked as if the horse was treading and stamping on the Bank. The statue, therefore, interfered with the harmonious geomancy of the new Bank building. Logically one could argue, however, that the statue was put up well before the construction of the building and if it was bad fùng séui for the Bank to face the statue, the designer could well have avoided disharmony by re-positioning the Bank. But as we have seen, fùng séui can be a political force in disguise, in this case expediting the erasure of a colonial symbol before the 1999 takeover.

The pulling down of the monument marked the process of 'decolonization within a colonial context'. This action can aptly be called an 'anachronistic decolonization' because it renders problematic ideas of a linear progress to postcoloniality – a topic in vogue in some Western academies. The removal of the equestrian monument before the demise of colonialism seems to underline a passage into a new era and the closure of a prickly historical age. However, it created an ambivalent scenario partly because it contradicts linear chronologies of colonialism – decolonization – postcolonialism. Macau is now strangely situated in a historically and theoretically problematic context which I would call a 'Pre-postcolonial' era from October 1992 until 1999. Although the oxymoronic rubric appears to be awkward and somewhat eccentric, it nevertheless precisely portrays the unique pre-postcolonial ambience in Macau, where the Chinese have already displayed in advance its 'legitimate' influence as symbolised by the Bank building. If the Amaral equestrian monument manifested the colonial power, the Bank building certainly represents China's overwhelming authority in Macau, which is also 'anachronistic' in the colonial milieu.

CONCLUSION

Architecture, as a cultural discourse, does not just exhibit the artistic expression of a certain epoch, but is also power-laden. The Bank of China Building in Hong Kong seems to use postmodern rhetoric, but it is in fact a modernist design and functions like a modernist building, lacking any kind of aesthetic populism and humanism. Although its 'sister' in Macau is kitschily topped by a prismatic triangular capital, it still resembles the modernist slab block model and is a postmodern simulacrum without novelty. Under the veneer of dubious postmodern architectural gestures, the two Banks' owners intriguingly display their resurgent ruling power in disguise. In fact, at least, the resurrected political power may also be symbolically suggested by the two Banks' monumental height–the tallest bank buildings in these two places. On a realistic level, however, the growing significance of the Bank of China in Hong Kong and Macau is suggested by the fact that it became a note-issuing bank in these two places in May 1994 and October 1995 respectively. By and large, the two buildings now stand as symbols of the importance of the Bank of China in international trade and finance, and also represent China's commitment to playing a key role in the economic integration of the two places after the resumption of full sovereignty.

In Hong Kong, the Bank of China Building's auspicious bamboo metaphor has been conversely interpreted by the local people as sinister omens, precisely because there is an obvious discrepancy between the architect's intention and the general public's perception of China. There is, therefore, a profound schizophrenic in the process of reunification of Hong Kong and Macau with China. During the 1980's, China exerted strenuous efforts to regain the sovereignty of these two places. The 1984 Sino-British Joint Declaration and the 1987 Sino-Portuguese Joint Declaration are wrapped in good intentions, to 'liberate' the colonial subjects from the grip of foreign usurpers/aggressors. It should have been a moment for celebration of territorial integrity and national solidarity since the shameful Opium Wars. But coming reunification instead unleashes unprecedented misgivings and stress about the future. Some Chinese show an unwillingness, if not phobia, of returning to the mother country. The Chinese state's efforts to resume the exercise of sovereignty and to oust the two colonial powers have not been met with applause and joy, but have triggered an emigration-mania, which reached its climax soon after the Tiananmen Square suppression of pro-democracy demonstrations in June 1989.[17] It is extremely ironical in colonial histories that the colonised subaltern citizens do not welcome decolonization and liberation, and much prefer foreign rule. The grandiloquent mission of historical recuperation from Western colonialism and imperialism is strangely displaced, becoming instead a possible threat to political stability and economic prosperity in these two places.

In Macau, through the cultural statement of fùng séui, the Chinese authorities successfully pressed for the early removal of the Portuguese colonial icon: the Amaral statue. This action at once complicates contemporary theories which see cultural phenomena delineated as linear epochal successions, and contradicts theories of postcoloniality. As Simon During argues, 'the notion of 'postcoloniality' carries with it a theory of history. It segments world history into three eras: the pre-colonial, the colonial and the postcolonial itself. The will to use the term 'postcolonial' is not simply driven by a need for narrative order and global harmony, but contains a political promise of liberation' (During, 1992:339). The 'post' does not signal an 'after' but rather mark spaces of ongoing contestation enabled by the process of decolonization. 'Postcoloniality' obviously connotes a condition that is evenly developed rather than internally disparate, disarrayed or contradictory. The term 'postcolonial' therefore embraces a temporal connotation which implies a progression of events marking history as a series of stages along an epochal road from the 'pre-colonial' to 'colonialism', 'postcolonialism' and 'neo-colonialism'. However, the removal of the Amaral statue does not signal a phase of immediate 'liberation'. These cultural theories cannot be neatly mapped onto Macau.

By examining the two Bank of China Buildings in Hong Kong and Macau, we can see that political power can be 'textualized' in architecture. In the main, these two towering Bank buildings suggest a complicity between power politics and culture, and evince a symbiotic relationship through artistic creation and architectural expression. The two Bank buildings are fashioned by professional views as well as political ideologies, and the different histories of Hong Kong and Macau are also willy-nilly articulated by the Banks' fùng séui disputes. They are not just high-tech towering edifices but are also ideological constructs which metonymically represent the resurrection of the repressed power, and reveal political wrestling in the disguise of postmodern fad, in the crucial years leading up to the return of Hong Kong and Macau to China before the end of the twentieth century.

NOTES

1 The Bank of China was formally established in 1912 by the new Republic of China and was a branch of the 'Central Treasury' possessing semi-government status. After the establishment of the People's Republic of China in 1949, the Bank assumed its role as the state's international bank in

1953 and gained a monopoly over all foreign financial transactions. In 1980, the Bank received its new statues through the State Council; it was described as a state-owned socialist enterprise. It is now one of the largest and the most important banks in China. See David Strohm, 'The Bank of China: A Review of its Role and Function in the People's Republic of China and the Hong Kong/Macau Region', Discussion Paper, (Macau: The University of East Asia, China Economic Research Centre, 1989).

2 The phrase 'postmodern architecture' first appeared in Hudnut's essay, 'The Post-Modern House', which was reprinted in Joseph Hudnut (ed.), Architecture and the Spirit of Man, (Mass.: Harvard University Press, 1949), p. 109–19.

3 In particular, the International Style, which took shape in America and Europe during the 1930's, developed a kind of formalistic rigidity in architectural features and showed a close relationship to Cubist and formalist developments in painting. Its advocacy of purism was partly a reaction against nineteenth-century eclecticism.

4 The Bank of China (BOC) was established in Hong Kong in 1917. The BOC Group in Hong Kong comprises 13-member banks, operated under the supervision of the Bank of China, Hong Kong & Macau Regional Office. On the role of BOC in Hong Kong, see David Ho Tai Wai, 'A Study on the Corporate Strategy of the Bank of China Group in Hong Kong in the Run-up to the twenty-first century', unpublished M.B.A. Dissertation, the University of Hong Kong, 1993.

5 Not true to the name, the 78-storey Central Plaza is not located at Central District, but at Wanchai. It now ranks the fourth tallest building in the world after the Sears Tower (Chicago 1974), the World Trade Centre (New York 1973) and the Empire State (New York 1931).

6 The Bank of China group is second only to the Hongkong and Shanghai Banking Corporation in Hong Kong.

7 Fung seui (literally, wind [and] water) is the Chinese art and science of placement that uses design, ecology, intuition and common sense in order to create harmony and to bring health, wealth and happiness, but also embraces competition and conflict resulting in strain. Maurice Freedman contends that it is a sort of 'science' which should be exempt from the description 'superstitious', and it must be part of Chinese religion. See Maurice Freedman, 'Chinese Geomancy: Some Observations in Hong Kong' and 'Geomancy', in G. William Skinner, The Study of Chinese Society: Essays by Maurice Freedman, (Stanford: Stanford University Press, 1979). It is, however, considered a popular Chinese magical system, serving the function of relieving anxiety and tension. See Charles F. Emmons, 'Hong Kong's Feng Shui: Popular Magic in a Modern Urban Setting', Journal of Popular Culture, Vol. 26:1, Summer 1992, p. 39–49. Although fung seui is considered a type of geomancy, a way of divining based on the earth, Stephen Feuchtwang points out that it might be called 'topomancy', as it involves reading the significance of landscape (topography) and of architecture rather than the earth or dirt itself. See Stephen D.R. Feuchtwang, Anthropological Analysis of Chinese Geomancy, (Vientiane, Laos: Editions Vithagna, 1974), p. 224.

8 Government House was declared 'historical building' by the Antiquities and

Monuments (Decoration of Historical Building) (No. 6) Notice 1995, published in the Hong Kong Government Gazette on 29 September 1995. On the history and transformation of Hong Kong governor's residence, see Katherine Mattock and Jill Cheshire, The Story of Government House, (Hong Kong: Studio Publications Ltd 1994).

9 During a personal interview in January 1996 with Dr Ho Tao (who was entrusted with the renovation of Government House for Governor Chris Patten in 1993), he reiterated that the changing of the shape of the fountain during David Wilson's tenure was mainly a fung séui issue. Ho co-initiated and designed the Hong Kong Arts Centre (completed in 1977) and won the territory's highest architectural honour, the silver medal, from the Hong Kong Institute of Architects in 1978. Adopting the city flower of Hong Kong – the Bauhinia – as a central theme, he designed the flag and emblem for Hong Kong Special Administrative Region which will be officially used on 1 July 1997.

10 For example, Chris Patten has been dubbed by his opponents as 'a prostitute' and 'a man condemned in history'.

11 In a telephone interview with two staff members of the Public Relations Office of the Bank of China, they unanimously said that the Bank building was not involved in the game of feng seui as widely speculated, rather they emphasised the 'official' information given in the Profile of the Bank of China Tower.

12 The Bank of China was established in Macau in 1950.

13 With regard to the problematic issue on the sovereignty of Macau, see Camões C.K. Tam, Disputes concerning Macau's Sovereignty between China and Portugal (1553–1993), (Taipei: Yung Yeh Publishes Ltd 1994), and Robert W. Usellis, The Origin of Macao, (Macau: Museu Marítimo de Macau, 1995).

14 Remo Riva, director of Hong Kong architects P & T Group, is one of Hong Kong's leading architects. He won the highest architectural honour, the silver medal, from the Hong Kong Institute of Architects in 1993 for designing the postmodern Entertainment Building.

15 The second tallest building, Luso Building, completed in 1983 with 26 floors, was at that time considered by the planners to have exceeded a desirable height.

16 Vicente Nicolau de Mesquita was the governor of Macau after the assassination of Amaral in 1849. He successfully invaded Baishaling, near Macau, and consolidated the Portuguese ambition to exercise sovereignty over Macau de facto. His statue, put up in 1940 in the square facing the Leal Senado, or the Royal Senate, was considered the very emblem of Portuguese imperialism and suppression, and was destroyed by the local Chinese during the anti-Portuguese outcry on 3 December 1966, known as the '123 Incident' in Macau.

17 On the impact of the return of Hong Kong and Macau to China, see Albert H. Yee, A People Misruled, (Singapore: Heinemann Asia 1992), and Jay Branegan, 'Perils of 1997', Time, 13 May 1991.

REFERENCES CITED

Architectural Record
1985 The Logic of Eccentricity. Vol. 173, September 1985.
Architecture and Urbanism
1986 The Hongkong Bank. No. 189, June 1986.
Bakhtin, Mikhail
1986 The Problem of the Text in Linguistics, Philology, and the Human Sciences: An Experiment in Philosophical Analysis. *In* Speech Genres and Other Late Essays. Austin: University of Texas Press.
Bank of China
1991 Pictorial Album: Bank of China Tower Hong Kong. HongKong: Bank of China Hong Kong-Macau Regional Office. Bank of China Building
1987 Hong Kong: General Fact Sheet. Hong Kong: Joint Sole Letting Agents.
Batalha, Graciete
1987 This Name of Macau. *In* Review of Culture (1st Edition).
Branegan, Jay
1991 Perils of 1997. Time, May 13.
Chung, Wah-nan
1989 Contemporary Architecture in Hong Kong. Hong Kong: Hong Kong Museum of Art.
Cremer, R. D.
1991 Macau – City of Commerce and Culture. Hong Kong: API Press Ltd.
Davey, Peter
1990 Another Prize for Pei. The Architectural Review 188.
During, Simon
1992 Postcolonialism and Globalization. Meanjin, Winter.
Emmons, Charles F
1992 Hong Kong's Fung Shui: Popular Magic in a Modern Urban Setting. Journal of Popular Culture 26 (1).
Fanon, Frantz
1971 The Wretched of the Earth. Harmondsworth: Penguin Books.
Feuchtwang, Stephen D.R.
1974 Anthropological Analysis of Chinese Geomancy. Vientiane, Laos: Editions Vithagna.
Freedman, Maurice
1979 Chinese Geomancy: Some Observations in Hong Kong. *In* The Study of Chinese Society: Essays by Maurice Freedman. G. William Skinner, ed. Stanford: Stanford University Press.
1979 Geomancy *In* The Study of Chinese Society: Essays by Maurice Freedman. G. William Skinner, ed. Stanford: Stanford University Press.
Hanna, Willard Anderson
1969 A Trial of Two Colonies: Portuguese Macao and British Hong Kong. East Asia Series XVI. No. 1 (Macao).
Harvey, David
1989 The Condition of Postmodernity. Oxford: Basil Blackwell Inc.

Ho, David T.W.
    1993   A Study on the Corporate Strategy of the Bank of China Group in Hong Kong in the Run-up to the twenty-first century. Unpublished M.B.A. Dissertation, The University of Hong Kong.

Jencks, Charles
    1977   The Language of Post-Modern Architecture. New York: Rizzoli.

Jameson, Fredric
    1984   Postmodernism, or the Cultural Logic of Late Capitalism. New Left Review 146 (July-August).

Keih Man No. 77, November 21, 1992. (in Chinese)

Klotz, Heinrich
    1988   The History of Postmodern Architecture. London: The MIT Press.

Lambot, Ian & Chambers, Gillian
    1986   One Queen's Road Central. Hong Kong: South China Printing Co.

Lee, Adam
    1992   Statue Taken Down in Macau. South China Morning Post,October 29.

Mattock, Katherine & Cheshire, Jill
    1994   The Story of Government House. Hong Kong: Studio Publications Ltd.

McLeod, Mary
    1985   Architecture. In The Postmodern Movement. Stanley Trachtenberg, ed. Westport: Greenwood Press.

Metropolitan Weekly (The). December 23, 1995. (in Chinese)

Mimar Architecture in Development
    1988   Hongkong and Shanghai Bank,Hong Kong.Vol. 17, March.

Ming Pao Daily News. December 10, 1993. (in Chinese)

Ming Pao Daily News. March 26, 1995. (in Chinese)

Olderr, Steven
    1986   Symbolism: A Comprehensive Dictionary. Jefferson: McFarland & Co. Inc.

Prescott, Jon A.
    1993   Macaensis Momentum. Macau: Hewell Publications.

Profile of The Bank of China Tower.

Saussure, Ferdinard de
    1974   Course in General Linguistics. London: Fotona.

Strohm, David
    1989   The Bank of China: A Review of its Role and Function in the People's Republic of China and the Hong Kong/Macau Region. Macau: The University of East Asia, China Economic Research Centre (Discussion Paper).

Tam, Camões C.K.
    1994   Disputes Concerning Macau's Sovereignty between China and Portugal (1553–1993).(A revised Ph. D. Thesis) Taipei: Yung Yeh Publishers Ltd. (In Chinese)

Usellis, W. Robert
    1995   The Origin of Macao. Macau: Museu Marítimo de Macau.

Venturi, Robert
    1977   Complexity and Contradiction in Architecture. New York: The Museum of Modern Art.

Venturi, Robert et al
    1989   Learning from Las Vegas: The Forgotten Symbolism of Architectural
         Form. Cambridge: The MIT Press.
Waring, Philippa
    1993   The Way of Fung Shui: Harmony, Health, Wealth and Happiness.
         London: Souvenir Press Ltd.
Wesley-Smith, Peter
    1992   Identity, Land, Fung Shui and the Law in Traditional Hong Kong.
         Law Working Paper Series Paper No. 5. The University of Hong
         Kong.
Yee, Albert H.
    1992   A People Misruled. Singapore: Heinemann Asia.

INTERVIEWS

Ho, Tao. Personal interview. January 17, 1996.
Public Relations Office. Telephone interview. February 2, 1996. The Bank of
China Head Office, HK.

6

TREADING THE MARGINS
PERFORMING HONG KONG

Rozanna Lilley

REPETITIVE HISTORIES

The prophets of doom and the seers of success have lately been busily making predictions about Hong Kong. A process of reification has been at work wherein the present is construed not simply as the here and now but a moment that must be dated and called the 'late-transitional' phase, a moment pregnant with potential meanings. When British colonisation ends in 1997 Hong Kong will become a Special Administrative Region of China, governed by a vision of reunification which is guided by the dream of an essential difference between Western capitalisms and the People's Republic. This dream is called 'One Country, Two Systems'. Initially conceived by Deng Xiaoping to settle the question of Taiwan (Sum 1995:96), the fantasy has become a formula which states that for fifty years following the transfer of sovereignty China will continue to practice socialism while Hong Kong will keep its capitalist systems and lifestyle.

What I want to draw attention to here is the way in which the potential meanings of this late-transitional phase tend to have been reduced to an oppositional discourse pitting, for example, Chinese accusations of neo-imperialism against United States grandstanding about human rights abuses. This opposition involves a repetitive history which, unwilling or incapable of imagining new political forms, takes its participants along the well-trodden paths of the past, paths sign-posted 'liberal-democratic' discourse for some, 'post-Maoist' discourse for others. The various positions which can be taken on China's resumption of sovereignty over Hong Kong, whichever terms they are couched in, can always be shown to articulate visions of history which deepen this repetition through an essentially political affirmation or repudiation. The acrimonious polemicising of the Cold War may be over but the essential core of the old positions remain. Both socialism and capitalism remain profoundly dependent upon each other for their self-definition. If you follow the other path you will step towards irrationality and malevolence. So many fears and desires are invested in this doubling, and in the particular ways in which this mirroring is played out in debates about 1997, that each time these roads predictably open in front of us, we must assume that other destinations and other modes of travel have been closed off. What I want to ask is, given the tenacity of this discursive dichotomy, how is it possible to intervene in such an 'overdetermined circuit' (Chow 1993:15)?

If you bear in mind Governor Patten's democratisation rhetoric[1] which, I should add, has operated entirely within the confines of an executive-led government (Sum 1995:71), and China's stress on the role of Hong Kong in bringing to partial fruition its nationalist dreams of reunification and of replaying the glories of a splendid past, you will begin to sense the extraordinary tenacity of the restrictions on imagination activated here. The consequences of walking these well-worn roads is to obscure plurality, fragmentation and heterogeneity and, no less importantly, to stifle thoughts that might give rise to differently envisioned modes of life.

That these thoughts have been stifled rather than suffocated, is evident from the work of a handful of theorists commentating on and formulating the issue of Hong Kong identity in ways which resist dominant conceptualisations. Lee (1994), for example, argues the case for a 'hybridised cultural register' in the territory which consciously displaces idealist demarcations between the East and the West in the interests of forging a strategic political identity. Chow makes a stronger plea for this type of strategy. She writes:

> it is the tactics of dealing with and dealing in dominant cultures that are so characteristic of living in Hong Kong. These are the tactics of those who do not have claims to territorial propriety or cultural centrality. Perhaps more than anyone else, those who live in Hong Kong realize the opportunistic role they need to play in order, not to "preserve", but to negotiate their "cultural identity".
>
> (Chow 1993:25)

For Chow (1993:92,97,140), this identity is strategic because of its instability. The utopia of opposition and the possibilities for difference

125

can be located in the perpetual modification of 'being Chinese' beyond the confines of national boundaries.

In this paper I would like to extend the direction of Lee and Chow's work through a consideration of Hong Kong performance group, Zuni Icosahedron. More specifically, I link the problems raised by their reception, on the part of both theatre critics and audiences, to questions of language and to some of the issues raised by Castoriadis in his provocative analyses of 'the imaginary'. When Castoriadis writes of a 'radical imaginary', he refers to the 'elementary and irreducible capacity of evoking images', to the 'originary faculty of positing or presenting oneself with things and relations that do not exist' (Castoriadis 1987:127). He also employs a more common usage of the term as a way of considering shifts in meaning and slippages which allow a movement away from the repetition of canonical significations. It is this interest in slippages, and especially in the ways in which 'the effect of the imaginary *outstrips* its function' (Castoriadis 1987:131), that I wish to pursue here.

In the course of this pursuit, Zuni Icosahedron has been chosen for investigation because, I believe, they provide instances of a form of representation which resists closing itself into a system, which is not dogmatic but problematic. Their repeated privileging of questioning speaks usefully to the late-transitional phase and suggests the necessity for new modes of thought and representation which cut across the certainties of both totalitarianism and liberal democracy. While we need to be aware of the limitations of Zuni's disjunctive work, we also need to acknowledge that within the hegemonic parameters in which the company operates they provide audiences with other points from which to start, conjuring hazy outlines for new conceptions of 'Hong Kong identity'. What is perhaps most pertinent for anthropologists here is the indigenous argument that Hong Kong people are in a privileged position to examine Chinese and Western culture in a critical way; that the very lack of an established identity is an asset.

In Hong Kong, the situation of being between cultures, identities, countries is producing its own mode of expression – unresolved tensions between continuity and disruption, between fragmentation and homogeneity characterise these articulations. These are the fractal patterns which anthropologists try to specify through terms like 'syncretism', 'creolization' (see Gilroy 1992:192), 'hybridity' or, more recently, 'discrepant cosmopolitanisms' (Clifford 1992:108). In this sense, Zuni Icosahedron's work is an invitation, and sometimes a demand, to reconceive familiar notions of nationalism and ethnicity.

REVOLUTIONISING HONG KONG THEATRE

Currently in Hong Kong there is a very self-conscious attempt on the part of some cultural workers to create and encourage specifically local forms in the performing arts. This call for indigenous modes of representation occurs within a context wherein the gravity and civilizational value of Western and Chinese performing arts are continually mobilised. Government funding is predicated on supplying the imputed need for this civilization and cultural policy has largely attempted to enforce these reference points. Groups which are engaged in the search for indigenous modes of representation strive to undermine assumptions about the aesthetic superiority of canonical versions of both Western and Chinese high culture and to produce work which decenters these received categories and is of immediate relevance to local people (see Lilley 1991, 1995). Zuni Icosahedron is the most extravagantly controversial group in the territory committed to this task.

Zuni Icosahedron was founded in 1982 and, since that time, the company has presented more than fifty productions and over two hundred performances. Zuni have become something of a legendary fringe institution within the territory's performing arts scene but have received their greatest critical accolades performing overseas – in Taiwan, Britain, the United States and Japan. Financially they rely on support from the Urban Council and from the Council for Performing Arts in the form of small project grants but the prospect of dissolution always looms. Indeed, for members, it forms part of the very horizon of commitment.

Zuni began to gain greater audience popularity in 1987 with *Romance of the Rock*, a production which drew its title from Cao Xueqin's classic Chinese text *The Story of the Stone*. During that year over 22,000 people bought tickets to Zuni shows. Since then, audience numbers have fluctuated but, as artistic director Danny Yung points out, the company is, at times, more popular than either the Hong Kong Dance Company or City Contemporary Dance Company.

Many, though not all, members of Zuni are persons we might loosely call 'intellectuals'.[2] In Hong Kong, this intellectual stance is generated from a strong sense of 'in-betweenness', of being interstitially placed between China and Britain, and is partially a response to state and quasi-state cultural apparati through which both of these powers propagate Oriental and Occidental cultural forms. It is also driven by cosmopolitanism, by the double vision and aesthetic stance of openness to divergent cultural perspectives which this 'in-

127

betweenness' fosters. This cosmopolitanism is not fortuitous. Hong Kong owes its existence to its positioning at an economic and political crossroad and, nowadays, is an important channel between centres and peripheries within wider international and regional systems (see Hannerz 1992:201). It is, quite literally, Hong Kong's business to be open. Furthermore, thousands of Hong Kong's families have strong links abroad, not only with mainland China but with diaspora China, made up of about thirty six million people scattered throughout the world (Kim & Dittmer 1993:277). The heightened awareness of cosmopolitanism within Zuni Icosahedron, and the metacultural position that this encourages, is derived from the above factors and from the internationalisation of art and culture generally. It is also intensified by the biographical histories of many senior members as people who have, at times, sojourned in various parts of diasporic China and returned home to find that the easy sense of the taken-for-grantedness of one's own milieu is no longer available to them, that encounters with contrasting perspectives have rendered them permanently sceptical.

In their application for a seeding grant to the Council for Performing Arts in 1991 the company suggested:

Performing arts in Hong Kong, until the beginning of the nineties, sadly, can by and large be described as "traditional" – either inheriting directly from Chinese culture or taking its roots in Western civilisation, lacking its own identity.
Zuni Icosahedron, now in its tenth year, has always aimed at bringing to Hong Kong an original force in creativity . . . It is with this idea in mind that Zuni performs as a "laboratory" . . . ultimately striking a unique language.

(ASG(D) 1991:1)

This defence of Hong Kong's self-image, in the form of a reaction against cultural domination from the West and China, is combined with an avowed concern to publicise 'minority interests' in the territory. Edward Lam[3], a company founder, put it to me like this:

Due to the existence of Zuni at least more people, especially people in the cultural scene, are more aware of the words "alternative" and "minority" and I think it is Zuni – absolutely, it is Zuni – who bring out these concepts. There is no other company that has been so persistent in promoting an alternative culture, in raising the voice of minorities, in reminding society that minorities should not be neglected. So the performing arts and the publicity and promotions around all these pieces have become a very important tool by which people understand the significance of minority interests in Hong Kong. That is a very big step that Zuni has achieved although not much credit has been given to us.

It is with these twin notions in mind – creating a unique local identity and defending minority interests – that Zuni claims to have achieved a 'revolution' of Hong Kong theatre (ASG(D) 1991:3). In the following section I will investigate this rather bold claim through a consideration of some of the stylistic hallmarks of the company.

ZUNI STYLE

In conversation, artistic director Danny Yung refuses to associate the company with any particular style but, if pressed, stresses that he is interested 'in basics more than particulars . . . in form more than contents', that he wants to explore the "impressionistic" and the "emotional"' (Program Notes *Decameron 88*). This exploration involves the creation of performance pieces stretched between theatre and dance, between Chinese and Western imagery. Zuni's desire to create a uniquely Hong Kong performance style has thus led to an excavation of disparate images and sounds deriving from foreign and Chinese sources. This layering effect, an uncovering of colonial history, is bound together by the use of ordinary, everyday movements, gestures and props.

Critics have responded differently to these performances. Reviewing *Decameron 88*, Andrew Kwong of the *Hong Kong Standard* (22/6/88) writes that the production:

carried all the hallmarks of Zuni: a bare stage, costume in black, white or some other neutral colours, characters aimlessly walking up and down the stage or running perimetrically and diagonally, hysterical cries which are irritating rather than enlightening. In this production the unconventional was crowned with a total absence of the spoken word (apart from some fragments of a live recording of the Legislative Council in session). Movements of the players occurred in a highly aleatory manner, and neither reason nor imagination would provide the key to what was happening on stage.

While some critics deny that Zuni productions have a 'subject', constraining themselves to 'implications' (e.g. Winterton *South China Morning Post* (*SCMP*) 21/9/1988), the following examples will give the reader some idea of how the company manages to relate the meaning of diverse texts to the social, political and cultural circumstances of Hong Kong. *Decameron* was said to be about the Black Death and about public fears and expectations in the homestretch to 1997, with voiceovers about ensuring stability and prosperity filling the auditorium and a bed at the side of the stage symbolising Taiwan (*China Post* 23/8/1988:9; *Hong Kong Standard* (*HKS*) 18/6/1988; *SCMP* 21/9/1988). *Romance of the Rock* linked the plight of Black Jade, the neglected granddaughter of the literary saga, with the sufferings of Mainland writers and artists during the Cultural Revolution (*SCMP* 27/2/1987:20). The political implications of *Sunrise* became increasingly explicit, with a mixture of oral and written dialogue referring to the Legislative Council's controversial Powers and Privileges Bill (1985).[4] Conjunctions of past and present are proclaimed, fictional histories form analogies with contemporary hopes and tribulations and the power of theatrical experience, imagery and mood to construct political consciousness is asserted.

However Zuni productions do not embrace any functional calls for specific political actions. They are intended as a space for questioning, an arena in which people are encouraged to construct their own interpretations from minimal forms. Yung's own attitude to audiences is related to his concept of 'sincerity'. Convinced that conventional works domineer and bombard, he tries to develop:

> a relationship of trust between audience and performers, of faith. You have to believe in whatever you see. Otherwise you would not be sitting there. And you have to believe in what you do. Otherwise you would not be standing there. Anything else is just a superficial interaction or transaction.

As critics never tire of pointing out, many of these characteristics are not new within the context of international performing arts. Zuni's work could, for instance, be linked to the detachment called for in epic stage-craft, the gestic theatre developed by Brecht in which the audience, instead of identifying with the characters, is educated to be astonished by the representation of conditions (see Benjamin 1968:150–154) until the familiar becomes strange, until inattention is jolted towards an historicising of the everyday (Blau 1982:18). More frequently, though, Zuni is linked to Western Experimental or Alternative Theatre,

Happenings and the whole flurry of radical performance activity during the rebellious 1960s. Some suggest that Zuni's immediate mentors come from more recent innovators, artists like Robert Wilson from the United States or Germany's Pina Bausch (*South China Sunday Morning Post* (*SCSMP*) 7/1/1990). The possibilities of a stylistic connection with Japanese theatre are rarely explored. Remarkably, the correlations with classical Chinese aesthetics are also little mentioned – the presentation of discontinuous images not unlike a Chinese poem, the importance of empty space and silence in bringing a performance to life, and the consequent stress on minimalism which attributes great weight to the active role of audiences in constructing their own interpretations are all relevant here (Leys 1988:21,23,36–37).

It is not my intention to enter into this debate about potential origins. What I do want to point to is the way in which such histories are used to suggest that there is something inauthentic about Zuni, something outmoded or plain suspicious. Rosamund Yu, writing for *Bazaar* (Dec 1990) put the case rather mildly: 'It's food for thought that Lam and Zuni have used seemingly Western forms to question Western colonial hegemony in Hong Kong'. Local critic, Winterton, reviewing *Sisters of the World United* in 1987, was more patronizingly virulent about the matter:

> It all seemed very worthy. But repeated stage images of involuntary self-denial, and symbolic gestures expressing emotional impotence plucked out from any narrative context, have ceased to be "progressive" decades ago practically everywhere else in the world . . . I have sat in a cellar while the actors shovelled earth on to the skylight in Poland, been locked into a lift with a ghost in Holland, seen *Hamlet* done as vaudeville, *Macbeth* played by three actors fixed together like Siamese twins, watched horn-players descend from a cathedral roof in pink overalls, been fed blue cake by a man with a live rat peeping out from his sleeve . . . seen Scott's expedition to the South Pole done on an ice-rink and watched fake decapitations. Whether I've loved them or loathed them, one thing is certain – I've never forgotten them. I won't say I can remember nothing of Zuni's meanderings on a too-large stage on Wednesday night . . . [but] *Sisters of the World United* was paler than life.
>
> (*SCSMP* 11/10/1987)

An essay by Zhang (1992) might help to solidify the company that well-travelled Winterton has here almost evaporated into the realms of insignificance. Writing about the series of campaigns against Western 'spiritual pollution' and 'bourgeois liberalisation' that have marked Chinese political affairs since the end of the Cultural Revolution, Zhang proposes that the travelling of Western theory to China is part of an active opposition, an act of antagonism in the face of institutionalised officialdom. Calling on the work of satirical author Lu Xun, the term 'grabism' is deployed to suggest the entirely different situations and purposes which Western theory speaks to in the Mainland. According to this analysis, the grabbing of Western theory through translation is a 'liberating' influence in a China mired in 'a completely threadbare and ossified theory of class and class struggle that reduces all literature and criticism to a number of rigid formulas' (Zhang 1992:109).

Zhang's argument can be applied with equal force to Zuni Icosahedron's 'grabbing' of foreign performing arts theory and practice. This application acquires an oppositional status in the midst of Hong Kong's mainstream performing arts scene which draws its strengths from the master narratives of Chinese and European tradition (see Lilley 1991 & Lilley 1995). Put more prosaically, this is an observation that while art forms may originate in a specific social context, they are not tied to that context – they make take on different functions in different places and times (Burger 1984:69).

During an interview which appeared in *AsiaWeek* (20/4/1984:94) Yung was asked whether he felt that Asian performers are too influenced by the West. He replied: 'In a bicultural environment we have a bicultural product – and there's nothing wrong with that . . . There are many avant-garde creators in New York who have digested Asian thought and art forms'. Or as Lu Xun pithily put it, 'the fact that we eat beef and mutton does not mean that we are turning ourselves into cows and sheep' (cited in Zhang 1992:120).

In fact, Zuni encompasses a variety of performance styles depending on the director involved. Most of the work I have been discussing is attributable to Danny Yung. Yung has the highest profile and is the strongest guiding hand of the company. It is his works that have toured overseas. I hope it has become clear by now that Yung's performance pieces are marked by a contemplative resonance, sometimes labelled sterile formalism by his detractors, a cool yet impassioned visual seduction. The astringent grandeur of these compressions can be contrasted with Edward Lam's proliferating expansions.

Lam was originally involved with more conventional theatre plays and had a kind of conversion after seeing Yung's work. He became Yung's most able protege but gradually went on to develop a very different approach. While there is a concern within the company to preserve the formal appearance of mutual good feelings, the two directors have become increasingly antagonistic. We are not only dealing with differences in style here, with the ways in which Yung's obsessive work solidifies against interpretation while Lam's is more accessible.

Both directors embrace forms of emancipatory politics, but Yung's concerns are more to do with the fixities of Chinese tradition, the conditions that enable hierarchical domination and the possibilities of Hong Kong identity, of a particular ethnicity, within these constraints. Lam, in his major pieces *How To Love A Man Who Doesn't Love Me* (1989) and *Scenes From A Man's Changing Room* (1991), is more overtly interested in sexual politics and gender differentiation, particularly in exploring gay issues in Hong Kong. His is a politics of self-identity that has an almost social documentary edge, aimed at constructing a self-defining history against the institutional and cultural stereotypes which afflict homosexual men in Hong Kong. These somewhat different approaches currently sit uneasily together within the company's repertoire. More generally, a determination to explore the conditions of perception and reception combined with an interest in more specific critiques are the axes around which Zuni turns, revolutions which are as frequently strained as they are smooth.

The breach between Lam and Yung is indicative of a broader split in the current political strategies adopted by concerned locals. In one definition of emancipatory politics, typified by Lam, the focus for critiques of illegitimate domination centres on a valorisation of differences, of 'minorities'; in this case, sexual difference and the need to overcome discriminatory attitudes towards homosexuals. On the other hand, there is a broader political agenda which seeks to examine the bindings of tradition, of the past, thereby preparing the new or allowing a transformative approach to an as yet undetermined future (see Giddens 1991:210,211). This is the approach taken by Yung in his stage journeys. This is the China Hongkongese must return to but by another route; the China of politicised memories and desire.

For Yung, minority politics smacks of tokenism. The familiar mantra of women, students, artists, workers, greenies and gays cannot address the big picture.[5] Although he takes an intense interest in elections and lobby groups and encourages, sometimes unsuccessfully, other Zuni members to do the same, he locates the site for 'real' politics beyond the governmental sphere. While Yung's productions seek to politicise any and all of the actions of the British administration or the Chinese

Communist Party (CCP), he treats these as symptoms of contradictions located at a deeper level. It is this use of the governmental as a reflexive target of self-problematisation (see Hunter 1992:367) that allows some members a disenchanted withdrawal from formal politics and others a fervent pledge to engage in political activities without any appearance of overt discord.

ENGAGING THE AUDIENCE

Zuni's placement of themselves as practising an autonomous 'high' art in opposition to companies given over to the ideological reproduction of society, their pursuit of originality and denigration of conformism, have resulted in accusations of having an 'insulting disregard for the audience' (*SCMP* 27/12/1985), of staging a 'confrontation' between performers and spectators (*Tsin Pao* 28/6/1988). Many company members take the elitist view that the masses seek distraction whereas true art demands concentration from the viewer. In their 1991 application for a seeding grant Zuni listed as one of its objectives 'serving' the audience in a more positive manner in contrast to merely 'entertaining' the community (ASG(D) 1991:1).

Zuni members express this viewpoint in a variety of ways. One woman said to me that Hong Kong Repertory Company was 'not no good, just traditional'; that 'most of their performances are just the same', 'just to make you laugh'. Yung is more balanced in his public statements:

> There are two kinds of performing arts. One kind belongs to the museum which we can all go to and appreciate. It is like looking at porcelain: a summary of our history, our background. The other kind is actually moving, going on, expanding, relating, develop-ing. I think I am more interested in the second, although I can see that the first is important.
>
> (Hackett 1990:33)

If Yung tactfully suggests ossification in Chinese and Western tradition, placing himself as part of a movement towards innovation, Lam, with typical confidence, at one time suggested that the response of audiences was, to a certain extent, irrelevant. In a newspaper interview he had the following statement attributed to him: 'Unlike other commercial groups which have to pander to the audience's tastes in order to secure a good box office, we are a sponsored group and therefore we can stage our performances in any way we feel like regardless of whether people understand them or not' (*SCMP* 4/9/1986).

Obviously there is a tension operating here between Zuni's belief that they are respecting and caring for audiences and the perception of others that this elitism is alienating. Frequently audiences do dislike Zuni productions. Some find an almost masochistic pleasure in their own bewilderment. Witness these meanderings from Zheng Jingming in the *Weekend Herald* (3/7/1988):

> If you are not perplexed after you watch Zuni's performance, I would feel worried. The feeling of being perplexed proves that you have tried, though failed, to find the answer. This is the normal reaction of normal people. That you feel you know the answer could mean that either you are above worldly considerations or you are dreaming during the performance. It is, in fact, a self-persecution to watch Zuni's performances. You have to enter a state of depression, constantly wrestling with your own thinking, trying to interpret the successive symbols . . . Faced by Zuni's obscure ideas it is natural that we are perplexed, or even angry, feeling that we have bought two difficult hours with our own money.
>
> A few days ago after I finished watching Zuni's *The Decameron*, my ears were filled with the audience's complaints . . . Zuni's performance appeared to bring a nightmare to the audience. Relief came only after the show. What the hell does Zuni's performance want to say? There would be no answer if you insisted on asking Zuni . . . Therefore quite a number of drama critics are of the opinion that Zuni's attitude has distanced itself from the folk. It is destructive, rather than constructive.
>
> This kind of criticism reflects only the critics mentality. They regard the audience as being three years old. To be honest, those soap-opera-type of dramas can only dull the audience. An approach like "this story teaches us that . . ." can only raise up a lazy audience.

Though the account is ambivalent, it demonstrates a willingness to accept Zuni's elusive pedagogy, an admiration for the discipline of their abstractions. Ironically, I think that this appreciation of Zuni's instruction is much greater in the Chinese language press because, while the content may be vague, the attitude has affinities with socialist philosophies of art and performance as educational tools. This notion also has some currency in the West but seems to be more readily accepted by Zuni audiences than might be expected elsewhere. The genuineness of people's desire to understand and to be taught is part of an acceptance of a marked pedagogical strain in contemporary Chinese artistic policy. And, in the Chinese language press, the circulation of these ideas, affects reviewers whether they write for Taiwanese, Mainland or independent publications. Ceasing to be a particular theory professed only in mainland China, the value of a distinctly pedagogical artistic practice has so affected language and ideas that it has become a constitutive part of the Hong Kong cultural landscape.

However, another critic of the same production, while indicating the same genuine quest for comprehension, believes he fails precisely because the form is too Western, too modern:

> This is the second time I have gone to a Zuni performance. The first time I watched *October* at the Shatin Town Hall. After the performance, several ladies asked me about my impressions. I simply said, "I don't understand". An old hand of the drama circle said: "You will understand more if you watch Zuni's performances more often".
>
> Yesterday, I went again to Zuni's performance. Still I failed to understand. Fortunately I met a very famous figure in the field of performing arts. He told me: "This type of drama has become very popular in the United States. It is the avant-garde type". I am still very perplexed. Maybe I am too old-fashioned.
>
> I did not want to give up. I must be able to find someone among the audience who could understand. While I was looking around, Mr Xu Guanglin came along with several young men. I dragged him out, asking: "What does this drama mean?" "Oh, we are just discussing that. Let's have something to drink first", said Mr Xu. We sat in a restaurant for two hours. We raised many questions. Several times we thought we could not continue the discussion.
>
> (Zhu Ke *The Mirror* 1984)

If Zuni aim to imbue an attitude of questioning, in this instance they certainly succeeded. One might note, though, that what is being questioned is the methodology of Zuni rather than current social circumstances in Hong Kong. In this sense, the company could be described as creating a disposition towards doubt which partially rests on the instability of attraction/repulsion to critiques addressed to Hong Kong Chinese couched in what is perceived to be a Western form.

Of course, critics are a particular case and most tend to admire Zuni, particularly after their overseas touring. Many are in awe. One dance critic I was attending Cantonese language classes with was too terrified to review a Zuni production. The mythos had grown around the company that they were not interpretable, particularly to foreigners. Some react negatively to this 'off-limits' quality – the most vicious attacks I have read were published in English language newspapers. I have already given some examples of these vilifications but the following will serve to jolt the reader's memory – 'boring, cold, authoritarian . . . rich kid's aloof play' (Winterton, *SCMP* 21/9/1988) or, rather more absurdly, 'Zuni performers were like characters out of Roger Corman's movie *Night of the Living Dead* . . . Everything was below a threshold of discernible stimuli' (Borek, *HKS* 1/5/1991). A number of issues and neuroses are played out in these critical commentaries. If Chinese critics sometimes feel they do not understand Zuni's productions because they are too Western, Western critics fear they lack understanding because they are too Chinese. There is an element of resentment here, common to many expatriate discourses in Hong Kong. But there is also a counter strategy of claiming superior knowledge of 'avant-garde' performing arts, of suggesting that Zuni have appropriated something which is not rightfully theirs and which, being Chinese, they do badly anyway.[6]

Critics everywhere have a fundamental role in producing legitimate classifications of artistic value. In Hong Kong, however, this role is somewhat attenuated. Critics cannot make or break a show because productions simply do not run for long enough. Even six performances would be a lengthy season. Reviews do not generally appear until a few days after opening night and audiences thus must decide whether to buy a ticket prior to the publication of a review. In the long term, though, critics do form the basis for the recognition of performing groups and for the further accumulation of their cultural authority (see Verdery 1991:189). Zuni have managed to sidestep this process to some extent through their 'political' reputation and their handling of specific controversies. This gives them an advantage over other local performing arts companies because they have largely managed to create and control their own media profile based on specific interventions that are deemed newsworthy.

PREPARING THE NEW

On occasion, Zuni members express a feeling of inadequacy about their own productions, a fear of the social ineffectiveness of their medium.

Mathias Woo suggested to me that art as an institution in Hong Kong neutralises the political content of individual works, saying that sometimes he thinks, 'Oh, God. There are so many problems in the world, in Hong Kong, should I put in an effort to do a performance?' Yung has also expressed this uncertainty:

> Worrying about the limitation, asking questions, circling around day in day out doesn't help a bit as it's not going to lead us anywhere. And the stage becomes a cage. With only worry and questions.
> (Program Notes *Days and Nights of Abstinence* (*DNA*) 1990)

In answering these concerns it would be possible to argue that Zuni's style is emancipatory in itself, that its nonorganicity permits the breaking up of ideologies. But we do not have to refer only to structural principles and formal characteristics. Content is equally at issue. Zuni frequently use the stage as a source of counter-information about events in the territory, exposing repression and bureaucratic high-handedness.

Most importantly, though, the value of Zuni Icosahedron lies in their advocacy of a perpetual state of questioning within a polity which encourages passivity and paralysis through a combination of conventional Chinese formal constraints on behaviour which endorse the maintenance of social order and British colonial policies which, until recently, have allowed locals little say in the running of their own city. Zuni member David Yeung gave me an insightful description of the company's rupturing practices:

> We are not a political group trying to put propaganda on stage but we do have a political consciousness that we try to express in a creative way on stage. We try to introduce an open-minded point of view, both for the audience and for ourselves. Also we try to talk about history, we try to talk about the environment affecting people and that environment can be Hong Kong or China. We are not trying to propose propaganda but we are trying to open people's minds so that they can see. We talk about chauvinisms, we talk about the passiveness of people towards the environment, their country, history.
>
> The form is a kind of revolution for Hong Kong audiences. It is very important for everyone to see their life, the standard of tradition and the history of Hong Kong and China. We are trying to break rules in the theatre and also in normal life, to show that we are not passive. We are trying to do something.

Yung is more succinct in his discussion of the same issue: 'The local education system forces everything upon you, making you memorise, and lays down a value system for you so that you won't challenge it at all. People say 'I don't understand' as if everything they watch has to be understood' (*HKS* 31/10/1989).

Zuni's remorseless destabilisation of canons is about creating an alternative form of representation, a new place from which to speak. Other performing groups like Sand & Bricks or City Contemporary Dance Company (see Lilley 1991) are also engaged in this quest. But it is Zuni's project of reclaiming, reinflecting and questioning history and tradition for the conditional present that has attracted the greatest publicity and the most polarised responses. Their pillaging of tradition, their parodies and their allegories construct a hybrid Chinese/Western theatre/dance form. Tracing the original sources from which this hybridity emerges is a challenging intellectual exercise. But the essential point to consider is not these originating moments. Rather, we should recall that it is Zuni Icosahedron which has effectively publicised an interrogative space which allows other positions to emerge and made visible the hegemonic parameters of Chinese and Western tradition.

Although the defining characteristics of Zuni's work remain difficult to capture, all of their performances are bound together by dramatic analyses of oppression and subjectivity, the intertwining of culture and power at the level of emotion and bodily expression – the loci where forms of domination become entrenched through being interiorised. What I remember most clearly from their shows is the incessant turning things over, knowing there will be no last word or easy solution. Their depictions of unspeakable closures almost return the viewer to silence, but not quite. And here, the sparse use of dialogue is necessary. Confronted by dominant cultures which repress the articulation of a specifically Hong Kong experience, their struggle is, as Williams has described the emerging identities of new social groups, 'at the very edge of semantic availability' (cited in Rutherford 1990:22). Thus they opt for the imagistic, recreating everyday movements and gestures occurring in daily practice. They are concerned with what cannot be put into words and this silence is eloquent.

The eloquence of silence is also, I suggest, intimately tied to the problematic status of Cantonese (see Bolton & Hutton's chapter in this volume). In Hong Kong Cantonese, not Mandarin, is the language primarily used by over 98 per cent of the population (Chen 1993:521). Stigmatisation of this language has been standard practice. In post-war years commentators, for example, suggested that local plays could not be written in Cantonese because there were 'limitations' to the language; it was 'slovenly' and an inadequate vehicle for the expression of emotional depths (Tsim 1968:23). With hindsight this notion appears extraordinary. Today more new works than translations are performed and the appropriateness of Cantonese as a medium of local expression is no longer at issue.[7]

Nevertheless, we need to bear in mind that the 1982 Constitution of the People's Republic stipulates for the first time that Mandarin is to be promoted across the country (Chen 1993:508) and detractors now argue that the common use of Cantonese in Guangdong public life is 'inhibiting socialist construction' (Erbaugh 1995:91). The Basic Law, which is a framework for the governance of the territory after 1997, allows for the official use of English and Chinese language 'by the executive authorities, legislative and judicial organs' (1990 Article 9). The ambiguous use of Chinese language or *jùngmàhn* in this document would seem to tacitly tolerate Cantonese. However, locals are frantically attending Mandarin classes in anticipation of a marked shift in this direction.[8]

Compounding these complications, is the fact that, until the early 1970s, English was the sole written language for virtually all formal occasions in Hong Kong and is embedded in administrative practice. Despite the promulgation of an Official Languages Ordinance in 1974, which gave parity to the use of Chinese and English, the civil service is still criticised for being slow in the promotion of the former (Chen 1993:532–533; *SCMPIW* 22/4/1995:11). An overwhelming majority of secondary schools continue to use English as the primary medium of instruction. This results in what Lee (1994:14) has termed a 'schizophrenic educational environment' where, within the classroom, students and teachers make frequent use of code shifting from English into Cantonese (Scollon 1995:9) and, outside the classroom, speak only Cantonese. While commentators predict an increasingly trilingual society in the territory, it is evident that language use has become both politically charged and highly demanding.

Chow (1993:147,160) has pointed out that inarticulateness is a way of resisting the talking function of the state, of refusing to participate in patriotic rhetoric. In Hong Kong, silence can also mark a refusal to be coopted into the monotonous affirmation of the dominant values of socialism and capitalism, a desire to disengage with the mutually defining relationship of these categories and the disparate visions of the irreversibility of historical processes that both categories promote. Instead of making predetermined speeches, instead of accepting the domination of the Hong Kong imaginary by inexorable conclusions which promise utopia or tragedy, instead of reciting the school texts laboriously learnt by heart, people may choose not to say anything.

This abandonment of words bespeaks vulnerability. It is as if, every coordinate buckling around them as 1997 draws closer, living in Hong Kong has become a constant navigation over the fault lines of tradition. The felt experience of Zuni performances depend on this quickening incertitude in which only a promise of problematisation is held out for the audience to grasp. Indeed, Zuni members take the fact that there is no finished edifice, that what is encouraged is the work of potentially endless reflection, as a sign of their own aesthetic and ethical superiority amongst other local cultural producers.

What makes Zuni's work a valid confrontation of the problems posed by the frontiers of the history Hong Kong people are living through is not any particular message that they convey to audiences but the interrogation which it is and to which it gives rise. Their performances do not unveil some occulted truth. They are a continual process of interrogation, destined to ambiguity in their desire to eliminate closure and completion, prohibited from absolutising their results. The most important 'message' that this process can convey is that there is no one good regime, that history is indeterminate and, as Castoriadis (1987:190) has so cogently expressed it, 'not the actualisation of pre-determined possibilities'.

Zuni Icosahedron's work is intimately related to changes currently taking place in Hong Kong. When local legislators voice their criticisms or issue their demands, they are not only calling for specific policy changes on the part of the administration. They are implicitly demanding the right to criticise and to make demands, a right which disrupts the logic of both colonialism and totalitarianism. Zuni's performances do not necessarily express these values as such. Rather, their work emerges in a space opened by them, and their formal values of questioning and interrogation, along with their utopian sense of future possibilities, are resonances of the optimisms and fears of the late transitional phase. Their attempts to represent Hong Kong experience in its often contradictory multiplicity, to convey the translations between and across cultures which are constitutive of the daily lives of Hong Kong people, tends to reveal the presence of social power in places where it had been practically invisible and inaudible. Zuni's vigorous defence of their right to perform involves the right of others to watch and intends a future in which expression is multiplied instead of frozen in the wastelands of politically useful art.

THE INDETERMINATE FUTURE

Concerned with shoring up a social space separated from state power and with nourishing a variously defined autonomy, Zuni Icosahedron are proposing a reformation of Hong Kong performing arts at every level, aesthetically and politically. The dimensions of the problems they are dealing with are enormous. Zuni are attempting to construct a unique Hong Kong identity, come to terms with history, keep a divided company together, avoid the use of highly trained professionals, develop a new audience, educate the public and alter the economic structure of performing arts in Hong Kong.

The group is too unknown to achieve all this; their performances will never be manna for the masses and they will inevitably fail from overextension. However, while I, as an academic analyst, may suspect that I am treading the slippery terrain of fantasies of radical consciousness, Zuni members and supporters believe that they are treading the margins of the possible and that the whole point of the exercise is the expenditure of effort.

The question here is to what extent a disposition towards doubt, an encouragement of questioning and hence of greater individual autonomy can cancel the effects on people's lives of the oppressive structures of the society in which they live. Yung admits to a cynicism about the political system and a consequent desire to use the freedom of the stage as a kind of last resort. His attitudes about the relationship between the wider polity and his own cultural products are difficult to pin-point because he wisely refuses to separate the two, relying on the old metaphor of the world as a stage to articulate his position:

> What's on stage is just as important as what's off stage. Tiny stages and enormous stages, political stages and historical stages, they're all waiting alike for us to acquaint, to stroll about, and to explore. Waiting for us to participate and experience . . . What a stage offers is space – with less function/mission/significance in mind, maybe we'll dig up more unknowns.
>
> (Program Notes *DNA* 1990)

If Yung believes in anything, he believes that Zuni Icosahedron speaks for the future. In conversation once on the Star Ferry, he spoke to me about the unique cultural position of Hong Kong, arguing that the impending horizon of 1997 now provides a source of continual ferment in the territory, an experience which is not a revolution but a 'condensed evolution'. He compared Zuni's performances to the types of cultural events that occurred in Russia during the October Revolution and in China just prior to and after 1949. Later he added:

> The most valuable thing is not only that you have the drive to express and articulate your experience and to analyse and then edit your ways of presentation but also it is that you can always step out again and this is what makes an artist. Being a bicultural person is really a plus. Because you can switch from one language to another language in order to relate in a new way. Through that whole social process we learn faster, we are more sensitive and have more acute vision.

Zuni provide a very concise picture of the acknowledgement of the bindings of Chinese tradition, a recognition of the relevance of their British history and a rejection of nationalism in favour of an unstable and fragile notion of 'Hong Kong identity' that has some roots in an ethnic idea, in that it primarily speaks to Hong Kong Chinese, but is utterly disassociated from any overt discourse of ethnicity. There is nothing apologetic about this stance and the following comment from Edward Lam may help to capture the sense of freedom, of entrepreneurial adventure, that this process entails:

> We are entitled to borrow so many things from the outside because we don't have this burden about being Chinese. Whatever we see we can borrow and turn it into something in a very Hong Kong style. Like the way they make clam spaghetti.
>
> (*TV & Entertainment Times* 12–18/8/1991:17)

In their excavation of disparate source materials, their presentation of bits and pieces of history, scraps of culture, in their silent gestures, Zuni diligently dismantle the authority of the master narratives of Chinese and Western tradition.

The condensations and displacements which Zuni offer their audiences are designed to alter perception. But we obviously cannot predict how and to what extent for whom. Indeed, in the absence of any genuine party politics in Hong Kong, in the lack of institutional foci with much independence from Britain or China, no dissenting voices in the territory stand much chance of becoming a chorus (see Verdery 1991:365).

However, groups like Zuni Icosahedron might be said to have a properly revolutionary significance because their work presupposes – over and above the individuals performing on the stage, speaking pompously about the virtues of the CCP, cursing propaganda and thought control, advocating democracy and greater citizen participation, making decisions without consultation – a rupture with the dominant regimes of the imaginary and a movement towards an unknowable future. It is the effective presence of this future in anticipation, the subtext of the ineluctable and uncertain prospect of 1997, which forms the base line for drawing new maps and Zuni inhabit this borderland culture area populated by Hong Kong Chinese unevenly assimilated to dominant nation states (see Clifford 1992:110), slipping between nation, ethnicity and identity in their repeated efforts to question the politics of tradition, of historical memory, of location, of the new.

ACKNOWLEDGEMENTS

Thanks to Neil Maclean for repeated assistance with editing a rather unwieldy manuscript and to the editor and readers who provided many useful comments. Earlier versions of this paper were delivered in the Anthropology Department of the University of Sydney and at the annual Australian Anthropological Society conference. I thank the people who contributed to those seminars. The fieldwork on which this research is based was made possible by funds provided by the Research School of Pacific and Asian Studies, Australian National University and by the Department of Employment, Education and Training. I am also indebted to the Australian Federation of University Women for a bursary and to Macquarie University for a Research Fellowship. All translations of original Chinese material in this paper were energetically undertaken by Jiang Ren.

NOTES

1 Patten has articulated a change in Britain's decolonisation rhetoric away from 'convergence' to a promotion of citizen participation in the interests of defending and creating 'democracy and rights' (Sum 1995:77). In, for example, a speech broadcast on Radio Television Hong Kong, Patten replayed a familiar liberalism which has very effectively forged the fiction of a society spontaneously organised as a result of free competition in which the state played the minimal role of ensuring that the rules of the game were

respected. The innovative element here is a move away from much touted generalisations about the apathy of Hong Kong people. For Patten, the economic success of the colony can only be preserved if the creative participation of the population is recognised and encouraged. Moral protection in the guise of a stimulation of active participation has become the exit-in-glory motif (Sum 1995:72). Scorning the notion that Hong Kong people are 'consumers of goods, but never of ideas', by remarking 'You don't need to be a Marxist to know that that's twaddle', Patten argues that the territory will not fundamentally alter 'if the men and women who live here don't want it to change'. 'Be positive and act positive too' he enthuses. In this way, listeners are reassured, Hong Kong will be 'a free, prosperous, decent society, living with the rule of law under a Chinese flag' (*South China Morning Post International Weekly* (*SCMPIW*) 8/4/1995:11).

2 Here I follow Hannerz's distinction between 'intellectuals' and 'intelligentsia' wherein both terms refer to people who are preoccupied with ideas but the latter tend to be more bound by paradigms and institutional constraints. Indeed, Hannerz's description of intellectuals is a very apt account of the type of theatrical work that Zuni are engaged in. He writes: 'It is the business of intellectuals to carry on traffic between different levels and fields of meaning within a culture, to translate between abstract and concrete, to make the implicit explicit and the certain questionable, to move ideas between levels of consciousness, to connect ideas which superficially have little in common, to juxtapose ideas which usually thrive on separateness, to seize on inconsistency, and to establish channels between different modes of giving meanings external shape ' (1992:139).

3 Lam now has his own dance/theatre company, called 'Edward Lam's D.T.', in Hong Kong.

4 The original draft of this bill gave the legislature the right to deny the public entry to council meetings, prohibited the publication of reports of proceedings held in camera and created a set of defamation offences including 'intentional disrespect' (*Far Eastern Economic Review* 27/6/1985:36).

5 The vital issue of audience responses to Zuni productions is addressed in my forthcoming book, *Staging Hong Kong: Gender and Performance in Transition*, Curzon Press. There I argue that the generally appreciative response of audiences to this company rests on their valuation of the demand for thinking and for questioning and on their insistence on heterogeneity and the refusal of precise meaning.

6 See Lilley 1994 for a sustained analysis of a Zuni production in which feminist issues were repeatedly hijacked by supposedly larger concerns, such as sovereignty transferral.

7 Erbaugh (1995) reports that the economic boom in southern China is rapidly enhancing dialect prestige. Television commercials in the Mainland employ Cantonese speaking actors to impart a sheen of sophistication to their products and travellers fake Cantonese accents in the hope of better service (Erbaugh 1995:89).

8 Currently, though, even among Hong Kong secondary and college students, less than ten per cent report any competence in Mandarin (Erbaugh 1995:80,87).

REFERENCES CITED

Application for Seeding Grant (Dance)
1991   Hong Kong: Zuni Icosahedron.
AsiaWeek. 1984.
Bazaar. 1990.
Benjamin, W.
1968   Illuminations. New York: Schoken Books.
Blau, H.
1982   Take Up the Bodies: Theater at the Vanishing Point. Urbana, Chicago, London: University of Illinois Press.
Burger, P.
1984   Theory of the Avant-Garde. Minneapolis: University of Minnesota Press.
Castoriadis, C.
1987   The Imaginary Institution of Society. Cambridge: Polity Press.
Chen, P.
1993   Modern Written Chinese in Development. Language in society 22:505–537.
China Post. 1988.
Chow, R.
1993   Writing Diaspora: Tactics of Intervention in Contemporary Cultural Studies. Bloomington & Indianapolis: Indiana University Press.
Clifford, J.
1992   Travelling Cultures. In Cultural Studies. Grossberg, L., Nelson, C. and Treichler, P., eds. Pp. 96–116. New York, London: Routledge.
Erbaugh, M.
1995   Southern Chinese Dialects as a Medium for Reconciliation within Greater China. Language in Society 24:79–94.
Far Eastern Economic Review. 1985.
Giddens, A.
1991   Modernity and Self-Identity: Self and Society in the Late Modern Age. Cambridge: Polity Press.
Gilroy, P.
1992   Cultural Studies and Ethnic Absolutism. In Cultural Studies. Grossberg, L., Nelson, C. and Treichler, P., eds. Pp. 187–198. New York, London: Routledge.
Hackett, L.
1990   Search for Status: Zuni Icosahedron. In Zuni Icosahedron. Hong Kong: Zuni Icosahedron.
Hannerz, U.
1992   Cultural Complexity: Studies in the Social Organization of Meaning. New York: Columbia University Press.
Hong Kong Standard. 1988, 1989, 1991.
Hunter, I.
1992   Aesthetics and Cultural Studies. In Cultural Studies. Grossberg, L., Nelson, C. and Treichler, P., eds. Pp. 347–372. New York, London: Routledge.

Kim, S. & Dittmer, L.
  1993 Whither China's Quest for National Identity? *In* China's Quest for
        National Identity. Dittmer, L. & Kim, S., eds. Pp. 237–290. Ithaca and
        London: Cornell University Press.
Lee, Q.
  1994 Delineating Asian (Hong Kong) Intellectuals: Speculations on
        Intellectual Problematics and Post/Coloniality. Third Text 26:11–23.
Leys, S.
  1988 The Burning Forest: Essays on Chinese Culture and Politics. London:
        Paladin Grafton Books.
Lilley, R.
  1991 The Double Bind: Performing Arts in Hong Kong. The Australian
        Journal of Anthropology 2(3):293–306.
  1994 Chronicle of Women: A Hongkong Story. The Australian Journal of
        Anthropology 5(1–2):86–112.
  1995 The Absolute Stage – Hong Kong's Revolutionary Opera. Social
        Analysis 38:76–91.
The Mirror. 1984.
Program Notes.
  1988 The Decameron 88. Hong Kong: Zuni Icosahedron.
  1990 The Sixth Year of One Hundred Years of Solitude – Days and Nights
        of Abstinence. Hong Kong: The Urban Council.
Rutherford, J.
  1990 A Place Called Home: Identity and the Cultural Politics of
        Difference. *In* Identity: Community, Culture, Difference. Rutherford,
        J., ed. Pp. 9–27. London: Lawrence & Wishart.
Scallon, R.
  1995 Plagiarism and ideology: identity in intercultural discourse. Language
        in Society 24(1–28).
South China Morning Post. 1985, 1986, 1987, 1988.
South China Morning Post International Weekly. 1995.
South China Sunday Morning Post. 1987, 1990.
Sum, N.
  1995 More than a 'War of Words': Identity, Politics and the Struggle for
        Dominance During the Recent 'Political Reform' Period in Hong
        Kong. Economy and Society 24(1):67–100.
Tsim, T.
  1968 Chinese Theatre in Hong Kong: Proceedings of a Symposium,
        November 22–23, 1968. Hong Kong: Center of Asian Studies,
        University of Hong Kong.
Tsin Pao. 1988.
TV and Entertainment Times. 1991.
Verdery, K.
  1991 National Ideology Under Socialism: Identity and Cultural Politics in
        Ceausescu's Romania. Berkeley: University of California Press.
Weekend Herald. 1988.
Zhang, L.
  1992 Western Theory and Chinese Reality. Critical Inquiry 19:105–130.

GENDER AND KINSHIP

7

NEGOTIATING TRADITION
CUSTOMARY SUCCESSION IN THE
NEW TERRITORIES OF HONG KONG[1]

Selina Ching Chan

INTRODUCTION

This paper examines the customary succession pattern in today's New Territories. The investigation is based upon information collected during one year of anthropological fieldwork conducted in a lineage village of Fanling Wai in the New Territories of Hong Kong during 1991 and 1993. The Fanling Pang lineage is one of the five big lineages in the New Territories (Baker 1968). According to the Pang's genealogy, the lineage was originally from Chaozhou. In 1190 A.D., the Pangs moved into the northern part of the New Territories of Hong Kong.

Based upon figures collected for 1992, there were approximately three thousands Pangs in total. Around 640 households, half of the population reside in Fanling Wai. The remainder are in Europe: in the United Kingdom, Belgium, Holland, Germany and Sweden. These people have sought work in Europe since the late 1950's. Many of them worked in restaurants. The influence of these villagers has brought the outside world to the village. Meanwhile, the New Territories have undergone rapid economic development and urbanisation. Under such circumstances, are lineages still 'traditional'? Are villagers still practising customary succession as has been portrayed by anthropologists and sinologists in the past?

In this paper, I will discuss first the traditional picture of customary succession. Then, I will delineate the substantial content of the inheritance pattern claimed as 'traditional' by villagers today. Through analysing the ways in which traditions are interpreted differently by villagers in distinct contexts, I will examine villagers' attitudes to inheritance issues. Interpretation of the legitimacy of granting inheritance to daughters in the form of cash will be investigated, as well as the reason why land and housing is strictly forbidden as a form of inheritance on the part of daughters. My discussion will refer in particular to the retention of idealised and over-structured aspects of custom derived from the legal order – the New Territories Ordinance.[2]

TRADITIONAL PICTURE

Anthropologists and sinologists have claimed that Chinese practise patrilineal inheritance pattern.[3], According to Shiga, Chinese inheritance, *gaisihng* has three modes of expression (1978:126). These are the names of individuals, property and sacrifices. Only sons can carry on the descent line, perform sacrifice, and continue the relationship between themselves and fathers or ancestors. Property is divided equally among all sons. Parents have no wish to favour any one of their heirs. Indeed, the Chinese inheritance pattern is structured by the principle of descent ideology (Chen 1984, Chun 1990). Property served as a *jóu* which belonged to the family and provided funds for ancestral sacrifices. The estate must also be retained within the clan through inheritance by male heirs. The Chinese succession pattern and its relationship with descent ideology can be defined within the context of two native terms: *hei* and *fōhng* (Chen 1984, Chun 1990).

Hei in the present context refers to the 'shared and transmitted substance' which passes from father to son (Chun 1990:20). Chun pointed out that hei serves as the basis of a symbolically constituted relationship between father and son, as well as between brothers (with extension outward) through a common father. It points to the continuous sharing of substance from father to son in every generation into the indefinite future, which diachronically runs through the whole lineage, and epitomises the descent ideology. Synchronically speaking, all sons share the same quantity of hei derived from the father, whether or not they have the same mother. Chun (1990) argues that the equal sharing of hei by each son actually forms the basis of equal inheritance. Or, in more direct terms, the equal sharing in the inheritance of property is formed on the basis of the holding of a fōhng status by each son, as claimed by Chen (1984). Fōhng is a native concept which relates closely to patrilineal descent. Fōhng denotes the descent status which a man holds by virtue of his being a son. All brothers constitute separate fōhng, and they all share equal right to the father's property (Chen 1984). In other words, it is the descent status which determines the son's rights over his father's property. In this way, it is understood that male offspring, whether of the principal wife or the secondary wife, share the same right of inheritance (Evans 1973:26, Jamieson 1970:16).

However, the pattern of equal division of inheritance among sons is an ideal model. In practice, R. Watson (1985:107) has pointed out that among the Ha Tsuen villagers in the New Territories neither the wealthy landlords nor the landless poor necessarily practised equal inheritance. She argues that a son is entitled to his inheritance only if his status is validated in the eyes of the community through the celebration of particular rituals (1985:109).

In the case of daughters, they are supposed to be 'married out'; as such, they are not entitled to inherit the family property. Freedman (1966:55) has claimed that daughters have no further economic claims on their natal families, although they may receive gifts from their families. Goody (1990:89) further pointed out that marriage defined the limit of effective claims of daughters on family property. Meanwhile, Goody (1990:79) also argued that daughters receive pre-mortem inheritance at marriage in the form of a direct dowry. In the 1970s, the dowry in Ha Tsuen was composed mainly of furniture such as cupboards and chairs, and clothes and jewellery; and earrings, rings, bracelets and necklaces. Sometimes a young servant girl was given (R. Watson 1985:131-2). Dowry in Fanling in the 1990s is mainly in the form of jewellery: gold and sometimes diamonds. Villagers claim that a proper dowry is necessary to make their daughters 'look good and decent' when entering their husbands' families. The meaning of dowry is however different from that of the inheritance. More significantly, the amount of the dowry – jewellery or cash – given to daughters is not comparable with the amount of the inheritance – land and cash – given to sons. Indeed, neither the meaning, nor the amount, of the dowry in Chinese society implies a form of pre-mortem inheritance to daughters.

Goody (1990:89) further argued that an exception exists in cases where daughters were needed to ensure the continuity of the family line. He argued, 'where a women (sic) continue to have a substantial claim on their parents after marriage, they "inherit" as well as take a dowry' (1990:89). In fact, it is not the daughter who inherits her parents' property and carries on the descent line in uxorilocal marriage. It is her son who inherits the property by means of 'indirect adoption', taking the surname of the natal family, and thus carrying on the descent line. In other words, uxorilocal marriage has no correlation with inheritance on the part of a daughter.

Indeed, daughters do not hold descent status and therefore are generally not entitled to have any share of the inheritance. R. Watson (1985) pointed out that women in the Ha Tsuen Teng lineage in the 1970's generally had no rights of inheritance.[4] Nevertheless, my findings in the New Territories in the 1990's show that, for daughters, marriage does not entirely end the claims on the estate of natal families. By investigating the following ethnographic case in detail, I will argue that there has been a subtle change of the attitudes of villagers on the issue of inheritance.

INTERPRETING TRADITION - CASH FOR DAUGHTERS

A. Ethnographic discussion

As shown in Diagram 1, A died, leaving widow B and their only child, daughter C, in the mid-1970's. Following Chinese custom, women (wives and daughters) could not inherit A's property. A's property, composed of land and houses was used to set up a jóu, or trust. This jóu, was named after A. The income from the trust was mainly in the form of rent collected from the house and land. Similar to other jóu, on the one hand, income derived from the jóu went towards the maintenance costs for widow B and daughter C; on the other hand, the income also made it possible for widow B and daughter C to worship A and A's ancestors. Following the conventional practice, widow B became the manager of A's jóu.

A few years later, in 1978, widow B also passed away, leaving behind the married daughter C. C had married a man from another village in the New Territories and had moved to reside in England with her husband. Since she was far away from Fanling, it was inconvenient for her to manage and collect the income of A's jóu properly and efficiently. She therefore wanted to dissolve A's jóu, so that she could inherit the property which was in the name of A's jóu.

I then asked the villagers if it was proper to request the dissolution of a jóu. The village representative explained that

> she is now the only person of her family. It is practically inconvenient for her to manage the jóu in England, so why shouldn't she dissolve the jóu?

Diagram 1

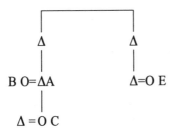

Other villagers who were listening to the story agreed with him. They told me that the continued existence of the jóu was not at all important. They further explained to me that the dissolution of jóu does not necessarily lead to an end of the worshipping of ancestors. Indeed, jóu is not the end, it is only a means for venerating ancestors.

For the villagers in Fanling, however, the controversy arose over the choice of a legitimate person to inherit the land and property of the jóu. C, as a married daughter laid a claim to the property. Her act however was not in accordance with patrilineal 'theory' in which daughters after marriage did not have any claim on family estate. The reason she gave was that she was the most '*chān*', the person most closely related to her father. In this context, chān was interpreted as a close relationship defined in terms of blood ties and sentimental filiation. The villagers seemed to support her claims entirely.

However, A's closest relative E, an aunt of daughter C, strongly opposed C's claim to A's property (Diagram 1). Interestingly, aunt E's petition was also based on an interpretation of the native concept of chān. She said that a 'married-out daughter' – *ngoi ga néuih* – was 'spilt water'. 'Married out daughters' are members of their husbands' families and therefore they do not belong to their natal families. E therefore claimed that 'married out women' were no longer chān, that is, related closely to their natal families. Her argument that a daughter after marriage should not lay claim to the property of her natal family accords with the traditional picture summarised by Goody (1990:89). E further pointed out that as a 'married in woman', she herself belonged to the husband's lineage, that is, to the Pang. Thus, she was chān, closely related to the Pangs, and in fact, the closest person to A. Her interpretation, followed the tradition of *yíh chān kahp chān*, 'succession by the closest relative'. As a widow of the Pangs, she claimed that, in accordance with tradition, she should be the person who received the family property if the zu was going to be dissolved. Meanwhile, she also suggested that she should be the trustee of the family's property also in accordance with 'tradition'.

Interestingly, the Village Council and the other members of the lineage did not accept aunt E's interpretation. The Village Council argued that, in accordance with tradition, only male descendants were closely or directly related with A. The Village Council said that only if E had a son might she lay claim to property on behalf of her son, because the son was a person who held descent status at the Pang lineage. A woman, lacking any male descendant, was in no way chān, closely related to A.[5] The argument rested on the basis that a woman could never be close to her husband's patrilineage without having an intermediate bridge in the form of a son. Thus, the Village Council decided that aunt E should not have any priority over daughter C to the claim, and in fact, it simply dismissed her claim.

Although the aunt sought support for her claim by protesting to the highest political organisation of the New Territories villagers, Heung Yee Kuk, this organization simply recommended that the Village Council re-examine the case in detail. At a later stage, aunt E considerably modified her claim and simply wanted the house, but not the land.

Nevertheless, both daughter C and the Village Council still disagreed with aunt E's second proposal. The Village Council strongly supported the claims of daughter C by agreeing with C's interpretation of the sacred principle of chān, and thought that the property of A's jóu should in its entirely be given to her. This shows that daughter C's claim to the property of her natal family was not related to her marital status. This finding is, however, in contrast to past research indicating that marriage ends a daughter's claim to the property of her natal family.

At the same time, villagers told me that the transfer of ownership of the landed property and the house from the deceased father to the daughter presented legal difficulties. This was because the pattern of succession in the New Territories had to follow the 'customary way'. According to section 13, Chapter 97 in the New Territories Ordinance, it stated that,

> In any proceedings in the High Court or the District Court in relation to land in the New Territories, the court shall have power to recognize and enforce any Chinese custom or customary right affecting such land.

Interestingly it was the villagers who told me this legal restriction. The Village Council then created a delicate arrangement. On the one hand the daughter did not become the real owner of the house and land of A's jóu, but on the other, nor was the jóu dissolved. Instead, the Village Council appointed the daughter as the trustee so that she could receive income from the house and the land. This arrangement guaranteed that the returns from the property of A's jóu would be given to daughter C, yet, it did not violate the law. As explained by the villagers, after obtaining the trusteeship, the daughter could sell the land of A's jóu to the private sector or to the government. Only in this way could daughter C inherit all her father's property, but in the form of money.

A further consideration in this whole dispute is the arrangement of old houses – *jóu ngūks* – where ancestors have lived. The jóu ngūks are situated in the oldest part of the village and are special to the villagers. The jóu ngūk has domestic shrines. and the names of patrilineal ancestors from the last three to five generations are placed on a large piece of red paper as a form of paper tablet facing the door. In other words, the intimate connection between the newly-dead kinsmen and the living is revealed in the old houses (Freedman 1958:85). Indeed, the jóu ngūk is a medium connecting descendants and their ancestors. It is, therefore, special, and should always be passed on to lineage members only. Daughters are not members of the patrilineal descent group, and thus they are not allowed to inherit these houses.

In this light, according to the villagers, daughter C is the most chān, the closest person to A, and therefore should have the right to live in the house, but she should not be the owner of the house. Daughter C, as mentioned earlier, is actually living in England with her husband. Yet she neither wanted to leave the house empty, nor rent it, nor sell the jóu ngūk. Instead, she decided to give the house to a distant relative, H, as a gift because C had a good relationship with H. Nevertheless, the reason put forward in public by the Village Council was that 'he is a person bearing the surname of the Pang; therefore, he is entitled to have the house.'

B. The contested concept of chān – closeness

Daughter C and aunt E both claimed that they were the closest person to A. Their arguments were both rooted in tradition. In different ways, they are both active participants and interpreters of the tradition bearing the native concept of chān. Chān, however, is interpreted of both patrilineally ideology and bilaterally. It is this inherent ambiguity and

157

flexibility that offers villagers the space to interpret and reinterpret the tradition.

Although the above case is the one in which a daughter inherits her father's property in the absence of sons, the absence of a son or adopted son is not the prime reason for granting the property to the daughter. Today, the motivation for granting the property to a daughter is closeness in terms of sentimental filiation and blood relationship. This is a general attitude which is not restricted to this particular case only. In my conversations with the villagers, it was very common to hear villagers saying:

> both the daughter and the son are mine. They are chān, related to me equally in terms of closeness. The daughter should obtain my property too.

Apparently, in supporting daughter C, the Village Council ignored the fact that she was somebody outside the patrilineal category, a 'married out' daughter. In other words, the sentiment derived from the bilateral relation is increasingly important relative to membership status in the patrilineal descent group. It has become as powerful as, or more powerful, than the descent status in entitling a person to receive a substantial part of the inheritance. Similarly, the selection of the particular distantly-related male member – H – was also due to sentimental links between C and H although this act was publicly justified by H's being an agnate of A.

In some other contexts, chān was interpreted as closeness in terms of the descent ideology. In other words, having or being a male descendant is an important basis for defining 'the relative closeness' to somebody. This is true when daughter C decided to give the house to H. The reason put forward to the public was that H was a male member of the Pang. Similarly, when the Village Council argued against the claim of aunt E over A's property, aunt E's not having a son excluded her from having A's property. Interestingly, a few years later, aunt E obtained an adopted son, and then wanted to claim A's house on behalf of her adopted son. The adopted son should have been the ideal person to succeed to A's house if descent status was of prime importance. The villagers, however, ignored her claim and said that the file was closed and that no more changes would be allowed.

What is most interesting about this whole case was that villagers selectively interpreted and reinterpreted different interpretations of chān on different occasions in order to justify both parties' claims to closeness to father A. Manipulation and selective interpretations of the concept led to different results. Significantly, none of the parties condemned the validity of the other's interpretation of 'tradition'. Indeed, what these contemporary attitudes of the villagers reveal is that interpretation of chān as closeness in bilateral terms can serve as a legitimate basis for the claiming of substantial inheritance.

C. The legitimacy of granting cash to daughters

As has been discussed earlier, in deciding that daughter C should inherit all of A's property, villagers did not give the land and house directly to C. Instead, A's property was ultimately given to C in the form of cash. Part of the reason given by the villagers was that it was inconvenient from a legal perspective to change the ownership of land. Cash is by nature liquid in form, flowing from one hand to another among the villagers, and can be given to anyone. Daughters are chān, closely related to the father, and therefore could be entitled to have the property of the father in the form of cash.

According to the villagers, the legitimacy of giving property in the form of cash to daughters is related to the income division in the jóu trust. Unmarried and married women are nowadays entitled to share in the cash income from a trust in Fanling village, and there is strong support for villagers' disposal of cash to daughters at a domestic level. In the following section, I intend to discuss in detail how the trust distributes its income.

The jóu organization customarily held a large amount of land. The income of the jóu was mainly in the form of rent collected from fields. In the past, the income was just enough for ancestor worship in spring and autumn, and also for the distribution of pork to villagers at the end of the year (Baker 1968:62). Owing to the increase of the value of land and the large amount of land sales since the 1970's, these trust organisations have become very rich. Today, the income left after deducting expenditure for annual worship is huge. This large amount of income is therefore divided among descendants.

Antony Dicks the legal expert on Chinese customary law, argued that jóu property had its origin in family property, and therefore the only way to divide the family property is per stirpes (Wong 1990:28). In practice, it is common for the jóu properties to be divided on a per stirpes basis and also on a per capita basis. Some of the income was used to buy roast pork for ancestor worship, and some for education and the relief of poverty on a per capita basis. Nevertheless, this per capita basis in the past referred only to men. Baker (Kan Fat-tat v Kan Yin-tat), as a lineage expert, was summoned to court to give opinions regarding the customary way of dividing money in trust. His opinion was,

> the deliberate removal of such property from the main stream of the family property and the fact that it was intended to be perpetual and inalienable and certainly not meant to be divided, show that if and when there should be division, the correct mode of division of family property . . . should not apply or at least would not necessarily apply.

> (1987:542)

Thus, Deputy Judge Robert Tang QC (Kan Fat-tat versus Kan Yin-tat 1987:543) and Selby (1991:63) concluded that there was no single correct mode of distribution according to Chinese custom. Nevertheless, it was widely agreed that, per capita basis means men only and not women.

Today the practice of the division of trust income is still based on per capita and/or per stirpes. Villagers in Fanling Wai told me that, today, half of the income of the trust is distributed per stirpes, and half among villagers per capita. Nevertheless, the content of the per capita structure is different from that in the past. The per capita distribution includes not only sons, but also unmarried daughters and married-in women. Thus, these women obtain a share of cash equal to that received by men. The villagers, male and female, were aware of this difference, and often told me proudly that they were very 'democratic' and 'fair' to women. Indeed, women's claims for money from the family or lineage property is a new development. After years of disputes concerning the method of dividing profit from the trust, the Sheung Shui Liao lineage had finally come to a new conclusion, namely that 'married-in' women or unmarried daughters were entitled to have half a share of the per capita portion while men had a full share.

Interestingly, villagers neither did see the present practice of the division of trust income as a change of tradition, nor did they point out that the content of per capita had changed. Instead, villagers implied that the whole thing was 'traditional' by referring to the 'traditional' structure of per stirpes and per capita in the division of the income in the 'traditional setting' – the trust organization. The fact that women are eligible to enjoy cash benefits from lineage property has become a very important phenomenon for the villagers. It has become a strong basis for villagers to claim that it is legitimate for daughters to obtain a cash inheritance from their fathers.

NEGOTIATING TRADITION: THE INFLUENCE OF THE LEGAL ORDER

A. Fossilised custom vs. commoditization of land and housing

Since the New Territories is a leased territory; legally speaking, the colonial government must respect the way of life of the villagers. Thus, there is a persistence of customary law in the area, particularly concerning inheritance. By the enactment of the New Territories Ordinance, the British government codified Chinese succession with reference to a particular historical point, the Qing dynasty in particular, law and custom as it existed in 1843, with some parts having 'its own Hong Kong flavour' (Lewis 1983:357). In practice, 'customary law' as perceived and referred to by the colonial government has changed little from the days before the British occupation.

According to Selby, the basic principle of customary succession as interpreted in legal procedures is,

> daughters could not succeed as owners of land, because, on marriage, their land would become their husband's property (and after his death, their sons'); thus land would be lost from the clan's shared wealth. The same principle also applies to widows, although less strongly if it was clear that they would never remarry. In the Ching (Qing) dynasty, even when landowners exceptionally made provision in a will for their wife or daughters to succeed to their property, that was not considered enough to override any claims by legitimate natural sons.
>
> (1991:71–2)

In customary law, the widow may only be the manager of her late husband's property, and she may claim for her maintenance and for that of her children. Daughters and widows were thus not fully entitled to lay claim to the land and houses of the father or husband in the absence of a will. If the daughter or the wife were to apply and successfully obtain the Grant of Probate or Letters of Administration within three months of the death of the deceased, the daughter or the widow might, theoretically, be entitled to have the inheritance. Nevertheless, according to the legal experts, the Grant of Probate and the Letters of Administration are practically impossible to obtain within three months of the death of the deceased. In addition, even if a daughter to whom letters of administration have been granted applies to have the estate of the deceased registered in her name, the Land Officer cannot approve the application because it will be contrary to customary law (Selby 1991:47,76). Moreover, if male descendants or agnates opposed inheritance by the daughter, they could certainly prevent it.

An interesting point is that the imposition of a British administration has resulted in a stricter adherence to 'Chinese law and custom' in the New Territories (Nelson 1969:12). It upholds the 'norm' of 'tradition' in the Qing days with few changes. Nevertheless, in areas other than the New Territories in Hong Kong, after the enactments of the Marriage Reform Ordinance 1970, the Deceased's Family Maintenance Ordinance 1971, the Legitimacy Ordinance 1971, the Married Persons Status Ordinance 1971, the Probate and Administration Ordinance 1971, the Affiliation Proceedings Ordinance 1971, and the Intestates' Estates Ordinance 1971, men and women have equal rights to the inheritance. Similarly, mainland China had already abolished the Qing law of customary succession by the enactment of the Civil Code of the Republic of China in 1930, and the Marriage Laws of the People's Republic of China in 1950. Ironically, the colonial government has continued to enforce 'Chinese' customs and traditions in the New Territories and has, through its legal apparatus, rigidified them to the point where they are markedly different from the original customs which were by nature flexible and diverse.

The legal order is based on the assumption that land is inalienable and perpetual. This assumption was to a large extent true in the past. The importance of not leaving land to non-lineage members may be understood in the specific context of an agrarian society in the New Territories. The agricultural economy was based upon highly fertile soil for rice growing, with its comprehensive irrigation systems actually predisposing local communities of agnates to arrange themselves into large settlements (Freedman 1958:129). Villagers, as peasants, were 'tied' to the land and therefore had a strong attachment to native soil (Fei 1949, Potter 1978, Redfield 1959). Indeed, land ownership was one of the important bases for competition between villagers. Land owned by one lineage within the precincts of the village was therefore not easily sold to other neighbouring lineages. Sale of land did occur, but only in the case of an urgent need for a capital sum, for example, to build or repair an ancestral hall (Selby 1991:63).

This underlying symbolic and practical value of land in customary law, however, contrasts with modern life in today's New Territories. The New Territories area has undergone tremendous transformation through modernisation and town planning in the past thirty years. Occupations in the village have diversified and most of the villagers are working in the city. Many of them even work abroad (the result of emigration since the 1950s). In 1992, only one couple in the village, who had retired from England, were farmers.

Not surprisingly, the symbolic value of land has been changing owing to this transformation from an agrarian community to a non-agrarian one. In the 1960s, Potter (1968:101) reported that villagers of the Teng lineage in Ping Shan, in the New Territories, planned to sell a large quantity of landholdings. Other members of lineage, however, were reluctant to approve the sales of land. But their reluctance to sell the land to non-Teng people was not due to the threat of violating tradition. Rather, as pointed out by Potter (1968), it was because they were afraid that other members of the group were secretly going to make more money from the sale than they did. This shows that, already in the 1960s, the symbolic meaning of the land was no longer the reason which led villagers to disagree over the passing of land to outsiders. It had been replaced by concern over individual profit.

Similarly, village life in the Fanling area has also witnessed tremendous changes in recent decades. Since the late 1970s, the villagers have started to sell large areas of land surrounding the core area of Fanling Wai. Thus, the land surrounding the village which was originally kept for farming is now put to other uses. Consequently, the 'territory' of Fanling Wai is now quite small (Map 1). And today sales of land near the village are no longer exclusively held by lineage members. Villagers do not condemn themselves for not following the 'traditional' norm or discouraging the sale of land to non-Pang people. Indeed, land has simply become a commodity with the villagers primarily being concerned with searching for a better price in sales of land.

Similarly, the meaning of another kind of landholdings, houses, is also changing. Villagers claimed that these should be kept in the hands of the patrilineal Pang member for ever. Villagers explained that, if daughters succeed to houses from their fathers, their children, bearing the surname of another group of people, will succeed to their mothers' houses. These non-Pang descendants will be living in the village in later generations, and thus, Fanling Wai will no longer be a lineage. The reality is however different from the theory.

To further understand this, we have to investigate two types of houses as classified by villagers. The first type is jóu ngūk, literally meaning 'houses of the ancestors'. This is the oldest type of house in the village, built when the Pangs first settled there. These have been repeatedly built and rebuilt over succeeding generations. At first, they were just one

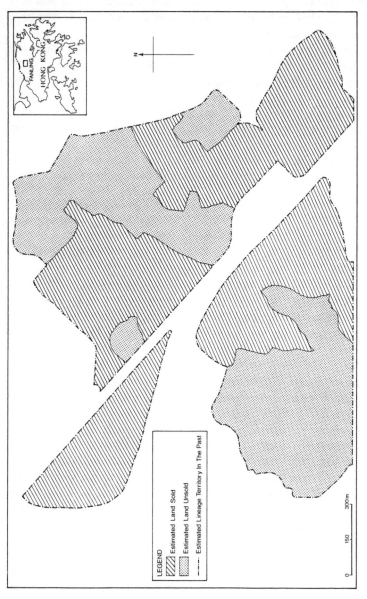

Map 1: Estimated Scope of Land Sales

LEGEND

▨ Estimated Land Sold

▦ Estimated Land Unsold

–··– Estimated Lineage Territory In The Past

0   150   300 m

storey high; later further storeys were added. Now they commonly have four storeys, reaching the maximum height allowed by the government's regulations. The second type is *ding ngūk*, literally meaning houses of the *dings*, males. Ding-ngūks, small houses, are a product of government policy. The 'small house policy' started in the 1960's, and was institutionalised in 1972. The policy laid down that only indigenous male villagers who had reached the age of 18 years were eligible to apply for a piece of land on which to build a house for their own usage. The house area could not be bigger than 700 square feet and should not be taller than 25 feet.

At first glance, villagers told me that both jóu ngūk and ding ngūk were not allowed to be passed on to non-Pangs, and were not allowed to be sold as well. Upon further investigation, I discovered that ding ngūk could be sold, whereas jóu ngūk should not be sold. Villagers argued that jóu ngūks were different from ding ngūks. Jóu ngūks are houses passed down from ancestors and, therefore special.

Ding ngūks, according to villagers, are new houses only. Today, it is not unusual to observe villagers manipulating the traditional patrilineal ideology in order to obtain a piece of land from the government in order to build a house, but not for their own use. Many of the houses are built for renting to outsiders, or even for sale. All villagers build three storeys in order to maximise the use of the height of 25 feet. Each floor is usually built as an independent flat with bedrooms, dining room, kitchen, and bathroom. In 1992, the rent of a single floor of a new small house was 7,000 Hong Kong dollars per month. Or each flat could cost about 2.7 million Hong Kong dollars if sold. I heard of several cases of ding ngūk sales in the village. Advertisements by property agents displayed in the village concentrate particularly on the sale and purchase or renting of the ding ngūk. For the villagers, the sale of the ding ngūk is perfectly acceptable. Not only this, but villagers also told me that some of the villagers had sold houses to others before they were even built. In other words, ding ngūk are not inalienable and do not necessarily pass onto patrilineal members.

Regarding the jóu ngūk, or old house, one further case of a Pang widow and her only daughter is worth considering. The married daughter, who lived in the city, decided she could no longer let her mother live alone at the jóu ngūk. There are three floors in this jóu ngūk. The widow used to live on the ground floor, and the second and third floors were rented to others. The rent was collected for the maintenance of the widow. The daughter wanted to move her mother to live with her in the city, she therefore decided to sell the old house. The house was in fact not registered in the name of the married daughter but under the name of the jóu of her deceased father, with her mother as a trustee. The daughter acted on behalf of her mother in deciding how to dispose of the house. The house was finally sold to a distant relative in the Pang lineage for 120,000 Hong Kong dollars.

The attitudes of villagers towards the sale of the jóu ngūk in this case are illuminating. Villagers explained to me that it was 'necessary' for the daughter to sell the house and seemed to view the sale as the only available option. They told me that if the widow had not sold the house and had not taken the cash, her daughter might not be able to afford to support her living in the city. The villagers therefore thought that it was perfectly reasonable and natural for a daughter to take money from the sale of the house. The sale of the jóu ngūk, however, contradicted the norm prohibiting such sales. Surprisingly, none of the villagers to whom I chatted condemned or even attempted to condemn the action of selling the jóu ngūk.

More interestingly, villagers also told me that if nobody in the village wanted to buy the house, they also had no right to oppose her selling it off to others. They explained to me that if they had stopped the daughter from selling the house, the daughter would not be able to afford her mother's living in the city. Then, those who had stopped the daughter from being a filial person would be castigated. In reality, nobody wanted to bear the responsibility of paying to support the old lady and thus they kept quiet. It was imagined by the villagers that if they opposed the sale of the house, the daughter could say, 'right, I will not sell the house, but you will have to cover the cost of taking care of my old mother.' Thus, faced by conflict between observing tradition and avoiding the economic burden, villagers chose a pragmatic solution rather than strictly following tradition. Interestingly, they also cite tradition – filial piety – as a justification for the daughter's sale of the house while at the same time violating another tradition – selling the jóu ngūk.

To summarise, the symbolic meaning of land and housing is fading. They are no longer strictly inalienable. Perhaps, the jóu ngūk to some degree still occupies a symbolic place for villagers. Villagers were concerned about whether the jóu ngūk was sold to a Pang or not. This was however not the reason for which ding ngūk and land are no longer passing on in perpetuity to lineage members.

Ironically, the New Territories Ordinance, Chapter 97 still assumes the inalienable and perpetual nature of land ownership. Legal experts argued that the passing on of property to outsiders and unmarried women or widows who may subsequently remarry would threaten the social cohesion of the village community (Selby 1991:76–77). In reality, the inalienable and perpetual nature of land ownership no longer conforms with today's demands. It represents the ideal expectation of a former era. Reality shows that there is a marked discrepancy between the assumption of the inalienable and perpetual nature of land as implied by the legal order in the New Territories Ordinance, and the real social situation.

More interestingly, the respect of custom, as enforced by the legal order, applies only to the issue of land (land and housing), and not to other forms of property. Although landholdings are symbolically important for the lineage organization in the Southeastern part of China, the customary succession pattern in this area did not draw a sharp distinction between landholdings and cash. The legal order of the colonial government has, however, led to a stricter observation of custom in relation to the disposal of land and housing. Meanwhile, the disposal of cash is not under the control of law, and therefore enjoys a greater degree of flexibility. In other words, it is the colonial government which has drawn the distinction between land and housing and other aspects of inheritance.

B. The structural conformity

It is interesting that there is a parallel between villagers' attitudes and the legal order. Ignoring the fact that tremendous amounts of land and housing are sold to private sector and the government, villagers claimed that land should be kept in the hands of the Pangs and should only be given to male descendants. They claimed that daughters were supposed to be married out. Daughters therefore should not hold any lineage land, otherwise the land would finally pass on to hands of outsiders.

More interestingly, the legal aspect – the New Territories Ordinance – is in daily conversation widely invoked by villagers in support of their interpretation of tradition. It is not uncommon to hear villagers saying, 'this is our tradition, not giving women a piece of land. The New Territories Ordinance also stated it.' Indeed, the Ordinance was highlighted by villagers as representing village tradition. This awareness of legal restrictions by the villagers in the New Territories contrasts sharply with what has been observed in some of the previous research into villagers in Chinese society. C. K. Yang's (1959:92) research in the village of Nanjing, and Myron Cohen's (1976:9) studies in a Taiwanese village, revealed that these villagers were ignorant of the law of the state. In the New Territories, R. Watson (1986:109–110) also showed that villagers in Ha Tsuen were ignorant of, and indifferent to, laws concerning inheritance in the 1970's. In those areas and in those days, it was the community and not the state which sanctioned inheritance practice.

Today, the force of sanction however comes neither purely from custom denoted in the law nor from the village. The form of tradition implied in the legal order is verbally strictly followed by the villagers. But the substantial content of the tradition may not be strictly followed. As shown in the case of daughter C, although the clansmen and the Village Council in the New Territories took the side of the daughter and wanted to give all the property of father A to daughter C, the ownership of the house and land of father A was not transferred technically to C. In other words, villagers followed closely the provision of the New Territories Ordinance, but at the same time, the substantial benefit of the land was given to the daughter without hesitation.

The technical arrangement, to set up daughter C as a trustee, was invented by villagers to ensure that daughter C was able to benefit from father A's property. This process was an active interpretation of villagers' customs and a reinterpretation of the government's legislation concerning those customs. Nevertheless, having a daughter as a trustee was not a 'traditional' practice. As past research shows, only wives, widows who had not remarried were trustees (Selby 1991:73). The right of married-in women to act as trustees was derived from their being members of their husband's patrilineage. Daughters, however, were supposed to be married-out, and therefore did not belong to their natal families. This distinction between the status of daughters and married-in women as referred to in aunt E's interpretation of chān, has also been noted by anthropologists. R. Watson (1985:135) claimed that in the 1970's daughters among the Ha Tsuen Teng were considered to be transient members of their natal households. M. Wolf (1972:32) in discussing the membership of a lineage, with reference to the possession of ancestor tablets, also claimed that a daughter who died before marriage would not have a tablet on her father's altar because she was not a member of the family. Therefore, only widows could be trustees, and daughters were excluded. In this case, villagers are making use of the traditional institution of the jóu but giving it new content by having daughter C as a trustee.

Indeed, not giving land and housing to daughters conforms to customary practice as codified by the legal order. Nevertheless, conformity is now only formal, and not substantial, as the benefits can be passed on to the daughter in the form of cash. Today, it is not uncommon to hear villagers in their mid-50s and younger saying that:

fathers could deliberately sell their land or house first. The property is thereby converted into cash, and, thus, daughters may legitimately receive the cash. So daughters are able to obtain a considerable amount, equal or similar to that received by a son.

This is distinctively different from the 'traditional' practice. Some told me that they would give a cash lump sum to their daughters while they would only give houses or land to sons. There are, however, still some villagers who give neither cash nor houses and land to daughters.

CONCLUDING REMARKS

To conclude, rural communities in the New Territories have undergone tremendous changes since the last century. Today, land and housing are no longer inalienable, even as an ideal. Housing and land are to a large extent similar to cash. The perception of land and housing implied in the New Territories Ordinance now lags far behind practice. The maintenance of the normative aspect of custom and tradition upheld in the Qing dynasty has, in practice, not accommodated social change. For administrative and technical purposes, the legal order has also distorted and ossified the dynamic nature of 'custom'.

Today, with increased commoditization of housing and land in the New Territories, there is a negotiation between the 'conservative' legal order – the sacred representation of idealised custom – and a relative 'reformative' social reality. Daughters are increasingly favoured with granting a share of family property in the form of cash. As my case study reveals, the customary concept of chān is interpreted differently in different contexts. Today, the concept of chān, signifying a close relationship interpreted in terms of descent ideology, is not the dominant force which structures the inheritance practice. The interpretation of chān as closeness in terms of sentimental filiation and blood relationship can now be as powerful as that derived from descent ideology. Consequently, the marriage of the daughter does not affect the degree of chān, closeness with her natal family, and thus, marriage does not end the claim of the daughter to the property of the natal family. Such attitudes mark a difference from customary practice in the past, and they also contradict the procedures dictated by legal order which claims that daughters should be contradict inheritance. Indeed, willingness to grant substantial inheritance to daughters implies a newly-emerging, subtle, gradual, yet significant, change in concepts of kinship.

NOTES

1 Special thanks go to Carol Jones who has kindly given me her advice and helped me to have access to a lot of useful legal documents. I also owe thanks to Rubie Watson and Yunxiang Yan.
2 The legal order discussed here is the one before the reform initiated by the Legislative Council in 1993. Outraged attitudes of the villagers toward the amendment of the Ordinance will be discussed in tradition inherited, tradition reinterpreted: A Chinese Linage in the 1990s, (Chan 1995).
3 Baker (1979:9); Cohen (1976:70); Gallin (1966:145); Jamieson (1970:25); Shiga (1978); M. Yang (1945:83); C.K. Yang (1959:92); Lewis (1983:369), R. Watson (1985:107).
4 According to Qing law, only when a son or adopted son could not be selected from the clan, when all eligible lawful male relatives, including agnatic relations were absent, and when the male line of the family had become extinct, daughters of the intestate were entitled to divide the family property between themselves (Jamieson 1970:25; Shiga 1968:127; Van Der Valk 1956:118). When it came to inheritance, daughters occupied a subordinate rank compared with other male relatives in the father's patrilineage. Van Der Valk (1956:119) pointed out that in practice, in the northern part of China, women's opportunities for inheritance were not completely obstructed.
5 Aunt E adopted a son in 1983. But the whole controversy took place in 1978, and the Village Council refused to re-consider the case in 1983, claiming that the case was already settled in 1978.

REFERENCES CITED

Baker, Hugh
    1966   The Five Great Clans of the New Territories. Journal of the Hong Kong Branch of the Royal Asiatic Society 6:25–48.
    1968   Chinese Lineage Village: Sheung Shui. Frank Cass & Co Ltd: London.
    1979   Chinese Family and Kinship. Macmillan Press: London.
Chan, Selina Ching
    1995   Tradition inherited, tradition reinterpreted, tradition reinterpreted: A Chinese Lineage in the 1990s. Oxford: DPhil. Dissertation (unpublished).
Chen, Chi-nan
    1984   Fang and Chia-Tsu – The Chinese Kinship System in Rural Taiwan. Yale: Ph.D. Dissertation (unpublished)

Chen, Chung-min
    1985 Dowry and inheritance. *In* The Chinese family and its Ritual Behaviour. H. J. Chang & C. Y. Chang, eds. Pp.117–127. Institute of Ethnology Academic Sinica: Taipei.

Chun, Allen
    1990 Conceptions of Kinship and Kingship in Classical Chou China. T'oung Pao 76:16–33.

Cohen, Myron
    1976 House United, House Divided: The Chinese Family in Taiwan. Columbia University Press: New York.

Evans, Emrys, D.M.
    1973 The New Law of Succession in Hong Kong. Hong Kong Law Journal 3(1):7–50.
    n.d. The law of Succession in Hong Kong: Current Problems and Possible Reforms. Law lectures for practitioners.

Fei, Hsiao-tung
    1939 Peasant Life in China: A Field Study of Country Life in the Yangtze Valley. Routledge: London.

Fei, Hsiao-tung and Chang Chih-i
    1949 Earthbound China: A study of Rural Economy in Yunnan. Routledge: London.

Freedman, Maurice
    1958 Lineage Organization in Southeastern China. The Athlone Press: London.
    1966 Chinese Lineage and Society: Fukien and Kwangtung. The Athlone Press: London.

Goody, Jack
    1990 The Oriental, the Ancient, and the Primitive. Cambridge: University Press.

Haydon, E.S
    1962 Chinese Customary Law in Hong Kong's New Territories: Some Legal Premises. (unpublished)
    1962 The Choice of Chinese Customary law in Hong Kong. International and Comparative Law Quarterly. 11:231–250.

Jamieson, G
    1970 Chinese Family and Commercial Law. Vetch & Lee Ltd: Hong Kong.

Jones, Carol.
    n.d. Women and the Law in Colonial Hong Kong (unpublished).

Howarth, Carla; Jones, Carol; Petersen, Carole; and Samuels, Harriet
    n.d. Report by the Hong Kong Council of Women on the Third Period Report by Hong Kong under Article 40 of the International Covenant on Civil and Political Rights (unpublished).

Kan Fat-tat v. Kan Yin-tat
    1987 Hong Kong Law Journal 516–545.

Lewis, D. J
    1983a Requiem for Chinese Customary Law in Hong Kong International and Comparative Law Quarterly 347–379.

Liu, Wang Hui-chen
  1959   The Traditional Chinese Clan Rules. Augustin Incorporated Publish-
          er: New York.
Marriage Reform Ordinance. 1970.
Nelson, H.G.H.
  1969   British Land Administration in the New Territories of Hong Kong,
          and its Effects on Chinese Social Organization (unpublished).
New Territories Ordinance 1984.
Ocko, Jonathan.
  1991   Women, Property, and Law in the People's Republic of China. In
          Marriage and Inequality in Chinese Society. Rubie Watson and
          Patricia Buckley Ebrey, eds. Pp. 313–546. California: University of
          California Press.
Pasternak, Burton.
  1972   Kinship & community in Two Chinese Villages. Stanford University:
          California.
Potter, Jack.
  1968   Capitalism and the Chinese Peasant. University of California Press:
          Berkeley and Los Angeles.
Probate and Administration Ordinance. 1971.
Redfield, Robert
  1959   Peasant Society and Culture. University of Chicago Press: Chicago.
Selby, Stephen
  1991   Everything You Wanted to Know about Chinese Customary Law (But
          were Afraid to Ask). Hong Kong Law Journal 21(45):45–77.
Shiga, Shuzo
  1978   Family Property and the Law of Inheritance in Traditional China. In
          Chinese Family Law and Social Change. David Buxbaum, ed.
          University of Washington Press: Seattle.
Strickland, G.E
  1948   Report of the Committee on Chinese Law and Custom in Hong Kong.
          The government Printer: Hong Kong.
Valk, Marius Hendrikus van der
  1956   Conservatism in modern Chinese Family law. Leiden: Brill.
Watson, James L
  1975   Emigration and the Chinese Lineage: The Mans in Hong Kong and
          London. University of California Press: Berkeley.
  1982   Chinese Kinship Reconsidered: Anthropological Perspectives on
          Historical Research. China Quarterly 92:589–622.
Watson, Rubie
  1984   Women's Property in Republican China: Rights and Practice.
          Republican China 10:1a:1–12.
  1985   Inequality among Brothers. Cambridge: University Press.
Wilmshurst, D.J
  1980a Report on the Erosion of Chinese Customary Succession in the New
          Territories. (unpublished) RC/NW1/477/80.
Wolf, Margery
  1972   Women and the Family in Rural Taiwan. Stanford Press: California.

Wong, Belinda
  1990 Chinese Customary Law – An Examination of Tsos and Family Tongs. Hong Kong Law Journal 20(1):13–31.
Yang, C.K
  1959 The Chinese Family in the Communist Revolution. Cambridge Press: Massachuetts.
Yang, Martin
  1956 A Chinese Village: Taitou, Shantung Province. Columbia University Press: New York.

8

JYUHT FÒHNG NÉUIH
FEMALE INHERITANCE AND AFFECTION

Eliza Chan

In December 1993 a Female Inheritance Movement began in Hong Kong. It is a feminist Movement through which 'rural'[1] women are struggling for their inheritance rights in terms of gender equality and human rights. This demand for female inheritance rights is a bold claim, since the patrilineal rule of inheritance is still a deeply entrenched custom. Newspaper reports depicted these women as fighters against 'Chinese tradition', i.e., male inheritance. However, through an examination of the women's narratives, we shall find out that the women's claims for inheritance rights are not so easily characterized as a denial of 'tradition'. By appealing to 'affection', the indigenous women sought to justify their apparently 'unconventional' claim through their manipulation of 'tradition'. The participants in the Movement (known as jyuht fòhng néuih) do not have any brothers who can inherit family property. This paper aims at exploring the reasons why 'affection' had been used by these jyuht fòhng néuih to justify their inheritance rights.

BACKGROUND OF THE MOVEMENT

In 1994, a group of indigenous women who had been legally banned from inheritance rights (because of Chinese customary law) successfully brought about a legal change which gave daughters and widows rights to inherit their families' properties. The indigenous women's demand for inheritance rights had been overlooked until it was articulated through the Movement, which attracted an unanticipated spate of public attention. A woman's demand for the right to manage family properties

174

has been documented before, but it is only now after forty years, that such a voice can be heard clearly (Hong Kong Law Reports 1967:367–389). Previously labelled as a 'family-dispute-only', the women's demands for inheritance rights could, for the first time, be expressed in the language of universal justice, and therefore was able to mobilise support from a vast range of social groups. Besides the indigenous women themselves, a number of other social groups also participated in the Movement, thereby greatly enhancing the range of resources able to be tapped by the women. These groups included feminist activists, reporters, legal practitioners and politicians. The Female Inheritance Movement was able to elicit the support of such an eclectic mix because, on top of female inheritance rights, the Movement was conceived of as a champion for gender equality and human rights as well.

'Indigenous residents' of the New Territories are barred from female inheritance (following Chinese customary law), while residents living in the rest of Hong Kong have never been subject to such a constraint. In order to understand why the New Territories have been governed by Chinese customary law, we need to take a look at Hong Kong's history at the turn of this century.

In 1898, the Qing Dynasty 'ceded' the New Territories to the British, on condition that the British respect Chinese customs in the New Territories (Lockhart Report 1900), and therefore a New Territories Ordinance was signed. Before 1994, there were two sets of inheritance rules prevailing in Hong Kong: the 'British law' (applied in the urban areas) and the 'Chinese customary law' (applied in the New Territories). Under Chinese customary law, indigenous women in the New Territories could not inherit their fathers' properties, even if their fathers only had female offspring, and were willing to give the properties to their daughters.

There have always been complaints about female disinheritance in the New Territories since the two sets of inheritance rules in Hong Kong have been in force. Yet the government did not deal with the issue until September 1993, when it was revealed that even the non-indigenous residents in the New Territories (those who lived in government estates) were subject to the New Territories Ordinance, meaning that they had to comply with Chinese customary law as well (United Daily News, 11 September 1993). The New Territories were once predominantly occupied by indigenous residents; but during the past two decades, the New Territories have witnessed a huge influx of people from the urban areas. Yet although they were not indigenous residents, they still had to comply with the New Territories Ordinance, meaning that the fathers could not pass their properties to their daughters.

To resolve the problem, the government proposed to exempt the non-indigenous residents from the New Territories Ordinance. Some Legislative Councillors, who supported human rights and gender equality, urged the government to expand the exemption to the indigenous residents as well, so that urban and rural Hong Kong would share the same rule of inheritance. In December 1993, an 'Anti-Discrimination Female Residents' Committee' was organised by six indigenous women (who were the most vocal among the indigenous women) together with some social workers. Demonstrations and seminars were held.

Those who opposed female inheritance stressed that female inheritance would destroy the clan system, since the women were going to marry 'outsiders'. Many of the indigenous residents come from single-surname lineages, which are patrilineal, and characterised by corporate landholding and ancestral worship. The group which objected most forcefully to female inheritance was the Heung Yee Kuk (the Kuk), an organisation formed predominantly by male indigenous residents, which is responsible for informing the government on the matters relating to indigenous residents. Some people in the Kuk feared that female inheritance would lead to a disintegration of corporate landholding, since the female lineage members would marry 'outsiders' bearing other surnames.

Despite vehement opposition from the Kuk, the New Territories Ordinance was successfully amended in 22 June 1994. The amendment stipulates that women, whose fathers pass away intestate after 22 June 1994, are legally entitled to their fathers' properties as well. Yet this did not directly benefit the majority of the women participating in the Movement whose fathers had passed away before that date.

THE MEANING OF JYUHT FÒHNG

As mentioned earlier, most of the participants in the Movement are jyuht fòhng néuih. Jyuht fòhng néuih refers to the daughters who do not have any brothers in their immediate families, and therefore have no one in the family to continue the male line. Jyuht fòhng is literally a genealogical term describing the situation when the male line cannot be continued. According to Chen (1984), '*fòhng*' literally means 'bedroom of the married sons'. 'Fòhng' represents a conjugal unit with unmarried sons, excluding the daughters. When sons get married, they form separate 'fòhng'. Daughters are supposed to be 'absorbed' into

Diagram 1: Jyuht Fōhng Néuih and Rule of Inheritance

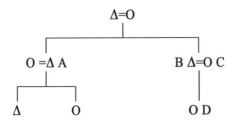

their husbands' fòhng'. It represents a father-son affiliation that informs the formal rule of inheritance. *Jyuht* means 'terminated' in Chinese. When both words come together, they refer to the termination of that father-son affiliation.

Referring to Diagram 1, B, C and D constitutes a jyuht fòhng family. A is the nearest male kin able to inherit B's properties, since D is a daughter who cannot inherit her father's properties. Most of the participants in the Movement resemble D's situation. It is not normally acceptable for D to claim her inheritance rights through her ties with her father, B, since such ties do not tally with the 'father-son' affiliation. Female inheritance is impossible according to the structural principle of 'father-son' affiliation.

The participants in the Movement did not choose to defy the patrilineal rule of inheritance (which followed a father-son pattern). They opted for a daughterly identity – jyuht fòhng néuih identity – which responded to the women's need to fight for their rights, and at the same time (the women hoped) would engage them in a dialogue with their natal kin. Contrary to the mass media/activists' view, the jyuht fòhng néuih did not regard a complete denial of the lineages' customs as favourable to their interests. By justifying their inheritance rights through 'affection' they hoped to prevent a confrontation between village kin and the women themselves.

AFFECTION

The women expressed a deep emotional attachment toward their natal families, especially their fathers. A structural-functional view of the lineages sees women as temporary residents whose membership and loyalty shifts as they 'marry out'; in fact daughters (even married ones) have always maintained close ties with their natal families. If such ties have always been regularly sustained, it is worth considering the significance of 'affection' in justifying women's rights in their natal families.

Jack Goody criticises the view that Chinese women have to cut all ties with their natal families after getting married, and therefore give up all claims to their inheritance rights in their natal families (1990:55). According to Goody, both daughters and sons inherit, but at different points in the life-cycle – daughters through their dowry at marriage, sons at the time of their fathers' retirement or death. This Goody calls 'diverging devolution' of property (1990:2). While this cultural principle affirms the validity of female inheritance it does not clearly specify the nature of that inheritance as it does with sons. The size of the dowry partly acts as a symbol of the family's social status and the desire to demonstrate that status therefore ensures for most women a reasonable dowry. But there also seems to be an 'arbitrary' component to female inheritance which allows space for the expression of filial affection. Thus, to prove their legitimacy as inheritors, women in their narratives expressed their *affection* toward their fathers (the patriarch) rather than the mothers, as a way of advancing their claims.

In the context of this Movement, 'affection' helps the women to 'bypass' the restriction of 'formal kinship', while on the other hand 'adhering' to the patrilineal principle of 'formal kinship' and 'tradition'. I would like to discuss Ellen Judd's article on 'Niangjia' (literally natal family), and the relevance of applying her theoretical framework in understanding the relationship between 'affection' and 'tradition' (1989).

Judd's fieldwork was conducted in Shandong, North China, where she discovered that married daughters did continue to maintain ties with their natal families. Such ties with their natal family apparently upset the 'official kinship' of the patrilineal community, but the compromise was, that the women usually stayed in their marital homes during the calendrical rituals, while visiting their natal homes at other times. According to Judd, there were two systems: the 'official model' (the believed-in model that inhibits married women from visiting their natal homes) and 'practical kinship' (the practice of married women visiting their natal homes). To this she adds the notion of 'customary practices' which

allow a range of kinship practices to occur and have legitimacy. The legitimacy acquired from observing custom is not of the same quality nor is it a substitute for observing the norms of the official model. However, it is sufficient to raise certain strategies from what would otherwise be a level of individual self-interest, idiosyncrasy, or exception to a level of expected and legitimate practice.

(1989:538)

It was precisely to the 'custom' of 'affection' that the women in the New Territories appealed. Judd's article, therefore, gives us a better picture of why indigenous women pursued their inheritance rights through affection, while at the same time recognising the importance of male inheritance. As mentioned earlier, the women admitted that they would not fight for their rights if they had brothers in their immediate families who could be legitimate inheritors. While the women affirmed the importance of the 'official model' (male descent and inheritance), they also sought to achieve their goals through strategies (i.e. affection) which were not institutionalised and not integrated into the 'official model'.

I will discuss 'affection' with ethnographic examples in the sections to come. Talking to the six indigenous women who actively participated in the Movement, and listening to their narratives, I found out that these women also used 'affection' to explain why they themselves should be the legitimate inheritors.[2]

'Affection' is not simply an emotional attachment that should be taken as 'natural' between the two generations. There are some groups of people who are more socially able to justify their rights via 'affection'. We are going to compare the different consequences of evoking an 'affectional bond' by daughters with brothers, and the jyuht fòhng néuih who do not have any brothers. What we are going to see is that, it is socially acceptable for jyuht fòhng néuih to justify inheritance rights through 'affection'.

Daughters with brothers were generally not active in the Female Inheritance Movement. This is because daughters competing with their brothers for their inheritance rights would soon be the target of criticism, and would attract less sympathy. The reason many people sympathised with the jyuht fòhng néuih, was that the male inheritors in their cases were not the women's brothers, but their cousins and uncles who were not fulfilling their duties to take care of the widows and the unmarried daughters.

The only participant in the Movement with a brother is Wei-lan, and she was once acidly criticised by her fellow villagers and the Kuk members for being 'money-minded': they believed that she should not eye the family property as long as she has a brother in her immediate family. In a television program, Wei-lan's brother apologised publicly to the leader of the Kuk, swearing to cut off ties with his sister. A further complication was that many women in the New Territories did not welcome female inheritance because they were afraid that their husbands' sisters would demand a share of their parents' properties. The jyuht fòhng néuih, daughters (without brothers), did not have to face the pressure from their immediate families because many of their family members had already passed away. Without voices of protest from the natal families, the jyuht fòhng néuih were less likely to be discredited when they justified their rights in terms of affection. In their own terms, they were fighting for their family properties, so that these properties would not flow into the hands of another family (the uncle's or cousin's family). Affection is a natural psychological attachment of all people engaged in social ties. However, 'affection' could also be deployed strategically as a justification of rights.

The jyuht fòhng néuih adduced different levels of understanding to justify their inheritance rights. On one level, jyuht fòhng néuih identity was a chosen identity. But besides their jyuht fòhng néuih identity, the women also had the chance to learn about the feminist understanding of their grievances, as set forth by the social workers and Legislative Councillors who focused on the patrilineal setting. 'Affection' therefore, has not been the only resource the women can deploy. On another level, the jyuht fòhng néuih's emphasis on affectional bonds reflects the impact of the social institution of the lineage on their choice of an identity.

The jyuht fòhng néuih identity emphasises affection partly because, within the lineage setting, women had no other means (socially and legally) to validate their legitimacy as inheritors. Formal inheritance rules recognise the father-son affiliation principle, which rules out women as inheritors. Though customary law ideally states that unmarried daughters (including jyuht fòhng néuih) should be maintained by the inheritors, the obligation has never been seriously supervised by the government or the villagers. Ideally, the jyuht fòhng problem can be conveniently solved by adopting a boy who should be a close relative bearing the same surname (Watson 1975). It is also assumed that once the adopted son inherits the land, he will deploy proceeds from the land to sustain the widow and her unmarried daughters. Many people (including the village elders whom I interviewed) had assumed that the elders might press the adopted sons to fulfil their responsibility toward their adopted parents. In fact, the men's obligation toward the unpropertied female kin has never been legally ensured. Without any reliable foothold from where they could assert their rights, the women could only draw on notions of 'affection' and 'loyalty', which were external to the formal inheritance rule and the colonial government's legal requirement.

AFFECTION DENIED

'There is no one as unfortunate as I am, my father is poor and my mother is poor.' A-tai's folksong started with these two lines.[3] Being born into a poor family and being brotherless are considered very unfortunate. Besides explaining their misfortune in terms of 'fate', these women believed that their misfortune has been inflicted upon them by specific 'culprits'. The most likely culprit is the closest male kin eligible to inherit the family property. The women not only saw themselves as victims of their wicked relatives, but also victims plagued by their cohorts, in-laws and even neighbours.

One way of explaining to themselves why they were jyuht fòhng néuih was to blame relatives, especially those most eligible to inherit, for all their misfortunes. Some women originally had brothers but they had died at a tender age and some blamed relatives for this. Some of them also thought that their fathers' deaths were caused by these relatives. A-tai and Mei-yi were among those whose brothers had passed away at an early age. A-tai said that her uncle (father's brother) and aunt had always wanted to take away her family's properties, so they were always looking for a chance to get rid of her little brother. One day while the little boy was grazing the cattle, the cattle roamed into his aunt's field. The aunt was furious and growled at the boy. She stamped her hoe several times, while the little boy was standing next to her. The little boy then contracted a high fever and passed away in a few days. A-tai thought that her aunt intentionally scared off his soul, since a child's soul was very vulnerable and could be easily scared off by vicious curses.

Mei-yi was one among three daughters in her family. Her parents' only son died of meningitis. Soon after his death, they adopted a teenage boy whose surname was the same as Mei-yi's, but that boy was just a friend's son, and not a relative. When the adopted son got married, he and his wife moved to Mei-yi's place. Mei-yi's 'sister-in-law' was described by Mei-yi as a 'bad' woman. She suspected that her father's death was caused by the 'sister-in-law', for there was no one around the house except this woman when he died there.

Oi-lee had a similar experience. Like A-tai, Oi-lee also came from a terminated fòhng or jyuht fòhng. She said that when she was a little girl of about 10, her elder sister was already married, so no one could take her to the mountains to collect firewood. The responsibility then fell upon the shoulders of her aunt (father's brother's wife). But this aunt turned out to be a very mean person who also tried to murder Oi-lee, at least in Oi-lee's opinion. Her aunt took Oi-lee to the riverside and threatened to leave her there for the tigers. Another aunt heard what the first aunt said and reprimanded her. Oi-lee also had a brother but he died in a plague during the Japanese Occupation. At that time, malaria and other types of epidemics were rife in the New Territories.

Aside from the would-be inheritors, the stigma of jyuht fòhng néuih was used to explain the tension between the women and the significant others at different stages of their lives. Aside from the patrilineal uncles and cousins, the significant others included 'sisters' who were the women's female kin of the same generation. A-tai remembered how she was ridiculed by one of the 'sisters' when they were small.

That woman was the most beautiful girl in the village, and there were many girls following her. She was rich and pretty. Once she asked me in front of other sisters, 'A-tai, why do you always wear that old suit?'[4] I felt so humiliated. Now when I met her again, I asked her why she said that. She said she was just joking.

A-tai thought that the girl made that insulting remark because she was a jyuht fòhng néuih who did not have any natal kin to fall back on. A-tai thought that the relatives looked down on her family, because there was 'nobody'[5] in her natal family.

The women got married at an early age, usually around 15. For those who did, the jyuht fòhng néuih identity was used to explain why they did not get along well with their husbands and in-laws. For those who remained single, the jyuht fòhng néuih identity justified their remaining single. As I have said earlier, jyuht fòhng néuih identity was redefined at each stage to explain the undesirable situation each woman had to confront.

Let me give two examples. A-tai's relationship with her parents-in-law was very poor. Her mother-in-law always scolded A-tai; rather than supporting A-tai, her husband ran away from home instead, leaving A-tai and her children in the hostile home. Since her mother-in-law refused to take care of A-tai's infants, A-tai asked her mother to babysit them. A-tai's mother, in return, had to depend on her only daughter, for the nephew who inherited her properties did not take care of her. A-tai felt extremely sorry for her mother who had to live with her. 'If she had a son, my mother would not have to suffer,' A-tai mused. She then finally decided to divorce her husband and left the village. I then asked A-tai the immediate cause that agitated her to fight for her own independence. She said, '[My mother-in-law] scolded me, "*jyuht doih!*".[6] This phrase is a Cantonese derogatory term which is used to curse people. When I asked A-tai why her mother-in-law did so many horrible things to her mother and children, A-tai said, 'Because I didn't have any relatives.'

Mei-yi remained single and is 42 years old. She was the only daughter in the family who did not get married. She had been introduced to several men but she rejected them all, because Mei-yi thought that they were just trying to marry an obedient 'slave' who would serve them, rather than marrying a wife out of affection for her. Her other reason for choosing not to marry, was that her mother needed to go to the hospital for regular checkup. Since she was the only girl at home she had to take care of her mother. Her two elder sisters were already married, and her youngest sister was, according to Mei-yi, an 'extrovert' whose heart was 'out there' rather than at home.

Instead of merely focusing on the situation of their own families, the women talked at great length of their situation as victims who were denied affection within both their natal and marital villages.[7] The victimisation as discussed in these women's narratives was not a general sense of victimisation, but rather involved a specific victimiser (usually the cousin or the uncle, and/or the uncle's wife). For example, in the court case 'Li Tang-shi versus Li Wai-kong and the Attorney General' (Action No. 1763 of 1967), the widow Li Tang-shi accused the nearest male kin and the District Officer of removing her from trusteeship of her dead husband's properties, without her approval. She maintained that she should be the sole trustee of her husband's properties. Since her husband's properties were held as 'Tso'[8] properties, the Court had to decipher the meaning of 'Tso' before the hearing could proceed.

Expert evidence was solicited, and the judge finally decided that once properties were subsumed under the category of 'Tso', they became family land ('family' meaning 'clan', in contrast to 'private' and 'personal'). Based on that definition, the widow could not dispose of the properties independently. There was pressure for the widow to compromise with the village elders on the management of the properties. In 1969, the widow appealed against the judge's refusal to declare that the land was not 'Tso' properties. The judge said that there were only two alternative ways the properties could be handled: either the properties should be devolved on to the nearest male kin, or a 'Tso' should be set up. There was no way she could claim the properties for her own use. Expert evidence supported the view that the properties of a dead man without sons would turn into ancestral properties of the whole clan. If properties were classified as 'clan' land, then the woman's autonomy in managing the properties was lost, as seen in the above court case. But it would be too simplistic to assume that the women were completely vulnerable to pressure from village kin. The women could protect their properties from encroachment by complying with the ideal of corporate ownership. In the above court case, both the plaintiff (the widow) and the defendant (the nearest male kin) wanted to monopolise the management of the properties, hoping that these properties would become personal properties. Being categorised as 'Tso', the properties ceased to be the widow's personal properties; on the other hand, this also prevented the nearest male kin from disposing of the land as if it was his own, or managing the land as if he was the sole owner. The attachment to the lineage was, therefore, a tactic for fending off encroaching male kin. Village elders also deployed 'lineage tradition' strategically; failure to observe ceremonial duties was adduced by the village elders to invalidate the widow's legitimacy as trustee of her husband's properties. Participation in lineage rituals and the principle of corporate ownership became the vehicles through which women and their male kin articulated claims for inheritance rights. To honour the custom (be it genuine or lip service only) was a prerequisite to sustaining their rights in the lineage.

By the same token, the jyuht fòhng néuih's discontent could only be wrapped in the language of personal relationships, dyadic and specific. In this way, their complaints were directed towards particular people and not the 'tradition' of the lineages. As far as their interests were concerned, the women still wanted to be regarded as lineage members. A-tai was once very upset by the fact that she was not invited to the opening ceremony of an ancestral hall in her natal village. She knew that some other women (generally known as 'sisters') of her generation were invited; one of them, like A-tai herself, was also divorced. Divorce was a disgrace to the conservative villagers. But A-tai thought that her divorce could not be the real reason why they removed her from the invitation list. Most probably, her natal kin (the village elders in charge of the ancestral hall) rejected her because her relationship with the villagers was not as strong as the other woman who was rich and always maintained close contact with the villagers (playing mahjong with them). A-tai assumed that if she herself had been rich, and kept in touch with her 'sisters' who still lived near their natal village, then perhaps she too would have been invited.

The jyuht fòhng néuih, like the widows, did not wish to abstain from all ties with their male kin, especially the village elders. Sustaining a congenial relationship between the village elders and the woman herself was crucial if she wanted to protect her properties. Should the women really be able to inherit their fathers' properties, they would consider the ties with their natal kin important. One woman said, 'I don't want to live next door to an enemy.' This woman arranged an out-of-court agreement with her cousin (who inherited her father's properties), and her mother complained that she was too lenient to her cousin because she did not demand enough. The woman, however, thought that she could not push her cousin's back against the wall. She foresaw that she and her mother would be living in the village anyway, and her cousin would be her neighbour, a potential enemy if she stretched the limits of their relationship.

THE LOYAL 'PROTECTOR' OF FAMILY PROPERTIES

It is noteworthy that at the beginning of our conversations, three out of six women lamented the death of their little brothers. If these little brothers had not passed away, then the women and their natal families would not have to go through the humiliation of being jyuht fòhng. Nearly all the little brothers who died young were dearly remembered by the women, for they were 'obedient and kind'. According to the women, the key point is that, the boys were legitimate inheritors not only because they belonged to the male sex, but also because they were 'obedient and kind'. The present inheritors by contrast were described as 'ungrateful' and 'malevolent'. If one criteria of inheritance rights was obedience and affection, then the women themselves should be eligible too, they seemed to claim.

Mei-yi's narrative is the best example of the jyuht fòhng néuih romanticising their little brothers. When I asked her to briefly describe her family background, she said,

I originally had a little brother. My parents were superstitious. Little brother was sick, so we took him to Pok Oi hospital. Before that, he had had a temperature, and my parents just prayed to their gods. This time, prayers didn't work. I was, 8 or 9. I can only vaguely remember. From dawn to dusk they were burning incense and praying zealously. After 24 hours, they sent him to hospital . . . he died . . . it must have been meningitis. I loved him very much. He was a very good child. I always put him on my back. I treated him like precious jewellery. After his death, my parents' temper changed drastically. They treated the girls even worse.

Compared with her little brother, her adopted brother[9] (a non-relative) was a greedy man whose presence in the household purely served the purpose of justifying his inheritance rights, and Mei-yi had to protect her family properties from him. Mei-yi thought that he only cared about money because Mei-yi's sister had once asked him to give her a piece of land to build a three-storey house, but he rejected the request. This man also occupied the best room in her house, and her bedroom was on the top floor which was hot in summer and cold in winter. Mei-yi seemed to think that if the little brother had not died, then she and her sisters would not have been treated so badly because he was 'obedient and kind'. Mei-yi had all the characteristics of a filial child, in her terms, as she was 'attached to home' (*chì gà*). Mei-yi also thought that she had to *chìgà* since she had to protect her family properties from the greedy adopted son. Indeed not only the jyuht fòhng néuih thought that obedience was one criterion of inheritance rights, but also those daughters who contested with their brothers for inheritance rights also appealed to the same criterion. Wei-lan was the only participant who had brothers, but she did not get on well with them. She complained of their 'rudeness' and 'disobedience'. Customary rights required the brothers (or those who inherited) to take care of the unpropertied, e.g. the unmarried daughters and widows. The 'bad' brother did not provide for her livelihood although she remained single. Wei-lan said,

My elder brother was followed by my two sisters. Little brother unfortunately died. My younger brother (i.e. the dead boy) was very obedient. My elder brother is now very disobedient, because he knows that it is up to him to give my mother face.

Wei-lan said that daughters were more obedient and that their hearts were with their parents. She said that she had to give up the opportunity to marry when she was young, all for the sake of making enough money for the weddings of her two brothers. She also gave up a well paid job in Kowloon, because she wanted to use more time to take care of her mother who had had a heart attack. Her affection for her mother was rewarded in 1980, when Wei-lan had to attend a medical conference in Japan, and her mother gave her $5000 for travelling expenses. 'It is very extraordinary for a village woman to give you all her money, because she is very careful with her money.' This generosity was to Wei-lan a token of love and a recognition of her loyal affection toward her mother.

The story of Wei-lan suggests that the notion 'daughters are more loyal than sons' is a well-organised idea. There are many traditional stories extolling the obedience of daughters circulating in the South China region.[10] Comparing themselves with the rebellious brothers, the jyuht fòhng néuih thought that they were more filial and, therefore, were in a better position to protect the integrity of the family properties. A-tai publicly accused her uncle (who inherited her father's properties) of spending money on prostitution and gambling. The jyuht fòhng néuih, though married, argued that 'good daughters have to take care of both families' (hó néuih gu léuhng gà: the natal and marital families).

AFFECTION BETWEEN FATHER AND DAUGHTER

'That woman didn't know who her father was. She was beaten up very often, her mother and grandmother often beat her', Suk-fen described the childhood of a girl who was abused by her adopted family. Common stereotypes of adopted daughters depicted them as starved, caned, overworked, and worst of all, fatherless.[11] The jyuht fòhng néuih, compared with the adopted daughters, were in a better position – at least they knew who their fathers were, as one jyuht fòhng néuih put it. The connection with fathers could eventually justify their inheritance rights. When the jyuht fòhng néuih had to justify their claims for inheritance rights, they would have to prove, in their narratives at least, their eligibility as inheritors through their hard work and devotion to their families, especially to their fathers. The narratives of the women Suk-fen, A-tai and Mei-yi best illustrate this point.

To prove her ties with her father, Suk-fen had to resort to the documents about her father, and those documents bore her signature. In 1984, Suk-fen's father passed away. Suk-fen told me in great detail the things she had done after her father's death. Not only was Suk-fen responsible for arranging her father's funeral, she also had to take care of the funeral of her paternal grandmother, though there were other male kin around. Being an indigenous resident, her father was allowed to be buried on the hillside nearby where other non-indigenous residents were not permitted access, for the hillsides were 'Crown Land'.[12] Suk-fen showed me the documents of her parents' burials – among them was a map which bore her signature. 'My relatives said that I was the adopted daughter, see, here's my name. What they said is garbage!' The burial site was circled on the map, and next to it was her signature. Suk-fen told me that the first time she went to the mortuary in the hospital to sign the death certificate, she was appalled by the creepy atmosphere there. She emphasised to me that she had to take a look at the corpse to ensure that the dead body was her father.

Soon after her mother's death, her relatives (paternal cousins) claimed that her mother had adopted them as sons, and successfully transferred all properties, bypassing Suk-fen's approval. When Suk-fen reproached them, they said that Suk-fen was just an adopted daughter. Suk-fen did not have any birth certificate to prove her identity (applying for a birth certificate fifty years ago was not a customary practice). The only thing that Suk-fen could use to prove her identity was the documents that she showed me. She tried to get two villagers to serve as witnesses, one of them a non-indigenous resident. The other witness was a native of that village but did not bear the lineage's surname, and that witness' ancestors were considered the 'inferior people'.[13]

In a patrilineal society, it is understandable that if a woman wants to establish her rights, she needs to justify her rights with reference to a male figure because many rights are only conferred through the male line (the father-son affiliation). Though jyuht fòhng néuih were supposed to be cut off from the corporate kin group, it does not mean that the women themselves would necessarily comply with such genealogical principles. Instead, the women thought that they had to sustain ties with natal kin if they wanted to protect their interests. Affiliation with fathers was not only proved by documents, but was also sought through expressions of the way father and daughter felt towards each other. The fatherly figures were usually the 'good guys', while the bad guys were usually the mothers. Fathers were the benevolent men who protected the girls from mothers who drove the daughters to harsh menial labour.

Suk-fen recalled one day that her mother beat her for stealing a piece of brown sugar, and Suk-fen was so scared that she hid in the bushes nearby. When her father returned at night, he looked for Suk-fen. When he knew that his wife had scared off the girl, he scolded his wife and then went to find her. According to Suk-fen, her mother, was ungrateful. She was also old-fashioned and she did not allow her daughter to study in school, despite the fact that the father consented to it.

A-tai called her mother a 'slave driver'. Like Suk-fen, A-tai also paid a lot of attention to her father's funeral in her narrative. When A-tai recollected her father's death, the details were so precise that it sounded as if the whole incident had just happened days ago. Since A-tai's family was very poor, they did not even have the money to prepare for the Chinese New Year. Her father therefore asked her to borrow money from her uncle. She told me the request was rejected. Finally, her other uncle loaned her some money, and her father tried his best to cook the last meal for himself. A-tai still remembers the ingredients of the dish her father prepared 40 years ago. The day when her father died, A-tai dragged him down from his bed and dressed him in his best clothes, for they could not afford to buy the proper clothes worn by the dead. When she kept vigil over the corpse, there were no other people except the musicians in the band.[14] A-tai felt that her uncle should be there too. At that time, A-tai was only 12.

According to Chinese customs, it is usually the eldest son who hosts his parents' funerals. But A-tai insisted that even daughters could host their fathers' funerals. The ritual, literally 'shouldering the flag and buying water' (*dàam fàan máaih séui*), was commonly regarded as the son's responsibility. In case the dead person did not have a male successor, the closest male kin should host the rituals. To perform this duty was to fulfil the responsibility of a successor who was entitled to inherit the properties. No male kin was willing to perform this duty for A-tai's father. A-tai, on the other hand, regarded the hosting of this ritual as proof of her entitlement to inheritance rights.

Indeed daughters playing host at their fathers' death rituals was not uncommon, at least this is what the indigenous women claim. According to A-tai, there were particular procedures to follow when the daughter had to perform this ritual. The daughter had to tie a red belt around her waist, so as to keep off the 'killing air' (*séi hei*) of the corpse.

The jyuht fòhng néuih had other ways of demonstrating ties with their fathers other than documents and formal rituals. All these means were used to solicit social recognition of their identity as their fathers' daughters (contrary to the adopted daughters who did not know who their fathers were). Some women would go back to their fathers' graves or to their fathers' homes to cry to their hearts' content. A-tai usually visited her father's grave during the Ching Ming Festival and the Chung Yeung Festival, which traditionally were occasions for sweeping the ancestral graves. However, A-tai would also go to cry in front of the grave apart from the above two festivals. She would also do so during emotional crises.

When she first participated in the Movement, her natal villagers saw her appear on the T.V. screen, criticising the uncle and cousin for taking away her properties without taking care of her mother. They were angry with A-tai for taking such a high profile, and since her relatives regarded inheritance dispute as a family matter, they thought that A-tai was making a fuss about it in public. The New Territories villagers were also afraid that female inheritance would be a prelude to government attempts to scrap other privileges granted to the indigenous residents. For these reasons, they rang up A-tai and scolded her for 'creating troubles in the New Territories'.

When A-tai received these calls (usually made by her 'sisters' or aunts), she was extremely upset. A-tai demanded that her cousin take care of her mother, and be responsible for her mother's burial in the future. All these demands were, according to A-tai, legitimate and reasonable. She assumed that her villagers would support her, but on the contrary, they did not sympathise with her. She then went to her father's grave and cried, singing the folksongs which recounted her unhappy childhood, hostile marital home, the cruelty of her fellow villagers and the ingratitude of her cousin. As her father's grave was just 200 meters from the nearest homestead in her natal village, her lament was more than just a personal carthasis, it was also a public performance.

It would be far-fetched to suggest that all jyuht fòhng néuih rationalises their father-daughter connections in the same way. The women interviewed came from different backgrounds, and this affected their ways of expressing the affectional bond.

AFFECTION AND INDIVIDUALS

Each woman's age, religious beliefs and personality affected their articulation of their affectional bond.

I started to pay attention to the women's religious beliefs when I was invited by an indigenous woman to accompany her to visit a spirit medium (*mahn máih pó*).[15] Not all jyuht fòhng néuih consulted the spirit mediums, as some younger jyuht fòhng néuih were Protestants. Out of the six women, those who consulted spirit mediums were the older ones. The two younger women in their early forties were Christians; the youngest woman (34 years old) did not have any religious beliefs.[16]

The older women who visited spirit mediums were in their fifties and seventies. By consulting spirit mediums, they were looking for means to support their claims for inheritance rights, claims which their fellow villagers did not support.

In January 1994, when the Movement just took off, A-tai went to spirit mediums; she wanted to ask her father some questions. As A-tai's mother was gravely ill, she wondered if her father was going to 'take away' her mother. A-tai also wanted to ask her father if her demand for inheritance rights was 'too much', since A-tai's natal kin said she was being 'ungrateful' by participating in the Movement. When spirit mediums fell into a trance, she started speaking Cantonese and later switched to Hakka (A-tai's father was a Hakka, and spirit mediums was also a Hakka).[17] Spirit mediums (speaking in Hakka, in the persona of her father) reminded A-tai of the deaths of her seven siblings, as well as her father's miserable burial. Her 'father' also encouraged A-tai to fight for her own rights. A-tai became emotionally disturbed on being reminded of this part of her childhood. Listening to her own story from a third person (who impersonated her father) reaffirmed her participation in the Movement.

Sometimes spirit mediums were not needed to prove the ties between daughters and their fathers. Ghost stories were used in some cases. Once I and the indigenous women were talking about ghost stories. Suk-fen said,

> My old house is haunted. My cousin took away the house from me, and rented the house to a couple. The couple soon moved away, because they saw my parents' ghosts coming home hand in hand. Now the house is still empty.

The ghosts were quiet, but to Suk-fen, they conveyed a message loudly and clearly: the house belonged to Suk-fen's parents, and no one could stay there except their daughter, i.e. Suk-fen. Though the house was renovated, the ghosts could still recognise the house and groped their way back from the murky underworld. No matter what became of the house, it was always her parents' home (and Suk-fen's home too, since it was her natal home). Suk-fen told us that her daughter had stayed there before, but that her daughter never met any ghosts. Suk-fen and her daughter had the blessing of their ancestors' ghosts to be the legitimate occupants.

Unlike Suk-fen and A-tai who were ten years older, Mei-yi and Wei-lan had more access to a variety of religions. Both Mei-yi and Wei-lan believed in Christianity. Wei-lan once quoted the Bible to prove that female inheritance was 'correct'. The setting of the story was Exodus. She did not give me the exact quotation, but stressed that the most important point was that Moses did not object to female inheritance. She also said that the Jewish synagogue 2000 years ago had forbidden women to voice their opinions, but that the Christian Church now allowed women to speak out. The biblical reference showed that 'tradition' could be amended. She said that she had times of self-doubt during the course of the Movement, but in her prayers she received a clear signal from God that she should carry on fighting for her rights. Wei-lan relied on the 'Father in Heaven' when she was in doubt, while A-tai and other older women would seek spirit mediums to speak directly with their 'fathers in Yellow Spring' ('yellow spring' is the Chinese translation of the underworld).

Besides being a devout Christian, Wei-lan is also very patriotic. She addressed Dr. Sun Yat-sen as 'The Father of the Nation' and his wife 'The Mother of the Nation'. Inside her clinic hung a painting of Dr. Sun Yat-sen's wife. Wei-lan, sitting under the painting, rested her chin on her hand, expressing surprise when I asked her who that person in the painting was. China's history of turbulent revolutions had impressed Wei-lan deeply. 'When I was in primary five, my teacher told me that Hong Kong would no longer be a colony in 1997. At that time, I thought that 1997 would release me from my brother's threat,[18] since there would be no 'Qing Law' after 1997'.[19] Her seniors, Oi-lee, Suk-fen and A-tai did not have the chance to receive primary education, and would not deploy 'objective' historical events (as well as nationalistic sentiments) to justify their rights. But the older women, through spirit mediums, could feel that they had their fathers' direct consent to their participation in the Movement.

Siu-ling was the youngest indigenous woman in the Movement. She said that the village she lived in was not far away from the urban areas, and her fellow villagers were not as 'stubborn' as those villagers who resided in remote areas. The proximity between her village and the urban areas allowed her villagers to have better working and education opportunities. Siu-ling herself was a good example: she went to a Catholic college and then to a famous university, and eventually worked as a news reporter.

As a jyuht fòhng néuih, Siu-ling did not see the jyuht fòhng néuih problem only as a personal issue. One reason was that her father was quite 'liberal'. She admitted that although her 'uncles' sometimes would tease her father lightly for having no male offspring, her father did not exert any pressure on her mother and on his daughters. She thought that her father's liberal attitude was due to his exposure to the outside world; her father enjoyed travelling a lot. Siu-ling was grateful for having had such a father. There were also no uncles or cousins who claimed to be her father's legitimate inheritors. As a news reporter, Siu-ling had a strong sense of social awareness, and for her the jyuht fòhng néuih problem was a social one as well as a personal one. Siu-ling's perception of the Movement and her way of articulating the father-daughter relationship was very different from other jyuht fòhng néuih. According to her, principles of gender equality and human rights, on top of her father's approval, justified women's inheritance rights.

From the above discussion we can see that individual differences – age, education, religious beliefs and personality – shape the jyuht fòhng néuih's articulation of their affectional bond with their fathers, an apparently 'natural' psychological response. From the mysterious and hair-raising ghost stories to socialist ideals – the women's narratives reflect the wide range of resources they can deploy. There was no standardised way of expressing the affectional bond; there was also no single best way to express it. Given the diverse way in which the affectional bond was articulated, we can conclude that its expression is not a carefully calculated formula to win sympathy.

CONCLUSION

The jyuht fòhng néuih in the Movement were clearly not submissive village females who accepted without doubt the 'customary rule' of male inheritance; if they were, the Movement would never have come into existence. However, they were not 'enlightened' women, inspired only by feminist ideals and human rights. It would be untrue to claim that the Movement marked a 'revolutionary' change in the lineage's patrilineal outlook. Yet, even if the lineage's patrilineal organisation persisted, the women could still strive for their interests by manipulating the 'formal rule'. The assertion of inheritance rights through affectional bonds obviously recognised the need to maintain ties with fellow villagers. Although the women did not strictly comply with the father-son affiliation principle, the strength of patrilineal influence still dictated the women's strategies for realising their rights. Thus, women could well be reinforcing the claims of a patrilineal system by asserting their inheritance rights through affection.

NOTES

1 The difference between the 'urban' and the 'rural' is a geographical distinction, rather than a difference in lifestyles, since the populations in the New Territories and urban Hong Kong both receive the same education, watch the same T.V., and enjoy equal job opportunities. Related to the term 'rural women' is 'indigenous women'. 'Indigenous residents' refers to the population living in the New Territories since 1898, and their patrilineal descendants. In 1898, the New Territories were leased to the British, therefore the original population in the New Territories were branded 'indigenous residents', in contrast to the colonial rulers.

2 These interviews were conducted after the amendment was passed. It should be noted that their views on 'affection' were expressed after their inheritance rights were legally recognised.

3 Folksongs used to be sung among the female indigenous residents in the New Territories. There were bridal songs and funeral laments. These songs are not popular now, and only some old women know how to sing them. A-tai learned the songs from her mother. A-tai also sang this folksong during the demonstrations.

4 Girls at that time wore loose-fitting pants and tops.

5 'Nobody' (*mòuh yàhn mòuh maht*) here metaphorically refers to the fact that the women did not have any male successors in the immediate families. The women thought that families without male successors were considered to be vulnerable.

6 'Jyuht doih' (a Cantonese phrase) meaning the male line is terminated and is similar to 'jyuht fòhng'. This anathema is regarded as very vicious.

7 All women were married into other indigenous families in villages, instead of marrying into non-indigenous families.

8 Expert evidence in the court proposed that the word 'Tso' was attached to the name of a dead man who died without a son, and the properties would be registered under the man's name and the character 'Tso'. The properties were used to finance ancestral worship, and managed by his widow, who acted as the trustee.

9 Mei-yi's brother was adopted into her family in his teens. Normally, only little boys are adopted to make sure they will have more attachment with the adopted family.

10 Among these stories is one which tells the tale of an obedient and clever daughter who saves her mother. Her mother was ordered by a god to cook nine dishes. Her mother was extremely worried about it since she did not have enough money to buy sufficient ingredients for the nine dishes. The clever daughter then prepared the nine dishes with only one kind of vegetable called '*gieu tsoi*' (Hakka), together with other simple ingredients. She used 'gieu tsoi', for 'gieu' rhymes with 'nine' in Hakka. This story was supplied by Ms. Wong Yuk-yan, who lived in a village in South China. She was already 82, and the first time she heard of this story was when she was still a girl, living in Mei Xian (Mandarin), a region in North Guangdong. Other popular stories about obedient girls are abundant, such as stories about 'Hua Mu-lan' (Fá Muhk Nàahn) and Guan Yin (Gùn Yàm). Hua Mu-lan was the daughter of a man who was conscripted, but too old to join the

army. Hua Mu-lan replaced him and passed as a man for 20 years. She finally became a general and at last disclosed her real identity. The story is set in Yuan Dynasty (1276–1386 A.D.). Though this story did not originate in South China, people in the South know this story very well. Guan Yin, a goddess, is believed to be a filial daughter who saved her father's life.

11 I checked up the synonyms of the word 'helpless', and discovered that one of the synonyms was 'fatherless'(there was no 'motherless' on the list). The stereotype of a 'fatherless' girl as 'helpless' is not particularly Chinese. (Longman Synonym Dictionary, 1986).

12 Crown Land means the land owned by the government.

13 Inferior people (hái fù) are also known as little people (sai màhn). They were the servants of the powerful lineages. For further information please refer to James Watson's 'Chattel Slavery in Chinese Peasant Society: A Comparative Analysis' in American Ethnologist, 15, 1976. Also see his 'Transactions in People: the Chinese Market in Slaves, Servants and Heirs' in Asian and African Systems of Slavery, edited by James Watson, University of California press, 1980.

14 During a traditional funeral, a band of musicians are present all through the rituals.

15 A spirit medium is usually an old woman. She does not work in a temple but offers services at home. Clients get in touch with her through friends and relatives. People who want to talk to their deceased close relatives can seek her consultation. After falling into a trance, she will impersonate the dead relative. The charge of each service ranges from $200 to $700.

16 The correlation between age and religious belief is just specific to the six women I interviewed, and should therefore not be generalised to all indigenous women.

17 The spirit medium spoke in Cantonese, perhaps because of my presence. She might have assumed that I only understood Cantonese. The code-switching between Cantonese and Hakka reflects how spirit mediums 'departmentalised' A-tai's experience: the present and the past. She used Cantonese to talk about the present and the future, and Hakka when talking about the past.

18 Wei-lan was the only woman in the Movement who had brothers.

19 China and Taiwan repealed Qing Law long ago.

REFERENCES CITED

Baker and Feuchtwang, eds.
    1991 An Old State in New Setting. JASO.
Baker, Hugh
    1966 The Five Great Clans of the New Territories. Journal of the Royal Asiatic Society (Hong Kong Branch) 6:25–47.
    1968 A Chinese Lineage Village–Sheung Shui. Stanford University Press.
Chen, Chi-nan
    1984 'Fong' and 'Chia-tsu': The Chinese Kinship System in Rural Taiwan. PhD dissertation. University Microfilms International.

Hong Kong Government
    1953   Chinese Law and Custom in Hong Kong. Report of a Committee
            appointed by the Governor in Oct, 1948. (Also called the Strictland
            Report).
Chun, Allen
    1990   Policing Society: The 'Rational' Practice of British Colonial Land
            Administration in the New Territories of Hong Kong c. 1900. Journal
            of Historical Sociology 3:401–422.
Devault, Majorie L.
    1990   Talking and Listening from Women's Standpoint: Feminist Strategies
            for Interviewing and Analysis. Social Problems 37:96–116.
Endacott, G.B.
    1958   A History of Hong Kong. Oxford University Press.
Faure, David
    1986   The Structure of Rural Chinese Society. Hong Kong: Oxford
            University Press.
Faure, David; Hayes, James and Birch, Alan
    1984   From Village to City. Hong Kong: University of Hong Kong.
Freedman, Maurice
    1958   Lineage Organisation in Southeastern China. Athlone Press.
Frice, T.; Axinn, W. and Thornton, A
    1993   Marriage, Social Inequality, and Women's Contact with Their Natal
            Families in Alliance Societies: Two Tamang Examples. American
            Anthropologist 95:395–419.
Gallin, Bernard
    1960   Matrilateral and Affinal Relationships of a Taiwanese Village.
            American Anthropologist 62:632–642.
Giddens, Anthony
    1984   The Constitution of Society. University of California Press.
Goffman, Irving
    1959   The Presentation of Self in Everyday Life. Doubleday Anchor Book.
Goody, Jack
    1990   The Oriental the Ancient and the Primitive. Cambridge: Camridge
            University Press.
Hong Kong Law Reform Committee Reports
Hong Kong Law Reports
    1946   pp. 58–67.
    1967   pp. 367–389.
    1968   pp. 542–578.
    1969   pp. 628–641.
Judd, Ellen R.
    1989   Niangjia: Chinese Women and Their Natal Families. The Journal of
            Asian Studies 48: 525–44.
Legislative Council Handsard 1990–1994.
Legislative Council Sessional Papers
    1899 & 1900 (including The Lockard Report)
New Territories Ordinance 1910.
Sacks, Karen
    1982   Sisters and Wives. University of Illinois Press.

Salaff, Janet
    1981   Working Daughters of Hong Kong: Filial Piety Or Power In The Family.Cambridge University Press.
United Daily News, Hong Kong
    11/9/1993   Female Family Members Do Not Have Inheritance Rights.
Watson, James and Rawski, Evelyn eds.
    1990   Death Ritual in Late Imperial China. California: University of California Press.
Watson, James L.
    1975   Emigration and Chinese Lineage: The Mans in Hong Kong and London. Berkerley.University of California Press.
    1976   Chattal Slavery in Chinese Peasant Society: A Comparative Analysis. American Ethnologist 15 (4).
    1980   Transactions in People: The Chinese Market in Slaves, Servants, and Heirs. *In* Asian and African Systems of Slavery Chinese. James Watson, ed. University of California Press.
    1982   Chinese Kinship Reconsidered: Anthropological Perspectives on Historical Research. The China Quarterly 92:589–622.
Watson, R. and Ebrey, P. B.
    1991   Marriage and Inequality in Chinese Society. University of California Press.
Watson, Rubie
    1981   Class Differences and Affinal Relations in South China. Man 16:593–625.
    1985   Inequality Among Brothers. Cambridge University Press.
Wesley-Smith
    1980   Unequal Treaty—1898–1997. Oxford University Press.
Wolf, Arthur P. and Huang Chieh-shan
    1980   Marriage and Adoption in China, 1845–1945. Stanford University Press.
Wolf, Diane
    1990   Daughters, Decisions and Domination: An Empirical and Conceptual Critique of Household Strategies. Development and Change 21:43–74.
Wolf, Margery
    1972   Women and the Family in Rural Taiwan. Stanford University Press.
Wolf, M. and Witke, R., eds.
    1974   Women in Chinese Society. Stanford University Press.

9

MOTHERHOOD IN HONG KONG
THE WORKING MOTHER AND CHILD-CARE IN THE PARENT-CENTRED HONG KONG FAMILY

Diana Martin[1]

At one time pregnancy and childbirth were women's unique and most important contribution to the continuation of the family and to its economy. Repeated pregnancies with their associated hazards occupied a considerable period of a woman's life. Whereas childbirth remains a woman's unique contribution to the continuation of the family, it no longer dominates her existence in the developed countries, including Hong Kong, where the desire to produce many children has given way to the aim of producing one or two who will be upwardly mobile. The decline of the pronatalist ethos of the Chinese, combined with the availability of effective contraception has reduced the birthrate in Hong Kong to one of the lowest in the world. From a figure of 35 births per thousand population in the 1960s, it is currently 12 per thousand. This means a total fertility rate per woman of 1.3. (Hong Kong Social and Economic Trends 1982–1992, Census and Statistics Department 1993). Despite a lingering preference for sons over daughters, this preference does not seem to be strong enough for most parents of daughters to continue to have children in order to try to have a son. Clearly there are other priorities such as being able to give one's children a good education, and a decent material standard of living. It is generally now considered hard work to bring up children.

It is my contention in this paper that the Hong Kong mother's identity as a worker is stronger than her identity as a mother; in other words her commitment is primarily to her wage earning work rather than to the nurture and raising of her child or children. This primary commitment is demonstrated by the mother's rapid return to work, and by her emphasis that this is what she would rather do even if she did not work for financial reasons. Where this is a financial possibility, the work of childcare is readily delegated to a paid childminder. In Chinese culture the main thrust of childcare has been, and on the whole still is, supervision and discipline with very little overt emphasis being placed on affection or the closeness of the relationship between mother and child. New mothers have said to me that looking after a baby is a 24 hour a day shift involving hard and dull work. In their view it is a job that is far better done by someone who has experience and who will do it for 24 hours a day five or six days a week in her own home. Above all the task of looking after a baby seems not to be perceived as primarily the mother's duty. As another anthropologist of Chinese society, a Chinese-American woman, remarked to me: 'Once the mother has had the baby her job stops there' (Koo 1993). This attitude would certainly make it possible for a mother to hand her baby over to the care of someone else without feeling guilty or torn between the roles of worker and mother.

Moreover Hong Kong is a society with a very competitive lifestyle. Accommodation for the aspiring middle-classes is expensive, as are many of the goods and services targeted at them. Although it seems that the generations keep in close touch, and that even after marriage the younger generation honour their financial obligations to their parents, the predominant family form is now nuclear.

There are two related themes to be looked at here. One is the practice and perception of women (and wives and mothers) in the labour force, and the second is the readiness with which the baby is consigned to another caretaker. Clearly the former cannot easily take place without the latter although the reverse is less true. It would however appear that the traditional Chinese pattern of childcare, which in a somewhat different form continues in Hong Kong today, makes it very possible for large numbers of women to remain in the work force after they have had children.

WET-NURSES AND FOSTER PARENTS

It must be said that the care of babies by other than their mothers is not particular to the Chinese. It seems to have been widespread among the upper classes of England and France in the seventeenth and eighteenth centuries (Stone 1977; Badinter 1980; Fildes 1986) although there were always those who condemned the practice, Rousseau, in France, being one of the most adamant that women should nurse their own children

(Aries 1960:362). Wiesner writes that, in Europe, although the wealthy would hire a wet-nurse to come into their own homes, others would send the baby to the wet-nurse's home for two to three years. Far from seeing it as a sign of lack of maternal feeling, Wiesner considers that it 'actually stemmed from the fact that nursing was incompatible with many of [her] familial and social duties' (1993:71). Resident nannies were also common until relatively recently in the English upper classes to allow the mother to pursue her social life and her role as wife or companion to her husband. In the West, possibly since Bowlby's writings in the 1950s (arguing that babies need the constant care of their mothers in order to thrive) and the ensuing reactions to his ideas, there is a continuing debate about whether the mother should be the exclusive caretaker of her child, what are the disadvantages or benefits to babies/small children of unrelated childminders, or nurseries (Bowlby 1953; Birns and Ner 1988). It is a very emotional issue in the West, and the perceived needs of babies will often depend on whether or not the writer/researcher has a feminist standpoint (by which I mean whether or not she regards the woman's interests and 'rights' as paramount). It is safe to say that there is, for the most part, no such debate in Hong Kong. Neither feminist issues nor issues to do with the rights of the child are in the forefront of public consciousness in Hong Kong as they are in the West. There is no law against sex discrimination in Hong Kong, for instance, although this is being discussed at various levels.

In a study of West African parenthood and fostering, Esther Goody discusses the prevalence in many parts of the world of delegating some of the tasks of parenthood, and the reasons for doing so (1982). It may be to establish ties between adult kin and children, or between adults, as among the Gonja of northern Ghana, or to create links based on sponsorship as in the Balkans. When the child is fostered at a later age it can be seen as an apprenticeship in specific skills or as a way of socialising children by adults who will be less indulgent than the natural parents. Goody also mentions the adoption of little daughters-in-law by the Chinese of Taiwan, extensively studied by A. Wolf and Huang (1980). The intention was that these girls would later marry the son of the house, thereby avoiding both the expense of bringing an adult bride into the house, and the conflicts endemic in the traditional mother-in-law/daughter-in-law relationship.

Carsten, in an article about fostering children in Pulau Langkawi, discusses the different kinds of arrangements made and the reasons for these (1991:425–443). At the time of her study about a quarter of the children in the village were not living with both their parents.

The old European institution, mentioned above, of babies boarding at the home of a wet nurse is also another instance of the delegation of some of the parent's – here specifically the mother's – roles.

I should like to use Goody's framework to maintain that in Hong Kong many families, in effect practise a partial form of what Goody calls 'nurturant fostering' from when the baby is a few months old to the age of between two and three years. That the child returns to its own home at that age in order to go to kindergarten, may be because it will anyway spend the major part of the day away from home, or it may be because of the very great emphasis placed on education which will be elaborated on later in this paper. The reason for the 'nurturant fostering' seems to be largely pragmatic and primarily to enable the mother to return to the workforce. It does not, as far as I know, create any lasting ties or affection between the minder and the infant, or the minder and the parents. The relationship is predominantly a financial one (even though many child-minders will say that they are looking after a baby 'for a friend', and she may even be a distant relative), and the child supposedly returns home at weekends and on public holidays. This is an area which could well be worth further study. Sixteen years ago, I lodged for a few months with a young woman whose husband was away at sea. She had a twenty-month old daughter, and to earn some extra money, she also took on the care of a one-month old baby boy during the week. I recall that on more than one weekend the parents telephoned to say that they were too busy to take their baby home.

That it is assumed that the ties between a child and an unrelated child-minder can be cut without perceived problems or trauma on the child's part was demonstrated to me by the following case. A social worker, specialising in the placing of children for adoption, told me about an eight year-old-boy for whom she was trying to find an adoptive family overseas (the assumption being that no Hong Kong family would wish to adopt a boy of such an advanced age). He was the son of a single mother who had placed him as a baby in the care of an elderly lady. For a year the mother had paid the baby-minder, but had then discontinued payment and effectively disappeared. The baby-minder had continued looking after the boy for eight years, out of affection, according to the social worker. But she had eventually become too old and ill to continue and the child had been handed over to the care of the Social Welfare Department. I asked whether the boy was continuing to see the old lady before he went overseas. The social worker told me that he was not because they did not encourage it as it was better to cut all links and have a clean break.

Since the reason that babies are looked after by people other than their parents is in order that their mother should return to paid employment, I shall first look at women in the work-force in Hong Kong society.

WOMEN IN THE WORK FORCE

The entry of Chinese women into the industrial labour force in pre-Communist China, post-Communist China, Hong Kong, Taiwan and Singapore has been well documented. In spite of the traditional value that women should not be seen outside the home (Pruitt 1945; Ba Jin 1931) it is now taken for granted that women work outside the home before marriage, after marriage and, increasingly, in the growing white-collar class, after they have children. In 1992 the overall percentage of women (aged from 15 to 65 and over) in the labour force in Hong Kong was 46.2% (compared to 78% for men), a figure which had been fairly constant over the previous ten years. The highest percentages of women's participation in the labour force are those of women aged 20 to 24 (82.5%) and 25 to 29 (79.1%). These figures presumably do not take into account unofficial work, such as baby-minding, or self-employed entrepreneurial type jobs (Hong Kong Census and Statistics Department 1993:14). Women's participation in the labour force equals that of Japan, and is among the highest in Asia, with married women joining at a faster rate than single women (Ho 1984).

In present-day Hong Kong where a dense population inhabiting a small territory renders almost all resources scarce except for opportunities for employment, and where children therefore continue to be seen as resources (as it is assumed that they will study hard at school and get a well-paying job), it seems to be nearly a cultural norm for the mother to continue in paid employment. It is certainly the case, for instance, that where a couple wish to adopt or foster a child the full-time employment of the mother is no impediment in the eyes of the Hong Kong Social Welfare Department. However, the scarcity of government-operated child care centres[2] and the expense of hiring a childminder (from HK$3,000 to HK$4,000 per month) means that re-entering the work force remains an ideal mostly pursued by the white-collar employees who can earn enough to make paying for child-care a feasible option. Manual workers who themselves earn about the same or barely more than a baby-minder stay out of the workforce and look after their children and express regret that they have to do so.

THE RETURN TO WORK OF THE HONG KONG MOTHER

At the end of the *chóh yuht* (the month after childbirth during which the mother's lifestyle is restricted) most mothers I talked to express great relief and pleasure that they can once more live normally. Within about six weeks of the birth most once more return to full-time work. This, as I have already said, seems to be a matter of personal preference as well as financial necessity. Working has in nearly all cases certainly predated marriage and motherhood, and has carried with it many implications about women's role in the family. Exactly how young married couples organise their finances is something that would be well worth studying as is the power balance of the family. Journalistic reports suggest that even in professional couples the husband is still regarded as the head of the family and that the wives still expect them to be the major breadwinners.

Well before the mother returns to work she has to make provision for someone to look after the baby. Many had however not made any firm arrangements up to the time when they were in hospital with their new-born baby. The wealthy will take out a contract to employ a live-in Filippina domestic helper (of whom there are about 125,000 working in Hong Kong) who will take care of all the household chores. The minimum salary for a foreign domestic helper is currently HK$3,500 per month. Free food or a food allowance is also provided by the employer as is a return flight home every two years and free medical care. The majority will employ a baby-minder, which in terms of salary costs nearly as much but accommodation and additional perks do not have to be provided. As one might expect, the preferred baby-minder is a member of the family: a paternal or maternal grandmother, a sister or sister-in-law. Sometimes however relatives are not available because they are themselves working outside the home, already looking after children/grandchildren, too old, or living in China or even in some cases have emigrated to the USA or Canada. These were all reasons given by informants. In the case of a relative not being available, an unrelated person will be sought as caretaker. As I have said, few women seemed to consider using government creches or baby care centres, and the reasons for this should be investigated. The unrelated caretaker will be found either through friends or by advertising. Women I talked to did not have any specific characteristics in mind that they required of a baby-minder, a few of them seeming satisfied to find someone who was clean and did not smoke. The baby is nearly always looked after away from its own home in the home of the baby-minder. One mother, married to a professional man, told me she would not want a stranger coming to her own home to look after the baby. There was a certain irony in trusting someone with her baby whom she would not trust in her home.

Although some babies are cared for outside on a daily basis, and are taken home in the evening by their parents, many will remain at the baby-minder's flat for the whole week. This was the intention with a substantial number of my informants. The parents will then collect the baby on Saturday and return it on Sunday evening. The baby is likely to continue to spend five or six days out of seven at the baby-minder's house until it is two or three years old and can go to kindergarten. Mothers say that the baby suffers no ill effects, although mothers whose friends have put their babies in care away from home say that their friends found that their babies had difficulties settling back with their own parents. These are obviously subjective opinions possibly to justify a course of action. On the topic of European children remaining at the wet-nurse's home for two years where affective ties may well have been created between nurse and infant, Goody comments: 'In the context of the divisibility of parent roles it is striking to see that none of these studies describes the integration of the returned two-year-old as a problem. While such difficulties may well have occurred, but not been recorded for the twentieth-century analyst, it would appear that this was not *seen as a problem* at the time' (1982:25). Evidently the same is true of present-day Hong Kong families who place a child in some one else's home.

The cost for weekly baby-minding in Hong Kong is, as already stated above, from about HK$3,000 to HK$4,000 a month plus the cost of milk-powder and disposable nappies. If the median Hong Kong household salary is currently about HK$11,000 a month (1991 Census), this is clearly a substantial outlay. In all the cases that I have come across a grandmother or sister is paid the same, the reasoning being that she would otherwise be gainfully employed in some other capacity. It should also be borne in mind that the older generation are seen as having few obligations towards the younger one, especially after its members have reached adulthood. Although the outlay is more or less equivalent to the salary earned by a Filippina maid (Chinese maid or *'amàh'* are nowadays scarce and much more expensive), most flats do not have the space to accommodate an extra person.

It seems to be, on the whole, those mothers who can only find low-paid unskilled work who remain at home to look after their children. They simply cannot afford to pay for outside baby-care, but often express the preference for going out to work. The working mothers seem to regard the weekly separation with equanimity, although in fact those whose baby is lodged with grandparents may well eat all together after work if the location is convenient. They say 'Of course I will miss him/ her but I have no choice'. They maintain, in addition, that there is . nothing to be enjoyed about being with a baby, that it is very hard work for 24 hours a day. I have never heard a mother express the idea that she did not want to miss anything of her child's development, or that it was in any way the mother's duty, let alone pleasure, to be the primary caretaker of the baby.

An administrator of my acquaintance who was the mother of a baby girl sent the baby to be looked after by her mother in a housing estate some way away. Her comments to me about the situation clearly demonstrated her priorities. 'I would like to take care of my baby', she told me, 'but I have no time'. When some time later she and her husband emigrated to Canada, the toddler was left in the care of the grandparents until such time as the couple were settled. 'It doesn't matter now' a mutual friend commented to about the separation of the 18-month-old from her parents, 'but it won't be too good when she's older'.

THE ROLE OF THE MOTHER IN HONG KONG CHINESE CULTURE

A Hong Kong Chinese obstetrician working in his own private practice told me about a difference he had observed between his Chinese and Western patients who came to his clinic for a scan or amniocentesis. These are all women with professional husbands. On the form they are required to fill in and sign is a slot for 'occupation'. Those Western women who are currently not working outside the home write 'mother'. Their Chinese counterparts leave the space blank. He said to me: 'Chinese women don't want to rear their children any more'. There is an old Chinese saying that it is the duty of a woman to support her husband and teach her children. Certainly those women among my informants who chose (either by default or because their husbands wanted them to) to remain at home with their children, claimed that they were doing so to supervise the children, and because a mother's care made the children more obedient and less rebellious. Many said that it was the husband who wanted the mother to stay with the baby.

Another concern that was expressed to me by the new mothers in the various hospitals, is that they do not know how to take care of a baby and that it is therefore better if someone else with experience does the job.

That this view is not a new one is evidenced in Flora Baber's and Elaine Field's observations in the late 1960s in their survey of infant care in Hong Kong. They write: 'There is a belief among the Chinese community that an institution calling itself a nursery, or an individual caring for a small number of children in her home, is better equipped to care for a young infant than is the child's own mother particularly if the child is her first. This idea is prevalent throughout all social strata, rich and poor alike, and there are innumerable 'nurseries' of varying standards, from very good to appallingly bad, to cater for them' (Field and Baber 1973:38).

There is still at least one private hospital in Hong Kong where parents can leave a new-born baby for maybe one or two months so that it can receive the expert and hygienic care of the nursing staff. The service is less prevalent than it was about ten years ago. It currently costs about HK$1,000 per day.

It is interesting to note by way of comparison that Margery Wolf found the same reliance on the 'expert' among women in China in the 1980s. She asked urban women how they felt about their children being in a nursery all day or being looked after by the older generation. The responses were that 'they said they didn't really know anything about taking care of children and grandmother had a lot more experience'. A surgical nurse whose child was in day care said, 'I was trained in medicine, not child care. They are trained in child care'. When I asked about the psychological effect on the infants, the majority of the women seemed puzzled and some explained that 'at that age (until two or three) children don't care who is around as long as they get fed' (M. Wolf 1985:120). This last observation is certainly echoed by what mothers and others have said to me in Hong Kong.

In China the one-child policy is a factor that has affected the way people wish to rear their children. Elisabeth Croll writes that 'parents fear that the single child may be lonely, spoilt and selfish, or may suffer ill-health, an accident or even death' (Croll 1985:231). She goes on to say that the investment in a single child has led to a certain amount of interest among urban families in child development and a demand for 'theoretical knowledge and practical aid in child-rearing'(1985:231). Here too Croll observes the faith vested in the expert:

> Because of their widespread fear that the child will be spoilt and selfish, the demand for child-care outside the family unit has increased in the past four years both because parents want company for their child and because of greater trust in

professional care. In the Evergreen Commune on the outskirts of Beijing] the belief in the superiority of professional care had risen to such heights that many peasants there preferred to place their children in the village kindergarten as weekly boarders than leave them all day with a doting and untrained granny.

(1985:231)

Implicit in this preference is that the affection of the grandmother is of far less value to the child than 'expert' care. It also appears that Chinese women on the mainland, like their Hong Kong counterparts are not disturbed by separation from their very young children. This does not necessarily mean that individual mothers, or even the majority of mothers, may not be deeply distressed by such separation, but it is clearly not a value that is part of the cultural construction of mother-infant relations. (See also Shih Ming Hu 1988).

It is ironic to note that the commitment of women to their work, and the substantial reduction in the number of offspring, which have been instilled in China by socialist ideology in the interests of reconstructing China, have come about in Hong Kong through laisser-faire market forces. (See Gates [1994] for a similar situation in Taipei). A comparative study of expectations of child-minders and child-care facilities in China and in Hong Kong would perhaps reveal many interesting differences and similarities that might be either caused by or occur in spite of the very different political ideologies at play.

WHAT ARE CHILDREN FOR AND WHAT DO THEY NEED?

In a recent survey carried out by a team of Taiwan researchers on behalf of the China Times Weekly on sexual attitudes and behaviour in China and Taiwan, it was found that in Taiwan, 36.2% respondents agreed that the purpose of having children was to continue the lineage, and in China 25.5% said that it was to 'ensure someone to provide for parents when they retire' (South China Morning Post 30/10/93). The Potters, researching in rural Guangdong, state that 'In having children, the villagers see a solution to their wish for care, rather than thinking of themselves as assuming responsibility for another. The child is to care for the parent in the future' (Potter and Potter 1990). Many Hong Kong people would probably also agree with those ideas, although I do not know of any survey or research which has been conducted on this issue.

One could, therefore, characterise the Hong Kong family as 'parent-centred', rather than as 'child- centred'.

Why people in any culture have children is obviously a very complex matter, and even more so in modern times when births can be planned and spaced often with a high degree of success. One of the themes that arises out of this study is that of instrumentality in relation to having children. By instrumentality I mean having children in order to have specific and explicit goals. The age-old preference for sons over daughters is one example of such instrumentality. The preference transcends any personal preference of the mother, as, in many cases, she knows she will be blamed for producing a daughter. Sons are preferred, typically and in the traditional scheme of things, because, on the ideological and religious level, it is they who continue the family line and keep up the worship of the ancestors. On the practical level, it is the sons, and especially the oldest one , who is responsible for the care of his elderly parents, and for whom they will bring in a daughter-in-law who will see to their daily physical needs as well as the more long-term aim of producing grandchildren. The plight of old people who have no sons has often been lamented and is still sympathetically viewed in China. Margery Wolf (1985) gives the example of a couple in China who tragically lose their son in an accident, and who, in spite of the fact that they have a daughter, are given permission to have another child in the hope that it will be a son.

However, although children are thought to be potentially very useful to the family when they have reached adulthood, or at least the ability to work, it would seem that their needs when they are small are regarded as very basic. They need to be fed, kept warm, kept clean, and kept safe from illness and danger.

Few writers have looked at the details of child care (mostly assuming that this is carried out by the mother) or looked closely at how a child is regarded in Chinese culture. Barbara Ward is one who has looked at ideas about children among the Hong Kong villagers with whom she lived in the 1950s (Ward 1985).

M. Wolf has also written about child training in a village in Taiwan in the 1960s (1970:37–62). Her argument is that child training is training for adaptation to the complex of relationships that make up adult family and village life in Taiwan.

In present-day Hong Kong children are expected to attend kindergarten at around 3 years of age, to learn and to do homework. Mothers will say that even very small babies are 'naughty' if they cry or will not sleep. In fact it is the most common response to the question

'How is your baby?'. When adolescent children are enquired after, their parents invariably pronounce them 'lazy' with a shake of the head. Both epithets are a way of being modest about one's children as it is not done to boast about one's own, but it also reflects the high aspirations many parents have of their children's' behaviour and performance.

A consideration of motherhood is inevitably intimately linked with the social construction of the infant, its characteristics and needs and how these change over time. How the infant and child is viewed leads on to how parenting is regarded. As has already been suggested, the Chinese family is parent-centred rather than child-centred. Hence babies and small children adapt to the parents' routine, sometimes to the extent that they are sent to a weekly babyminder, until they are old enough for a kindergarten at two to three years of age, so that they do not disturb it at all. A mundane consequence of this adaptation to the adult lifestyle is that small children routinely go to bed at the same time as their parents, and are to be seen late at night in the streets and in restaurants. Many Chinese parents express astonishment at what they regard as the very early bedtime of English children in the territory.

In the long-term, the structure of the family is such that the child is expected to please the parent, to fulfil certain expectations as it grows up, and finally, to take responsibility for the care of the parents in their old age. This last expectation is to some extent changing in Hong Kong as ideas of economic independence are gaining ground and expressions of intergenerational conflict are coming out into the open. The allocation of government resources to contribute to adequate old age pensions is currently much debated in the Hong Kong Legislative Council.

Chinese writers stress that the emphasis within the family is on the welfare of the group. Given the continuing lack of emphasis on the individual, and especially the individuality of the child, the parenting of infants and small children can be characterised in Hong Kong Chinese culture as protective, and then later on, as the child grows bigger and is expected to take more responsibility for its actions, as directive. In Western culture, I would characterise the *ideal* style of parenthood as interactive. These are, of course, best thought of as emphases rather than as absolute categories. In Western parenting there is also, as there must be, a certain amount of protection, and later on direction. An example of directive behaviour in infancy is shown, however, in the common way of toilet-training. Beatrice Kit-May Hung, in her research on early mother-infant interaction, describes how the mother makes certain different sounds (a hissing sound or a humming sound) when she wants the child to urinate or defecate. Hung comments that unlike the British or American idea which is to help the toddler control his/her own bodily functions, the Chinese idea is that the mother determines when these should happen (Hung 1983).

In Hong Kong Chinese parenting, the lack of emphasis on interaction and communication is lamented in a forthcoming paper based on a survey by Justina Leung, etc. (1994) and others, including Susanna Tsoi who runs courses on parenting (for parents). Tsoi has also published two books. The first is called *A Mother's Personal Jottings* (1991) which sold 3,000 copies in its first edition and over 4000 in its second edition. A second book on sex education *That Which Bewilders A Child* (1992) has sold 6,000 copies and has just been approved for sale in China. Tsoi stresses the need to spend time with children, the need to take a firm stand over issues the parent considers important. She feels that currently Hong Kong parents relate to their children 'on materialistic terms', buying them things at weekends to compensate for the time spent away from them during the week. I queried with her the notion that parenting has taken a downturn in modern times, in view of the fact that modern parents mostly shared their parents with several other siblings. Her answer was that because many Hong Kong parents shared their parents they themselves do not think that their children have the need of intensive parenting. My interpretation is also that the younger parents may not have the model of intensive parenting.

It is notable that there is a good deal of physical distance between parents and children in a Hong Kong Chinese family. Although parents, inevitably, have a good deal of physical contact with very small children, inasmuch as they are carried around a good deal, this is discouraged after the age of five or six, or when the child no longer needs to be carried. Susanna Tsoi agreed with my observation, but had no explanation. She did not disagree however, when I suggested family hierarchy as one possibility, and the extended family with the need to inhibit incest as another. It is an area which would be well worth investigating fully.

EXPECTATIONS OF CHILD CARE

Unlike in the United Kingdom, there is no law in Hong Kong requiring the registration of those who care for fewer than six children for monetary reward. Nor is there a law against leaving small children locked up alone at home, although this topic is the subject of a certain amount of debate in the newspapers and at official levels. As already stated, most mothers did not have a very clear idea of the kind of woman they wished to employ as their child-minder, perhaps preferring to trust the recommendations of friends of relatives, or their own judgement when meeting a potential child-minder.

The Family Welfare Society, a government-subvented body which belongs to the Hong Kong Council of Social Service, has produced three pages of guidelines both for parents and child-minders. The opening recommendation is that parents and child-minder should be clear about all the arrangements before they come to an agreement. This is followed by recommendations about the kind of woman suitable to do the job and her ideal circumstances. She should be healthy, mentally stable, should not have bad habits such as smoking or playing mah-jong, should be patient and enjoy being with children, should be loving and responsible, have a suitable education (this is not defined), and enough time. The second section deals with safety in the home. The emphasis is on a child having a safe place in which to 'learn and rest'. Section three asks how much the potential child-minder knows about children. Caring for the child and teaching him or her are emphasised, as is communicating with the parents about the child. The rest of the section is concerned with giving the child balanced meals, dressing the child in clothing appropriate to the weather, concern with hygiene and safety, talking to the child and trying to understand him or her, administering suitable rewards and punishments so as to maintain a balance between spoiling and excessive severity, giving the child time for work and for play so as encourage his or her own thinking. The fourth section deals with the need for a child to get used to the strange environment in the absence of the parents. Parents and child-minder should arrange that the child meets the child-minder and sees the new environment before going there alone. For her part the child-minder should make sure that she knows about the child's needs and habits, likes and dislikes and fears. The final sections returns to the relationship between the child-minder and the parents, re-emphasising that all expectations and practical arrangements for normal living and emergencies should be clearly understood by both parties. The pamphlet ends by stating in quotation marks that the term for child-minder *doi móuh* means replacing the mother or deputising for the mother.

Much of this is relevant when the child is starting with a child-minder at the age when he or she has already established ways and patterns. Many of the babies of my informants however went to a child-minder when they were from one to a few months old. The pamphlet expresses a common-sense approach to the matter and it would be interesting, although difficult, to find out how much of its advice is adhered to.

The Family Welfare Society also sponsored a report on children who were being looked after by child-minders (1986). The study was motivated by the realisation that although it has been generally known that children are being placed in the care of 'child caring agents e.g. relatives, friends, or persons with whom they have no relationship . . . little is known about the pattern of such care, the factors that determine the parents'choice and the level of satisfaction they have regarding the type of care rendered' (1986:5). The predominant reason for the parents'of the 155 households interviewed placing the child with a child-minder was so that they could both work. Parents interviewed, 57 per cent of whom had secondary education and 7 per cent post-secondary education, were asked to choose among various priorities in child care. The physical health of the child was given as first priority by 70 per cent of the respondents, intellectual development by 36.8 per cent, and love and care by 34.1 per cent (1986:41). It is of course quite possible that 'love and care' are considered as being properly given by the parents and not the child-minder, but in that case the child is required to do without it as an active ingredient in its life for a week at a time. However, the co-ordinator of the research, Diana Mak, writes:

> It is, however, a bit disappointing that so few respondents (53 respondents or 34%) identify "love and care given to the child" as among the first three priorities. One wonders to what extent this is due to the way affection is expressed in the Chinese culture or whether this is due to the unawareness of the respondents of this element as an important attribute to child care. The latter point seems to be supported because the respondents have generally demonstrated a low attention index towards their children in the minder's care.
>
> (1986:120)

By this last comment is meant that many parents do not see the need to visit their children or take them home at weekends. It tended to be factory workers who had lower scores in this area, for which their 'lower education and knowledge in child care' is held responsible (1986:76). Implicit in these observations is the idea that love for one's children is connected to knowledge and educational level rather than being something natural and spontaneous.

TWO HONG KONG WORKING MOTHERS AND
THEIR CHOICE OF CHILD CARE

I shall illustrate the choices made by two Hong Kong mothers with the stories that they told me.

The first one, Agnes, works in a skilled job as a garment pattern cutter for a workshop which makes up samples. I was introduced to her by her boss, an Englishwoman who knew of my research interests. I met Agnes at her workbench during the lunch hour. She was happy to talk and the conversation was in English. She is forty-two, and had twin girls about twenty months old who had been born after their mother had had treatment for fertility after seven years of marriage. When she knew she was having twins she had hoped to have one of either sex. There was no pressure on her to have sons, she said, because her husband was the youngest of four sons and her mother-in-law already had 'lots of grandsons'. She is the second child and eldest sister of two boys and five girls. Her parents are both dead, her mother having died when the twins were nine months old. She had given birth in a private hospital close to where she lives, because of its proximity and because she had 'heard nothing bad about it'. She had the babies by Caesarian section, because of which she had not been able to see them for the first two days as she had been in bed on a drip. But her sister had visited her and seen the babies so that she knew they were normal and healthy and she was not anxious about them. She had not tried to breastfeed them because by the time she had got to see them they had already been given bottles. Anyway she did not think she could manage to breastfeed twins. Her mother-in-law was also against the idea saying that all her children had had canned milk. Agnes had left hospital after seven days but the doctor had suggested that the twins should remain for longer saying that she would find it very tiring to look after them. In the end the babies had stayed in hospital for an extra ten days (at a total cost of over HK$6,000). Agnes had not known why it was thought necessary to keep the babies in hospital and suggested to me that maybe it was for the paediatrician's own purposes (i.e. the fees). She had visited the babies daily and helped to feed them. Once she had returned home she had employed a *pùih yuht*[3] for a month. She had postponed her return to work because she had had difficulty finding good child-minders. The twins are cared for by different people under different arrangements. Twin A comes home every evening and Twin B stays with her minder all week (Agnes' terms). I was interested to know how she had decided which one was to sleep at home and which one to stay at her minder's house. Agnes replied that her sister-in-law had told her that her fourteen year-old daughter said she liked Twin B better because she looked more like her father (i.e. the fourteen year-old's uncle and therefore perhaps more like a member of her family). She then went on to tell me that Twin B was better-looking, although Twin A was not bad looking, and that Twin A had more understanding (*tùhng sih*). None of this added up to how the decision had been made although the fourteen year-old niece's comments seemed in some way to have been influential. Maybe Agnes found it convenient to dissociate herself from the decision. In fact, she told me that she had wanted both twins to board weekly but that her husband had wanted to have one of them at home in the evenings. Many women who are not returning to work give as one reason for this course of action that the husband wants the mother to look after the child.

The minder who looks after one twin all week is her brother-in-law's wife. She is clean and experienced, but Agnes does not like her attitude, and does not think she is very nice. 'Quite mean' she told me. 'She should be content because I take back the baby every holiday' said Agnes. But apparently if she collects the baby after 6 p.m. on Saturday evening the baby-minder is not pleased. The arrangement was initiated by Agnes's husband who is doing business with the baby-minder's husband who is also his younger brother. This is perhaps a case where family connections (and business interests) override the choice of someone whom Agnes might find personally more acceptable. She pays the minder HK$ 3,400 per month plus the cost of milk and nappies which she estimates at about HK$540 per month.

The other twin, Twin A, is looked after close to home by an unrelated minder. She is a woman Agnes knew as a machinist in a factory ten years ago, and whom she ran into by chance again some time ago. She is in her forties. Agnes takes the baby back in the evenings. She pays her HK$2,000 per month.

Twin B will come back to live at home probably next autumn, when she will be nearly three and about to start kindergarten. Agnes does not want the twins to be separated in the long term, she says. They talk to each other a lot and seem happy to see each other at week-ends. Agnes has not decided whether at that point she will give up work, or employ a Filippina maid, or entrust the children to an after school care centre.

Agnes said she was happy to have twins, and she was not planning to have any more children. She also said she was quite happy to have daughters because she thinks it is easier to get on with a son-in-law than a daughter-in-law. She is of the opinion that because daughters will go to work and earn a salary they will be just as good at looking after their mother in her old age as a son.

The other mother, Lai-ying, had just had her first child, a daughter, when I met her. She is twenty-nine and works as a clerk. She gave birth in a charity hospital where my first meeting with her took place. The baby was not with her as she was having light treatment for jaundice. Lai-ying was giving her bottles but said that when they got home she wanted to breastfeed her as she had read that it is better for the baby. She was intending to return to work at the end of her maternity leave. She was planning to find a neighbour to look after the baby in the daytime and anticipated that this would cost about HK$2,000 a month.

Three weeks later, in May, my assistant and I went to visit her at her privately-owned flat in a not very modern building in North Point in the middle of a busy street market selling vegetables, fish and other fresh and dried produce. The flat was very small and dark and the room where we talked was piled high with files and bits of dismantled electronics. The air-conditioner was on. Decorating the wall were large, poster size, soft-focus photographs of Lai-ying in a white wedding dress. These were lit up by spot-lights. Dressed in pyjamas, four years after her wedding, the Lai-ying who greeted us provided quite a contrast to the implied romance of the photographs. Her sister, who normally did part-time domestic work, but who was currently without work was staying with her for the month to look after her. The *mùhn yuht* banquet (held one month after a baby's birth) was to be the following Sunday and Lai-ying was looking forward to it as after that she would be free, she told us, from the restrictions of the *chóh yuht*. She would be able to drink soft drinks and eat ice-cream again. Currently an experienced neighbour was helping to bath the baby. Not for money, out of neighbourliness, I was told. Lai-ying was due to return to work on 25 May, and at that time the baby would go to friends in Kowloon for the week and return home at week-ends. It was going to cost HK$3,200 per month plus the cost of milk and nappies. In response to my asking how she felt about the weekly absence, she replied that she had no choice because she had to work in order to earn some money. She preferred to go back to work, she said, as a baby is very troublesome. She added that she would rather have found someone to look after the baby in the day-time but that she had been unable to find anyone to do so. Having a baby is so much trouble that she is not sure she wants another one.

Her sister joined in the conversation and told us that she had not worked for two years after her own son had been born ten years ago. She had looked after him herself and then at the age of two he had gone to a nursery to encourage him to get on with other children and to get knowledge from books. She had not enjoyed looking after him, she said, but she had had no choice as she had had no work at that time and therefore no income with which to pay someone to do it for her.

CONCLUSIONS

It can be seen that the 'nurturant fostering' practised by some Hong Kong families, bears little resemblance to the model put forward by E. Goody or by Carsten. It seems to be resorted to purely as a practical arrangement that benefits the parents' life-style. It could also be, as has been suggested to me (Evans 1995 personal communication) that the distancing of the parents in this way makes the child easier to control because of a deep-seated fear of abandonment. On the whole, those mothers I talked to who can afford paid baby-care would rather return to work. This is not to say, as Tam has pointed out to me (personal communication 1995) that there are not undoubtedly women whose priority it is to spend a good deal of time with their child for the first few years of its life, and who feel torn and guilty if they do not do so. Further research is needed to find out what ideas and values inform their decision and influence their feelings in this direction.

At present in Hong Kong it is not difficult to find a middle-aged housewife whose children are grown-up or at secondary school to take on the job. For some reasons it seems to be harder to find a daily care-taker. However it is possible that the mothers actually (secretly?) prefer to have the baby away for the whole week. That way they do not have to look after it in the evenings when they return home tired after work. Nor is their sleep disturbed at night. In professional families where there is a resident maid, it is commonly the maid who attends to the baby at night. It is perhaps significant that it is fathers, who, although they play with their babies and clearly enjoy being with them, play a minor part in the fundamentals of child care, who seem to want the baby to spend more time at home. It would be interesting to know more about what fathers say about child-care arrangements and how much influence they have over the decision. As I did not meet fathers I cannot comment on how strongly the fathers may have wished to keep the baby at home, nor how much the issue is one of gender politics. (See Gates [1994] on how couples in Taipei negotiate the number of children born.

The relationship between the experiencing of emotion and the ways in which it is expressed and acted upon is complex. What the long-term consequences are of the baby-care arrangements discussed above and of the mother's attitude to her own identity and of the mother's and society's perception of the needs of the infant is undoubtedly also a very complex matter and well beyond the scope of this study. It could also be asked to what extent has many professional women's relative lack of emotional (if this is indeed the case) and practical involvement enabled them to do well in their careers and to become more self-confident and satisfied individuals. That these areas should be researched is without much doubt.

NOTES

1 This paper is based on a chapter from my doctoral thesis (1994) and forms part of a wider study of pregnancy and childbirth in Hong Kong. For the most part, my informants were about two hundred new mothers whom I interviewed in person (from January 1991 to June 1992) with the help of a Cantonese female assistant in the maternity wards of three hospitals (chosen to represent intakes of low-income, middle-income and higher-income women). We subsequently visited about fifty of these women in their own homes for further discussions about a month after the birth of the baby.

2 A call to the Senior Information Officer of the Social Welfare Department Public Relations Office ascertained that there are currently day places (8 a.m. to 6 p.m.) for 34,000 children aged from 2–6 in government and government subvented day care centers. These charge around HK$1,300 a month. They do not cater for babies so would not therefore help the mothers who return to work at that stage.

3 A woman employed especially to look after the mother and baby in the first month after childbirth. They are paid a good deal more than a regular domestic helper. They seem to be quite scarce in modern Hong Kong and very few women in my study had recourse to one.

REFERENCES CITED

Aries, Philippe
 1960   Centuries of Childhood. Harmondsworth: Penguin Books.
Badinter, Elisabeth M.
 1981   The Myth of Motherhood: An Historical View of the Maternal Instinct. Souvenir Press.
Ba Jin
 1931   Family. New York: Anchor Books, Doubleday and Co.
Birns, B. and Dale F. Hay et al
 1988   The Different Faces of Motherhood. New York: Plenum Press.
Bowlby, J.
 1953   Child Care and the Growth of Love. Harmondsworth: Pelican Books.

Carsten, J.
  1991   Children In Between: Fostering and the Process of Kinship on Pulau Langkawi, Malaysia. Man 26:425–443.
Croll, Elisabeth, Delia Davin and Penny Kane et al
  1985   China's One-child Family Policy. London: Macmillan.
Evans, Grant
  1995   Personal Communication.
Family Welfare Society
  1986   An Exploratory Study on Parents' Choice and Satisfaction on Childminding in Hong Kong. Hong Kong.
Field, C. Elaine and Flora M. Baber
  1973   Growing Up in Hong Kong. Hong Kong: Hong Kong University Press.
Fildes, Valerie
  1986   Breasts, Bottles and Babies. Edinburgh: Edinburgh University Press.
Gates, Hill
  1993   Cultural Support for Birth Limitation. In Chinese Families in the Post-Mao Era. D. Davis and S.Harrell, ed. Berkeley: University of California Press.
Goody, Esther N.
  1982   Parenthood and Social Reproduction. Cambridge: Cambridge University Press.
Ho Suk-ching
  1984   Women's Labour Force Participation in Hong Kong, 1971–1981. Journal of Marriage and the Family 46(4):947–953.
Hong Kong Census and Statistics Department
  1991   Hong Kong 1991 Population Census Summary Results. Hong Kong.
  1993   Hong Kong Social and Economic Trends 1982–1992. Hong Kong.
Hung, Beatrice K.M.
  1983   Mother-Infant Interaction and the Infant's Social Development in the First Half Year of Life. Unpubl. M.Phil dissertation. University of Hong Kong.
Koo, Linda
  1993   Personal Communication.
Macfarlane, Alan
  1986   Marriage and Love in England: Modes of Reproduction 1300–1840. Oxford: Blackwell.
Mause, de L.
  1974   The History of Childhood. New York: Psychohistory Press.
Potter, Shulamit Heins and Jack M. Potter
  1990   China's Peasants: The Anthropology of a Revolution, Cambridge University Press, Cambridge, UK.
Pruitt, Ida
  1945   A Daughter of Han: The Autobiography of a Chinese Working Woman. Stanford University Press.
Shih Ming Hu
  1988   The Chinese Family: Continuity and Change. In The different Faces of Motherhood. B. Birns and D. F.Hay, ed. New York: Plenum Press. South China Morning Post. Hong Kong.

Stone, Lawrence
  1977 The Family, Sex and Marriage in England 1500–1800. London: Weidenfeld & Nicolson.
Tam, Maria S.M.
  1995 Personal Communication.
Tsoi, Susanna
  1991 A Mother's Personal Jottings. Hong Kong: private publication.
  1992 That Which Bewilders the Child. Hong Kong: private publication.
Ward, Barbara E.
  1985 Through Other Eyes. Hong Kong: Chinese University Press.
Wiesner, M.E.
  1993 Women and Gender in Early Modern Europe. Cambridge: Cambridge University Press.
Wolf, A. and C.S. Huang
  1980 Marriage and Adoption in China,1845–1945. Stanford: Stanford University Press.
Wolf, Margery
  1970 Child Training and the Chinese Family. *In* Family and Kinship in Chinese Society, M. Freedman, ed. Stanford: Stanford University Press.
  1972 Women and the Family in Rural Taiwan. Stanford: Stanford University Press.
  1985 Revolution Postponed. Stanford: Stanford University Press.

RELIGION AND BELIEFS

10

TRADITIONAL VALUES AND MODERN MEANINGS IN THE PAPER OFFERING INDUSTRY OF HONG KONG

Janet Lee Scott

Over the past few years, an increasing number of newspaper and magazine articles, as well as television and radio programs concerned with local affairs, have devoted much attention to the question of the preservation of Hong Kong's cultural heritage. While much of this attention is directed to the protection of antiquities (monuments and archaeological sites), increasing concern has been expressed over the survival of traditional arts, crafts, and lifeways. It would appear that an ever-increasing number of citizens are convinced of the importance of what they term traditional Chinese culture (in all its manifestations) to modern Hong Kong life and are arguing strenuously for its preservation or revival. As suggested elsewhere in this volume, this may be seen as symptom of Hong Kong's modernity. However, we need to understand the living context in which an item of material culture, an element of belief, a set of actions, or a historical monument is set, and for this what is required is an understanding of the meaning attributed to these things by participants. Indeed, without such a context, the significance to modern life of the entire complex referred to as 'traditional Chinese culture' cannot be evaluated.

Some insights may be gained by a brief examination of one facet of the most 'traditional' of areas – the realm of ritual and worship and the repertoire of material culture that complements it. More specifically, it would be helpful to focus attention on two familiar Hong Kong scenes, two enduring realms of meaning – the world of death rituals and paper offerings for the departed. In Hong Kong, offerings for the dead are characterized by their abundance and great variety in form and style. Large amounts continue to be made and burned to the departed. Why should this practice continue? One interpretation suggests that contemporary urban Chinese are motivated by a desire for reciprocal enrichment; great giving to ancestors results in great receiving on the part of the descendants. It is also said that the variety of offerings reflects the materialistic orientation believed to be characteristic of the society as a whole. However, this paper will explore a parallel explanation that connects this practice to another realm of motivation, one that may then allow further reflection on the first concern – the place of traditional thought and practice in the modern Chinese world.[1]

FUNERALS AND DEATH RITUALS

Recent scholarly efforts have re-examined and re-emphasized the importance of death ritual for the understanding of the design of Chinese society. They have concluded that the underlying structure of funerary rituals, with their accompanying elements associated with settling the soul after death, were (and are) conducive to cultural unity across the Chinese social landscape. With the acceptance of a sequence of culture-wide funeral rituals, ethnic groups could practice a wide variety of burial customs, yet continue to identify what they did as 'Chinese' (Watson and Rawski 1988). As Watson observes, 'The system allowed for a high degree of variation within an overarching structure of unity' (1988:16). For our purposes, gifts and materials offered to the dead seem to be a most significant part of the the funeral ritual sequence and the rituals of commemoration which follow. While food offerings may be both abundant and various in form and complex in meaning (Thompson 1988, Ahern 1973), there are other goods and offerings that are normally made to the departed. It would seem from all this that funeral customs are not only a most meaningful complex for the understanding of human behavior, but that funeral offerings, an integral part of such customs, are themselves of great significance. To better comprehend the nature of the funeral offerings and appreciate their significance to the discussion of tradition and contemporary Chinese identity, a brief overview should be made of the world of paper offerings currently available in Hong Kong.

THE WORLD OF PAPER OFFERING

Residents of Hong Kong and short-term visitors alike sometimes notice, at the curbside or at street corners, tall metal containers full of ashes, charred sticks, and the fluttering bits of colored paper – the remains of items recently burned. The visitor to Hong Kong may be puzzled and wonder what the original objects were, how they appeared before being consigned to the flames, and, even more likely, why such things were being burned at all. Had the observer arrived earlier at the scene, however, he or she would not only have observed small groups of people watching over the burning. By inquiring further, the observer would quickly come to know what residents already understand – that the individuals concerned with the proper burning of the materials are the close relatives of someone recently deceased. They will also have learned that the items piled on the street next to the ovens will be burned as paper offerings, for use by the deceased in the world that they inhabit after death.

These items, the large and diverse collection of items for the dead, are but one part of an important and complex category of Chinese material culture – the paper offerings purchased for offering to gods, to ghosts, and to the ancestors (for the classic discussion on these categories, see Wolf 1974). These items can best be seen in context of the religious observances characterizing the ritual cycle of the lunar year. Overall, there are a great number of occasions for which paper offerings of some form are appropriate. While individual worshippers understand and conform to the general expectations of worship accompanying both events of the ritual year and the more unusual events, each worshipper may make offerings according to his or her level of devotion and individual perceptions of the occasion and of what and how much is appropriate to offer.

A visit to any of the urban retail shops selling paper offerings will reveal a great and bewildering variety of beautiful items,[2] often elegantly designed and crafted, always colorful. A typical paper shop is crammed full with materials used in worship. From floor to ceiling, wall shelves on all sides of these shops are stacked with the different varieties of paper offerings arranged according to the festival or occasion in which they are used, or by whether the item is one of those for everyday use, or one needed for a more rarely occuring purpose. The floor space in front of the shelves usually accomodates larger stacks of hand-assembled worshipping packs, or open cardboard boxes or bins overflowing with bulkier or pre-packed items. Even the ceiling space cannot be wasted and is put to use for the hanging of paper clothing bundles, small items modeled on bamboo frames, plastic bags filled with packages of gold or silver money, circular lucky basins trimmed with gold paper money, and other items. During the weeks preceding the New Year, the ceiling also supports a dazzling, eye-catching array of the complex and beautiful golden flowers, or *gām fā*. In even the smallest paper shop, a considerable amount of the full paper repertoire may be viewed, along with stacks of the many varieties of incense, incense burners, lotus lamps and old-style red candles, painted and three-dimensional images of dieties, prayer beads, new style red household-sized burners for offerings, and other worship-related items also for sale. Hong Kong paper offering shops present a true feast of color and design, and it is not surprising that visitors and tourists are tempted to venture in to see what is available.[3]

Most shops serve a regular clientele of local residents, providing materials for their daily worshipping needs and for observing the special celebrations which highlight the year-long ritual cycle. While not all customers are equally knowledgable about the background and use of these items,[4] nor are they always fully conversant of all details of their meaning and iconography, it is correct to say that most purchasers understand their general use and their significance. Most also feel that, as an integral part of worship, offerings should be made and used. Samples of worshippers and shopkeepers all agreed that such offerings were to be used regularly. 'Regularly' in this context means that the 'average' worshipper or customer purchases on a recurring basis, the exact time (perhaps every two weeks) depending on the amount used. The amount used depends, in turn, on the individual offering style and personal habits of the worshipper. Regular worshippers purchase proportionately more supplies during the periods immediately preceding major events of the lunar calendar, such as the New Year, *Ching Mihng*, and the Yùh Nàahn Festival. For example, during the Ching Mihng festival, customers purchase additional packages of clothing and other personal items to send to the deceased.

THE VARIETIES OF PAPER OFFERINGS

The paper offerings for the dead are fabricated in workshops still operating in Hong Kong as independent companies, or as an adjoining sections of an established retail shop selling paper items for everyday worship. Most of the offerings for the dead form part of a larger division – what informants refer to as 'pitched' items – within the full repertoire of paper offerings. Pitched items are those built up on a frame of bamboo strips covered with paper.[5] Each retail shop or workshop prepares and has printed a list of their products from which the customer may choose. If unclear about these offerings, customers can ask advice from the master or owner, may observe items in the process of manufacture in the shop, or consult a photo album with pictures of items crafted in previous orders. The current repertoire of paper offerings as grave goods, or gifts for the dead, is both variable and complex, but may be divided into two large categories.[6]

The first comprises what could be termed the 'basic set'. This includes items made in a style reminiscent of an earlier period of Chinese history-perhaps the middle to late Qing or early Republican-when the design of furniture, clothing, and other everyday items was markedly different from today's items. Other items in this set seem to be created from beliefs about the soul, what it requires, and what it encounters in its travels; again, it is difficult to determine from which period such beliefs have been taken. While the actual number of items listed therein varies somewhat from shop to shop, there is considerable agreement on a list of approximately ten to thirteen items. For example, one workshop listed the basic set as the following: A dragon tablet, a pair of items consisting of the immortal crane and its accompanying catkin fan, one set consisting of a red and a white fan, one bathing pan, a package of bathing clothes, a pair of mountains in gold and silver, a sedan chair, and the image of the hell-breaking spirit. Also included are: the platform for looking back on one's home village, a pair of male and female servants, a pair of bridges-one gold and one silver, a Chinese-style safe to hold personal items for the deceased, a red cabinet for storing clothing, a car, a Western-style multi-floored house with a garden, a pair of storage chests for the gold and silver money , a television set, and an additional set of a seven foot gold bridge and a silver bridge. Many of these items are crafted to conform to old fashioned images. For example, the male servants are often dressed in Qing or Republican era costumes; often the grey or blue long jackets with stand-up collars, worn with matching trousers, black cloth shoes and a Western-style hat. Female servants are attired in the side-closing jackets, trimmed with paper rickrack, trousers, with their hair done up in chignons.

Other shops had more or less extensive product lists. In addition, while informants never suggested that any of the items lacked significance or importance, these owners of workshops and retail outlets understood that not everyone could afford to purchase all the items listed. While not excessively expensive, a full set of items might be too much for very poor families to offer.[7] Accordingly, families need not make a full purchase; only certain of the items available would be considered to be of greatest importance. For example, refering to the preceding offerings list, only the first seven items were considered by the shop master to be of greatest importance. It should also be noted that this workshop placed the house and the car on the 'second' list of items to secure; most place these on the first list of necessary items and most customers do order at least one house and one car for the deceased. Similarly, a number of shops would not list the television set as so important, but some do. This indicates some variations of opinion among the shops or workshops as to the arrangement of items which appear on the list, and further, on the content of the item list itself. The reasoning behind this is not completely clear and needs further study; certainly, the items which are associated with the rituals held during the funeral are of great significance. It is also clear that there is some ambiguity about how 'old' things can be; cars are not usually thought of as ancient artifacts. However, the car can be viewed as simply a modern substitution for the sedan chair, which is itself an earlier representation of an even older theme of providing transportation for the dead in the other world.

In addition to the basic set just described, there is a second large category of items which could be termed the 'items of everyday use'. This category contains a number of sub-divisions. First, there are the special items that are made up to accomodate the particular wishes of the customers. These might include the life-sized, or nearly life-sized replicas of what the deceased possessed in life, what he or she desired to possess in the otherworld, or what the family of the deceased wished to provide. Most often, this category includes additional cars, houses and other buildings or even, although more rarely, animals. All of the shops were prepared as well to make up variations of the Street of the Dead, an actual city street made up with all the shops and places necessary for continuance of ordinary, everyday life. It is clear that families concerned with the comfort of their deceased family members, and possessed of suitable finances, can order anything that can be thought of – this category of paper offerings being infinite in content.

A second sub-division, and a more common section of this second category, is the cluster of what could be called 'daily necessities'. This category is extremely popular, with many retail paper shops displaying considerable numbers of prefabricated examples packed and ready for purchase. Such items are to be burned at the end of the official funeral observances or later, during other festivals such as Chìng Mìhng. It includes three identifiable groupings. First, there are the various electrical appliances and gadgets, including fans, rice cookers, television sets, telephones, VCRs, irons, computers, calculators, refrigerators and so on. A second grouping consists of paper clothing (of prefabricated or custom design), underwear, hats, shoes, handbags, schoolbags, jewelry and all manner of items for personal use.[8] A final grouping takes up the items of personal finance – the check books, savings books, ETC cards for the withdrawal of money from money machines, and credit cards, all drawn on the Bank of Hell. The credit cards, it should be noted, bear the image of the God of Hell, and in color and design are very similar to the American Express card; providing an otherworldly twist to their advertising slogan, 'Don't leave home without it'.

This sub-division of daily necessities is the most elastic and ever-expanding in its content; whenever a new item of technology, or a new and improved version of an existing item, appears, it is made up and ready to supplement, or even replace, the existing version of the same item reflecting an earlier style or technology. The flexibility shown by this sub-division is understandable as a process of adaptation within a category, in which the general content is retained, but the specific item or items within may be modified or even eliminated. This process applies, for example, to some of the items in the classical category of the basic set. The houses and cars, found in the basic set but of obviously modern form, still reflect the general category of housing and transportation, categories of grave offering with an ancient history, and as such are appropriately placed within this sub-set. Nevertheless, the introduction of new items and replacement of the old is definitely more marked in the daily necessities sub-division, where technological and stylistic change is more rapid. For example, while standard desk telephones have been available for some time, retail shops have begun to offer mobile phones. A similar situation held for the replicas of the battery-operated calculators, which were replaced in some shops by full-sized replicas of computers, and for the old style stereophonic systems, supplanted by working (i.e., containing moving parts) examples of compact disc players. Even clothing design, which in appearance is somewhat more conservative, shows the effects of this change; shops display high heeled shoes and the latest in sports shoes (complete with real or string shoelaces) alongside traditional cloth (but made of paper) slippers.

It should be clear from the preceding that paper offerings for the dead consist of a large and complex sub-category of the total repertoire of paper offerings. As a genre of material culture, it is a sub-category characterized by great elasticity of its boundaries and a seemingly-infinite capacity to absorb new elements of material culture, and their accompanying changes in technology. It encompasses the most up-to-date items, yet also contains and preserves the more old-fashioned elements embodying in their form and meaning allusions to times gone by. Yet, with all this variety, there is little tension or contradiction among the objects, the combination of which apparently troubles none of the purchasers, who consider the objects quite proper, both socially and ritually. What are we to make of this combination – is this a reworking of traditional culture into a new vehicle for the satisfaction of contemporary needs? And, does this repertoire of paper offerings for the dead provide any useful insights into what things are significant to the role of tradition and the maintenance of 'Chineseness' in the Hong Kong context?

OFFERING CONTENT

Evaluating the design and content of the paper offerings for the dead calls to mind two preliminary observations. The first is whether the common contrast 'East' and 'West', an overarching feature of discourses on Hong Kong life – discussed in the Introduction to this volume – is of any value in this context. It seems clear from purchasers' behavior that, in this regard, there is no serious contradiction, because according to shopkeepers, their customers purchase (for eventual burning) all new items with little hesitation. They do not think of them as being divided along an East-West axis, or even as 'Western' at all, for items adapted from both sources are subsumed under the overriding category of 'proper offering', and are understood as such by the purchasers. As the repertoire has for some time included items of clearly imported technology, the allusions to westernization and modernization are there, but do not seem to be of special importance for understanding consumer acceptance.

Secondly, in the world of paper offerings for the dead, traditional patterns, while well represented, cannot be characterized as totally conservative and resistent to new items. The old-fashioned paper offerings for the dead, represented by the anciently-attired servants, the silver and gold bridges, and the cranes, are in one sense never really at risk. They can comfortably coexist with newer items because these classical elements of the paper offerings for the dead are firstly, offered as part of the funeral rituals performed at regular intervals after death, and as such are set temporally and functionally within a somewhat different frame than are the electrical appliances and other items in the category of everyday goods. The classical items are part of the rituals to settle the spirit of the dead within the underworld, and thus, are still vital. The items of everyday use are offered regularly thereafter for the continued comfort of and use by the dead (although it appears that some purchasers burn some of them with the classical items burned at the funeral rituals). Thus divided, the different categories of items satisfy demands of different stages of the process of the funeral and are equally necessary, but are not in conflict. It is also clear that, under the heading of 'proper offerings', modern items of technology may be transformed and provided with a new identity and meaning as grave goods. The larger categories of items generally remain intact while what changes is the form and variety of items within the category. Very old categories of offerings may then be retained, with their specific contents altered, a process which perhaps continues to echo Watson's insight into how the system allowed for a 'high degree of variation within an overarching structure of unity' (1988:16).

It would seem that this transformation of new items into proper grave offerings has been effective; even those long dead accept these items, just as the living residents of Hong Kong are quick to adapt to, and use, all manner of new technologies. In this sense, the continuity of the dead and the living – long stressed by observers as an element of funeral belief and one which stresses social continuity – is again maintained in the attitude of those making these offerings to the dead.

SPIRITUAL MATERIALISM AND CONSPICUOUS CONSUMPTION

However, is all this simply a reflection of a 'culture of affluence', as one Hong Kong scholar describes it (Chan 1994), the predictable results of a form of spiritual materialism or a Hong Kong reformulation of the old adage into, 'You can take it with you' (even if you never had it in the first place)? This 'driven by consumerism' interpretation of the materials requires some consideration. Many studies on Hong Kong life have emphasized the importance of material values among the population (for example, Hayes 1975; Mitchell 1969; Chaney 1971). Speaking of Lee, Cheung and Cheung's 1979 study of life satisfaction, Lau Siu-kai observed, 'Lee, Cheung and Cheung (1979), for example, found that the degree of life satisfaction among their Chinese respondents was positively associated with the level of material well-being enjoyed by them. Furthermore, this relationship was independent of sex, age, and educational status, thus attesting to its all-pervasive nature' (Lau

1982:69). Lau himself devised the phrase 'the fetishism of material wealth', explaining its rise in terms of the conditions of the original immigrants, the commercialization of *Gwóngdùng*, the lack of moral constraints in a migrant society, and the absence of other channels for self advancement (Lau 1982:69–70).

Whether materialism is a key concept in understanding the dynamics of contemporary Hong Kong society is highly debatable and outside the scope of this paper, but for the purposes of examining the paper funeral offerings it must be given some attention. It has long been understood that Chinese funerals are complicated and expensive affairs; along with marriage and birth, they are one of the critical rites of passage demanding proper observance. This is true not only in Imperial China but also in contemporary Chinese societies. While earlier accounts make clear the financial burden funerals imposed on the family of the deceased, a reference to the situation in the modern state of Singapore may be instructive. 'One of the most striking features about Chinese death rituals in Singapore is the astronomical sum of money spent to ensure their performance. It is not uncommon for families to spend the equivalent of $20,000 to $30,000 to enact these rituals. The average family spends between $10,000 and $20,000. Even poorer Chinese families desire and attempt to make the death rituals as elaborate as possible' (Tong 1993:130). In Hong Kong, funerals can also be quite expensive, with a custom-built Chinese style coffin costing as much as HK$800,000. It is not inconceivable for the wealthy to spend in excess of one million Hong Kong dollars.[9] In short, funerals could be seen, along with weddings, as amazing examples of conspicuous consumption.

If for the moment it is accepted that Chinese funerals are, by their nature, expensive, then paper offerings should also be affected. First, in terms of sheer quantity and variety, it is clear that much is already available, new items are being added, and the potential for more is there. The price for a basic set has varied, from roughly HK$1,000–2,000 in 1989 to HK$4,000–5,000 in 1995. Of course, the price for a single funeral set is quite variable, and has no set upper limit due to the potential for special orders and custom-made items. As said earlier, what limits there may be would be subject only to the value placed on labor and the quality of raw materials. Hong Kong residents, increasingly affluent, are also able to purchase more and finer items for the departed, to the extent that the dead could theoretically live in the underworld even more luxuriously than they did during their lives on earth. Noting again the common practice among paper offerings workshops of refering customers to photo albums of previously ordered items, it is also possible that this practice acts as a subtle impetus, not only to the continuing introduction of new items into the repertoire, but also for the influencing of customers to have fabricated what others already have – a spiritual form of 'keeping up with'.

Hence, the increasing elaboration of offerings may have much to do with a general acceptance of social expectations of heavy spending and conspicuous consumption – an influence from materialism and the culture of consumption on the conduct of funerals and the choosing of funeral offerings. For example, the purchasers may be motivated by the desire for public display of family wealth or for praise from observers noting the lavish displays of offerings to be burned. On the one hand, while it is clear that purchasers of paper offerings do not do so for their own use (no matter how elaborately offerings are made, or how much they cost the purchaser, paper offerings absolutely cannot be worn or used by the living), the objects are, nevertheless, on display for a period of time before burning, and in rural areas may be moved in a procession to the burning site (Hase 1984:158), giving observers ample time to note the quality and quantity of the offerings, relative to the status of the individual being buried. This practice has also been noted in Singapore: 'These items are put on display and burned in open spaces, in full view of the public, demonstrating the virtue of the family in offering elaborate sacrifices, and thereby enhancing their own social status' (Tong 1993:149). It has also been observed that individual family members may wish to take photographs to remember what was offered, or to send to relatives for their approval.[10] In the urban areas of Hong Kong, there is less, if any, practice of parading items, but passers-by can, if they chance upon the burning, observe the number and quality of items to be burned.

THE QUESTION OF CARE

Despite the persuasiveness of the preceding line of inquiry, an equally, if not more promising parallel explanation for the persistence of paper offerings lies in the deeply-rooted belief about the care due to ancestors. 'The Chinese believe in a future state somewhat similar to that existing on earth, and therefore treat their dead with a view to preparing them for the exigencies of the next world and supplying them with the various articles of luxury and necessity which they trust will be translated in the spirit land for the use of the manes-or ghost of the deceased-by the modern process of burning paper offerings of such articles' (Williams

1976:109–110). This conception implies a view of the underworld wherein such articles have a place, not simply as objects, but as necessary foundations for the comfort and succor of the departed. No matter how small or how large the family fortune, how minimal or how advanced the level of education, family members of the deceased will endeavor to provide materials for the comfort of their departed loved ones. As seen, retail paper shops sell a wide variety of materials designed to ensure a comfortable life for the deceased. For example, families can purchase full sets of clothing in every style, from formal to sports clothes, complete with paper underwear. Shops now have available pre-pack sets of items for personal grooming (including toothpaste, toothbrush, and glass), adornment (sets with watch, rings, and earrings), and relaxation (including paper tea sets, and packets with paper replicas of cognac, Coca Cola, and the glasses in which to drink them). The sum of these items, when combined with the items already described, suggests a high level of concern for the comfort of the departed, as well as a desire to reproduce as carefully as possible their original living environment. Providing for the dead, in short, still exerts a powerful influence on Hong Kong residents. Informants have made clear their beliefs that they would feel uneasy without giving paper offerings. That the demand is still strong is also reflected in the comments of many of my respondents, masters of the craft, who believed that the trade in creating these objects were not in any immediate danger. As one explained, 'A bit over ten years ago, I had the thought that maybe we couldn't keep working any more after another ten years because these items might not be so necessary. But now, ten years after I wondered about that, I can't manage all the orders I get'.

Yet, a further question remains. Is it possible that family members are burning great and variable amounts of paper offerings not only for the care of the dead, but also for the care of the living-in short, are these material benefits reappearing in another form? The giving of gifts, the burning of grave goods to the departed, is generally portrayed as an extension of the belief in the continuity of the ties between the living and the dead, a belief already described as a key element of Chinese funeral ideology. Not only has emphasis been placed on these ties, but even more importantly, on their reciprocal nature. As Watson has observed:

> Closely associated with these ideas of social continuity is the final, and some might say the most important, feature of the Chinese ideological domain: the idea of exchange between the living and the dead. Death does not terminate relationships of

reciprocity among Chinese, it simply transforms these ties and often makes them stronger. A central feature of Chinese funerals and postburial mortuary practices is the transfer of food, money, and goods to the deceased . . . . In return the living espect to receive certain material benefits, including luck, wealth, and progeny.

(Watson 1988:9)

Similar observations have been made by scholars investigating the link between the making of funeral offerings and the confirmation of legal heirs and inheritance. The transfer of goods is critical, in that it not only satisfies the obligation to provide for the deceased, but at the same time ensures that the givers-the potential heirs of the deceased-are able to claim their rights to inherit the property of the deceased (Johnston 1910, Ahern 1973). Further, the giving of offerings may have a beneficial effect on the status of the ancestor himself, for offerings proclaim the ancestor to be a 'property-owning spirit, as a person without property cannot conceivably bercome an ancestor' (Tong 1993:145).

However, the offering of goods is not only efficacious for the claiming of rights to inherit and for the ancestor to be deemed capable of providing an inheritance, but may also affect the nature, content and value of the inheritance itself, in both its material and nonmaterial dimensions. An interesting depiction of this sentiment may be found in Tong Chee Kiong's analysis of contemporary Singaporean funerals, in which it is understood (at least privately) by the mourners that a number of benefits may be obtained by correct management of death:

I suggest that what is important is not simply the inheritance of the property of the deceased, but also the potential for greater benefits that motivate the descendants to spend so much money. It is believed that by converting the deceased into a rich ancestor, the now well-off ancestor will see fit, and is in fact expected, to return the favour and reward descendants with even more wealth.

(1993:153)

This line of thought, emphasizing the (perhaps privately or uncon-sciously-held) view that enriching the ancestors enriches the descendants and that providing for the ancestors 'pays off', is most persuasive and does allow for a clearer understanding of the amount of paper offerings given to the dead. However, to fully comprehend the Hong Kong experience, a parallel explanation, that of 'ethical

235

imperatives superior to egocentric motivation' (Tong 1993:154) must be explored.

The responses of my urban informants suggest that for them, enriching the dead provides benefits, but not ones that only allow them to gain materially or socially. What happens is that, by providing for the departed through grave goods, the giver is satisfying the demands of filial piety, one most important aspect of social virtue in Confucian thought. There are ample indications that this thinking has far from disappeared in modern Chinese contexts, including that of Hong Kong. For example, in social surveys conducted in 1985 and 1986, Lau Siu-kai and Kuan Hsin-chi discovered that a very high percentage of the population (87.6% in the 1985 sample) either strongly agreed or agreed that the first thing necessary to ensure a good society was to have everyone practicing filial piety. In both surveys, respondents were adamant that care of parents was of primary importance (Lau and Kuan 1988:59). While in the same surveys, repondents displayed more ambiguity regarding their behavior and obligations towards other relatives, such results suggest the continuing strength of the concept of filial piety. Similar results were obtained in a later social survey of 1990, in which the majority of respondents (56.1%) agreed that children must support their parents (Lee 1992:22). Indeed, numerous authors would affirm *the concept* of filial piety, and the resulting emphasis on providing parental care and respect, to be of greatest importance, not only for the continuation of Chinese social life, but for life in the modern world overall.

Overwhelmingly, my respondents declared that burning paper offerings to the ancestors was important. Most comments fell into five categories: that providing such offerings was a long-standing Chinese practice, that one needed to show respect to the ancestors, that providing offerings expressed devotion and respect and reflected the sincerity of the person making the offering, and that the practice allowed for psychological comfort or the easing of one's heart. As one lady expressed it, 'Offerings are necessary to show our sincerity and devoutness and the ancestors need it. We must respect them and help them to have a better life'. The emphasis on a better life is the key. The primary motivation for burning so many items, and for continuing to send new and up-to-date versions of items previously offered, is that families want the dead to be comfortable in the other world, that they want the dead to have the kind of life they enjoyed while living. Indeed, the enriching of the departed, the efforts to enable them to live well beyond the grave, is a manifestation of family members wanting the best for their departed kin. Individuals take care of their relatives, especially their parents, while they are living, and provide the latest in comforts for them as they can. Why should they not do the same after these relatives depart for the next world?

Further, no matter how important these offerings were considered to be, the majority of respondents also declared that the ancestors would not necessarily bless them more if they gave more offerings. That is, they saw no automatic or necessary link between the amount of offerings rendered and the nature of benefits to be obtained, nor did they perceive any relationship between the quality or the costliness of the offerings and the level of benefits to be gained, if any. In fact, a number of informants were perplexed that such an idea could be held; some vaguely remembered hearing of such motivation, but did not believe it. Even further, respondents saw no direct relationship between offering gifts to the ancestors and obtaining any benefits whatsoever; their explanations indicate that a majority had delinked the two issues.[11] This de-emphasis on the potential for gain on the part of the one making the offerings is also echoed in the responses of the minority of respondents who felt it was not necessary to give paper offerings at all; their views were that the state of mind was most important and only small, simple items like flowers or incense were enough to reflect this. The giving of offerings was seen as vitally important, unquestionably necessary, to the majority of respondents, but not because so doing would influence the ancestors to provide more benefits, or any benefits at all.

What emerges from respondents' comments is their sense of the rightness of providing material support to the departed. While this is done for the purpose of providing a comfortable existence for the departed, the giver is also comforted when giving, the act of giving itself springing from the intent, the state of mind of the giver. As informants explain, this 'state of one's heart' is most important and takes one into a far different realm from that of status seeking, or the expectation of gain.

RETHINKING THE OFFERINGS

Given such sentiments, it seems clear that a useful perspective on the continuing provision of paper offerings for the dead is one that sets the sentiment of care for ancestors in a new form. These objects of material culture are not simply one more example (albeit an otherwordly one) of conspicuous consumption or the desire for gain, but reflect the love of the departed and the deeply felt need to provide for them, to make them safe, secure and comfortable, even 'happy' if this is possible, in the next world. Urban families who may no longer have a domestic altar in their homes, nor regularly visit ancestral temples to participate in rites, nevertheless purchase the larger items of the classical set at the time of the funeral, to offer them at the appropriate time within the ritual sequence. They then can add materials from the selection of everyday items and continue to send items year after year. They may take comfort, secure in the knowledge that they are performing what is not simply correct or expected but right in both traditional and modern senses; love for family members spans both past and present. Seen in this way, it may be suggested that the repertoire of paper offerings persists, grows and continues to be important, even in this ultra-modern example of contemporary urban life, because it provides a framework for the expression of one element still important to the understanding of modern Hong Kong Chinese identity-the concern for family-which may in other contexts appear to be obscured or questioned.

While existing discussions of the form and content of modern Hong Kong identity (Baker 1983; Chan 1994; Lau and Kuan 1988; Chan 1986) either set aside or do not fully address the place of traditional thinking or of traditional elements in the identity configuration, this discussion of paper offerings suggests that more explorations in this area would be worthwhile. Certainly, it would seem from the comments of my respondents that our views of the mindsets of urban residents may also need to be approached more carefully, lest observations in one realm (general consumerism) unduly channel our thinking in another (the motivations for providing for the dead). Returning to the observation on cultural preservation which began this essay, the continued existence of the paper offering industry attests to the strength of belief underlying it and the importance of such belief to the complex termed modern Chinese identity. Certainly, the realm of paper offerings can be seen as a form of culture in process, in which an established area of traditional culture can not only survive but can expand, playing a vital part in a modern urban context, as an expression of an enduring and valued complex of behavior.

NOTES

1 Research in this paper was supported by an Earmarked Grant for Research (HKBC 3/88, RSC/88–89/02) from the (then entitled) University and Polytechnics Grants Committee. The author wishes to express her gratitude

for such generous support. Thanks is also due to the research assistants: Ms Florence Lui Yuk Lin, Ms Elizabeth Lai Ching Man, Ms Brenda Cheung Lai Shan, and Mr. Timothy Tsang Ching Chuen. Special gratitude is due to all the paper shop owners and workshop managers, who so generously gave of their time and expertise. Data collected for the project was obtained using a variety of research techniques: survey, interview, specimen collection, observation, and photography. The data for this essay was taken from the project data base which includes: in-depth interviews conducted at seventy-five retail paper shops, ten paper offerings wholesalers, and eight workshops for the dead; 282 in-depth surveys of users of paper offerings; a matching sample investigating young people's knowledge; and nearly 1,000 indicative surveys conducted at temples. A collection of nearly 1,500 specimens of paper offerings has also been collected for the project. The author is grateful for criticisms of previous versions of this paper provided by Prof. Gene Blocker, Dr. Michael DeGolyer, Dr. Grant Evans, Dr. F. Lauren Pfister, Prof. James L. Watson, Prof. Rubie S. Watson, and the anonymous reviewers.

2 Observations made in southern Taiwan would suggest that the paper offering repertoire of the retail shops is less extensive than that on offer in Hong Kong; on a visit in March of 1995, the author noted no more than twelve varieties available for sale in shops in Tainan. This evaluation does not hold for the paper replicas observed in use during temple rituals , however, which appear to be both extensive and elaborate. Nevertheless, this observation is quite limited and it is clear that a fuller exploration of the relationship between and the comparison of, materials used in Taiwan and Hong Kong must be done.

3 Some shopkeepers, recognizing the sales potential of the visitor, have made efforts to learn basic English terms and descriptions of many items. During one interview in the Yau Ma Tei District in 1992, for example, the author was asked by the shopkeeper to write down suitable English names of the paper items tourists had asked about.

4 While most customers have a working knowledge of which paper offerings to use for which purposes, most of those who have questions seek advice from the shopkeeper on what to purchase. Generally, customers ask about what to use for illness, accidents, or rarely-performed rituals, although exactly what customers need to know would would vary from shop to shop. Examples given from shopkeepers make clear that amount or accuracy of knowledge cannot be easily correlated to age and experience alone; many shopkeepers said that their younger customers were as knowledgable as the elderly purchasers. The same can be said for gender, which in the opinions of the shopkeepers is also not a deciding factor in either the knowledge about, nor the purchase and use of, paper offerings.

5 Paper replicas to be burned for the dead are only one part of the category of pitched paper items. Other categories include: the flower cannons (*fā paau*), made for the worship of Tin Hau; golden flowers (gām fā), employed as offerings and adornments for the gods; paper lanterns of all varieties, but especially the lotus lanterns made at the New Year; and pinwheels (*fûng chè*), purchased at the New Year as a sign of renewal and good luck.

6 There is no agreement among informants, whether from workshops or retail paper shops, on a single overarching scheme for classifying the repertoire of

paper offerings. The author has identified one large subdivision between pitched and non-pitched (printed or painted) items. Referring to items for the dead the former category would include the three-dimensional offerings made up on frames-the cars, servants, cranes, and large household goods. Within the latter category, there is even less agreement about how to divide the items within, but items such as everyday and special offerings, charms, paper clothing, and money are commonly found. For this paper, the author is dividing the offerings for the dead into what may be termed the 'basic set' and the 'items of everyday use', which itself is further subdivided into special items and daily necessities (itself further divided into three groupings).

7 The cost of a basic set varies according to the level of quality, the materials used, and the amount of labor and time spent on special designs. In 1989, a basic set could be purchased for HK$1,000–2,000, with as much as HK$10,000 or more for very elaborately-made sets. In 1992, the price of a basic set of thirteen items had risen to 'a few thousand dollars' as one master put it, meaning, HK$4,000–5,000. Prices for 1995 remain roughly the same.

8 Some masters made wonderfully designed and crafted items. One lady shopkeeper interviewed made paper clothing so fine and detailed that each piece could be worn everyday by the living; she was justifiably proud of the quality of her garments.

9 In the November 26, 1995, edition of the Sunday Morning Post Magazine, (of the South China Morning Post) an article on modern Hong Kong funerals lists one funeral parlor as selling custom-built Chinese-style caskets for HK$800,000 (approximately US$100,000 at the exchange rate of 8:1). Most families, more often favoring cremation now, are content with simple models retailing for somewhat less than HK$20,000 (or US$2,500). Either way, when added to the costs of other elements of the funeral ceremonies, a large bill can be expected.

10 Dr. Lauren F. Pfister, personal communication, 1995.

11 It should be noted in this context that informants expressed similar views towards the offerings made to the gods.

REFERENCES CITED

Ahern, Emily M.
    1973 The Cult of the Dead in a Chinese Village. Stanford: Stanford University Press.
Baker, Hugh D.
    1983 Life in the Cities: The Emergence of Hong Kong Man. China Quarterly 95:469–480.
Chan, David K.K.
    1986 The Culture of Hong Kong: A Myth or Reality. In Hong Kong Society: A Reader.Alex Y. H. Kwan and David K. K. Chan, eds. Hong Kong: Writers and Publishers' Cooperative.

Chan Hoi-man
  1994 Culture and Identity. *In* The Other Hong Kong Report. Donald H. McMillen and Man Si-wai, eds. Hong Kong: Chinese University Press.
Chaney, David
  1971 Job Satisfaction and Unionization. *In* Hong Kong: The Industrial Colony. Keith Hopkins, ed. Hong Kong: Oxford University Press.
Hase, Patrick
  1984 Observations at a Village Funeral. *In* From Village to City. David Faure, James Hayes, and Alan Burch, eds. Hong Kong: University of Hong Kong Press.
Hayes, James
  1975 A Tale of Two Cities. *In* Hong Kong: The Interaction of Tradition and Life in the Towns. Marjorie Topley, ed. Hong Kong:Hong Kong Branch of the Royal Asiatic Society.
Johnston, R. F.
  1910 Lion and Dragon in North China. New York: Dutton.
Lau Siu-kai
  1982 Society and Politics in Hong Kong. Hong Kong: The Chinese University Press.
Lau Siu-kai and Kuan Hsin-chi
  1988 The Ethos of the Hong Kong Chinese. Hong Kong: The Chinese University Press.
Lee Ming-kwan
  1992 Family and Gender Issues. *In* Indicators of Social Development: Hong Kong 1990. Lau Siu-kai, Lee Ming-kwan, Wan Po-san, and Wong Siu-lun, eds. Hong Kong Institute of Asia-Pacific Studies, The Chinese University of Hong Kong.
Lee, Rance; Cheung Tak-sing and Cheung Yuet-wah
  1979 Material and Non-material Conditions and Life-satisfaction of Urban Residents in Hong Kong. *In* Hong Kong: Economic, Social, and Political Studies in Development. Tzong-biau Lin, Rance P.L. Lee, and Udo-Ernst Simonis, eds. White Plains: M. L. Sharpe.
Thompson, Stuart E.
  1988 Death, Food, and Fertility. *In* Death Ritual in Late Imperial and Modern China. James L. Watson and Evelyn S. Rawski, eds. Berkeley: University of California Press.
Tong Chee Kiong
  1993 The Inheritance of the Dead: Morturary Rituals among the Chinese in Singapore. Southeast Asian Journal of Social Science 21:130–158.
Watson, James L.
  1988 The Structure of Chinese Funerary Rites: Elementary Forms, Ritual Sequence, and the Primacy of Performance. *In* Death Ritual in Late Imperial and Modern China. James L. Watson and Evelyn S. Rawski, eds. Berkeley: University of California Press.
Williams, C.A.S.
  1976 [1941] Outlines of Chinese Symbolism and Art Motives. New York: Dover Publications.

11

SACRED POWER IN THE METROPOLIS
SHRINES AND TEMPLES IN HONG KONG

Graeme Lang

INTRODUCTION

Among the Chinese cities of Asia, Hong Kong has the most unfettered economy, and offers the best access to the sources of economic power. Hong Kong also has the most unfettered *religious* economy, and offers – for believers – the best access to the sources of *sacred* power. This chapter is about the temples and shrines which comprise Hong Kong's nodes of sacred power. It will also offer some comments on the future of temples and folk religion in Hong Kong.

SHRINES AND TEMPLES AS POWER-NODES

The capitalist metropolis is a maze of economic opportunities, but uncertainties and troubles afflict most residents (Mak and Lau 1992). Urbanites cultivate personal relationships for protection and for advantage, but social networks offer limited help in a crisis. Drawing heavily on such help may cause a loss of further network support. The city contains a scattering of secular power-nodes, but most are not accessible to ordinary residents. The few accessible secular power-centres provide little comfort for those who feel insecure, and offer little help for citizens in trouble. Neither secular power-centres nor personal networks, therefore, can cope with the volume of risks and troubles. Anxiety is endemic. Thus, there is a market for alternative methods of pursuing security and advantage. Gambling is one method. Religion is another.

Religion can be viewed as a system for getting access to alternative sources of power. When people cannot rely on network resources or secular power-nodes to help them with pressing problems, their needs create a market for other kinds of helpers. Attracted by these needs, religious entrepreneurs have created a world of invisible potencies, and offer their expertise in dealing with them, for which they are suitably rewarded by believers (Stark and Bainbridge 1987:90–104).

The cultures of many modern cities are still deeply rooted in earlier cultures in which such potencies were almost the only sources of accessible power outside of clans and social networks. In the villages, in the dark night when demons roamed spreading illness and misfortune, when storms destroyed dams and dykes, when pestilence ruined crops and killed animals, villagers turned to gods and spirits for protection. They had learned from religious specialists that gods and spirits could help them or afflict them, that they should be feared and must be honoured. Some of these gods were carried to the cities by migrants and religious entrepreneurs; some survived in local villages engulfed but not destroyed by the expanding metropolis.

Thus, scattered among the great concrete warrens of the city, and in the surrounding hills, are a large number of shrines and temples where such invisible powers can be tapped. These sites are doorways to a realm of spirits who may be induced to help and protect those who come bearing gifts and showing deference. All such sites are places where exchanges occur between humans, seeking benefit, and these invisible agencies.

ANCESTRAL ALTARS

The most common shrines in the territory are ancestral altars. The ancestors consume more incense each day than all of the other gods and spirits combined. Although not as powerful as gods, they might help their descendants in small ways if pleased and well-cared for, and may be a source of trouble if neglected. Offerings of tea and incense are made to sustain and please ancestors in thousands of households each day.[1] Periodic offerings of money, clothes, food, and durable goods are also required. In part, these offerings are intended to prevent the deceased from sliding into poverty in the afterlife. But the distress of the deceased might mean misfortune for descendants, and so these offerings are part of the exchange between humans and spirits which occur at all nodes of sacred power.

While the gods receive burnt offerings of gold paper, signifying gold bars, ancestors are also provided with *hell bank notes*. The practice of burning piles of afterlife-money for use by ancestors evidently dates from the beginnings of circulation of bank notes in China in the twelfth century (Hou 1975:35–6), and has continued into the modern era. In the densely crowded metropolis, the smoke from such inter-world transmissions of funds creates pollution at those times of the year when every family is engaged in sending such money to deceased parents and grandparents. In Taiwan, the city government of Taipei has tried to reduce the volume of smoke by issuing 'bank of hell' credit cards, so that a family could burn one of these instead of the usual large piles of paper currency.

To date, such an innovation has not appeared in Hong Kong. However, in other respects the worship of ancestors reflects the modernising of Hong Kong society. While the gods still ride around their territories in sedan-chairs – the most exalted means of transport at the time when their iconography and rites became fixed in old China – ancestors who lived in modern Hong Kong must be provided with a contemporary afterlife. Thus, offerings burnt for their benefit by their affluent offspring include paper models of air-conditioned houses, colour T.V.s, cars, watches, computers, and even jet airplanes. Hong Kong life has thus modernised the Hong Kong afterlife. Can the old gods in their mandarin robes and sedan-chairs really rule such a world? Indeed, what is the presence and fate of these old gods in the modern metropolis?

TEMPLES AND SHRINES: STATICS AND DYNAMICS

Most gods live in shrines and temples. Their fates are intimately linked to the fates of these sites. To survey shrines and temples properly, we need to classify them into types and discuss the functions and activities of each type. However, a static typology of shrines cannot capture the dynamics which operate over historical time-scales. I will begin with the 'statics': the main types of nodes of sacred power. In discussing each type, some of the 'dynamics' will also be indicated.

Types of deities

In the late 1970s, Keith Stevens counted nearly 400 shrines and temples in Hong Kong. About 135 were Buddhist or devoted primarily to

Buddhist deities such as *Gùn Yàm*, while only a small number were Taoist (Stevens 1980). More than 240 of the remaining temples and shrines were dedicated to deities from Chinese folk religion. Nearly 100 of them shelter gods and goddesses worshipped by people who derived part of their living from the sea (Stevens 1980:29), of which about 70 are devoted to the goddess *Tin Hauh*. The oldest Tin Hauh temple site in the territory apparently dates from 1266 A.D. (Watson 1985:302). Many of the villages in the inland New Territories[2] also built Tin Hauh temples, beginning in the seventeenth century, though they did not make their living directly from the sea. They adopted Tin Hauh, in part, because the goddess's cult was recognised by the imperial authorities. By embracing her cult the villagers could claim orthodoxy and adherence to the national religious culture and, not incidentally, politically correct allegiances. But they also believed and hoped that Tin Hauh would protect them from the coastal pirates and bandits who operated throughout the region (Watson 1985:308).

It is likely that all of the deities worshipped in Hong Kong were carried here by migrants from other parts of China. Even deities which appear to be local, such as *Tàahm Gùng* were brought from elsewhere (Siu 1987). Only the faintest traces of possibly original local gods and goddesses can still be found (see, for instance, Watson 1985:310–311).[3]

Following Stevens (1980), we may estimate that about 5% of the shrines and temples in Hong Kong are Taoist, about 35% are Buddhist, and about 60% are for deities popular among ordinary people but not necessarily among ordained clerics. The most striking differences between shrines are not in the types of deities worshipped in them, however, but in the size and constituencies of the shrines.

Types of shrines and temples

There are several ways to classify shrines and temples besides the types of deities represented and the religious affiliations of the shrines. One way is to determine the communities which they serve. Most temples are small and serve only the local neighbourhood or village. Others attract worshippers from a larger but still restricted community such as a group of villages or an urban district, or an ethnic group such as the Chiu Chow or the Fukienese. A few draw worshippers from the entire territory and from among overseas Chinese.

There are of course rough correlations between the constituency of a temple and its size and wealth. The smallest and most primitive shrines serve only the local neighbourhood, and contain some of the most primitive kinds of gods. At the other end of the scale are four or five massive urban god-palaces occupying an acre or more of land. Between the two extremes are more than three hundred temples ranging in size from a small hut to a large house. I will begin with the simplest and most primitive shrines, and conclude with the grandest and most magnificent.

The Earth God: Tóu Deih Gūng

The simplest shrines in Hong Kong, outside of the home, are the small open concrete boxes and platforms scattered throughout the urban and rural districts. There are thousands of these shrines in the territory. Most attract only people who live in the immediate neighbourhood. The most common deity at these shrines is the Earth God, or *Tóu Deih Gūng*

Earth God shrines are tended by residents in urban Hong Kong and in the villages of the New Territories. Many of these shrines consist of only a three-sided concrete box with a rock inside representing the deity. In a few urban districts, the Earth God sits in a free-standing temple, with the annual festival organised and managed by a local committee, usually chosen by lot – that is, 'chosen by the god' (Hayes 1983a). In the walled villages of the New Territories the Earth God shrine typically sat inside the tower at the gateway to the village (Stevens 1980:19). In rural China, the Earth God was petitioned for a good harvest (Chamberlayne 1993:71). Earth-god-districts with a radius of as much as three miles have been reported in China (Shryock 1931:129), but this is larger than most of the earth-god districts in Hong Kong.

The Earth God is like a low-level bureaucrat. In some parts of Taiwan births and deaths were reported to the Earth God at the same time that they were reported to the secular authorities (Wolf 1974:134). In one Earth God temple in Shau Kei Wan, local people offered a pig's head to the god on the birth of a son, and a chicken on the birth of a daughter (Hayes 1983a:129). The Earth God also monitors local residents. We might imagine him as a faceless being living in the shadows in each neighbourhood.

The Earth God must be honoured to induce him to protect the neighbourhood against the forces which might intrude and cause harm. These forces may include local ghosts. One Earth God temple in Shau Kei Wan, for example, is linked to the local *Yùh Nàahn* Festival, designed to feed and appease hungry ghosts, reportedly because of the many deaths in the area during the Japanese occupation: the Earth God is mobilised to help control and appease the spirits of these restless and homeless dead (Hayes 1983a:129). At some Earth God temples, the god

246

is also credited with protecting or rescuing residents of the district from a particular crisis such as an epidemic (Hayes 1983:121).

The Earth God has the most limited long-term prospects of any of the deities in Hong Kong. Plagues no longer threaten local residents. Ghosts are better cared for, now pitied more than feared, and in any case the city's bright lights drive them away without the Earth God's help.

A marriage and fertility shrine: the yàn yùhn sehk

Some prominent rocks are thought to be inhabited by potent spirits, and attract worshippers seeking some benefit from their power. The most striking of these in Hong Kong is a natural stone pillar jutting out above a walking path which snakes through the hills above the business district on Hong Kong Island. This pillar-shrine attracts women who want to find a good marriage partner (hence the name yàn yùhn sehk, or marriage-fate rock). It also attracts women who wish to become pregnant with a son. Petitions for a male child may be the earlier form of worship at this shrine.

Whatever the original nature of the spirit of the rock, some worshippers have humanised it by legendizing two lovers who committed suicide there, and who now, with the supernatural power which they earned by their tragic fate, are able to help petitioners. These two spirits are known to worshippers as *Sehk Gùng* and *Sehk Móuh*, the 'father and mother' of the site (Chek and So 1987). A nineteenth century observer recorded another tradition about the rock: that it was associated with immoral influences on the population, and that 'those who profit from immoral practices [presumably, prostitutes] actually go and worship that rock' (Eitel 1984 [1873]:43), a type of patronage which has evidently continued up to the present.

The shrine has no influential patrons, and is vulnerable in the event that planners conceive other uses for the site.[4] But it seems in no imminent danger of removal, and the trickle of female patrons will probably ensure that this extraordinary shrine survives into the twenty-first century. Standing behind this pillar, one sees the great modern towers of commerce rising up out of Hong Kong's central business district just below one of the most archaic cult-objects in the history of religion.[5]

Dragons of stone

The Hong Kong landscape also hides other primitive but potent forces. For villagers in the suburban districts, the mountains and valleys are charged with latent power. Specialists in *fùng séui* (literally, wind-water) sell to villagers their expertise in the analysis of this latent power. They tell villagers where to put their houses to take advantage of it, and how to avoid the calamities which could result from disturbing it.

The forces bound tightly into mountains and valleys may send destructive ripples through the lives of the village clans, causing innumerable misfortunes, if these forces are disturbed by bulldozers excavating the ground for roads or reservoirs. The determined resistance of the clans to some of these projects has thus caused the government to abandon or revise some excavations to avoid confrontations with anxious villagers. Occasionally, the government has paid for the services of a geomancer (fùng séui specialist) to make progress in negotiations with them (Hayes 1983c).

Some of the forces rippling through the landscape are personified as 'dragons', 'white tigers', 'crabs', and other extraordinary creatures. These forces are considered by fùng séui theorists and perhaps by most urbanites to be secular and mechanical, and are called by the names of sentient beings only as a metaphorical convenience. However, the concept of the 'dragon' in hillsides and mountains (Eitel 1984:17–19) preserves a vision of a powerful 'earth-being which must be propitiated. The ceremony of 'pacifying the dragon' (*ngòn lùhng*), which has survived into modern times in some villages in the New Territories (Ward and Law 1993:80) may be based on such a belief.

Above the level of spirits lurking in rocks, trees, and hills, we find local potentates who reside in dwellings like those of humans and are represented by human-like icons. The smallest of these dwellings are rooms or flats comparable to the dwellings of ordinary urbanites. The largest are comparable to the yamens of the mandarins in old China.

Neighbourhood and village temples

Some of the New Territories villages include a temple owned by the village. (The deed may indicate that a god is the real owner of the temple – but elders of the village serve as his trustees [Stevens 1980:29]). For example, the village of Tai Wai near Shatin includes a *Hàuh Wòhng*[6] temple at which only villagers worship (Hase 1984:130). The temple was supported in part by property owned communally by the villagers, including several village houses. Every ten years, the village holds a *jiu* festival, centred on the temple, to purify the village from accumulated spiritual pollution of various kinds, and to renew its pact with the gods.

The temple has a side hall dedicated to the founders of the village and to village heroes who died in its defence during earlier centuries when such villages might be attacked by rival villages, or by pirates. These village martyrs are worshipped in the side-hall on a certain day each year by village elders (Hase 1984:130). In a village such as Tai Wai, with sixteen different surnames by the 1890s, the temple has probably been used to promote village cohesion and identity (Brim 1974). If the god earns a reputation for particular benevolence, he or she may be invited by local people to serve as the god-father for some of their sons and daughters (e.g. Hayes 1983b:215).

VILLAGE TEMPLES AND URBANISATION

Sometimes the growing metropolis surrounds a village but does not destroy it, and the village and its temple can still be discovered nestled among the high-rise residential blocks, as in the case of the village of Nga Chin Wai and its Tìn Hauh temple, near Kai Tak Airport (Hayes 1983b:216).[7] In some urban districts, distinctive communal ceremonies also survived long after the village was engulfed by the city – but only if the older low-rise buildings and their family businesses also survived. A number of temples on the Kowloon peninsula built or rebuilt in the nineteenth century, such as the Gùn Yâm and Tìn Hauh temples in the villages of Mong Kok and Yau Ma Tei (Hayes 1983c, Chapter 3), once served as convenient meeting places for committees of local leaders when they gathered to decide on matters of general importance (Watson 1985:26). Such meetings first occurred to discuss and arrange communal rituals linked to the temple, but could easily be adapted to the resolution of other secular communal problems.

Many rural and village temples, however, have lost their communal functions and most of their constituencies during urban redevelopment. Some village or neighbourhood temples absorbed into the metropolis, however, continue to serve an important secular function even though their communal functions have disappeared and patronage continues to dwindle: they become colourful repositories of traditional culture, visited by tourists and the curious as much as by worshippers.

Temples as museums

A museum displays objects made by earlier generations of people. A good museum tries to provide some context for each object, to show us how it was used. So a museum is also an aid to the cultural memory of a society. Some local temples contain bells, drums, incense burners, and god-statues which would be eagerly acquired by real museums if they were for sale. The grander temples also preserve the architecture of temples and palaces in pre-modern China.[8] Some temples in China, such as the *Bak Dai* temple in Foshan, have survived difficult times in the P.R.C. because of their value as museums of cultural history. In Hong Kong, temples are not explicitly museums. But they serve this function nevertheless: for tourists, for local scholars, and for Hong Kong's young people. For some local people, to visit a grand temple is to savour the richness of Chinese cultural history, and thereby to nourish one's identity as a Chinese.

In addition to preserving artifacts and architecture, temples may also preserve reflections of the social system of old China. Some gods still dress and comport themselves like the mandarins on whom they were modelled. Some of them also preserve the memory of specific imperial officials. For example, the patron deity of the *Daaih Wòhng Yèh* spirit-medium temple in Kwun Tong described by Myers (1975) was said to have been, during his life on earth, an official of the Tang dynasty who was given a posthumous title by the emperor for his loyalty, filiality, and frugality. A scroll at the temple claimed that the memory and worship of this person had been brought to the area by a descendant during the Southern Sung dynasty. His worship was revived, after the temple became decrepit, by Chiu Chow migrants into the area after World War II (Myers 1975:20).

A temple may also preserve relics of the honour once accorded to long-dead imperial officials who performed some service for the local population. For example, a temple which stood in Sheung Shui until 1955 commemorated two seventeenth century officials in Guangdong who earned the intense gratitude of the local population by helping to convince the emperor to let them return to their villages after the coastal evacuation of 1662–1669 (Faure and Lee 1982). After the temple's destruction by fire in 1955, it was relocated to a small flat in Sheung Shui, where it survived into the 1980s. Worship at the temple by an alliance representing the major old clans in the area continued. Presumably, they resumed worship of these two officials at the shrine because they perceived some continuing benefit from doing so. But the temple is also a relic of the tumultuous political history of the region, and preserves a local reflection of these events for residents or scholars who may be interested.

The Tìn Hauh Temple complex in Yau Ma Tei also preserves some relics of folk religion which are extinct or fading toward probable extinction in the area. For example, it includes a shrine for *Sehng Wohng*, the so-called City God, and a rock representing the Earth God, though most people visiting the temple have little interest in these deities. The complex also includes a statue of Wong Tai Sin, wearing golden robes as his statues once did in China before all of the temples and statues to this god in China were destroyed between the 1920s and the 1950s (Lang and Ragvald 1993:Chapter 2). This is the only intact image of the god which preserves the original iconography of this god's cult in China. (All the other images of the god in Hong Kong are modelled after a painting of him in the main temple in Kowloon). The statue is a genuine museum-piece, valuable as a relic of an earlier and now extinct version of the cult of this deity.

From village temple to district temple

If a village temple is large enough, and by luck or strong communal support avoids destruction during urban development, it may eventually become a focus for worship among the urbanites who have moved into the area, and the village temple becomes a district temple with a much larger constituency of worshippers. It may thus escape the fate of other temples which attract fewer and fewer worshippers and gradually turn into museums. During this transition from village-temple to district-temple, control over the temple by the villagers may be challenged by other groups living in the area, as in the case of the Shatin *Chè Gùng* Temple, which was taken over by the Chinese Temples Committee after disputes between rival villages over control of the temple (see also Smith 1973, on struggles for control over a temple on Ap Lei Chau).

The powers and character of the deity may also change, as the temple acquires new patrons among the urbanised population of the district. As a particularly interesting case study, we could consider the Chè Gùng Temple in the New Territories.

Chè Gùng temple

This temple, located near the new town of Shatin behind the hills north of the Kowloon peninsula, would seem like any other district temple in the Hong Kong region except during the second and third days of Chinese New Year, when it attracts more than 100,000 worshippers. They come from all over the territory, and the crowds during these few days are exceeded only by the multitudes who press into the Wong Tai Sin Temple in Kowloon during the New Year period.

The Shatin temple had remained a rural shrine for local villagers for two hundred years, until epidemics in the nineteenth century induced the villagers to carry the statue of Che around the villages. The apparent success of this act in halting the epidemic may have led to the renovation of the shrine by the alliance of villages. In any case, the temple was used as a base for the *jiu* ceremonies (Issei 1989) which are held every few years to cleanse the villages of accumulated evil spirits.

The opening of the Kowloon-Canton Railway (KCR) at the beginning of the twentieth century brought a major change in the temple's fortunes. The temple was not far from the Shatin train station, and could now be reached easily from Kowloon. Indeed, it was probably easier to get from Kowloon to the Chè Gùng temple in Shatin than to reach the Wong Tai Sin temple in Kowloon, then separated from the main villages in the area by a kilometre of dirt roads and paths. The Chè Gùng temple keepers eventually added the concept of a brass propeller-wheel which could be turned to petition for a change of luck, and the shrine began to become well-known for this feature, and attracted those who had suffered reverses of fortune. The transformation of the KCR trains into a mass-rapid-transit system in the early 1980s, and the addition of a station at Tai Wai, a short walk from the temple, further increased its convenience for worshippers and it became a major pilgrimage site at New Year.

The god has proved able to attract a curious mixture of urban worshippers. Interviews at the temple[9] have shown that his worshippers now include drivers (possibly influenced by the fact that the character *che* means 'vehicle'), and government workers responsible for the difficult and sometimes risky task of policing hawkers (Che was a civil servant and a general, hence a very appropriate god for them, according to one of these hawker-control officers interviewed at the temple). Chè Gùng has also developed a reputation for helping gamblers and people involved in somewhat disreputable business dealings (known as *pìnmùhn sàangyi*),[10] perhaps because he is not burdened with the ethical doctrines which cluster around well-known Taoist and Buddhist saints such as Wong Tai Sin and Gùn Yâm.

Because of the extraordinary popularity of the Shatin temple among a growing number of urbanites, a new larger temple was recently built on the site by the Chinese Temples Committee, which spent nearly US$6 million on the project.[11] A giant new statue of 'General Che' now stands in this temple, while worshippers bang drums and turn wheels on an enlarged plaza outside the temple to attract the god's attention and to petition for better fortune in the future. Seldom has an obscure figure at an obscure rural shrine achieved greater renown in a shorter time. Only

Wong Tai Sin has had a more dramatic success from humble beginnings. But both cases illustrate how a well-placed and cleverly managed temple can achieve fame and success in the expanding metropolis.

IMMIGRANTS AND TEMPLES

The construction or reconstruction of temples in Hong Kong since the 1840s may have occurred more frequently during certain periods (Stevens 1980:26): the 1840s, when many immigrants from China entered Hong Kong; the 1870s to 1880s, with rising prosperity; the 1890s, particularly after 1894, during the waves of bubonic plague in the region; and the 1950s, when large numbers of immigrants again arrived from China. The period after the 1911 revolution also led to the founding of several major temples in the territory, as religious specialists and many others fled from conditions in China. Other waves of immigrants and refugees have also been associated with the opening of new temples. For example, Fukienese monks and nuns fleeing the attacks on shrines in Fukien during the Cultural Revolution in the late 1960s set up a number of apartment-temples in the Fukienese areas of North Point (Guldin 1977:122). In any case, except for the temple construction associated with the bubonic plague and with other epidemics, all of this activity was directly related to the arrival of immigrants.

Several of these new temples became nodes of secular as well as sacred power. The *Màhn Móuh* temple on Hong Kong Island, for example, was established in 1847 by two immigrants who became leaders, temporarily, of the Chinese community soon after the founding of Hong Kong. One had gained wealth and influence helping to provision the British forces during the so-called Opium War, and thereafter invested in local dwellings, a gambling house, and brothels (Smith 1971:81). The other had become wealthy as a contractor. They periodically held court in the Màhn Móuh temple, evidently deciding disputes of various kinds until the early 1850s, when the local shopkeepers elected a committee to meet in the temple and decide cases of public interest (Smith 1971:81). Perhaps the presence of the gods in the shrine helped to sanctify the proceedings and legitimate their decisions; with the gods looking on, what leaders would dare choose selfish interests over the interests of the community?

By the last decades of the nineteenth century, the wealthy directors of the Tung Wah Group of Hospitals had become the unofficial government of the Chinese community in Hong Kong and decided many matters of communal importance (Sinn 1989). It was no longer necessary for them to meet at the *Màhn Móuh* temple to carry out their deliberations, but they still went to the temple every year to celebrate the Spring and Autumn sacrifices to Confucius, following the custom of their contemporaries and peers, the magistrates in imperial China (Lethbridge 1978:62). The temple continued to provide a public setting for the display of their authority and power in the community.

The processes of invasion and succession described for urban inner-city neighbourhoods by urban sociologists occasionally have a counterpart in the succession of ethnic groups who control a local temple. If a community swells with migrants from a different home-county in China, the migrants may take over a feeble or decrepit local temple as their own (e.g. Myers 1975). If the local temples are too strongly held by existing communities in the area, the migrants build their own shrines nearby, in apartments (e.g. Guldin 1977:122), or on hillsides. This is especially likely where the religious practices of the immigrants were markedly different from those of the local Cantonese population, as with Chiu Chow migrants (Myers 1981). The hillside shrines may attract the hostile attention of the state (as it struggles to regulate squatting on vacant land), or of the proprietors of other local temples with which the new shrines begin to compete.

The 'squatter' temples survive only as long as they stand on land which is not immediately coveted by planners and developers, and some have been destroyed during urban development (e.g. Stevens 1980:7), to be rebuilt elsewhere only if the shrine had sufficient and reputable community support (e.g. Jen 1967:31). But not all temples started by immigrants are small and vulnerable.

The largest and most striking temples in Hong Kong were also started by immigrants. The most successful of these temples were established on large plots of land by religious entrepreneurs from China who had managed to line up enough financial support from interested patrons in Hong Kong (see Lang and Ragvald 1993; Tsui 1991). One of the major reasons for the success of these temples was that their founders had the vision and ambition to build shrines on large plots of land, rural at the time but close enough to the city to draw urban patrons, and which were eventually surrounded by the expanding metropolis. These shrines include the grand temple complexes of the *Sīk Sīk Yùhn* devoted to Wong Tai Sin in Kowloon, of the *Fuhng Yìhng Sin Gun* in Fanling, and of the *Chìng Chùhng Gun* in Tuen Mun. Of these, the most famous and popular is the Sīk Sīk Yùhn's Wong Tai Sin Temple.

In the urban environment, of course, high population densities can support a number of temples within a district, and can provide a high income for a successful temple. In this environment, the better class of temples compete with each other for patrons (Stevens 1980:5). Such competition can be documented in China from at least as early as the Sung dynasty (Katz 1992:208, citing Hansen 1991), facilitated by the polytheism of Chinese folk religion. In India, competition between temples can be extravagant and dramatic, as in the Spring Pooram festival in Kerala, where rival temples compete in a public display in which 'both will try to display the largest elephants, the best musicians, the most beautiful parasols, the most astonishing fireworks' (Miller 1988:612). In Hong Kong, the competition is less dramatic, but the organisations which manage these shrines are keenly aware of their competitors, which helps ensure that the shrines are as appealing as they can be with the funds available. These grand shrines draw worshippers from all around the territory. Many visitors are attracted to such a temple because it serves as an oasis of tranquillity and beauty, and provides a respite from the concrete canyons of the metropolis.

Thus, while most small temples in the territory are declining, the major urban god-palaces, along with a few conveniently reached suburban ones, have prospered. The organisations which operate those grand temples have grown rich on the services which they offered to the post-war generation of urbanites as they struggled upward in the general social mobility of the last four decades. In harmony with their religious belief, but also for the sake of harmony with their political environment,[12] these organisations channel a proportion of their wealth back into the community in the form of free medical services, schools, and homes for the elderly (e.g. Lang and Ragvald 1993:64–5). Thus, these temples now play a part in the circulation of funds in Hong Kong from private pockets through intermediary organisations and finally into public facilities (a part, however, dwarfed by the much more massive circulation of money through the Hong Kong Jockey Club's betting operations into public projects and services).

Unlike the old village and district temples which have been absorbed into the metropolis, these new urban god-palaces are able to attract the younger generation of worshippers (Lang and Ragvald 1993 chapter 5). They go to these temples to try divination using fortune-sticks (*kàuh chim*) to ask for help and guidance, and rely on the fortune-tellers at these temples to interpret the god's messages. The gods of these grand temples (aided immeasurably by the fortune-tellers based at these temples) thus become adept at dealing with the problems of modern urbanites, such as housing, investments, job choices, marriage, and career changes. With such services to offer, these temples are likely to have a strong presence as the major nodes of sacred power in the metropolis of the twentieth-first century.

SHRINES TO THE SUPREME DEITY, FOR THE PROTECTION OF THE STATE

The only major shrines in imperial China not represented in Hong Kong are those in which high officials conducted annual worship rituals of great importance for the well-being of the empire, such as the 'altar of heaven' complex in Beijing (Meyer 1991:80–99). Indeed, in such cities, temples and altars were often a key part of the design of the city. These shrines were used to ensure that the state preserved a harmonious and beneficial relation with the highest supernatural powers, represented abstractly by the term 'heaven' (*tin*). Major administrative centres of the empire in provincial capitals and county towns also had temples officially incorporated into the state religion. Hong Kong did not even have a county town; the villages in the region were nominally under the control of the nearest county seat in Hsin An – now called Pao An – in *Guangdong* province (Stevens 1980:32, fn.8). The official religion of the empire is thus conspicuously absent among Hong Kong temples.[13]

However, the St. John's Anglican Cathedral, not far from the Governor's residence on Hong Kong Island, may be considered to have served a nearly equivalent function for the ruling British elite up to World War II. The central location of the Cathedral indicates its importance to the early colonial government in Hong Kong, and it served nearly the same kind of function for the regime as Westminster Cathedral in London. Because the ruling elite was British rather than Chinese, we should expect, and indeed we find, a British 'altar of heaven' in the city.

Unlike the 'altar of heaven' in Beijing, however, the St. John's Cathedral also served individual interests and needs, in addition to those of the state. In this sense, it offered a far less lonely form of worship than that of the Emperor of China, who faced heaven, ultimately, alone.

THE FUTURE OF FOLK RELIGION IN HONG KONG

Many local temples and shrines have been adversely affected by urban redevelopment. Removal of old buildings to make way for the construction of new housing estates has resulted in the demolition of many temples. Some temples were rebuilt nearby with government funds, but have lost any communal functions and survive on the business brought by a relatively small number of local patrons. Many former patrons have been dispersed into new housing estates farther away, and cease to visit these shrines.

Urban development has also separated a number of temples catering to boat people from their natural clients. For example, some of the Tin Hauh temples were originally built near a beach for convenient access by boat, but vast land reclamation projects have cut them off entirely from any access from the sea. The changing geography of Hong Kong has masked the original geographical logic of many temples in this way (Stevens 1980).

A more serious problem for the future of most of the temples and shrines in Hong Kong is the decline of belief in 'folk-religion' among Hong Kong's young people. With each passing decade, there are fewer of them who are interested in what they consider to be archaic devotions. A survey carried out in 1988 shows the trend (Hui 1991). Among those over age 65, 46% believed in 'Chinese traditional religion', while 41% professed no religion (Hui 1991:105). By contrast, among people under 30, less than 2% believed in 'Chinese traditional religion', while about 70% professed no religion. By comparison with their elders, the young are overwhelmingly irreligious.

However, a thoroughly scientific world-view is not dominant anywhere in the world. Most people feel that science cannot explain everything. The gaps are filled by strange powers and strange beings which live within the local culture. For example, ghosts and supernatural warriors provide endless material for Hong Kong films and T.V. dramas, watched by the young as much as the old. Young people also occasionally hear stories about remarkable predictions by fortune-tellers. Thus, even the most irreligious of youth may be prepared to believe that fortune-tellers can sometimes predict the future, or that ghosts can sometimes afflict the living. Some youth experiment with the occult out of curiosity. Christian teachers may reinforce such beliefs by giving credibility to belief in demons and spirits.

Some young people are also attracted to Protestant religious groups which offer individual salvation and strong social bonds. Folk-temples cannot compete with a form of religion which offers close companionship with other fervent young people, lively singing and group activities, an intense personal relation with a caring supernatural friend/godfather, and the prospect of personal salvation with few conditions attached. It appears that Protestantism is growing among young people who have rejected the folk-beliefs of their ancestors.[14]

The trend is partly a function of education: the more educated the population, the fewer the people who believe in Chinese traditional religion, and the larger the proportion who believe in some form of Christianity (Hui 1991:107). Part of the reason for the impact of education is that many of the elite schools in the territory are Christian schools which promote Christianity, to varying degrees, within the curriculum. As the Hong Kong population becomes more educated, on average, with each passing decade, it is likely that the proportion of young people who are willing to support traditional religious practice will continue to decline.

However, some types of traditional religious practice will be carried into the twentieth-first century by communal and sectarian groups operating out of apartments or halls, and offering many of the same rewards and benefits as those offered by the evangelical Protestant groups.

HOUSE-SHRINES

Some religious practitioners who cannot raise the funds to build a temple manage instead to set up a house-shrine. These shrines are found in many of the residential districts (see, e.g. Guldin 1977:122), and cater to residents through specialised services and personal attention to their needs. The services may include looking after the tablets of a deceased family member (much cheaper than buying a gravesite), or providing spirit-writing oracles for petitioners, offering them medical advice and healing prescriptions, personal counselling, and careful predictions about their future. Some of these groups are novel and syncretistic, combining elements from several religious traditions (e.g. Tsui 1985).

Some of these house-shrines are linked to sectarian religious organisations based outside of Hong Kong. They occasionally receive important visitors from branches of the sect in other countries, and see themselves as part of an international network of believers. These sectarian groups are able to attract young people just as the Protestant evangelical groups have done, and for the same reasons. Like the Protestant groups, they offer communal solidarity and social ties (some extending beyond the city into other territories), desirable roles and leadership positions for laypersons, and a much more intimate and personalised communion with a god or gods than at most public temples.

They may also be able to provide various kinds of practical assistance. Like the Protestant house-churches, such groups are probably growing among urbanites also in China, for the same reasons (Chan and Hunter 1994; see also Seiwert 1981, on the *Yāt Gun Douh* sect in Taiwan).

House-shrines cannot easily be counted. They are usually invisible from the street, and may operate for years without being discovered by researchers. With the benefits and services they provide, their niche in the urban religious economy is secure, and their numbers will grow as it becomes more and more difficult to build a free-standing temple in a metropolis where, as local people say, 'a foot of land [is worth] an inch of gold'.

CONCLUSIONS

The cultural transition to a technical-industrial society has proceeded with increasing speed in Hong Kong over the past 40 years. The traditional society of the villages in the New Territories was protected from secular revolutionaries by a colonial regime which deliberately avoided interference with the rural customs and lifestyle of these villages for the sake of political stability. Hence, the villages preserved forms of folk-religious practice which were suppressed if not eradicated in China. But many of the smaller village and district temples which survived urbanisation have entered a long period of decline as their natural patrons are displaced, physically and socially, by the new populations and constructions of the metropolis.

The younger and better educated metropolitan dwellers neglect most of these older shrines, preferring the large urban god-palaces. Thus, the distribution of sacred power in the city is shifting. Some of the power, along with the money which such power attracts, are flowing away from many small old shrines and temples into a few large new ones.

In addition to visiting these temples, the younger urbanites also join apartment-cults and small Christian congregations. The spread of these groups shows that sacred power is mobile and opportunistic. If some of the power of these small groups derives from their creation of community, and if the need for community is increasing as the metropolis shrinks families and dissolves social bonds, they are likely to be more prevalent in direct proportion to continued modernisation.

Temples and shrines in Hong Kong, however, also serve as museums, preserving classical architecture, old visions of gods, and ancient religious practices. Their survival in the city provides exotic experience for both residents and tourists. Thus their value in the city is greater than the sum of the power which they offer to believers, and we can see them as nodes of cultural memory as well as nodes of sacred power.

NOTES

1 In the mid 1970s, a survey of households in Kwun Tong found that about 64% of them included an ancestral altar, while about 60% of the wives and 55% of the husbands in these households participated in the ancestral rites (Myers 1981:279). I do not know of a more recent comprehensive survey which can provide a current estimate of the number of households with such shrines. But many of the children of these families probably did not continue the rites once they moved into their own apartments, since only about half of children in households with such shrines in Kwun Tong in the 1970s participated in the rites (Myers 1981:280).

2 The New Territories comprises most of the territory of modern Hong Kong outside of Hong Kong Island and urban Kowloon. The area, inhabited largely by farmers and fishermen until the 1960s, now includes six cities and a large number of towns and villages. It was added to the territory of Hong Kong in two stages, in 1868 and in 1898. China will resume sovereignty over Hong Kong after the termination of the 99 year lease over most of this area which commenced in 1898.

3 In Ha Tsuen in the New Territories, oral tradition suggests that a local deity called 'Sand River Mother' was once worshipped there, but was supplanted by the later Tìn Hauh cult. The process is vividly illustrated by the local belief that Tìn Hauh had 'eaten' Sand River Mother, thus absorbing her powers as well as her duties (Watson 1985:310–311). This nearly extinct deity comes to life again only during the *jiu* festivals in the area, when she is invited back, in company with a flock of other obscure deities, to witness the operas organized for the festival.

4 According to Eitel (1873:43), some local residents in the nineteenth century believed that disturbing the rock could bring misfortune, and related stories of stonecutters who died suddenly after attempting to remove stone from around the base of the rock. Modern planners are not as easily intimidated by the rock's powers.

5 The rock is perceived by a number of observers as a phallic object, petitioned by women for fertility – and perhaps for vigorous male children – for that reason (e.g. Mo 1978:22). Phallic pillars are a very ancient type of cult-object in some societies, as in ancient Greece where the phallus was paraded in rites associated with fertility (Durant 1939:178,199,231). However, some worshippers at the yàn yùhn sehk may conceptualize its powers quite differently (as in the figures of Sehk Gùng and Sehk Móuh).

6 Hàuh Wòhng, according to a local legend, was a Sung dynasty official who arrived in the area not long before the fall of the dynasty in the thirteenth century.

7 Nga Chin Wai was still standing in 1995, but has been scheduled for removal in connection with urban redevelopment.

8 For example, the design of the Wong Tai Sin Temple, renovated in the early 1970s, was influenced by the design of temples and palaces in Beijing.

9 Interviews were conducted in early 1993 by a research assistant and by student interviewers as part of a project on folk religion supported by a small-scale grant from City Polytechnic of Hong Kong.

10 One worshipper interviewed at the temple in 1993 was asked what business he was in. He replied, 'electronics goods'. Doing what, asked the interviewer: manufacturing? sales? 'Smuggling', he mumbled after a pause.

11 The Chinese Temples Committee was established in 1928 to oversee and control temples in the colony. It manages or leases out a number of public temples, and collects rents or lease fees from persons to whom it allocates the day-to-day operation of the temples. The funds are used for occasional renovations of these public temples.

12 Since 1928, when the Chinese Temples Ordinance was passed, the government has had the right to expropriate any temples or shrines deemed to be operating purely as profit-making enterprises without substantial community support. Influenced by the passing of similar legislation in China at the time, and wary of the influx of religious entrepreneurs allegedly eager to 'exploit' the population's desire for religious services, the government did expropriate some temples, allocating their management and income to the Tung Wah Group of Hospitals or appointing temple-keepers directly. Of course, it is impossible in practice to distinguish 'profit-making' from 'genuine religion', since the two are inevitably intertwined. But organizations which manage highly profitable temples know that they need the government's good will to continue their operations without interference. Substantial investment of their resources in community services have proved to be a good way to foster such good will. Communal support for a shrine is also important. From the government's point of view, temples sit in a social field, and may have more or less 'weight' according to the breadth and power of that social field. Temples strongly supported may be left alone. Temples with little local support are vulnerable to take-over or removal. Temples which are the object of struggle among competing local groups are also vulnerable to takeover. Some shrines play little or no role in the communal life of a district. Other shrines are the focus of periodic communal rites organized by local committees for the benefit of a village or district. Such shrines have more weight in the social field than purely client-shrines, and their supporters have much more bargaining power with the government.

13 Some of the most 'imperial' of the Chinese deities have also not taken strong root in the Hong Kong context. The Jade Emperor, the highest supernatural official in the Chinese pantheon, is present in only a handful of lesser temples in the territory, accompanied by some of his ministers and officials (Stevens 1989:25), but he is too remote from the experience of the new generations of urbanites – too politically dated, perhaps – to retain their interest.

14 Data on Protestant Church growth are scarce. However, according to Luk Fai and Lee Kin-wah, in a Christian publication titled *The Challenge of the*

Nineties (Hong Kong: Hong Kong Gospell 2,000 1991:93–101), the number of Protestant churches in the territory grew from 610 churches in 1977 to 872 churches in 1990. The number of Sunday church-goers increased from 84,590 in 1985 to 124,900 in 1989, a growth of 47% in only four years. (I would like to thank Ko Tin-ming for providing me with these data). A survey of 1644 respondents in 1988 showed that about 7.2% identified themselves as Protestant (Hui 1990:104), a figure higher than the proportion of Buddhists in the territory, and nearly a third of the number who indicated belief in Chinese traditional religion (indicated by the response '*baai sàhn*'). Protestants are disproportionately found among those under age 30, compared with other religious believers (Hui 1990:105).

REFERENCES CITED

Abbreviations:
JHKBRAS = Journal of the Hong Kong Branch of the Royal Asiatic Society

Brim, John A.
    1974   Village Alliance Temples in Hong Kong. *In* Religion and Ritual in Chinese Society. Arthur P. Wolf, ed. Pp. 93–103. Stanford: Stanford University Press.
Chamberlayne, John H.
    1993   China and Its Religious Inheritance. London: Janus.
Chan, Kim-Kwong, and Hunter, Alan
    1994   Religion and Society in Mainland China in the 1990s. Issues and Studies 30:52–68.
Chek May Chee, and So Shiu Miu
    1987   Stone Worship and the Analysis of the Condition of Chinese Women. (unpublished) Department of Religion, The Chinese University of Hong Kong.
Choi, Chi-cheung
    1993   Studies on Hong Kong Jiao Festivals. JHKBRAS 30:26–43.
Eitel, Ernest J.
    1984   [1873] Feng-Shui: The Science of Sacred Landscape in Old China. London: Synergetic Press.
Faure, David, and Lee Lai-mui
    1982   The Po Tak Temple in Sheung Shui Market. JHKBRAS 22:270–279.
Feuchtwang, Stephan
    1992   The Imperial Metaphor: Popular Religion in China. London: Routledge.
Guldin, Gregory E.
    1977   Little Fujian (Fukien): Sub-neighbourhood and Community in North Point, Hong Kong. JHKBRAS 17:112–129.
Hansen, Valerie
    1991   Changing Gods in Medieval China, 1127–1276. Princeton: Princeton University Press.
Hase, Patrick
    1984   Observations at a Village Funeral. *In* From Village to City: Studies in

the Traditional Roots of Hong Kong Society. David Faure, James Hayes, and Alan Birch, eds. Pp. 129–163. Centre of Asian Studies, University of Hong Kong.

Hayes, James
1983a Secular Non-gentry Leadership of Temple and Shrine Organisations in Urban British Hong Kong. JHKBRAS 23:112–138.
1983b The Kwun Yam Tung Shan Temple of East Kowloon, 1840–1940. JHKBRAS 23:212–217.
1983c. The Rural Communities of Hong Kong: Studies and Themes. Hong Kong: Oxford University Press.

Hou, Ching-lang
1975 Monnaies d'Offrande et la Notion de Tresorerie dans la Religion Chinoise. Paris: Press Universitaire de France.

Hui, C. Harry
1991 Religious and Supernaturalistic Beliefs. *In* Indicators of Social Development: Hong Kong 1988. Siu-kai, Lee Ming-kwan, Wan Po-san and Wong Siu-lun, eds. Pp. 103–143. Hong Kong Institute of Asia-Pacific Studies, The Chinese University of Hong Kong.

Issei, Tanaka
1989 The Jiao Festival in Hong Kong and The New Territories. *In* The Turning of the Tide: Religion in China Today. Julian Pas, ed. Pp. 271–298. Hong Kong: Oxford University Press.

Jen, Yu-wen
1967 The Travelling Palace of Southern Sung. JHKBRAS 7:21–38.

Katz, Paul R.
1992 Changes in Wang-yeh Beliefs in Postwar Taiwan: A Case Study in Two Wang-yeh Temples. Journal of Chinese Religions 20:203–213.
1995 Demon Hordes and Burning Boats: The Cult of Marshall Wen in Late Imperial China. Albany, N.Y.: State University of New York Press.

Lang, Graeme, and Lars Ragvald
1993 The Rise of a Refugee God: Hong Kong's Wong Tai Sin. Hong Kong: Oxford University Press.

Lethbridge, Henry
1978 Hong Kong: Stability and Change. Hong Kong: Oxford University Press.

Mak, Jenny W.H., and Bernard W.K. Lau
1992 Stress as a Social Phenomenon in Hong Kong. *In* Indicators of Social Development: Hong Kong, 1990. Pp. 33–51 Hong Kong Institute of Asia-Pacific Studies, The Chinese University of Hong Kong.

Meyer, Jeffrey F.
1991 The Dragons of Tiananmen: Beijing as a Sacred City. Columbia, S.C.: University of South Carolina Press.

Miller, Peter
1988 Kerala: Jewell of India's Malabar Coast. National Geographic 173, May:592–617.

Mo, Timothy
1978 The Monkey King. London: Penguin.

Myers, John
1975a Hong Kong Spirit-medium Temple. JHKBRAS 15:16–27.

1981 Traditional Chinese Religious Practices in an Urban-industrial Setting: The Example of Kwun Tong. *In* Social Life and Development in Hong Kong. Ambrose Y.C. King and Rance P.L. Lee ,eds. Pp. 275–288. Hong Kong: The Chinese University of Hong Kong.

Roper, Geoffrey
1990 Report on Visit to Tai Hang Fire Dragon Dance, Mid-Autumn Festival, 1992. JHKBRAS 30:307–8.

Seiwert, Hubert
1981 Religious Response to Modernisation in Taiwan: The Case of I-Kuan Tao. JHKBRAS 21:42–70.

Shryock, John K.
1931 The Temples of Anking and their Cults. Paris: Librairie Orientaliste.

Sinn, Elizabeth
1989 Power and Charity: The Early History of the Tung Wah Hospital, Hong Kong. Hong Kong: Oxford University Press.

Siu, Anthony K.K.
1987 Tam Kung: His Legend and Worship. JHKBRAS 27:278–9.

Smith, Carl T.
1973 Notes on Chinese Temples in Hong Kong. JHKBRAS 13:133–139.

Stark, Rodney, and William S. Bainbridge
1987 A Theory of Religion. N.Y.: Peter Lang.

Stevens, Keith
1977 Under Altars. JHKBRAS 17:85–100.
1980 Chinese Monasteries, Temples, Shrines, and Altars in Hong Kong and Macau. JHKBRAS 20:1–33.
1989 The Jade Emperor and His Family: Yuh Huang Ta Ti. JHKBRAS 29:18–33.
1990 Chinese Local Semi-divine Deities. JHKBRAS 30:75–88.

Tsai, Wen-hui
1979 Historical Personalities in Chinese Folk Religion: A Functional Interpretation. *In* Legend, Lore, and Religion in China, Essays in Honor of Wolfram Eberhard on his 70th Birthday. Sarah Allan and Alvin P. Cohen, eds. Pp. 23–42. San Francisco: Chinese Materials Centre.

Tsui, Bartholomew P.M.
1985 Tan Tse Tao: A Contemporary Chinese Faith-healing Sect in Hong Kong. JHKBRAS 25:1–17.
1991 Taoist Tradition and Change: The Story of the Complete Perfection Sect in Hong Kong. Hong Kong: Christian Study Centre on Chinese Religion and Culture.

Watson, James L.
1985 Standardising the Gods: The Promotion of Tien Hou ('Empress of Heaven') along the South China Coast, 960–1960. *In* Popular Culture in Late Imperial China. David Johnson, Andrew J. Nathan, and Evelyn S. Rawski, eds. Pp. 292–324 Berkeley: University of California Press.

Watson, Rubie S.
1985 Inequality among Brothers: Class and Kinship in South China. N.Y.: Cambridge University Press.

Ward, Barbara, and Joan Law
  1993 Chinese Festivals in Hong Kong. Hong Kong: The Guidebook Company.
Wolf, Arthur F.
  1974 Gods, Ghosts, and Ancestors. *In* Religion and Ritual in Chinese Society. Arthur F. Wolf, ed. Pp. 131–182. Berkeley: University of California Press.

The 'Next Magazine' cover at the height of the rumour (13 November 1992). It reads: The Truth of the TV Ghost Advertisement Rumour'.

12

GHOSTS AND THE NEW GOVERNOR
THE ANTHROPOLOGY OF A HONG KONG RUMOUR

Grant Evans

In early November 1992 the Chinese population of Hong Kong was suddenly enthralled by a ghost story. In trains, buses, schools, offices and homes people swapped information, investigated and discussed the 'ghosts' which allegedly had appeared in a most unlikely location – a TV commercial. It was all very '*hóu kèihgwaai ge*' – very strange.

The rumour, like an epidemic, flared up at the beginning of November, reached a peak around the middle of the month and then abated, so that by December it had all but disappeared.

The rumour focused on two commercials placed on Hong Kong television by the Kowloon-Canton Rail Corporation (KCRC). One commercial, which ran for 30 seconds and which attracted most comment was of a group of very young children (ages 6–8) in a line, hands on each others' shoulders, playing trains. This I will call the 'ghost train' commercial. The second which ran for 40 seconds showed children playing a traffic light game – '*yāt, yih, sàam, hùng luhk dāng*'. Both of these commercials were made in 1991; the 'ghost train' had been on air in Hong Kong from May 1991 until June 1992, the second commercial from September 1991 to October 1992. So, they both had been taken off the air at the time the rumour erupted. The interesting question is, why, after all these months on air, did a powerful rumour suddenly attach itself to these commercials?

But first, what was the nature of the rumour and where did it begin, if anywhere?

Of course, there are various folk theories concerning the origins of the rumour. It is possible that the ghost story had been around for a while before November, and indeed some people claim to have first heard it some months before. However, these claims made at the height of the story cannot be checked, and we know that a feature of rumours is that there is a tendency for people to 'back-date' their knowledge of a particular story and consequently we have reason to be sceptical of such claims. Furthermore, we are really interested in why a rumour acquires mass circulation rather than origins.

Nevertheless, it does seem that the key take-off point for the ghost story was a radio programme on Commercial Radio Two on the 31 October, Halloween night, when the DJs Lam Hoi Fung and Kuok Man Fai, adepts of Hong Kong's *mòuh lèih tàu* ('nonsense') verbal repartee, were asking listeners to call in with ghost stories. One listener called in with a KCRC ghost story:

DJs: 'Happy Halloween! Hallo Bin Bin.

A: Happy Halloween! I am Dorothy. I want to talk about the commercial . . .

DJs: What commercial?

A: The commercial of the KCRC . . . The kids are playing 'Traffic Light', remember? . . . Some people saw seven kids altogether. One of them is strange. When the others are playing happily he is the only one with a very white face. This is very strange.

DJs: Yes. People are saying this outside.

A: Some telephoned to complain. But when a check was made the exact number of kids is only six . . .

DJs: One, two, three, four, seven, nine, six, twelve. I saw twelve kids! Why? Did you see the commercial yourself?

A: I felt something strange, but I didn't notice anything in particular.

DJs: You should go to the Consumer Council to complain.

A: Some people could see the kids bleeding from their seven orifices . . .

DJs: Who did you say was bleeding? Were the persons bleeding? Maybe you have a dirty TV screen. Did you see it yourself? It is strange.

A: I felt something strange, but it wasn't clear.'

Later that evening 'Christine' rang the same programme:

A: 'I want to talk about the train commercial. In fact it came from a report on the 60 minutes programme on an English TV channel a few days ago. They interviewed the director of the commercial. There should originally be six kids altogether.

> The second kid is obviously bleeding from the face, as can be
> seen on the TV screen . . .
> (Scary sound)
> DJs: Put on your pants . . . Yes, let's continue.
> A: It has been discovered that the commercial was filmed
>   somewhere in China. I don't know whether the kids are from
>   China or Hong Kong, but two of them died and four of them
>   have disappeared.
>   (Mysterious sound)
> DJs: Did you see the programme yourself? Or did others tell you?
> A: My friend told me all this today.
> DJs: So you are being deceived! Today is Halloween. Your friend is
>   just playing with you!'

Where these listeners got the story from we don't know, and perhaps can
never know. The 60 Minutes programme, we should note, does not exist.
But, the actual origin of the story is not all that important, even though
the origins of rumours fascinate people.

Despite the radio presenters' ironic and mocking tone on Halloween
eve the rumour sprang to life and on the following programme the DJs
felt compelled to play the following jingle:

> 'Someone in our audience on Halloween mentioned something
> about the KCRC commercial rumours on our programme. After
> that the news unexpectedly spread from one to ten, from ten to one
> hundred, from one hundred to one thousand, from one thousand to
> ten thousand. From slow to fast, from false to true, from true to
> very true, from very true to frightening.
>
> Unexpectedly, in this confusing time, not just one person, but
> children and adults alike from all over are inventing stories and
> associating thoughts. The young children are scared.
> We hope that we should have a proper attitude in the face of such
> rumours. Please remember do not hear, believe or spread news that
> is not real.
>
> But who is the one who tried to fool the people with evil words,
> making something out of nothing and setting the fire alight?'

From this point the story quickly spread into the press and television,
and fanned out into the Hong Kong population. Soon there was hardly a
Chinese person in Hong Kong who had not heard the rumour. In
contrast, and typically, the expatriate community remained largely

unaware of the scale of the rumour and it received little coverage in the English press.

There are many minor variations of the rumour, which is to be expected, because variations help keep the rumour alive. Variations give the illusion of having new information. In a sense, what happens with most rumours is that a core storyline crystallises, to which can be added small and often localised variations. There are many famous examples of this from elsewhere, and I do not need to go into them now (see Brunvand 1981). The core elements of the KCRC 'ghost story' were that one of the children in the line was a ghost (often identified as the third child in the line, sometimes the last), and that this ghost had caused the death of several of the children, and serious illness or disappearance of the others. Part of the 'evidence' for this was that the girl in front of the third 'ghost' child was bleeding from the mouth. Another piece of 'evidence' was that the childrens' feet appeared to not touch the ground. They drifted along like ghosts.

I should point out that generally I will treat the various sources I tap in Hong Kong as a single 'informant'. My reason for doing this is that rumour is a collective phenomenon and perhaps provides an insight into the 'collective unconscious' of, in this case, Hong Kong society. But in doing this we must keep in mind that it is a very special kind of 'public opinion' we are tapping. As anthropologist Peter Lienhardt comments, 'rumour has its associations much less in the field of logical thought than in the field of metaphorical thought. It is figurative. Hence the attitudes it expresses do not have to be consistent with each other. A bizarre set of 'facts' – and it has to be bizarre here for the rumour to work – is invented to fit in with the attitudes of the public' (1975:128).

So, what does this rumour tell us about Hong Kong society?

RUMOUR AND THE STRIVING FOR MEANING

To many people rumours and panics are irrational and meaningless. But psychologists, sociologists and anthropologists who have studied these phenomena see in them a social and cultural logic. Allport and Postman's late 1940s study *The Psychology of Rumor*, which arose out of the rumours that circulated during World War 2, saw them as an 'effort after meaning'. Rumours, they wrote, 'sometimes provide a broader interpretation of various puzzling features of the environment and so play a prominent part in the intellectual drive to render the surrounding world intelligible' (1947:45). Shibutani's sociological study called rumours 'collective problem-solving . . . men caught in an ambiguous situation attempt to construe a meaningful interpretation of it by pooling their intellectual resources' (1966:17). And Lienhardt writes that 'rumours of the more fantastic sort can represent, and may generally represent, complexities of public feeling that cannot readily be made articulate at a more thoughtful level' (1975:130).

When people are faced with missing details and secrecy then conditions are created for people to attempt to fill in the details in order to make the situation less ambiguous. These situations can be more or less extreme. The news we receive everyday through the mass media is selective, and therefore it always allows some basis for speculation. In fact knowledge of this selectiveness is the basis for much scepticism about the press. Such scepticism was voiced at the height of the rumour when the advertisement was re-screened to allay public fears. One rumour claimed that the ghosts had been edited out of the original version of the commercial. The more selective (censored) the news, the more room there is for speculative rumour.

One aspect of the striving for meaning is the attempt to discover the 'real' origins of the rumour, in order to prove that it did not just emerge capriciously from thin air, and with the hope of providing the rumour with some motivation. Only rarely, however, can the origin of a rumour be isolated. Most often, as in the ghost commercial rumour in Hong Kong, the source of 'hard information' about a rumour disappears along the endless trail of a 'friend of a friend of a friend told me'.

In studies of rumours elsewhere it has been found that 'explanations' will often attribute the rumour to malicious motives of rivals. Ronald Baker's study of 'The Department Store Snake' concerning K-Mart in the US says that 'several K-Mart managers . . . swear the story was started by a competing department store . . .' (1976:371). Similarly, in Hong Kong some commentators suggested that the 'ghost train' rumour was started by commercial rivals (a 'theory' which overlooked the fact that the KCRC does not have any rivals). Advertisers Olgivy & Mather, however, do have rivals and some hinted that 'jealousy' (*Eastweek* 12/11/ 92) over the success of the commercial caused them to spread the rumour. A similar allegation was made by the Teacher's Federation statement on the rumour (*Wan Wei Pao* 12/11/92). Still other 'origin' stories pointed more diffusely to the advertising industry. For example the *Tin Tin Daily News* (6/11/92) wrote: 'According to our investigations, the source of this rumour started with a preview of the concerned commercial. Among the previewers, a programme host and a columnist reported their discovery of "strange images" in the commercial. At first these stories were restricted to the "in" circle. But the story soon spread' (see also *The Metropolitan Weekly*, 14/11/92). Several of the people I interviewed about the commercial claimed to have a 'friend of a friend who works in advertising' (on several occasions there was confusion about whether the friend of a friend actually worked for O&M), and this person said that the ghost was real and that there was an attempt at a cover up. One story suggested that KCRC employees whose pay rise had been delayed were 'subtly' associated with the rumour (*Hong Kong Economic Journal Daily* 11/11/92). None of these 'origin stories' were ever confirmed. Nevertheless they continued to circulate at the time of the rumour because they offered an 'explanation' in terms of 'dirty tricks' between competitors. Others simply hinted darkly that 'evil people' started the rumour and were perpetuating it.

Other 'origin stories' claimed the rumour started in Sha Tin and Tai Po (*Hong Kong Daily News* 13/11/92), or started in the Tuen Mun area (*Fresh Weekly,* November, No.588), while yet another report said the source of the rumour was 'from a message left in a pager station' (*Ming Pao Daily News* 15/11/92). We shall return to such apparently senseless variations below.

There were also sober, 'rationalistic' attempts to explain the origins of the story. The *South China Morning Post* (14/11/92) reported: 'it began in the New Territories where television reception may not be perfect and may lead to "ghosting" of images on screen.' This was followed by several attempts in magazines and in TV programmes to explain the technology of editing, TV photography, and so on. But what these rationalistic interpretations overlook is the fact that the commercial was collectively appropriated to carry cultural, social and political messages. By way of comparison we can turn to a fascinating study of the introduction of photography into the United States last century by Barbara Allen who points out how the novelty of photography was used to articulate themes of spirit appearances, and so on. She writes: 'While the newspaper accounts marvel at the apparent wizardry of photography, the folkloristic accounts use the imperfectly understood photographic process as a vehicle for treating traditional themes such as love, justice, revenge, and retribution – human concerns far more lasting than technological wonders; . . . ordinary portraits become ghostly images, prepared glass plates [used in early photography] become windows and mirrors [in which images of ghosts are seen] . . .' (1982:101). Viewed in this light, attempts to give technical explanations in order to disperse the ghost rumour were beside the point.

MASS MEDIA & RUMOUR

Not surprisingly one of the themes in the debate surrounding the 'ghost train' commercial was the role of the mass media, especially as the rumour pivoted on a Television advertisement. As we all know there is an ongoing 'moral' debate in modern societies – not just in Hong Kong – about the impact of advertising on the minds and habits of people, and on young people in particular. The mass media penetrates the home and this is often perceived as an invasion of outside influences into the family. Perceptions of such influences were a subterranean theme in the 'ghost train' debate, and one writer spoke of media coverage of the rumour 'invading the family' (*Express News* 13/11/92).

However, in this case, no-one could seriously target such a 'cute, innocent' advertisement in terms of improper influence on the minds of youth. Public ire instead was directed by segments of the media at other segments of the media, joined by 'responsible' public figures, who attacked irresponsible reporting and sensationalism. Ching Kai Ming, writing in the *Hong Kong Economic Daily News* (17/11/92) called on the media to show some moral responsibility, and not just chase money: 'When discussing the social responsibility of the media some suggest that there should be self-discipline, but this could have political implications. Political self-discipline would inhibit the reporting function of the media: political self discipline would be media suicide. On the other hand, moral discipline ensures popular support for the media. To not emphasize moral discipline would be suicidal for the media too. Slow suicide. When the rumours were spreading and reaching their climax . . . the media should cooperate. But the fact is that the media has been fighting to search for the most sensational story.' But, as this commentary shows, there was also considerable sensitivity concerning the problems of political censorship, and lying at the back of this was anxiety about post 1997 Hong Kong.

Some of the strongest criticism, however, was directed at ATV who, in a special programme on the rumour, invited a *hei gùng sì fú*, Mr Ho, to comment on the commercial, whereupon he affirmed that there were ghosts. The Teachers Federation, among others, condemned the programme: 'We believe the electronic media is irresponsible. Their attitude in spreading superstition and in hurting the feelings of the children should be criticised. They should apologize.' (*Wan Wei Pao* 12/11/92)

There is no question that the mass media today can speed up the transmission of rumours through both straight reporting, and through radio 'hotlines'.[1] In the 'ghost train' story the mass media both recorded and further disseminated variations on the rumour. However, a closer analysis of the course of the rumour tends to contradict simplistic assumptions, made by many commentators on the media, of a passive public at the mercy of media interpretations. In the 'ghost train' rumour we see a complex interaction between a public actively constructing explanations of the rumour and media recording and re-ordering of that process.

Indeed, much of the rumour was spread by word of mouth, in schools, offices, on trains and buses and around dinner tables. As Jan Brunvand, author of *The Vanishing Hitchiker* (1981:11) writes: 'Apparently the basic human need for meaningful personal contact cannot be entirely replaced by the mass media and popular culture. A portion of our interest in what is occurring in the world must be filled by some face-to-face reports from other human beings.' These discussions produced continual variations in the detail of the rumour and kept it alive. The media in turn tried to keep up with these variations by occasionally attempting to systematise them, only to be eclipsed by new variations. In the process, however, the media no doubt communicated some new variations to people who had not yet heard them. This ongoing attempt to systematise the story is, in one sense, an attempt by the media to gain control over the story, and perhaps this is one reason why we begin to see the construction of obscure interpretations of the commercial. In his discussion of rumours in the US Donald Bird notes that people begin to invent complex numerologies or provide obscure interpretations for ordinary events (he refers for example to a rumour around the alleged death of then Beatles member Paul McCartney. The story was based, among other things, on the fact that he was not wearing shoes on the *Abbey Road* album cover), he writes: 'Some of these games appear to go beyond a search for understanding to a deliberate construction of obscure codes and meanings which arise not from lack of information, but rather, it seems, from a desire by participants to savour, toy, or manipulate the item under discussion' (1976:300). I would suggest that one of the things we are seeing in these obscure interpretations is an attempt by the public to maintain a discourse which is autonomous from the media. To some extent, this is a generationally specific autonomous discourse, something we shall return to below in the discussion of children.

Eastweek (12/11/92), *Fresh Weekly* (No.588, November 1992) and *The Metropolitan Weekly* (14/11/92) all provided systematisations of the rumour, reducing it to seven variations in the cases of the first two magazines, ten in the latter. The following is a typical example from *Eastweek*:

(1) Among the kids in the line playing the moving train game there was an extra girl (or shadow) at the end of the line. Some claimed that her face was bloody all over.
(2) The third boy in the line has a trace of blood on his face.
(3) All the children in the commercial floated along without touching the ground.
(4) The girl whose shoulders were being held by the extra girl died after the filming of the commercial.
(5) Among the six participating kids, four of them are reported to have disappeared, while the other two died for no obvious reason.
(6) Five of the ten children died after the filming.
(7) Babies cried after seeing the commercial, and children could see blood on the faces when it is played in slow motion.

In the other summaries there were further variations – rumours of the death of the director of the commercial, and so on. Such inventiveness on the part of the Hong Kong public kept the rumour moving at a cracking pace for several weeks.

We should not overlook the sheer thrill of participating in a rumour like this which helps to break the routine of everyday life. As one Hong Kong journalist half-joked it comes 'from the sense of entertaining oneself with pain' (*Hong Kong Economic Times* 11/11/92). Despite the fear associated with the rumour, for a short while it also created in Hong Kong's metropolis a sense of *communitas* and shared experience and knowledge, which conveniently did not impinge on anyone directly and so, in that way, was uncontentious. Thus the rumour was simultaneously a symptom of anxiety and an outlet for it.

THE NEW GOVERNOR

It would be absurd to claim that Hong Kong people were not anxious about the consequences of impending union with China in mid-1997 before Chris Patten made his fateful policy speech of 7 October 1992. Indeed, since the Joint Declaration between China and Britain in 1984 many people have been voting with their feet and leaving Hong Kong. But Patten's speech and China's strong reaction to it galvanised fears concerning Hong Kong's future. It was in this general atmosphere of intense political and social anxiety that the ghost rumour sprang into life.

The relationship between the general political context and the rumour was sometimes acknowledged in the press reporting at the time. *Eastweek* (12/11/92) was one of the first to make the connection: 'The ghost story serves as an alternative to the talks on the airport and the Governor and his policy.' On the following day, four separate newspapers made the connection. The *Hong Kong Economic Journal Daily News* (13/11/92) followed a similar line of thought to *Eastweek:* 'we lack something in common to talk about. The politics between the two governments are deadlocked. What else is more exciting than the eerie talks? . . . the kids are in China and are hard to contact, therefore the ghost story can become as horrible as it likes . . .'. In one of the reports that appeared in *Ming Pao* one writer commenting on the alleged "crowd psychology" of the rumour, claimed: 'People immigrating because of the 1997 issue is an example of 'crowd psychology' being developed into "hysteria"' (Education & Culture section 13/11/92). Another report in the same edition by Shek Kee drew attention to how small incidents can highlight the unsettled relations between China and Hong Kong. The writer refers to threats made to a Hong Kong actress, Wo Wai Chung, when she was in Beijing, and to the commercial.

> I have two apparently unrelated cases here. In fact they are both related in the sense that they both took place in China. The relationship between Hong Kong/Taiwan and China is growing closer. The award winning commercial was filmed in Beijing using Beijing kids. There is also another award winning commercial by Marlboro, this time of a spectacular Lion Dance and Drum Dance. These kinds of commercials arouse nostalgic and positive feelings toward the mainland. And it is a trend for stars to make money in the north. When communication begins at a fast pace it is not surprising to find a mismatch. And China herself is changing. There are no established rules to cater for the new, or to settle the old. Therefore, rumours will be generated . . . .

The writer in *Express News* (13/11/92) commented: 'The ghost story is much more mysterious than the political debate . . . We do not know if there are secret talks between the governments. But the commercial won even more attention than the political gossip.' Some days later *Eastweek* (19/11/92) rejoined: 'Everybody is frightened, afraid and excited at the same time, in another strong whirlwind after Patten's (*Fèi Pahng*) speech. The rumour of the KCRC commercial is a hundred times more marvellous than the Sino-British talks.' Pro-Beijing paper, *Wan Wei Pao,* suspected anti-Beijing motives behind not only this rumour, but others as well:

> The KCRC commercial used a few Beijing kids as the protagonists . . . A few years back, it was rumoured that children here were being kidnapped and taken to Shenzhen. Some people were in a panic and the image of Shenzhen was affected. The case died down slowly without any conclusion . . . Coincidentally, the various rumours are related to China. It is unclear whether the motive is to blackmail China, or to abuse the backwardness of the mainland's media.
>
> (15/11/92)

While no-one analysed the issue at length, and while it was not a main theme in the commentary on the rumour, various commentators did draw attention to the broader political context of the rumour.[2] This context included suspicions of the actions of both governments – 'secret talks' – and of course in the absence of openness rumours will, as we have seen, attempt to fill in the gaps in our knowledge either in a direct or displaced way. Secondly, and as *Wan Wei Pao* recognizes, the rumours do reflect a general fear, or at least suspicion, of Beijing among Hong Kong people. But, *Wan Wei Pao* embarks on its own political 'search for meaning' by seeking a political culprit for the rumours – a vain search, of course.

The many rumours one has heard in Hong Kong about the fate of unspecified individuals in Shenzhen are illustrative of this general projected anxiety. There are many stories of Hong Kong individuals being dragged into large limousines in the streets of the New Economic Zone, drugged, having organs removed from their bodies[3] and then dumped back on the streets again. One can only be amazed by the extent to which this implausible story is believed or retailed in Hong Kong (for reports of other stories concerning Shenzhen see *Eastweek* 19/11/92). The only thing which makes it intelligible is both a displaced anxiety about China and the sense of difference many Hong Kong people feel when they travel there, even to a place as close and as similar as the NEZ.

Ghost stories and rumours of various kinds circulate, of course, on the mainland.[4] Hong Kong television is watched in the NEZ and in Guangdong, so not only had many people there seen the 'ghost' commercial, but many had also heard of the rumour. In fact the rumour was reported in the *Shenzhen Special Economic Zone Daily* on 21

November 1992. Yet the rumour never took off there. I asked a friend of mine who taught at the University of Shenzhen to ask his students (at the beginning of December) what they had heard of the rumour and what they thought about it. Sixty-one gave written replies. Besides one student who wrote 'I am so stupid that I don't know anything about this story,' the other sixty had known about it for around one month. Most had heard about it from a friend, although some had received their information from either Hong Kong radio or television or newspapers. Forty-eight of the students thought it was 'nonsense', and some added 'striving after explanation' type reasons for the rumour, such as attempts by advertising competitors to slur the companies involved. Among the other 12 some wrote 'maybe it's true' or 'It makes me wonder what happened', through to simply 'it frightens me'. The rumour, however, did not develop into any kind of mass hysteria in Shenzhen and appears to have remained at the level of idle chatter.

The explanation for the different reactions to the rumour lies in the contrast between the political contexts of Hong Kong and Shenzhen. One may want to suggest, as did one of the Shenzhen disbelievers, that 'Hong Kong people are superstitious', but I think it would be difficult to argue that Hong Kong is more 'superstitious' than other parts of China (or any less!).

So, the new Governor's speech about democracy and political 'through trains', and Beijing's strong reaction to it, cathected with general anxiety about 1997 to send the 'ghost train' rumour racing down the tracks.

GHOSTS AND CHILDREN

A fundamental feature of the whole rumour was its focus on children – both on those in the advertisement, and a concern for the effect of the rumour on children in Hong Kong.

First, let's focus on the children in the commercial. Certainly before the rumour began the children were generally considered to be 'cute' (*dākyi*). Nevertheless, they were marked as somehow different. The designers of the advertisement set out to evoke a world of childhood innocence, a world we have lost. At the end of the 'ghost train' commercial we read the words: 'Trains. When you were small, they were wonderful. At KCRC we're working hard to keep it that way for you.' In order to find 'suitably innocent-looking kids' for the commercial the makers had to go to China. According to O&M's executive director,

'Hong Kong kids are too slick. They're more likely to play Ninja turtles than chugga-chugga.' (cited by Lim 1991:15) This idea was repeated to me by the company's senior copywriter for the commercial, K.C. Chang during an interview in December 1992. Hong Kong kids were, he said, too 'street-wise and too camera conscious.' So they went to Beijing where they selected the children from a kindergarten on the outskirts of the city. 'We chose some cute ones, but also some deliberately not cute. Such as the third kid in the line who has slightly bulging eyes, or the last kid who was chubby. We did not want kids who had a plastic look like in other commercials.' Their idea was, he said, to create a softer image for a faceless, large organisation like the KCRC. Greenish, sepia like tones were also used to evoke a sense of memory and nostalgia. And they were successful. Early reactions to the advertisement were positive. Lim, in his 1991 survey of Hong Kong advertisements cites a public relations person who placed the commercial at the top of his list: 'I never get tired of seeing it. It has a nice, nostalgic way of presenting children's concept of trains and linking it with the service of the KCRC. The music is also particularly good.' Another person he interviewed at the time responded: 'Kids these days won't play like this but those in their 30s and 40s will recall the days when they did.' (Lim 1991:15). And similar accolades were given to the commercial when it won advertising awards in May the following year.

The 'innocence' of the children in the commercial, their style of dress, the game, all marked them as somehow separate from Hong Kong kids, and this separateness, perhaps even strangeness, was one of the reasons the commercial became an appropriate vehicle for a rumour. Once the rumour had begun, this difference was highlighted in the media and by some of my informants. Some of the latter denied the children were at all 'cute', and said they were a non-Hong Kong idea of pretty kids. 'Their eyes are too big, they are too pale and their clothes are not pretty. The problem with the commercial is that there is too much green in it and green is a deathly colour. The children are too pale and ghostly.' Of course, here we have a retrospective view of the commercial which reconstructs an original perception of separateness as something now foreign and ugly.

The *Hong Kong Economic Journal Daily* (17/11/92) almost laments that 'Hong Kong kids are mini-adults . . . Only in Beijing could they find fresh and innocent kids . . . Everyone is impressed by the faces of the lovely and simple kids. In fact, the kids in the commercial, their costumes, movement and even facial expressions, are all different from the Hong Kong kids.' Similar ideas had been expressed earlier in *Tin Tin*

Daily News (10/11/92) where the kids used in the commercial were identified by name: 'The five kids in the "train commercial" are Wu Shong, Cheng Kin, Chiu Yu, Chiu Han and Chow Wai. They are naughty and cute. They are not mini-adults like Hong Kong kids. According to one crew member the kids are compliant, polite and cute. When they met ladies they would say, "Hello Auntie!". When they received a candy they said "Thanks Auntie!". When the assistant directress said she would like to be Wu Shong's Godmother, Wu replied: "I don't want a Godmother from Hong Kong". Why? The child replied: "Because Hong Kong people do not speak genuine Chinese".' Not only do these children mobilise feelings about a 'world we have lost', but perhaps even feelings about 'the country we have lost'. Indeed, Hong Kong's ambiguous relationship with China, is suddenly spotlighted by Wu Shong's barb about Cantonese not speaking 'real Chinese'.

The controversy surrounding the commercial mobilised views concerning children in contemporary Hong Kong, and anxieties about them. These anxieties have several sources: changing family relations in modern Hong Kong are leading to a gradual cultural reformulation of ideas parents have towards children. However, like everywhere, people feel they are stepping into unchartered waters and this in itself creates anxiety. Thus there are many attractions in reconstructing a fantasy of a more 'innocent' past. Second, Hong Kong society is beginning to experience many of the trials and tribulations of families in other modern industrial societies, and these are voiced in the debate over the commercial. People in Hong Kong are aware of the pressures on children to succeed in the modern world. This pressure along with others has been blamed for the rising rate of suicide among children up to 1992, and beyond. This too, created a general, diffuse feeling of anxiety.

Naturally, children represent the future, and so anxiety about the future of Hong Kong was therefore mediated via anxieties concerning children.

Take, for example, the following reflections by Lee Pik Wah writing in *Oriental Daily News* (21/11/92):

To be a child in modern times is not an easy job . . . This is a generation who lack childishness. They no longer have lullabies, cartoons or simple playthings. They have nothing to be nostalgic about when they grow up. The songs they sing are the love songs of the Karaoke, the films they see are full of bloodshed and violence, the toys they play with are complicated and expensive. Most of their games are the "fighting games". Children live in

280

crowded conditions with their families due to rising property values. They have no choice but to follow around the Filipino maid or the elderly when their parents go off to work. They meet their parents only once a week. They lack love, just like lacking oxygen. It is extraordinary that a TV commercial about kids playing a game could arouse such intense fear. When I hear friends talking about the situation of children I feel sorry for the poor kids. Eventually, even babies will not know what happiness is . . .

Others linked the issue to child abuse. The *Oriental Daily News* (26/11/ 92) noted the irony of the fact that the press release by O&M and the KCRC entitled "It is unfair to the innocent kids", was coincidentally the same title the paper used on the same day for a story on child abuse in Hong Kong. People may consider outsiders and the rumour spreaders as evil, but there are also 'evil parents in the world. And what about the rest of the six million other people here? Parents are quarrelling everyday. It is unfair for the kids.' In their ruminations on the effect of the commercial on 'the innocent children' still others complained that not enough attention was being paid by society to childrens' 'psychological well-being . . . For instance, our news stalls are one of the most filthy parts of our society. We have no choice but to look at nude photographs at the news stalls. To cite another example: we do not have censorship of comics which convey unacceptable messages to the youngsters' (*Hong Kong Economic Daily News* 17/11/92). The vulnerability of children was also focused on by the numerous reports of children being too scared to go to the toilet alone, or being scared to sleep alone at night during the height of the rumour. Indeed, this hysteria swept through the halls of the University of Hong Kong where students also reported being scared of going to the toilet and of gathering in groups in rooms to sleep together. And perhaps what is not too far from the minds of these students is their impending loss of 'sexual innocence'.

In some respects, therefore, the discussion of the rumour also took on features of a moral panic relating to young children.

There are many reasons why a society's anxiety should focus on its children. For a start they represent the future and cultural continuity. In the context of Patten's speech and feelings of insecurity about Hong Kong's future, it is not surprising that these anxieties should be re-channelled through children. Indeed, one may want to suggest that this kind of displacement is one consequence of the lack of democracy in Hong Kong, in that the political channels for expressing disquiet are restricted.

Around the same period there had also been growing concern about child suicides in Hong Kong. Many of these appear to be a result of growing strains and stresses within families and on individuals. Pressures to succeed at school, both peer and parental, is one source of strain. The other would appear to be the result of something like a 'generation gap' in Hong Kong where, within the modern nuclear family, ideologies of companionship and mutuality mix in confusing ways with lingering authoritarian parental attitudes. And in many families girls are still treated as less valuable than boys, while at the same time they are encouraged to succeed intellectually, which of course has an important impact on their self-esteem. The suicides also formed part of the background to the atmosphere surrounding the rumour, and in fact surfaced in the rumour itself. One of my informants retold the following story: 'The ghost is one of the children who was not selected, out of all the children that could have been selected for the advertisement. The child was scolded by his mother when he got home for not getting the job. Therefore, the child committed suicide and became a ghost and wreaked havoc on the other children.' One can quickly see in this story a re-cycled version of real events in Hong Kong where children have committed suicide after their parents have scolded them for poor school results. Several variations of the rumour speak of vengeance by a child who for one reason or another was excluded from being featured in the commercial. To give another example: 'A woman whose child had died two years before saw her child in the commercial. She consulted a shaman who told her that her child was very lonely and wanted to participate in the choo-choo-train game. The other children wouldn't let her join and so the child took revenge.'

Perhaps at an even deeper level there is an association of children with the dead. The fact that the rumour took off at the time of Halloween is very suggestive in this regard. Halloween is not well known in the Chinese community, but many people do know that 'the foreigners' have their own ghost festival – 'gwáilou gwái jit' – and as we have seen a radio station took this opportunity to ask its listeners to phone in with ghost stories. In the Halloween festival children dress up as ghosts or as the dead and are able, during this rite of reversal, to go and demand propitiation from adults who offer them sweets or money. They are placated in the same way as ghosts are in Chinese society and elsewhere, by making offerings to them. In his discussion of festivals preceding and associated with Christmas, Levi-Strauss has drawn attention to the fact that children are, by definition, uninitiated into adult society, and in important respects they remain at the margins of society. Thus, he asks, in festivals of the dead 'who can personify the dead in a society of the living if not those who, one way or another, are incompletely incorporated into the group, who, that is, share the *otherness* which symbolizes the supreme dualism: that of the dead and the living?' (1993:49). Children, or foreigners, or in the past, slaves, could all perform this role for 'the fact of being other is the nearest image we can get of death' (1993:50). I take Levi-Strauss's observations as suggestive because the boundaries between adulthood and childhood will be more sharply drawn in some cultures than in others.

Although there is no direct parallel role for children within, for example, the Chinese Ghost Festival that I am aware of, we can still reflect on the role of children as symbols of the culturally anomalous. The deaths of children and young people (especially women) before they become adults makes them potential 'hungry ghosts', a fear clearly expressed in the havoc allegedly wreaked by the child in the ghost commercial. People who die before they are fully incorporated into society are cultural anomalies and therefore most likely to become avenging ghosts. This is one of the central explanations for 'ghost marriages' in Chinese society (Martin 1991). The boundaries between adulthood and childhood remain strongly drawn in Hong Kong, although this is in the process of change. Indeed the renegotiation of relations between parents and children in modern Hong Kong probably heightens adult perceptions of 'lost innocence', and probably explains the references to Hong Kong children as 'mini adults' in the discussions around the rumour. There are other clues within the rumour itself that suggest that children, at least unconsciously, are somehow regarded as liminal. For example babies were said to cry uncontrollably after seeing the commercial (*Eastweek* 12/11/92). Others suggested that only people with 'yin eyes' (*yām ngáahn*) could see the ghost, and that children especially were able to see the ghost.

These distinctions between children and adults have further implications for the course of the rumour. Studies of urban societies have drawn attention to the existence of sub-cultures who have their own networks of communication, 'shared symbols and meanings, an esoteric language, cultural objects, a vocabulary of motives,' and so on (Laba 1979). And in their studies of urban folklore some have drawn attention to the fact 'that the young possess their own oral culture' (Opie 1980:65). Several have also referred to the importance of school children as a group for the oral transmission of rumours and urban legends (Baker 1969; Fine 1979; Kapferer 1992). Not surprisingly then, schools in Hong Kong became a hotbed for the 'ghost train' rumour.

Teachers from around the territory reported hysteria among students, and in response the Education Department Counselling Unit set up a hotline to deal with any problems (*Hong Kong Daily News* 13/11/92; *Ming Pao Daily News* 13/11/92 & 17/11/92). Indeed, it would seem that the rumour began among children and made its way into adult society.

Children in modern Hong Kong used telephones to stay in touch with school friends and others throughout the course of the rumour. Telephones were, of course, an important source of oral transmission for everyone. But what was abundantly clear was that there was a distinct child/youth based circuit for the rumour, and this in itself was a further source of anxiety for adults who were unable to control this autonomous source of authority.

Indeed, the visual imagery and theme of the commercial encouraged children to identify with it, but it was also evident from early on that younger people responded to it differently from adults. Lim in his September 1991 survey wrote: 'older viewers among the twelve polled understood the commercial better . . . a few of the younger women interviewed said they had to watch it several times before they realised what product was being promoted.' The nostalgic allusions made sense to the adults but not to the children, for whom the whole presentation was new, not nostalgic. Even the use of harmonica as background music was problematic. The association of harmonicas with steam trains was established as a musical trope within American popular music through black migration from the south to the north of the US and through blues music. Hong Kong adults may have been exposed to this musical trope and identified harmonicas with steam trains, but among my informants it seems that some of the younger children had no such nostalgic flash-back. Instead, they identified the harmonica only as the 'ghost music'. *Tin Tin Daily News* reported: 'Some children ran into their bedrooms and hid under the blanket when they heard the background music' (12/11/92). This contrasts with the advertising executive, cited above, who especially liked the music. Gaps in perception like this are, of course, unforseeable, but they do underline the separation of child from adult experience.

In her perceptive analysis of modern media panics Kirsten Drotner argues that children and youth are often the focus of these panics because in the modern world they occupy 'a pioneering cultural position' (1992:56). Media is youth oriented and this, she says, 'has not escaped adult attention' (1992:56). Therefore, 'On a *social level,* media panics basically attempt to re-establish a generational status-quo that the youthful pioneers seem to undermine' (1992:57). In fact, some of my older informants indicated that at times they would jokingly refer to the ghost rumour to scare younger children, thus using ghosts as a form of adult intimidation or discipline.

Children, Drotner goes on, are also panic targets 'because they inevitably represent experiences and emotions that are irrevocably lost to adults: one cannot go back in time and become a child again. Perhaps this common human condition becomes a particularly painful realisation in modernity because modernity is based precisely on evolution and a linear progression of time. To modern adults, children become captive symbols of what is lost not only in an individual sense, but in a social sense' (1992:59).

We can see from our analysis that children can become an extremely potent cultural symbol, and like most powerful symbols they articulate simultaneously several discourses, some of which cross-cut. *Children* as a potent polyvalent symbol is the reason why the KCRC's 'charming, innocent' commercial could become such an effective vehicle for Hong Kong society's anxieties.

RUMOUR 'RATIONALITY' AND 'SUPERSTITION'

The discourse on 'rationality' and 'superstition' surrounding discussion of the commercial is also very revealing. When the KCRC and O&M released their press statement denying the rumours of ghosts they argued that 'Rumours stop with rationality.' This sentiment was echoed by many other commentators, who in order to demonstrate their rationality pointed to the folly of previous rumours in Hong Kong. Or their rationality was couched in that of technology. The ATV programme on the rumour went to great lengths to demonstrate the various effects that could be achieved by modern photographic technology, methods of cutting, editing, varying shades of colour or speed, and so on. Or, for example, take the remarks of Dr Tso, a lecturer from the Chinese University who was invited by ATV to comment on the claims by *hei gùng* Master Ho that the light, floating steps of the children could not even be achieved even by a master of *hei gùng*, thus affirming the ghostliness of the children. Dr Tso remarked: 'please note that the advertisement is shown in slow motion. In slow motion everything is light. Next time you see him show it to him at normal speed, and perhaps he will reduce his suspicions.' And, so on. He also disputed Master Ho's specific claim that there were tree ghosts in the commercial: 'He said that there are two ghosts in the tree. I really cannot see any. It is just the shadow of the trunk.' Note the slight shift of meaning here; the existence of ghosts are not being denied, it is just that he cannot see the ones being pointed to by Ho. Indeed, Dr Tso is willing to agree that demons reside in trees. 'It is true,' he says, 'big trees might develop demons.' The important point here, of course, is that the representatives of 'rationality' do not deny the existence of ghosts, they simply deny the existence of these specific ghosts.

This contradiction was, culturally, not acknowledged and perhaps unacknowledgeable by most Chinese engaged in the debate over the ghosts. People who were calling on parents and adults to explain to their children that there were no ghosts in the commercial, were, by their actions, continually confirming the existence of the ghosts. For example, the host of the ATV programme mentioned above is well-known in Hong Kong as a strong believer in the spiritual power of *hei gùng* to overcome evil forces in the world. When, in late November he went to Beijing to locate the children in the commercial and interview and photograph them in order to 'rationally' dispel the rumour of their deaths, he carried with him Buddhist protective beads and a *fùng séui lòh gàang* (a geomancer's compass) for protection. 'He found a few tombs around the site [the original location for the filming], but nothing ghostly' (*Oriental Daily News*, 29/11/92). A Ms. Ho Kim Hong, the manager of the Public Affairs Department at the KCRC, in charge of helping dispel the rumour, saw its propagation as a kind of 'curse' on the children (*Ming Pao daily News* 17/11/92). And indeed, this is how the parents of the children felt and they could 'not understand why Hong Kong people had cursed their kids' (*Shing Pao* 29/11/92).

One parent explained the dilemma in a letter to *Eastweek* magazine (19/11/92) after watching a re-run of the commercial designed to dispel the rumour: 'The third kid in the line made me scared. It makes me shaky even when I'm writing now. How am I supposed to teach my children?'

Indeed, the whole campaign against the rumour within a cultural context which believes strongly in ghosts proved to be self-defeating. According to many people I interviewed, and according to press reports, on the night when the commercial was re-screened on 9 November many families gathered around their TV sets to watch the commercial. Some I interviewed videod the advertisement and played it back three or four times, each time debating the various rumour-theories concerning the ghost. Of course any child watching all this activity and attention to the commercial would in fact be observing adults taking the issue very seriously, thereby confirming that something important was afoot.

Naturally, the re-screening and the lounge-room discussion that followed served to allay some peoples fears.[5] But for many it simply scared them, as we saw above with the mother who wrote to *Eastweek*, or provided new impetus to the ongoing rumour. The next day at school, on the bus or train, or at work, people discussed yet again the commercial which had been played the night before, helping the rumour on its way.

In fact the discourse surrounding the commercial in a sense reflected a more general discourse concerning social and cultural change in Hong Kong: Modernity (or 'Westernization') versus Chinese 'tradition', or, modern 'rationality' versus Chinese 'superstition'. This discourse on Hong Kong is a complex and contradictory one, as we pointed out in the introduction to this book, for, depending on the context, modernity is regarded as either 'good' or 'bad', just as Chinese traditional ideas are regarded as 'good' or 'bad' depending on the context. In everyday life this discourse becomes especially complex because people unconsciously code-switch from one discourse to another. We can see this in the examples given above; people using the language of rationality but through their actions confirming 'superstitious' practices.

Rapid modernization may produce fantasies and anxieties about a total break with the past. Of course, such a radical break never happens. Nevertheless, while all modern societies celebrate change they simultaneously express deep anxieties about it. Such ambivalence seems to be part of the modern condition. In Hong Kong social change has occurred very rapidly, with processes that took hundreds of years in Europe being telescoped into three generations here, which in turn has produced significant generational shifts in experience. Elements of 'tradition' are, naturally, rejected or left behind in the process of change, others are retained and perhaps reinterpreted, or even re-invented, and they provide a sense of cultural continuity, as does the overlapping of generations. Not surprisingly this produces overlapping and cross-cutting discourses on tradition and modernity within the society at large and within the minds of the individuals within that society. In other words, individuals may, depending on the social context, express contradictory views concerning a particular social or cultural phenomena. This is one source of the complexities of inarticulable public feeling that, as Lienhardt suggested earlier, provide the fuel for rumours.

Illustrative of this ideological bricolage, for example, is the fact that *fùng séui sin sàang* (geomancers) and other experts in Chinese metaphysics were given significant roles to play in the debate over the rumour. In the ATV programme it is not unimportant that, formally, Master Ho's views were treated as equal with Dr Tso's, although the gestures and mannerisms of the presenters tended to at least genuflect in the direction of the higher prestige of the university academic.[6] Of course the intellectual elite of modern Hong Kong society publicly proclaim the scientific values of modernity, but many of them also 'listen' to the discourse of 'superstition'.

Psychologists were also consulted about the rumour, though the most they seemed to be able to say was that it was a matter of 'crowd psychology' and therefore 'irrational' (*Fresh Weekly*, No.588, November 1992; *Ming Pao Daily News* 13/11/92). The Education Department responded calmly and sensibly, and appealed to scientific rationality:

> The Education Department . . . thinks that the incident might well serve as a good lesson for the young people. Mrs. Lau Wing Man, Chief Inspector from the Education Department told the Media that the case may enable the children to realize that it was all merely a product of their imagination. Thus they may have learnt to distinguish similar problems in the future, with the help of newly acquired scientific minds.
>
> (*Ming Pao Daily News* 17/11/92)

By and large, however, the voice of a hegemonic rationality had relatively little to say about the rumour, and perhaps there was little it could say, and simply had to wait for the rumour to run its course and for the dominant modern rationality to re-assert itself. I should also say that the rational anthropological analysis offered in this article would also have had little effect on the course of such a rumour.

The other major protagonists in the debate were the traditional metaphysicians, and their participation was strongly criticised in some quarters. *Wan Wei Pao*, for example, criticising Master Ho's appearance on TV said 'it is common in Hong Kong to have such deceiving and disreputable men who deal in 'black magic' and fool people' (14/11/92). Master Ho's appearance on television, and the subsequent reporting of what he had to say in the press, was heavily publicised. As we have already seen Master Ho claimed the children must be ghosts because of their light steps. Could he see ghosts in the commercial? the presenter asked: 'I can see two, in the upper left-hand corner here [of the screen]. Let me put it this way, they are not ordinary spirits. Since this advertisement was made in the morning it is a time when ordinary spirits cannot appear, so these must be vampires.' The appearance of Master Ho on television legitimised his views and the cultural beliefs in ghosts among his audience.

A few days later he was asked to elaborate on his views by the *Oriental Sunday:* 'Look at their gaze, it is completely empty of childishness. Kids at that age cannot have that kind of gaze. Their souls and spirits are already beyond their control. The only one who looks natural is the first one. Maybe it is because his *'yùhn hei'* (core spirit) is stronger' (15/11/92). He then continues with an elaborate description of the different kinds of evil spirits, devils, vampires and so on who may be acting on the children.

The Metropolitan Weekly (14/11/92) asked the chief Buddhist monk of Sai Fong Temple to comment. He had not seen the commercial, but after the reporter explained the situation he replied that of course it was possible for spirits to appear in the film. 'Under what conditions?' the reporter asked: 'The spirits waiting to be reincarnated. They wander here and there, and may be seen by people by chance. Appearing on screen or in reality makes little difference.' As for the appearance of a child ghost: 'He may have been attracted by the laughter of the other kids, and joined the group without any intention to cause harm.' Can anything be done to appease this spirit? 'All we need to know is his name, or his photo, say prayers and give offerings for his sake.' He ended by saying that 'not everybody can see the ghost. Only small children and people with clear minds [in the Buddhist sense], and those who have "ghost eyes" can see them.'

But one of the most interesting contributions to the whole debate came from Lee Kui Ming, writing in the magazine *Strange News* (no.77, November 1992). He called for the immediate withdrawal of the commercial from TV and for an immediate cessation of discussion, 'we should forget the incident at once.' He too added his comments on the unsettled relations between Hong Kong and China and claimed that an unsettled heart will produce evil: 'The evil psycho of the city has been cast onto the KCRC, a rail linking up China and Hong Kong. It reflects the mind of the Hong Kong people. Everybody is passive and negative. We are full of "yin".' Unlike the rationalists Lee Kui Ming is convinced that there are ghosts in the commercial, but underneath his metaphysics there is in fact a compelling sociological logic:

The problem is that the commercial is "evil". The "evilness" in the commercial brings out the "monster" in the heart of Hong Kong people . . . The third child is possessed. He is covered with "yin air" (*yām hei*). The spirit belonged to an old woman, a deceased member of his family. People having the same "magnetic field" with the child will be able to see the spirit in the commercial. In fact there are spirits everywhere. The force of the "yin" will gradually increase as more and more people talk about it. Just imagine the situation when the commercial is played again! Six million people are pinning their eyes to the screen. All the "yin" forces are concentrated, and little ghosts will become large ghosts. This is the reason why the commercial has to stop.

If we ignore the metaphysics of this article we are in fact left with one of the most sociologically insightful pieces of the whole episode. Consider the logic: when people are disturbed due to the breakdown in relations between China and Hong Kong then in that context it is not surprising that their 'unsettled hearts' will be projected as something 'evil'; and secondly, that the more people watch and discuss the advertisement the more plausibility and power they will give to the rumour. Just stop everything, and it will stop. It is an interesting case of what anthropologists have observed elsewhere about shamans, that is, because they have their finger on the pulse of the society around them they are able to articulate its moods and motives most accurately, albeit in a specific rhetorical or metaphysical idiom which has to be deciphered by the anthropologist.

In this case, despite the subliminal sociological logic which no doubt makes the Lee's case more compelling to his audience, he in fact reconfirms the actual existence of the ghost and therefore helps the rumour on its way, adding his authority to its existence.

At the same time, however, each of these metaphysicians were participating in the society's striving for meaning by providing culturally recognisable explanations for the ghost thus asserting some cultural control, or imaginary control, over the seemingly inexplicable phenomena.

CONCLUSION: RUMOUR IN MODERN SOCIETY

Thus while it was the context of the new Governor's speech which galvanised this rumour, there were many other elements coursing through Hong Kong society that conspired to make the KCRC's 'cute' commercials an appropriate vehicle for the rumour.

Anthropological analyses of modern society are still relatively rare. For various historical reasons anthropologists have tended to leave the study of urban and modern societies to sociologists. But now that they are turning their gaze toward modern societies the corpus of anthropological work, with its cross-cultural emphasis, has primed anthropologists to see familiar human themes in what for others is at first culturally strange. In my own case, some years ago I published a book in which one of the central concerns was the study of the growth and spread of a rumour among a hilltribe group in Laos (Evans 1983:Chapter 6). Confronted with a rumour in modern Hong Kong, I was intrigued rather than mystified. Furthermore, compared with other fields of social science, anthropology has been more sceptical of the claims of modernisation theory concerning the emergence of a rationalised world in which religious or metaphysical thought is banished to the sidelines. Indeed, Ernest Gellner has said, 'it is possible that fully industrial society will exceed in ritual and doctrinal fantasy anything achieved by "primitive" society' (1973:133). So, in contrast to one expatriate writer in the *South China Morning Post* who was mystified as to why 'normally level-headed Hong Kong people' (14/ 11/92) were gripped by the ghost rumour, the anthropologist approaches it as a cultural puzzle.

Chinese society, modern or 'traditional', is not the only society which sees ghosts, and ghosts everywhere represent disharmonies and anomalies or provide explanations for random tragedies. For this reason they will not disappear from modern 'rational', 'scientific' societies because the workings of modern societies, and modern science, remain as mysterious and opaque to many of its members as the workings of the world did for many people in pre-modern societies, and tragedies continue to occur inexplicably and with seeming capriciousness. One might want to argue, however, that the Chinese have a higher propensity to see ghosts than some other people. The reasons for this are complex and are related to the cultural codification of ghosts in Chinese culture, and to the fact that, in Hong Kong at least, one has not seen concerted campaigns against superstition conducted by Church and State that we saw in Europe, although we have yet to understand the full cultural impact of the communist interlude on the mainland and its modernising campaigns against so-called 'feudal superstition' (see Siu 1989). Because ghosts are alien to ideas of order then perhaps societies which place a higher stress on order, like even modern Chinese societies do, are more likely to be haunted by fantasies of disorder.[7]

Anthropologists are prone to point out that people do not see just any ghosts, they see the ghosts that their cultures construct for them. These elements of cultural coding are, of course, part of the rumour we have been discussing. Historically, there has been a high propensity to see female ghosts in Chinese culture, and this has been explained by the anomalous position of women within the patrilocal and patrilineal family (Harrell 1986). In the rumour around the commercial one is struck by the attention paid to young girls. For example, it was often said that it was a young girl ghost who had joined the group of children, and attention focused on her alleged long vampire-like fingernails. Attention also focused on the girl who was said to be bleeding from the mouth. The focus was on females, although the reading was somewhat ambivalent – in some cases a girl was the ghost, in others she was one of the victims of the ghost, and sometimes this ghost was male. The ambivalence perhaps reflects changing evaluations of girls/women in Hong Kong society. Newspaper reports on the commercial often referred back to another rumour in 1983 when people saw the faces of foxes in the marble of a Wanchai building, and these allegedly were causing people to die. This also points to the re-cycling and re-formulation in an urban context of old Chinese cultural themes about fox fairies who lure men in particular to their doom. Further analysis of film, comics and other popular culture media would no doubt reveal modern refigurations of older ghost themes.[8]

Rumours circulate continuously in modern societies, though only rarely do they become full blown rumours. Special conditions are required for that. The modern mass media is obviously capable of speeding up the spread of a rumour, but as we have seen it can only imperfectly control it. In Hong Kong minor rumours surface all the time (*Next Magazine* 13/11/92; *TV & Entertainment Times* 23–29/8/93; *Varsity*, April 1994). These rumours emerge out of the gaps in our understanding and as expressions of inarticulate thoughts and feelings. Rumours produce a temporary integration of feeling without thought and in this sense are irrational. But ultimately rumours burn themselves out because they are unable to answer the questions they pose. The striving for meaning ends in incoherence.

The final episode of the 'ghost train' rumour resembled a farce.[9] Almost two months after the rumour had died down in the wider society it was debated in the Legislative Council on 17 February 1993. Mr Tik Chi-yuen said: 'the recent coverage on supernatural matters . . . will have undesirable psychological effect on children and my daughter is one of the victims', and wanted to know what action the government would take. Would it, Mrs Peggy Lam asked, consider 'prohibiting' programmes on 'fortune telling, supernaturalism, spiritualism, evil spirits and weird phenomena.' Veteran politician Mrs Elsie Tu for her part chose to dramatise for us the difference between the pre-TV generation and the modern generation because she, one of the very few in Hong Kong, had not heard of 'these advertisements that have been referred to'. In suitably sober tones, the Secretary for Recreation and Culture, replied that there is freedom of expression in Hong Kong and that no laws had been transgressed. 'However, I . . . remind those in the media to act responsibly and have regard to public sensitivity and feeling.' And so this rumour which so enthraled the people of Hong Kong for one whole month died a dreary death at the hands of the colony's politicians.

Finally, this article is pertinent to the long standing debate within anthropology concerning the role of 'insider' and 'outsider' analyses of a culture (Evans 1993:15–19). During the research for it one fact became very clear: almost every Chinese person I spoke with, from true believers in ghosts, to Chinese Christians (fundamentalists included), and academics, through to self-proclaimed atheists, all acknowledged at least the possibility of a ghostly realm. Earlier, in the section on 'rationality' versus 'superstition', I remarked that debate over the commercial took place within a culturally circumscribed logic which was self-defeating. So, perhaps it requires an outsider to recognize the importance of studying Chinese cultural beliefs in ghosts in modern Hong Kong. For, when all Chinese are only seeing ghosts then it is only a *gwáilou* who can see the cultural structure of the apparition.

NOTES

1 Unfortunately, except for the original Halloween radio programme I have little data on how the issue was discussed on radio talk-back shows, but see *Eastweek* (12/11/92) and *Next Magazine* (13/11/92) for some commentary on radio reporting. I have no reason to believe that the themes raised in these programmes were much different from the material I have managed to gather for this article.

2 There was one other way the politics of Chris Patten and the rumour intersected and that was a dispute between political pollsters concerning measuring Pattern's popularity. Mr Robert Chung of the Social Science Research Centre at the University of Hong Kong claimed that polls tended to become self-fulfilling prophecies, and compared them with the 'ghost train' rumour (*Sunday Morning Post* 29/11/92).

3 There has been a controversy over organ transplants in China, and significantly it is Hong Kong people who are the *recipients* of these organs (*Sunday Morning Post* 30/10/94; *Eastern Express* 24/11/94). Vague knowledge of the organ trade in China may provide the raw material out of which a rumour can be convolutedly spun, but it does not provide the motivation.

4 For example, the following rumour reported from Chongqing, south-west

China: "Terrified youngsters are refusing to go to school over fears that a child-eating robot is running wild . . . The US made robot favours victims wearing red clothes and has already devoured several children . . . Parents gave their children cloves of garlic and chopstick crosses to ward off the monster, causing a garlic shortage at markets, said the city's legal News' (*Hong Kong Standard,* 22/3/93). I will restrain myself from commenting!

5 The commercial was re-screened several times between 9 November and 19 November, alternating with the KCRC's new commercial featuring two young children, also from Beijing, on a pump trolley in a forest. This latter commercial attracted no interest, and continued to be screened.

6 As Freedman (1979) notes, in the past the geomancer was a respected person because of his association with the traditional literati, of which he was a 'pseudo member'. 'But the geomancer puts his metaphysic to common use. He mediates, then, between the two main strata of Chinese society, the learned . . . and the common; and occupies a status which is, in consequence, both hampered and advantaged by ambiguity' (1979:323). In modern Chinese society there has been a tendency to transfer some of the prestige of the traditional literati to University professors. Geomancers have retained some of their traditional prestige, certainly among ordinary people, but they have had to make strategic shifts in the direction of science. Thus, 'upper class' geomancers in Hong Kong like to present their knowledge as 'scientific', thereby bowing to the higher prestige of modern science.

7 After finishing this article I came upon an excellent study of ghosts in modern Singaporean society by a French anthropologist. See Gilbert Hamonic (1995).

8 For example, some 1994 programmes on Chinese TV have featured Chinese shamans in Malaysia who claim to be able to use aborted fetuses, no more than two hours old because they still have the spirit of life in them, which they then can raise as a spirit child who will do their bidding. What is immediately apparent here is the theme of the problems of child control in a world where they are felt to be increasingly beyond parental control, and secondly a wider debate about abortion (bearing in mind that the Shamans are in Muslim Malaysia, and Muslims object to abortion). This is only to suggest initial directions for interpretation.

9 In mid-December there was a highly publicised Christmas party for the children in the advertisement, with photos of them with Father Christmas, among others, to prove that they were alive. (See especially *Ming Pao Weekly* 21/12/92). But by this time the rumour had already exhausted itself.

REFERENCES CITED

Allen, Barbara
    1982   The 'Image on Glass': Technology, Tradition and the Emergence of Folklore.Western Folklore 41:85–103.
Allport, Gordon W. and Leo Postman
    1947   The Psychology of Rumor. New York: Henry Holt and Company.

Baker, Ronald L.
1969   The Face in the Wall. Indiana Folklore 2:29–46.
1976   The Influence of Mass Culture on Modern Legends. Southern Folklore Quarterly 40:367–376.
Bird, Donald
1976   A Theory for Folklore in Mass Media: Traditional Patterns in the Mass Media. Southern Folklore Quarterly 40 (3&4):285–305.
Brunvand, Jan Harold
1981   The Vanishing Hitchhiker: American Urban Legends and Their Meanings. New York: W.W. Norton and Co.
Drotner, Kirsten
1992   Modernity and Media Panics. In Media Cultures: Reappraising Transnational Media. Michael Skovmand and Kim Christian Schroder eds. London and New York:Routledge.
Evans, Grant
1983   The Yellow Rainmakers. London: Verso.
1993   Introduction: Asia and the Anthropological Imagination. In Asia's Cultural Mosaic. Grant Evans, ed. Singapore, Prentice Hall.
Fine, Gary Allen
1979   Folklore Diffusion Through Interactive Social Networks: Conduits in a Preadolescent Community. New York Folklore 5:87–126.
Freedman, Maurice
1979   Geomancy. In The Study of Chinese Society, Essays by Maurice Freedman. G. William Skinner, ed. California: Stanford University Press.
Gellner, Ernest
1973   The Concept of Kinship and Other Essays on Anthropological Method and Explanation, London, Basil Blackwell.
Hamonic, Gilbert
1995   Les Fantomes dans la Ville: l'example de Singapour. Journal des Anthropologues, No. 61–62.
Harrell, Stevan
1986   Men, Women, and Ghosts in Taiwanese Folk Religion. In Gender and Religion. C.W. Bynum, S. Harrell and P. Richman, eds. Boston: Beacon Press.
Kapferer, Jean-Noel
1992   How Rumors are Born. Society (July/August):53–60.
Laba, Martin
1979   Urban Folklore: A Behavioral Approach. Western Folklore 38:158–169.
Levi-Strauss, Claude
1993   Father Christmas Executed. In Unwrapping Christmas, Daniel Miller, ed. Oxford: Oxford University Press.
Lienhardt, Peter
1975   The Interpretation of Rumour. In Studies in Social Anthropology, Essays in Memory of Evans-Pritchard. J. H. M. Beattie and R. G. Lienhardt. Oxford: Clarendon Press.
Lim, V
1991   "The Hidden Persuaders", Sundary Morning Post Magazine (15-11-91).

Martin, Diana
    1991   Chinese Ghost Marriage. *In* An Old State in a New Setting. Hugh D.R. Baker and Stephan Feuchtwang, eds. Oxford: JASO.
Opie, Iona and Peter
    1980   Certain Laws of Folklore. Folklore Studies in the Twentieth Century: Proceedings of the Centenary Conference of the Folklore Society. Pp.64–75.
Shibutani, Tamotsu
    1966   Improvised News, A Sociological Study of Rumor. Indianapolis: Bobbs-Merrill.
Siu, Helen
    1989   Re-cycling Rituals: Politics and Popular Culture in Contemporary Rural China. *In* Unofficial China, Perry Link, Richard Madsen and Paul G. Pickowicz, eds. Boulder: Westview Press.

LANGUAGE

13

BAD BOYS AND BAD LANGUAGE
CHÒU HÁU AND THE SOCIOLINGUISTICS OF SWEARWORDS IN HONG KONG CANTONESE

Kingsley Bolton & Christopher Hutton

The frequency [of swearwords in Cantonese] is so high that ... some speakers of Cantonese [have remarked that]: (a) Cantonese sounds very "odd" and "obscene". (b) One out of three utterances by Cantonese people is "obscene"   (Tse and Yu 1980:50).

John Chen kept his polite smile but screw you he thought ... Screw you in spades. **Dew neh loh moh** on all your generations ...
                                                           (Clavell 1981:36).

In popular belief in Hong Kong, the use of swearwords (or *chòu háu*[1] 粗口) is associated with a number of partially contradictory, partially interlocking stereotypes. On the one hand, there seems to be wide acceptance for the notion that Cantonese, as a living, vibrant dialect, actually distinguishes itself from other varieties (particularly the standard varieties of Chinese) through its use of punning, double entendre, slang and racy word-play: an aspect of language often seen as 'naughty but nice'. At the other extreme, the use of swearwords is associated with insults, threats, male language at its most offensive, and the language of the labouring and criminal classes. It is 'bad' language used by 'bad people', with strong associations with 'nastiness' in a range of behavioural forms.

Whether we approach the study of 'bad language' from either a linguistic or anthropological perspective, there seem to be few easy answers on offer. Linguists and lexicographers have made various attempts to define precisely terms such as 'slang', 'argot', 'jargon', 'swearword' and 'cant' (Epstein 1994), but such taxonomies end up as futile attempts to legislate a parallel vocabulary to the one actually and historically in use. Allen's definition can serve as a point of orientation (Allen 1993:6):

> Slang is, at bottom, just a highly informal register of speech and does not differ from standard usages in any purely linguistic way. Slang shares indistinct boundaries with other informal levels of vocabulary, such as colloquial usages, subgroup argots, and regional, class and ethnic dialects. Slang is such a slippery concept that the idea of "popular speech", a broader concept that includes slang, is now preferred by many writers on language.

Allen speaks however of 'general slang', with its roots in the various sub-group languages of the city (1993:6): 'General slang is mostly words and phrases that have escaped from the myriad subcultures of society and found favor in wider usage'.

What seems to distinguish the situation in Hong Kong from the situation in Western societies is that there is much less official tolerance of bad language in the territory than is the case, for example, in Britain. Although censorship criteria appear to have relaxed somewhat since the 1980s, television and films in Hong Kong are still monitored closely. One important area of concern here is the so-called 'triad language' of Chinese criminal societies. Triad rituals and signs may not be shown, nor may triad language be used. The use of *chòu háu* is often seen as a marker of criminality or triad-membership, and official agencies tend to view the spread of *chòu háu* into the mainstream of Hong Kong society and its media as indicating a general crisis, as being symptomatic of a rising tide of social disorder and alienation. Nonetheless, triad language or triad-associated language is an important source of innovation in Hong Kong Cantonese. In an earlier paper, we discussed notions of 'bad' and 'banned' language in Hong Kong (Bolton and Hutton 1995). Our discussion there centred on the status of this 'triad language', and on the role of this sub-group language as a source of innovation for general slang in Hong Kong. Another target of censorship is the use of sexually-explicit taboo words, or *chòu háu*, which are still relatively strictly censored on television, in feature films, and the print media. One indication of the continuing enforcement of linguistic taboos is the simple fact that the five swearwords of the Cantonese *chòu háu* lexicon are rarely, if ever, found in print (these are the Cantonese equivalents to 'dick', 'cock', 'prick', 'fuck' and 'cunt', see section 3 below). Equally, it is also significant that even today no publisher has included any of the most commonly used core swearwords in a dictionary of Cantonese.

The current situation in Hong Kong is therefore in this respect analogous to that in Britain pre-1963, before the *Lady Chatterley* trial paved the way for the liberalisation of publishing norms with respect to the English swearwords listed above, as well as many more related items. What makes the issue more complex today is the fact that, however strict today, censorship has relaxed considerably from the more rigid norms of the 1960s and 1970s. This occurred particularly with respect to the classification of films in the 1980s, when a whole series of local triad films in the *Godfather* mould were filmed and marketed to packed houses in Hong Kong cinemas, and family audiences through video stores. The popularity of socially-realistic crime films of the 1980s, combined with the rise of comics depicting the same milieu, was both cause and symptom of a dislocation of the pre-existing organisation of language and social space.

Allen (1993:18) argues that one important conduit for the diffusion of slang in the United States of the 1940s and 1950s was the comic, but concludes that '[t]elevision has all but supplanted this role of the newspaper comic strips in the talk of the town'. However the comic book continues to be central to the popular culture of East Asia, with Japan exerting a powerful influence on graphic art in Korea, Hong Kong and Taiwan (Lent 1993). Glain (1994:1, 7) reported Korean anxieties in the face of Japanese comic books which threaten to 'fuel the demise of Korea's comics trade and the decay of Korean morality, according to an alliance of local cartoonists, censors and ethics groups'. Comic books, along with video games (Krakinowski 1994), loom large in the minds of psychologists, social workers and teachers in Hong Kong, who tend to see them as contributing to social alienation and delinquency (Mosher 1994).

The following scenario might therefore be adduced to explain the recent history of Hong Kong slang. What previously may have been the language of lower working-class males, criminals and construction workers became the texture of Hong Kong film and cartoon culture and the linguistic property of the Hong Kong people as a whole. Fairly rapidly, it seems, knowledge and/or use of slang, triad jargon, and even *chòu háu* spread to other social classes in Hong Kong, including middle-class males and middle-class females (even perhaps to the kind of 'straight' people, who in the dismissive words of the publisher of Hong Kong's most notorious triad comics, Cowman, 'split the bill at lunch', Mosher 1994). As a result, private space and public space were redefined, and the bounds of good linguistic order tested. For many, the spread of bad language can be linked to a wider social crisis, reflecting what Harris terms (1990:414) the 'social thermometer' view of bad language.

In this paper, we set out to deal with a range of questions relating to 'bad' language in Hong Kong. In Section 1, we discuss various anthropological and linguistic issues in the study of bad language. In Section 2, we focus on the sociological background to bad language in Hong Kong. In Section 3, we present the results of our own empirical work on this topic, which is based on a survey of 60 schoolboys, between the ages of 15 and 18. This section also includes a basic word list of 96 *chòu háu* items, which we believe provide the core of the *chòu háu* lexicon. Further analysis of these words, together with a commentary on the written representations is also provided. Section 4 comprises the conclusion.

ISSUES IN THE STUDY OF BAD LANGUAGE

The issue of bad and taboo language is surrounded by confusion and uncertainty. For some, insults, racial slurs and obscenities only have power so long as we fear and avoid them: 'the word's suppression gives it the power, the violence, the viciousness' (Bruce 1972:79). For others, swear words are an anti-language of non-conformity, a free domain not yet levelled by ideologically correct language planners (Epstein 1994:10, reviewing the *Random House Historical Dictionary of American Slang*): 'Perhaps the only thing to be said on behalf of political correctness is that, in an otherwise latitudinarian society, it may help to keep slang alive by sending it underground.' Both these views might be labelled liberal, yet they offer diametrically opposed views of bad language. As Harris puts it (1990:413): 'We may argue about bad language endlessly: but it is far from clear that anyone has any adequate theory about it as a form of linguistic behaviour'. In part, this confusion reflects the inability of linguistics to come to terms with the phenomenon of meaning in general, but it also reflects a sense that linguistic taboos are irrational (Trudgill 1983). Yet to call a belief or kind of behaviour irrational or illogical is a polemical admission that one does not understand it. Jay (1992:30) quotes Flexner as follows (1976:157):

> There is, of course, no logical reason why *fuck*, *screw*, *make* [...], or any other term should be "dirty", shocking, or taboo, no logical

reason why they should be considered any different than such synonyms as *copulate, sexual intercourse*, or feces. It's a matter of conditioning and etiquette.

What, one might ask, is the force of the word 'logical' here? Why 'of course'? Jay gives this quotation with approval, but he himself seems to contradict it in the introductory section of his book (1992:9):

> One can see that what is considered taboo or obscene revolves around a few dimensions of human experience and that there is a logic or purpose behind dirty word usage. They are not simply outbursts of hot air, devoid of meaning and communicative intent.

Is taboo a rational and comprehensible part of human social life, or is it a murky area where we are conditioned to accept a primitive belief in word magic otherwise absent from our modern philosophies?

Both Davis (1989) and Harris (1990) discuss the cricket test between England and Pakistan held in December 1987 where an altercation involving bad language led to play being suspended the following day (Davis 1989:1-2; Harris 1990:416-419). Subsequently, of the British newspapers, only the *Independent* printed in full what the umpire is alleged to have called the England captain, namely a 'fucking cheating cunt'. The editor of the *Sun* attacked the *Independent* for publishing the words in a family newspaper, and suggested that he should have used forms such as *f...* , *c...* instead. Harris remarks on the fact that there are not only taboos about the use of bad language, but also about its mention (he terms this a 'double prohibition', 1990:421). Mentioning bad language means making literal what is otherwise not heard as language with meaningful, referential content. To cite and discuss bad language foregrounds the literal meaning rather than its other functions. In this sense, bad language may be at its most shocking when it is written down and 'glossed', for in writing it down, its segmental 'reality' and literal meaning come to the fore. This factor will come into play below when we discuss some of the data we collected at a Hong Kong boy's school.

Harris' argument however takes on a twist when he argues that those who rail against bad language are those who have the most stake in it. The diffusion of swearwords into general use heralds, he argues, a breakdown of the distinction between public and private domains of life, and public and private English, one that 'automatically threatens the sacrosanct distinction between the rights of the individual and the rights of the community' (1990:420). The loss of this private world means the loss of a place into which one can withdraw 'into a world of inviolable, timeless privacy' (1990:421). Those who condemn bad language are those who most value it, since they are preserving a valued distinction: 'The epitaph on the tomb of British bad language in the 1980s should read: "Valued most by those who most vehemently condemned it" ' (1990:421).

This raises a complex and interesting issue. Censorship involves a recognition of the power of bad language. In this sense, it pays respect to that power and serves to bolster it. But censorship serves also to draw a line between different social domains, so that the language that can be overheard on the minibus or in the street is prevented from entering the public media and especially the private home (television is more heavily censored than film). Censorship marks out certain core areas of social space and indicates certain social groups as being in need of protection. The fact that children swear may not necessarily invalidate censorship, for in protecting them from bad language the censor is in effect protecting them from a loss of social orientation. The recognition that children themselves use bad language does not of itself invalidate special rules concerning their exposure to bad language.

In discussing these issues one should distinguish between four contexts in which bad language is used. The first is when swearing is used as an intra-group norm, when it appears as part of the routine speech of a particular group, where bad language reinforces boundaries between groups. One could imagine various levels of sensitivity among such 'foul language' using groups. Swearing may occur when there are no outsiders present, or in situations such as on the street or in public transport, where other people are only present as (involuntary) eavesdroppers. Some schoolchildren who swear in the school playground might drop the bad language from their speech when they are in the presence of a teacher or parent. Media representations of such groups (e.g. gangsters) will use slang and obscenity as a key element of characterisation ('realism'). The second case is the deliberate use of bad language to insult, threaten, shock or offend. An example would be a verbal attack on someone who does not use bad language and feels threatened by it, where bad language is used to break down social barriers temporarily, to violate someone's social integrity. The third is the use of bad or suggestive language in jokes or for comic purposes. Suggestive punning by comedians or *mòuh lèih tàuh* in Hong Kong films may be experienced as a pleasurable (and temporary) regression to a childish state. In some contexts (e.g. joke-telling in a group) people may be cajoled or prompted into laughing. The fourth context would be the use of swearwords to express strong emotions such as surprise or, as in the classic hammer-and-thumb situation, pain. Responses in Cantonese may vary from the mild (*pì kèi*) to the very strong (*diu* 閂) and may be gender-graded: *pì kèi* might typically be used by a young woman, and *diu* by your average male taxi driver. Young people may also often use the English 'Shit!', which is often claimed to be free of the heavier connotations of Cantonese equivalents. We could term these four uses of bad language *integrative*, *aggressive*, *regressive*, and *expletive*.

THE CASE OF HONG KONG

In Hong Kong one could study the issue of bad language at a number of levels. First, there is the question of the official policy towards bad language; second, the language behaviour of particular groups with regard to swearing; and third, informal attitudes to the acceptability or otherwise of using certain language in particular contexts. At first glance, swearing in Hong Kong seems to be the province of working class males. For example, an informant (a Hong Kong Chinese business executive) defined swearing as 'male language, taxi-driver language'. Received beliefs about Cantonese include the notion that it is particularly rich in swearwords and invective, but, leaving aside the difficulty of measuring such things, such a notion most likely reflects a set of cultural values operating within the pan-Chinese world. These values may be viewed by Cantonese speakers themselves with mixed feelings. As 'Chinese' they must accept the overall cultural pre-eminence of Mandarin and the associated modern standard written language and therefore the secondary status of Cantonese as a 'dialect'. As a non-standard language, it is thus a more private possession of the speakers, a purer identity marker. To the extent that Cantonese has gradually widened its functions within Hong Kong (to include the civil service, some lower courts, the Legislative Council and many other social forums formerly dominated by English) it is also a quasi-national language, studied by non-native speakers and with a wide number of different social functions (including high cultural functions such as formal reading styles for use in religious contexts, for reciting poetry, Cantonese opera, etc.). But, within the pecking order of languages, it still must give way in Hong Kong to the official languages of the present and future sovereign powers and can be emotionally set off against these two languages as a 'private' (and therefore 'vibrant', 'authentic', 'natural') language, even while serving many of the social functions of a 'high' variety.

However, many factors enter into the societal equation. One important issue that relates to language within Hong Kong is social mobility. A society with a relatively high degree of social mobility might be expected to place a great deal of emphasis on linguistic markers of social success, in the same way that Hong Kong people are stereotypically said to enjoy the use of material and portable status symbols such as expensive watches and mobile phones. But in terms of pronunciation, there is not the same social awareness of class markers in Hong Kong that one is alleged to find in Britain. The so-called 'lazy pronunciation' (*láahn yàm* 懶音)[2] is of concern primarily to teachers of Chinese.

This lack of clear class-related norms reflects in part the status of Cantonese as a semi-private language. However the use of 'foul language' may be such a class marker. A group of boys or men using 'foul language' among themselves in public may be marking themselves as marginal or deviant (junior triads, bad schoolboys, petty criminals), or as labourers with no pretensions to gentility or social mobility. But it seems that they are not always perceived as acting wrongly; for example, other 'respectable' passengers in earshot of a barrage of *chòu háu* in the minibus seem oblivious. The taxi driver involved in a near collision swears because that is what taxi drivers do in such situations. He is talking in the way that taxi drivers talk. There is an element of reassurance that the world is in place. In this context, swearing is not always 'matter out of place' (Douglas 1991). It is out of place when it is used to break down social boundaries, to insult or attack. But when overheard in the minibus, it may not be deeply shocking because it is not heard as communication, but as a part of a social role acted out and understood. Social boundaries are being strengthened. In a sense, the respectable can feel at ease in the presence of this language since it is not 'their' language and it is not directed at them or intended to include them. Everyone knows who they are and where they sit. One hypothesis would be that if the boundaries between these groups were less clear - perhaps in a society where there is a greater ideology of social equality - then this language would be threatening since there is no water-tight social-class division to keep it out. In Britain obscenities can be heard on national television and are printed widely in the media, but their use by a taxi or bus driver in public might well cause greater offence than in Hong Kong. It is also interesting to consider what it means to *overhear* bad language. To what extent do people know 'what the words (literally) mean' as opposed to their simply identifying the language as bad?

Other groups who reportedly use bad language in Hong Kong are 'Yuppie' foreign exchange dealers and other 'macho' type financial dealers; here there may be an attitude of indifference or hostility to traditional methods of social advancement or wealth acquisition and a cynicism about the social hierarchy (since a successful dealer can achieve 'unnaturally' rapid affluence). This language may serve to exclude outsiders, e.g. women, from fully participating in the institution, for women who swear seem to be involved in a more radical form of self-stigmatisation than men. But there are women who swear (some in an attempt to integrate into male culture in the workplace, Coates 1986:10), and others who do not swear but are not particularly offended by it or by discussion of it. Perhaps again some women recognise that swearing makes clear and secure a gender boundary with defined gender roles.

That swearing has made inroads into the general population can be seen from this comment from a female student at the Chinese University of Hong Kong, defending the production of a controversial campus newspaper called 'Little Door' (*síu mùhn bou* 小門報): 'I always hear male schoolmates speaking in foul language in the dormitory. Why can't this language be used in publications or in public?' (quoted in Tsang 1994:23).

SURVEY DATA:
THE LANGUAGE OF HONG KONG SCHOOLBOYS

As mentioned above, one important source of language data for our research was a questionnaire survey that was conducted at a boys' secondary school in Hong Kong. The background to this research was as follows. In order to investigate the use of slang and 'bad language' by Hong Kong schoolchildren, we decided to replicate an experiment discussed by Andersson and Trudgill (1990), in which British school children were asked to list expressions meaning 'stupid person'. The British survey produced a list of over 120 slang words. The twelve most frequently cited expressions were the following: *wally, stupid, dimbo, idiot, prat, dumbo, dickhead, dippy, dumb, silly, thicko,* and *nerd* (Andersson and Trudgill 1990:88-89). The field research for our survey of Chinese slang was largely conducted by a twenty-year-old Hong

Kong Chinese acquaintance of the authors. When informed by us that we intended to conduct questionnaire research at a Hong Kong secondary school, he suggested that we distribute questionnaires at his *alma mater*. The school in question was not one of the 'lower band' schools in the local hierarchy and was generally regarded as having a good academic reputation. It was also apparently renowned for the *chòu háu* resources of its pupils. This latter reputation may well be connected to the fact that it is an all-male school.

A short, single-sheet questionnaire was then prepared by the authors. The instructions to respondents on page one read as follows: 'This is a questionnaire about Cantonese slang and vulgar language [*chòu háu*] in Hong Kong. You have to write down your age, your form, and answer all the five questions.' To summarise, the five questions asked for (i) expressions meaning 'a foolish or stupid person', (ii) expressions meaning 'a bad or evil person', (iii) expressions used to insult 'a person you hate', and (iv) expressions used to tell someone to 'go away!'. The fifth question then asked respondents to indicate those expressions that they 'would not use themselves in everyday life'.

We later concluded that the first four questions worked rather well in eliciting a core corpus of slang and taboo language. The fifth question worked rather less well; largely because of the imprecision of the question. Our assumption had been that this question would provide some kind of rough guide to the 'taboo rating' of the words and expressions listed by the boys. In the event, the results were unclear: they might reflect perceived taboo norms, but might also reflect other reasons for avoiding an item. Some expressions, for example, might be regarded as dated or childish.

The questionnaire was administered by our informant to some friends within the upper forms of the school and, in turn, by them on a 'friends-of-friends' basis to a substantial number of older pupils throughout the school. The questionnaires were distributed and collected over a period of one week in March 1991. In all, 60 questionnaires were completed and returned. The majority of respondents (75%) were Form 6 pupils in the age range 17-18. Smaller numbers of Form 4 and Form 5 pupils (25%) aged 15-16 were also included.

The amount and quality (in terms of this research exercise) of language data collected was impressive and intriguing. Question 1 ('stupid person') yielded a total of 85 different items; Question 2 ('bad person') produced 96 items; Question 3 ('a person you hate') 52 items; and Question 4 ('go away!') 84 items. In all this produced a total of over

300 *chòu háu* and slang items, although many of these items occurred only once in the data.

In order to provide a clear and more focused analysis of the slang and taboo vocabulary collected, we decided to draw up a core list of *chòu háu* and slang vocabulary which included only those items which occurred more than twice in our data. Subsequent research suggest that this list does in fact hold up as a basic word list for Hong Kong *chòu háu* (although we shall later try to show that the items we have included here maybe further categorised into subtypes of *chòu háu* language).

Hong Kong slang and *chòu háu* - a basic word list

In the list below, all words and expressions occurring more than once in the survey are included in the list. The entry for each word includes the Chinese characters for each expression, the Yale transcription followed by a bracketed number indicating how many times a particular item was cited, a 'literal' translation into English, and an explanatory gloss. In all there are 96 items and expressions, which are set out in order of frequency in Table 1 overleaf:

TABLE 1: A List of Core Insults in Cantonese (*Chòu Háu* and Swearwords)

Chinese Characters	Yale Transcription	Literal Meaning in English	Approximate English slang equivalent
閪	díu (46)	fuck	fuck
仆街	pùk gàai (43)	fall down in the street	you bastard!
冚家剷	hahm gàa cháan (30)	whole family die	fuck you in the heart !
笨閪	bahn chaht (27)	stupid dick	stupid dick
閪樣	lán yéung (24)	prick face	prick face
閪開	lán hòi (17)	fuck away	fuck off!
豬兜	jyù dàu (16)	pig dish/bowl (pig penis)	silly willy
戇閪	ohng gàu (14)	stupid cock	stupid prick

309

賤種	jihn júng (13)	cheap species	scumbag
契弟	kai daih (12)	younger god-brother	homo
傻閪	sòh hài (12)	stupid cunt	stupid cunt
攔瘓	làan táan (11)	creep paralysed	creep
含撚	hàhm lán (10)	hold suck prick	cocksucker
戇居	ohng gèui (10)	simple-minded	moron
白痴	baahk chì (9)	plainly crazy	dimbo
閪種	hài júng (9)	cunt species	cunt
攔屍冚路	làan sì gaht louh (9)	creep corpse limp road	beat it, bozo!
收皮	sàu pèih (9)	withdraw foreskin	push off!
死開	séi hòi (9)	die away	piss off!
閪頭	chaht tàuh (8)	dick head	dickhead
	fàk òf (8)	fuck off	fuck off!
行撚開	hàahng lán hòi (9)	walk prick away	fuck off!
閪	hài (8)	cunt	cunt
賤人	jihn yàhn (8)	cheap person	scum
豬閪	jyù hài (8)	pig cunt	cunt
撚𡃁	lán díu (8)	prick fuck	fucking prick
磨碌	moh lùk (8)	short/medicore	shortarse
白痴仔	baahk chì jái (8)	plain crazy boy	thicko
臭閪	chau hài (7)	smelly cunt	stupid cunt
頂你個肺	díng léih go fai (7)	pierce your lung	screw you!
屎忽鬼	sí fàt gwái (7)	ass ghost	asshole
冚家鈴	hahm gàa lìng (6)	whole family bell	go to hell!
豬標	jyù bìu (6)	pig dart	stupid idiot
茂利	mauh léi (6)	prosperous profit	wally
戇閪仔	ohng gàu jái (6)	stupid cock boy	stupid little prick
仆街仔	pùk gàai jái (6)	fall down in the street boy	little bastard
笨賊	bahn chaahk (5) (c.f. bahn chaht)	stupid thief	stupid cretin
笨蕉	bahn jìu (5)	stupid banana	stupid moron
疙開	gaht hòi (5)	creep away	get lost!
走撚開	jáu lán hòi (5)	walk prick away	fuck off!

賤泥	jihn làih (5)	cheap soil	little shit
死劍	séi cháan (5)	dead spade	go to hell, you bastard!
狗賊	gáu chaahk (5)	dog thief	shithead
過主	gwo jyú (4)	across lord	push off!
閪仔	hài jái (4)	cunt boy	little cunt
賤	jihn (4)	cheap	cheap
豬	jyù (4)	pig	stupid pig
死仔	séi jái (4)	dead boy	little shit
笨閪	bahn lán (3)	stupid prick	stupid prick
笨閪閊	bahn lán chaht (2)	stupid prick dick	fucking stupid dick
蠢閪	chéun lán	stupid prick	stupid prick
痴閪線	chì lán sin (3)	crazy prick	fucking crazy
低能仔	dài làhng jái (3)	low ability boy	retard
賤格	jihn gaak (3)	cheap character	cheap bastard
豬嘜	jyù màk (3)	pig mark	wally
閪閊	lán chaht (3)	prick dick	fucking dick
閪閪	lán hài (3)	prick cunt	fucking cunt
欄開	làan hòi (3)	creep away	piss off
冇閪用	móuh lán yuhng (3)	no prick use	fucking useless
戇閊	ohng chaht (3)	stupid dick	stupid dick
戇閪閊	ohng lán gàu (3)	stupid prick cock	fucking stupid prick
收嗲	sàu dè (3)	shut chat	shut your face!
收閊皮	sàu gàu pèih (3)	withdraw prick skin	shut the fuck up!
死仆街	séi pùk gàai (3)	dead fall down in the street	fucking bastard!
屎	sí (3)	shit	shit
吔蕉	yaak jìu (3)	eat banana	fuck yourself!
笨閪	bahn hài (2)	stupid cunt	stupid cunt
笨蔗	bahn je (2)	stupid sugar cane	stupid wally
賊	cháak (2) (c.f. chaht)	thief	dick
痴線	chì sin (2)	nerves stuck together	crazy
低B仔	dài bì jái (2)	low ability boy	dummy
低閊能	dài gàu làhng (2)	low cock ability	fucking moron

311

低能	dài làhng (2)	low ability	idiot
返屋企咬蔗	fàan ngùk keíh ngáauh je (2)	go back your home to bite sugar cane	go fuck yourself!
廢柴	fai chàaih (2)	waste firewood	stupid wanker
閪種	hài júng (2)	cunt species	cunt
去仆街啦	heui pùk gàai là (2)	fall down in the street	drop dead, you bastard!
雜種	jaahp júng (2)	mixed species	bastard
做生日	jouh sàang yaht (2)	mark birthday	(I'll) get you, you bastard!
豬炳	jyù bíng (2)	inferior pig	thick as pig shit
瀨閪	láai hài (2)	lick cunt	fucking cunt
欄閪開	làan lán hòi (2)	creep prick away	fuck off
嘍揪呀	lau chàu àh (2)	provoking a beating	(you) want trouble!?
碌	lùk (2)	one (classifier for penis)	dick
冇腦	móuh lóuh (2)	no brain	dumb
懵閪	múng lán (2)	stupid prick	stupid prick
戇閪閪	ohng gàu gàu (2)	stupid prick	fucking cretin
戇閪	ohng lán (2)	stupid prick	gormless prick
仆開	pùk hòi (2)	fall down away	sod off!
死開	séi hòi (2)	die away	shove off!
食蕉	sihk jìu (2)	eat banana	sod you!
傻噏	sòh gèp (2)	stupid cunt	stupid cunt
傻佬	sòh lóu (2)	stupid man	wally
淫賤	yàhm jihn (2)	obscene cheap	leering
弱智	yeuhk ji (2)	weak intelligence	dim wit
弱智仔	yeuhk ji jái (2)	weak intelligence boy	dimbo

General commentary on word list

Timothy Jay, in *Cursing in America* (1992) attempts to provide a category analysis of various types of swearwords and taboo language. In brief, his taxonomy includes ten categories of cursing. These categories are: 'cursing' (in the sense of involving harm and injury to others), 'profanity', 'blasphemy', 'taboo', 'obscenity', 'vulgarity', 'slang', 'epithets', 'insults and slurs', and 'scatology'. There are obvious problems with this type of categorisation, however. There is an overlap between 'profanity' and 'blasphemy' in one instance, 'obscenity' and 'taboo' in another, and vulgarity with virtually every other category. In spite of these problems, however, some of the terms he discussed can be applied to the *chòu háu* data we are discussing here.

Crucially, it should be noted that at the core of our *chòu háu* list above is a set of items that are sexually taboo swearwords. These five key Cantonese swearwords (or *chòu háu jih* 粗口字) are *díu* 閪 ('fuck'), *chaht* 閪 ('dick'), *gàu* 閪 ('cock'), *lán* 閪 ('prick') and *hài* 閪 ('cunt'). Of the 96 expressions in the list, 36 of the items either comprise, or include, the five 'core' items of *chòu háu* vocabulary. The other 60 items on the list may be explained by such categories as curses (e.g. *hahm gà cháan* 冚家剷, *pùk gàai* 仆街), scatological items (*sí* 屎, *sí fàt gwái* 屎忽鬼), animal taboo words (*jyù dàu* 豬兜, *jyù màk* 豬嘜, etc.), or other categories of description (see section 3.5 below).

Díu 閪 ('fuck')

Díu ('fuck') is the most frequently cited expression, appearing in the list with a count of 46. All the *díu* expressions were elicited by question no. 3 ('the insult to someone you hate'). The range of expressions here often displayed almost Elizabethan flair in creative word-play. *Díu* expressions included both crudely explicit insults, as set out in Table 2, and the less direct insults that rely on word-play and puns, as in Table 3.

TABLE 2: *Díu* (i)

Díu léih.	閪你
'Fuck you'.	
Díu léih lóuh móu.	閪你老母
'Fuck your mother'.	
Díu léih hài hàhn.	閪你閪痕
'Fuck till your cunt's itchy'.	
Díu chaht baaul léih	閪閪爆你
lóuh móu go hài.	老母個閪
Fuck dick crack your mother's cunt.	

Óh díu léih lóuh méi,   我閪你鹵味

hóu m̀h hóu a?   好唔好呀？

'I fuck your mother, is that okay?'

Díu léih lóuh móu go   閪你老母個

chau fàa hài.   臭花閪

'Fuck your mother's smelly, flowery cunt'.

TABLE 3: *Díu* (ii)

Óh díu léih lóuh méi.   我閪你鹵味
'Fuck your old roasted meat'.

Tìuh leih móuh mòuh.   條脷冇毛
'Piece of tongue no hair'.

Sìu léih sou bóu.   燒你數簿
'Burn your ledger-book'.

Bìu, léih yáuh móuh.   錶，你有冇
'A watch, do you have (one)?'

Mahn hauh léih lóuh móu.   問候你老母
'Give my regards to your mother'.

Mahn hauh léih lóuh dauh.   問候你老豆
'Give my regards to your father'.

In addition, one boy displayed his literary aspirations in the submission of a short piece of doggerel, which is apparently sung aloud to the tune of 'Colonel Bogey':

Díu léih lóuh móu hahm gàa cháan,
閪你老母冚家剷，
Daai léih lóuh móu séuhng tìn báang,
帶你老母上天棚，
Gong hah yàt go yùhn jí dáan,
降下一個原子彈，
Jaa dou léih lóuh móu bin làan táan.
炸到你老母變欄癱。

In English translation, this reads a lot less smoothly as follows:

> 'Fuck your mother and may your whole family die
> Take your mother up on the roof,
> Drop an atom bomb from the sky,
> Explode it on your mother so she is paralyzed!'

Chaht 𨳍, *lán* 𨶙, and *gàu* 𨳊

Expressions using *chaht* 𨳍, *lán* 𨶙 and *gàu* 𨳊, all meaning 'penis', all proved popular amongst our schoolboy informants. *Bahn chaht* 笨𨳍 ('stupid dick') received 27 attestations; *lán yéung* 𨶙樣 ('prick face'), a score of 24; and *ngohng gàu* 戇𨳊 ('stupid cock') a score of 14.

Previous explanations of these terms (e.g. Tse and Yu 1980) do not provide a consistent translation for the three items. We now propose to introduce some lexicographic systematicity into the translation of these expressions, and suggest 'dick' for *chaht* 𨳍, 'prick' for *lán* 𨶙 and 'cock' for *gàu* 𨳊. This suggestion is largely motivated by a consideration of the translatability of compounds and derivations. Thus *bahn chaht* 笨𨳍 and *chaht tàuh* 𨳍頭 become 'stupid dick' and 'dickhead', and *ngohng gàu* 戇𨳊 becomes 'stupid cock'. This then leaves 'prick' for combinations like *lán yéung* 𨶙樣, *bahn lán* 笨𨶙, and *hàhm lán* 含𨶙, which may be translated as 'prick face', 'stupid prick'; and 'suck my prick' respectively.

Lán 𨶙 may also be used for a range of grammatical purposes. It can appear as a noun in *ngohng lán* 戇𨶙('stupid prick'); as a verb in *lán hòi* 𨶙開('prick [fuck] off'); and as an intensifier in *móuh lán yuhng* 冇𨶙用('no prick [fucking] good'). Its function in examples of the latter type is that of an intensifying morphological infix. We have other examples of this list, including *hàahng lán hòi* 行𨶙開 ('walk pricking away'), *jáu lán hòi* 走𨶙開('go pricking away'), *bahn lán chaht* 笨𨶙𨳍('stupid pricking dick'), and *làan lán hòi* 欄𨶙開 ('creep pricking away').

Hài 閪

Combinations using *hài* 閪 ('cunt') also proved popular. *Sòh hài* 傻閪 ('stupid cunt') gained 12 citations, *hài júng* 閪種 ('cunt species') 9, *hài*

閪 ('cunt') 8, *jyù hài* 豬閪 ('pig cunt') 8, *chau hài* 臭閪('smelly cunt') 7. Other expressions included *bahn hài* 笨閪 ('stupid cunt'), and *láai hài* 瀨閪 ('lick cunt'). As in English, this is the item that carries the heaviest taboo.

Other slang expressions

In the list of 96 expressions provided in table 1, 36 items, as mentioned earlier, include the five core *chòu háu* words. The other 60 items in the list would be typically regarded by most Hong Kong speakers as slang (*juhk yúh* 俗語) rather than *chòu háu*. They are of interest in their own right, as they can be loosely grouped into a number of distinct sets. One set would include pig words, e.g. *jyù dàu* 豬兜 ('pig dish'), *jyù bìu* 豬標 ('pig dart'), *jyù màk* 豬嘜 ('pig mark/brand'); a set similar to taboo words in other languages, using animal categories (Leach 1964). Another group relates to words with phallic connotations, such as *bahn jìu* 笨蕉 ('stupid banana'), *bahn je* 笨蔗 ('stupid sugar cane') and *yaak jìu* 吔蕉 ('eat a banana').

A further grouping is composed of words relating to physical or mental handicap. In this category we have expressions such as *baahk chì* 白痴 ('plainly crazy'), *chì sin* 痴線 ('crazy'), *dài bì jái* 低B仔 ('low ability'), *dài nàhng* 低能 ('low ability'), and *yeuk ji jái* 弱智仔 ('weak intelligence boy').

Finally, yet another category perhaps embodies a typically Hong Kong distaste for 'cheapskates' in all their forms. Thus we have *jihn júng* 賤種 ('cheap species'), *jihn yàhn* 賤人 ('cheap person'), *jihn nàih* 賤泥 ('cheap soil') and *jihn gaak* 賤格 ('cheap character').

Orthographic obscenity and Cantonese taboo language

The claim that the five *chòu háu jih* 粗口字 discussed above be regarded as the core items in the Cantonese lexicon of obscenity can be supported in a number of ways. One way of approaching this issue, however, is by looking at the written form of the language. In the case of the obscene lexicon of the English (and the written use of words such as *fuck*, *cunt*, *prick*, etc.), the last thirty years have seen a considerable relaxation in films, literature and even lexicography. Today even the *Oxford English Dictionary* carries a number of entries for each of these words. Other dictionaries, such as the *Collins English Dictionary* include multiple entries for such words and their derivatives. Oxford also publishes a dictionary of modern English slang (Ayto and Simpson 1992). This has been a rather recent process; but in earlier times, dictionaries of 'vulgar language' had included such items in their word lists. These *chòu háu* characters in Cantonese, however, have never to our knowledge found their way into print outside pornographic contexts. They are certainly not recorded in dictionaries of Cantonese. Our research into the spoken language shows that in speech the acceptability of such language varies according to the gender, setting and context, but in writing the use of *chòu háu* has hitherto been taboo. When the vernacular is transcribed, the 'real' obscene characters are avoided in favour of orthographic euphemisms of various kinds.

One medium where clear examples of this can be found is that of comic books. The publishers of these books, no doubt fearing the wrath of the Television and Entertainments Licensing Authority (the TELA) and, perhaps, awed by the power of taboo linked to the written Chinese language routinely avoid the use of 'authentic' obscene characters through a variety of written devices. Table 4 below sets out a list of the most commonly-occurring euphemisms:

TABLE 4: The Five *Chòu Háu* 粗口 Characters and Their Euphemisms

'Authentic' character (plus Yale) and English	Euphemism (plus Yale) and English
屌 (*díu*, 'fuck')	小 (*síu*, small) 嗱 (*nàh*) 挑 (*tìu*, to shoulder) fuck (*fàk*) X (*ìksih*)
閪 (*chaht*, 'dick')	七 (*chàt*, seven) Q (*kìu*) X (*ìksih*)
鳩 (*gàu*, 'cock')	鳩 (*kàu*, pigeon) 九 (*gáu*, nine) 狗 (*gáu*, dog) Q (*kìu*) X (*ìksih*)
撚 (*lán*, 'prick')	能 (*lán*) Q (*kìu*) X (*ìksih*)

閪 (*hài*, 'cunt').	西 (*sài*, west)
	Q (*kìu*)
	X (*ìksih*)

The question then begged is obviously this: if these authentic characters simply do not appear in dictionaries or in any other kind of print media, where then do they occur, and how are they recognisable as the real thing? The brief answer to the first part of the question is that they appear as graffiti, inscribed in toilets and on the seat backs of buses, and in the halls of juvenile courts, and as (the perhaps age-graded) secret language of schoolchildren in Hong Kong. The answer to the second part of the question is that one can tell that these characters are the 'real thing', because they are precisely the ones that are banned. While there is no list of forbidden characters and censorship in Hong Kong is context-sensitive to a degree, it seems likely that any comic book printing these characters would be classed as Category III under the Obscene Articles Ordinance (i.e. banned as obscene). However Hong Kong comics do use a range of graphic euphemisms.

In Table 4 above, *X*, *K* and *Q* are generic euphemisms, and take their value from the context, like the use of màt as in *màah màt fàahn* 麻乜煩. They can be pronounced as characters in their own right (*bàa kèi bai* 巴K閪, *bàa ìks bai* 巴X閪) reflecting actual speech forms. But in the case of *X léih lóuh móu!* X你老母(see figure 1, below) we are not being asked to imagine a triad member in full cry actually using a euphemistic form of this kind. A second category are the simplified versions of the full obscene character, with the 'gate' character removed and the 'phonetic' standing for the whole character. These simplified characters to an extent represent the pronunciation of the taboo character. Alternatively, characters with identical or related pronunciations are employed. Again these may reflect actual euphemistic speech patterns, or may simply be graphic euphemisms.

Euphemism can be defined as the replacement of a charged or taboo form by a relatively neutral one. As such it is a complex form of representation, since it both refers and avoids referring. It is easy to make fun of the futility of graphic conventions such as 'f---'; these euphemistic devices however, if nothing else, pay symbolic tribute to the established hierarchy of values (see Figures 1 and 2 on pages 372 and 373 overleaf).

In this connection it is important to stress the extent to which both the official world of government bodies, teachers' associations, concerned social workers etc. and the media underworld of lurid comics are operating with a shared value-system and within shared norms. In part this shared value system is the result of the coercive powers available to the TELA and the Obscene Articles Tribunal. The comics have to suppress the five forbidden characters in order to stay on the right side of the law. But there is nonetheless a shared cultural understanding between these two sides of society so commonly juxtaposed. There is an agreed hierarchy of linguistic values, and this consensus extends to the realm of ideology. Hong Kong comics often depict the dangers of dabbling in the occult, the risks for women of hanging around triads, the dangers of promiscuous sex, the possibility that pornography can lead to rape. Much popular culture of a melodramatic kind has the moral ambiguity of the fairy-tale. Little Red Riding Hood is a warning to young girls not to stray from the path, but it draws its excitement from the fear and danger. Beneath this overtly subversive sub-culture of triad glitz and sexual provocation is a conventional morality of sin, degradation and fall.

BAD LANGUAGE, BAD BOYS, AND THE BOUNDARIES OF POPULAR SPEECH

As a follow-up to the questionnaire research which yielded our survey data, we conducted in 1993 face-to-face interviews with five schoolboys aged between fourteen and fifteen years old. The five boys were all from lower-class backgrounds, were living in public housing estates and attending low-prestige secondary schools. They were recruited for the interviews by a student at the university, who was given the task of finding five lads who had reputations as 'bad boys' and who readily admitted to speaking *chòu háu*. The boys in question Big Ear, Leon, Meatball, Mikey and Raymond, were interviewed about their use of *chòu háu* and their perception of its role in their world, i.e. the world of housing estates, video games parlours, fifth-rate schools, and as it turned out, the world of gang-fights and triads.

Their experience varied somewhat. Generally, they all claimed that they learned to swear in school, as early as P6 (Primary 6), from friends and classmates. They also learned to read and write *chòu háu* from friends, comics, from graffiti in buses, toilets and in the juvenile courts. They used this language in conversation, for fun, with 'bad boy' friends, and when they were angry or in a bad mood. Usually they would not use *chòu háu* to parents or teachers, though Mikey claimed that he would use it with anyone he was angry with. They also reported that the girls in their gang also used *chòu háu* and accepted the use of this language by the girls. According to Big Ear, it was 'not a

FIGURE 1: Depiction of a Triad Fight in a Hong Kong Comic (Chinese original)[3]

FIGURE 2: Depiction of a Triad Fight (English translation)

problem ... [as] we're all bad people'. What emerged very clearly from the interviews was that these five boys all regarded themselves a 'bad boys'. In their view, 'good' standards in their school did not use this kind of language; highly educated people, like office workers and lawyers, did not use bad language either. Or at least, so they thought; Mikey and Meatball, on reflection, were unsure because '[w]e don't know any people like that, we're only guessing'.

On the question of censorship, three of the boys actually favoured more censorship of the media, asserting that the government should intervene to censor the mass media. Mikey was against all censorship, but Meatball was in favour of censorship of sex, but asserted that violence and bad language should be left alone.

Towards the end of the interview, Mikey admitted his own membership of a triad society (and the membership of the other four boys as well), and went on to give an explanation of the use of in the context of the triad societies activities in secondary school:

Dòsou dòu haih gànjó hàkséhwúi sìn góng ...dòsou haih óhdeih lìgo lìhngéi hohkdàk góng lè, tùngsèuhng dòu haih yahpjó hàksèhwúi sìn góng ge. Léih póutùng yàt go hohksàang móuh màt dím m$hwúih góng ...

多數都係跟咗黑社會先講...多數係我哋呢個年紀學得講呢，通常都係入咗黑社會先講嘅。你普通一個學生冇乜點唔會講...

In most cases those who use [*chòu háu*] are triad members ... most of those of our age who have learnt it usually also joined triad societies. Your ordinary students don't have to use these words.

The view from 'housing project hill' in Hong Kong seems fairly straightforward. *Chòu háu* marks out the 'bad boys' and 'bad girls' from the good students in school. It is the language of the their group, it is the language of their gang, it is the language of their jokes and insults (for comparison, see Labov 1962, on black street gangs in south-central Harlem). But what is more serious, more damning in a social sense perhaps, is that for these boys the use of *chòu háu* is effectively a badge of membership in a triad society, one stage away from pricking your finger and having your name 'written down' by a triad big brother.

With this social self-stigmatisation comes a parallel psychological effect. All the boys interviewed showed few traces of self-esteem or self-worth. They were, in their own minds, 'bad' children, 'bad' students and general 'bad people'. And this sense of their badness was confirmed to themselves by their membership of a triad society. They had all joined the society at the age of eleven, when entering the F1 class in secondary school, in order to get protection from bullies and other gang members. According to currently available statistics, crimes by young people are now reaching unprecedented heights. Much of this crime is associated with schoolchildren placed in the Band 5 category schools in Hong Kong (17,032 in 1993), who are classed as 'academically low achievers' and 'culturally deprived' (Fitzpatrick 1994:10).

We might now attempt to evaluate the use of *chòu háu* amongst this group. In our earlier paper (Bolton and Hutton 1995), we quoted a high-ranking officer in the Hong Kong police force explaining that 'triad language swims in a sea of *chòu háu*'. For Big Ear, Leon, Meatball, Mikey and Raymond the use of *chòu háu* in their world is a marker of class membership, specifically criminal-class membership. It is the language of their comic books, their video parlours, their street life; it is the language of their 'big brothers' who run the street gangs of school kids. This equation is not absolute; Mikey pointed out that not all students who use *chòu háu* are triad members. For these boys, *chòu háu*, has a clear *integrative* function; it is the language of bad boys, and also bad girls, though Meatball pointed out that in their group the girls use less *chòu háu* than the boys. When asked if they would let their sisters use bad language, they replied that if they were 'bad' girls they would allow it, but if they were still good girls, they would not. It also has an *aggressive* function: it is the deadly serious language of gang confrontations, street fights, and perhaps the occasional 'chopping'.

What seems most ironic about this view of themselves is the expectation that the 'good people' of Hong Kong - the 'office workers' and 'lawyers' - would never swear themselves or use *chòu háu*. As we indicated earlier, our belief is that Cantonese triad slang, street slang, and even swearwords, are a source of lexical innovation throughout the Cantonese vernacular generally, and throughout all classes of society. What will vary however is the range of contexts in which this occurs, and the frequency with which individual speakers will use this language.

What Mikey and the boys fail to recognise, with good reason, is that their speech, their *chòu háu*, their triad jargon and their slang may often provide the lead for the language of the middle class and the rich. The survey of the 'good' schoolboys shows that the language the 'bad' boys see as a mark of their own stigmatisation is actually the common property of schoolchildren, or at least schoolboys, across Hong Kong. An informant in the legal department of the Hong Kong government told us that lawyers had taken to expressing their frustration at the slow pace of the legal machinery through the regressive use of the phrase 'delay no more', which, pronounced in Hong Kong English, sounds not unlike *díu léih lóuhmóu* 閪你老母. The 'bad' boys are living in a social time-warp when they speculate that office workers and lawyers are *chòu háu* free.

Allen, commenting on the rise of New York slang between 1850 and 1900 and the interaction of categories like 'public' and 'private' with social class, concludes (Allen 1993:32) 'that the socially constructed reality of city life was just as often negotiated from below as imposed from above.' For Mikey and the boys, the fact that their language use may be the driving force behind Hong Kong vernacular Cantonese is not evident; it is not transparent to them. They showed no signs of linguistic invention and did not have any particular idea or theories about where the language they used came from. For, while from the outside, from the point of view of a sociolinguist like Labov, it may seem that adolescent bad boys are in the vanguard of linguistic innovation, conscious linguistic creativity in Hong Kong is the domain of media personalities like the *mòuh lèih tàuh* masters Lam Hoi Fung and Got Man Fai on Commercial Radio, and Stephen Chau, the film actor and media personality. Mikey and the boys are the embodiment of social passivity; they lack the assertive anti-identity of Labov's urban Black youths.

For the other social classes in the territory, the street slang of TV and movie culture has now entered the 'mainstream' of Hong Kong slang. Phrases like *kàu léui* 媾女 ('to chat up or chase girls'), *chyun* 吋 ('stuck-up, arrogant') and *giu gài* 叫雞 ('to go to a prostitute'), although risqué, are widely used and accepted. The *mòuh lèih tàuh* of the 1990s, according to some sources, originated in the street life of Hong Kong's less privileged citizens. But whatever its social origins, it became for a while the property of music radio and the Hong Kong film industry, and was accepted as a local 'nonsense speak'. While this variety of local slang left many educators and moralists aghast, it was a source of general amusement in the population as a whole, again *regressive*, again 'naughty but nice'. Behind *mòuh lèih tàuh* is *chòu háu*, since much of the word-play hinted at or played with suggestive puns, but in a way that escaped the conventional grading of slang from the colloquial to the obscene. An example of this from a list of fashionable slang published in *Next* magazine is the *mòuh lèih tàuh* expression *dáan ... léih go sàhn* 蛋...你個晨 ('egg your morning!') which parodies slang constructions such as *góng léih go séi yàhn tàuh* 講你個死人頭, *chòu háu* 'echo-expressions' such as *díng léih go fai* 頂 你個肺 (itself only recently acceptable in the media) and of course *chòu háu* itself.

An example of a *mòuh lèih tàuh* dialogue is the following from the Steven Chau film *Fight back to school* (*tòuh hohk wài lùhng* 逃學威龍), involving a search for a lost pistol:

> -- kéuih haih yàt jì sihn lèuhng ge chèung!
> -- chèung dòu yáuh sihn lèuhng?
> -- ngóh jì chèung bún sing sihn lèuhng gà ma, jeui pa lohk hái dì
> waaih hohk sàang sáu seuhng...

> -- 佢係一支善良嘅鎗!
> -- 鎗都有善良?
> -- 我支鎗本性善良㗎嘛，最怕落喺啲壞學生手上...

> -- It's a very kind pistol.
> -- Is there such as thing as a kind pistol?
> -- Its nature is kind. But I'm afraid that it will fall into the hands of
> bad schoolboys...

Behind this lurks not only the phallic associations of 'pistol', and the things that bad boys might do with it if they got hold of it, but also the familiar opening line of the *Three Character Classic* (*sàam jih gìng* 三 字經): *yàhn jì chò, sing bún sihn* 人之初，性本善. Thus both classical Chinese and *chòu háu* are 'behind' the word-play. *Mòuh lèih tàuh* 無 厘頭 plays with linguistic meaning and draws people into a set of puns and allusions that challenge conventional boundaries of what is proper and what is obscene. Unlike other forms of slang, its register is indeterminate, and it relies on hectic innovation and a sense of regressive spontaneity. It is also in this sense a parody of slang and of the devices of slang, including the punning 'sandwich' (the *kit hauh yúh* 歇後語 discussed in Baker 1991).

In Freud's discussion of humour (1905) the joke is, in effect, therapy for the dramatically socially mobile. It is a controlled regression which makes fun of unintentional slips of the tongue or behaviour and parallels psychoanalysis in that it aims to strip away layers of socialisation to get at some earlier, more primary, more authentic self. That self is a suppressed ethnic (Jewish) identity: vibrant, sloppy, noisy, indecorous, vulgar. There is also an element of aggression in the joke-telling process, since anyone who gets the joke and laughs has come out (or been 'outed') from the social closet. People are not neatly divided into the securely socially mobile and the insecurely socially mobile; the pressure in joke telling is both on the teller to solicit the laugh, to make the successful seduction and on the listener to understand and to allow the regression. When we laugh at a dirty joke or understand innuendo we are revealed as co-conspirators in the silence surrounding sex, death, or the particular taboo in question. This idea of a controlled slip of a tongue, a regressive performance can be applied to *mòuh lèih tàuh*.

We can think of *chòu háu* as a source of energy, an unspoken driving force not only behind *mòuh lèih tàuh* but Hong Kong slang in general. The schoolgirl who calls someone a *pì kèi* ('PK') is both avoiding using the 'full expression' *pùk gàai* 仆街 (one which lies on the borderline between *chòu háu* and slang) and drawing on its 'naughtiness'. *Chòu háu* serves as a badge of stigmatisation (but also of macho meanness) for the 'bad boys', the 49 junior triads; but for the middle-class Yuppie it symbolises social mobility. *Chòu háu* is no joke for Mikey and the boys; their experience of it is 'heavy'. But for the naughty boys of the elite secondary school it serves as much as anything as a mark of their social mobility. For these boys *chòu háu* is literally a laughing matter.

A strong underlying assumption behind modern linguistics is known as uniformitarianism (Sampson 1980:24). This basically is the belief that the same processes and forces are at work in all languages at all times, and in general is a working assumption about linguistic change (Labov 1994:23):

> To the extent that this principle depends on uniformities in the physiological basis of language, it must be correct, since there is no indication of differences between the linguistic past and the present in this respect. But the uniformitarian principle is more problematic where social differences are concerned, and we must be alert to its limitations...

Andersson and Trudgill seem however to apply this uniformitarian idea to the 'problematic' level of social differences: (1990:194-195): 'There is no reason to [...] claim that bad language threatens our society and civilisation. "Bad language" has always been part of our language and will be so in the future'.

Like many fundamental tenets of linguistics, the uniformitarian principle implies an attack on ordinary or 'lay' view of language. For example, in the face of the growing acceptance of bad language in the media, conservative critics often assert that standards are declining. Bad language is taking over and corrupting previously 'clean' aspects of public and private discourse. Harris (1990) accepts that bad language is spreading into new realms, but laments this as heralding a loss of its power to demarcate clearly distinct public and private spheres. So both Harris and conservative critics take a basically non-uniformitarian view of the question of bad language; but for Harris the spread of this language is not a symptom of its increasing power but of its waning potency. This is the logic behind Lenny Bruce's position: the more we repeat racial slurs, the faster they lose their power to shock and hurt. The uniformitarian linguist might predict that other racial epithets will arise in their place.

There are therefore here three basic views. One states that with the spread of bad language there is a rising tide of moral corruption; the second that with the spread of bad language there is an entropic decline in its ability to shock and an either desirable or undesirable decline in its taboo value. The third is that all societies have swearing and taboos and in some general sense there is little that can be done to change the situation, because this is the quasi-natural order of things. This being so, we should not get worked up about bad language. But on closer inspection the uniformitarian view looks a little like the entropic view, since if 'lay' speakers were to adopt this sanguine approach to bad language ('all societies have swearing, so what's the big deal?'), then clearly the nature of swearing would change. This is the complicating factor in any discussion of taboo and bad language. For the most part, linguists, even sociolinguists, tend to dismiss linguistic taboos on swearing as primitive or quaint. Sociolinguistic models are overwhelmingly 'consensus' rather than 'conflict' models implying uniform social attitudes, and they parallel a model of society found in Parsonian structural-functionalist sociology (Williams 1992:204), where individuals are depicted as in effect 'judgmental dopes' without insight into their own actions and beliefs (Heritage 1984:27). Anthropologists in recent years have, by contrast, become increasingly sensitive to their own impact on their object of study, and the 'new anthropologists' (Barley 1983, Geertz 1988, Sodusta 1993) take some pains to foreground their roles as 'professional strangers' (Agar 1980).

The complication comes when sociolinguists present a glossary of taboo language, as we have in this article by printing the 'obscene' Cantonese characters. The situation is rather as if an anthropologist, on being told that a piece of land was sacred, were to rush over and trample about on it. The regressive pleasure in playing with bad language should not obscure from view the fact that it remains a serious business for those who are still caught up 'in the culture'.

ACKNOWLEDGEMENTS

The authors would like to thank Mr. Wesley Wong for his sterling help with the early questionnaire research reported on in this chapter. We wish to thank Ms. Cynthia Mok of the Department of English, The University of Hong Kong, for her valuable assistance in administering interviews, and in the preparation of tables for this paper. Our thanks also to Ms. Katherine Chen for additional editorial assistance.

NOTES

1 The Yale transcription used here to transcribe Cantonese is one of many competing systems. The version used in this article recognises six tones: high (*màn*), mid-rising (*mán*), mid-level (*man*), low-level (*mahn*), low-rising (*máhn*), and low falling (*màhn*). In this article we transcribe *a* in open-syllable by *aa*.

2 The term 'lazy pronunciation' reflects a normative view of sound changes currently in progress in Hong Kong. These changes involve, for example, the substitution of *l* for initial *n* in words like *néih* 你 ('you') and *g* for *gw* in words like *gwok* 國 ('country').

3 The illustration on page 372 is taken from a popular 'triad' comic-book, *Gú Waahk Jái* ('Teddy Boy'), page 7, volume 1, in the 1993 compendium version. In a newspaper interview in 1994, 'Cowman' the owner-publisher of *Gú Waahk Jái* asserted that 'most of my readers are night people - bad people'. But in spite of this disclaimer, Cowman's publications seem to be reaching a much wider adolescent audience; in just one year (1995-1996), three films based on the *Gú Waahk Jái* comics have appeared in Hong Kong and have gained a popular following. Another of Cowman's triad comics *Gú Waahk N éui* ('Teddy Girl') has also been turned into a film.

REFERENCES CITED

Agar, Michael
1980 The Professional Stranger. Academic Press: New York.
Ayto, John and Simpson, John
1992 The Oxford Dictionary of Modern Slang. Oxford: Oxford University Press.
Allen, Irving Lewis
1993 The City in Slang: New York Life and Popular Speech. New York: Oxford University Press
Andersson, Lars and Trudgill, Peter
1990 Bad Language. Oxford: Blackwell.
Baker, Hugh
1991 The English Sandwich: Obscenity, Punning and Bilingualism in Hong Kong Cantonese. *In* Interpreting Culture through Translation. A Festschrift for D. C. Lau. Roger Ames, ed. Pp. 37-58. Hong Kong: The Chinese University Press.
Barley, Nigel
1983 The Innocent Anthropologist. London: Penguin.
Bolton, Kingsley and Hutton, Christopher
1995 Bad and Banned Language: The Censorship of the Cantonese Vernacular and Colonial Language policy in Hong Kong. Language in Society 24: 159-186.
Bruce, Lenny
1972 The Essential Lenny Bruce. John Cohen, ed. London: Macmillan.
Clavell, James
1981 Noble House. London: Hodder and Stoughton.
Coates, Jennifer
1986 Women, Men and Language. 2nd edition. London: Longman.
Davis, Hayley
1989 What Makes Bad Language Bad? Language and Communication 9: 1-9.
Douglas, Mary
1991[1966] Purity and Danger: An Analysis of the Concepts of Pollution and Taboo. London: Routledge: London.
Epstein, Joseph
1994 Raw, Ribald and Flip. Review of the Random House Historical Dictionary of American Slang, vol. 1. Times Literary Supplement (November) No. 478:9-10.
Fitzpatrick, Liam
1994 Dead-End Kids: Hong Kong's Alienated Youth. Eastern Express Weekend (1-2 October):9-13.
Flexner, S.
1976 I Hear America Talking. New York: Van Nostrand.

Freud, Sigmund
    1905 Der Witz und seine Beziehung zum Unbewussten. Vienna: Deuticke.
Geertz, Clifford
    1988 Works and Lives: The Anthropologist as Author. Stanford: Stanford
        University Press.
Glain, Steve
    1994 Korea's Angel Dick may not be Nastu Enough to Repel this Invasion.
        Asian Wall Street Journal (May 19):1, 7.
Harris Roy
    1990 Lars Porsena Revisited. In The State of the Language. Christopher
        Ricks and Leonard Michaels, eds. Pp. 411-421. London: Faber and
        Faber.
Heritage, John
    1984 Garfinkel and Ethnomethodology. London: Polity Press.
Jay, Timothy
    1992 Cursing in America: A Psychological Study of Dirty Language in the
        Courts, in the Movies, in the Schoolyards and on the Streets.
        Benjamins: Philadelphia.
Krakinsowksi, Leah
    1994 Space Invaders and the Rapid Heart Beat. Eastern Express (23
        February):5.
Labov, William
    1972 Language in the Inner City: Studies in the Black English Vernacular.
        Oxford: Blackwell.
    1994 Principles of Linguistic Change. Oxford: Blackwell.
Leach, Edmund
    1964 Anthropological Aspects of Language: Animal Categories
                and Verbal Abuses. In New Directions in the Study of
        Language. E. Lenneberg, ed. Pp. 23-63. Cambridge: MIT Press.
Lent, John.
    1993a The Renaissance of Taiwan's Cartoon's Arts. Asian Culture (Asian
        Pacific Culture) Quarterly 21:1-15.
Mosher, Stacy
    1994 Reading the Righteous Brothers. Eastern Express (12-13 February):
        4. Next Magazine.
Sampson, Geoffrey
    1980 Schools of Linguistics: Competition and Evolution. London:
        Hutchinson.
Sodusta, Jesucita
    1993 Into the Field: Applied Anthropology and the Dilemmas of
        Development. In Asia's Cultural Mosaic. Grant Evans, ed. Pp.
        324-344. New York: Prentice Hall.
Trudgill, Peter
    1983 Sociolinguistics: An Introduction to Language and Society. London:
        Penguin.

Tse Sou-Mee and Yu Tao-Lin
  1980 Semantic Functions of the Allegedly Obscene Particles "X" in Cantonese. Maledicta: The International Journal of Verbal Aggression 4:45-51. [Second author's name is a pseudonym]
Tsang, Annette
  1994 Breaking through the 'Door'. Underground newspapers at the Chinese University put freedom of expression to the test. Varsity (Department of Journalism and Communication at the University of Hong Kong) 4:22-24.
Williams, Glyn
  1992 Sociolinguistics: A Sociological Critique. London: Routledge.

GLOSSARY

a màh 亞

Bāk fòng yàhn 北方人

báau yí jek 胞衣跡

baai sàhn 拜神

chān 親

Chìu Jàu lóu 潮洲佬

Chìu Jàu Wá 潮洲話

Chìu Jàu yàhn 潮洲人

Chè Gùng 車公

chèuhng sàam 長衫

chì gà 孻家

chì tóng 祠堂

Chìng Chùhng Gun 青松觀

chìng lèuhng chàh 清涼茶

Chìng Mìhng 清明

chìng yiht 清熱

chòu háu 粗口

chóh yuht 坐月

dàam fàan máaih séui 擔幡買水

daaih luhk yàhn 大陸人

Daaih Wòhng Yèh 大王爺

dākyi 得意

ding 丁

ding ngūk 丁屋

doi móuh 代母

Fā Muhk Nàahn 花木蘭

fā paau 花炮

Fèi Pahng 肥彭

fōhng 房

Fūkgin yàhn 福建人

Fūkjàu yàhn 福州人

fùng chè 風車

fùng séui 風水

fùng séui lòh gàang 風水羅更

fùng séui sin sàang 風水先生

gaisìhng 繼承

gām fā 金花

géi jí 杞子

gieu tsoi [H] 韮菜

Gùn Yàm 觀音

Gùn Yàm Duhng Sàan 觀音洞山

Gwàan Dai 關帝

gwáilóu 鬼佬

gwáilóu gwái jit 鬼佬鬼節

gwāi lìhng gōu 龜苓膏

gwāt yuhk [C] gud ngyug [H] 骨肉

gwokgà 國家

gwóngdùngwá 廣東話

Gwóngdùng yàhn 廣東人

Gwóngfú yàhn 廣府人

Gwóngfújàu 廣府州

Gwóngfúwá 廣府話

Gwóngjàu yàhn 廣州人

Gwóngjàuwá 廣州話

Haakgà yàhn 客家人

Haakgà 客家

Hahmùhn yàhn 廈門人

hái fù 下夫

Hàuh Wòhng 侯王

hei 氣

hei gùng sì fú 氣功師傅

Hèung Góng Yàhn 香港人

hó néuih gu léuhng gà 好女顧兩家

333

Hohklóu 鶴佬

hohng 行

Hóiluhkfùng 海陸豐

hóu kèihgwaai ge 好奇怪嘅

jingfú 政府

jiu 醮

jóu 祖

jóu ngūk 祖屋

jùngmàhn 中文

jùngyèung 中原

jyuht doih 絕代

jyuht fòhng néuih 絕房女

kàuh chim 求籤

lèuhng chàh 涼茶

Máhn 閩

màhn juhk 民族

mahn máih pó 問米婆

màhn móuh 文武

mòuh lèih tàu 無厘頭

mòuh yàhn mòuh maht
無人無物

mùhn yuht 滿月

néih haih māty éh yàhn
你喺乜嘢人

ngóh haih Gwóngdùng yàhn
我喺廣東人

ngoi deih yàhn 外地人

ngoi sáang yàhn 外省

ngoi ga néuih 外嫁女

ngòn lùhng 安龍

pìnmùhn sàanyi 偏門生意

Póutūngwá 普通話

pùih yuht 陪月

Sīk SīkYùhn 嗇嗇園

sáangsìhngwá 省城話

sai màhn 細民

sài yàhn 西人

sài yī 西醫

sehk gùng 石公

sehk móuh 石母

séi hei 殺氣

Seuhnghói yàhn 上海人

síu sok màhn juhk 少數民族

sūk pòh [C] sug po [H] 叔婆

Tàahm Gùng 潭公

téhnggà yàhn 蛋家人

tìn 天

tìnhái 天下

Tin Hauh 天后

tòhng 堂

tóu deih gūng 土地公

tùhng hèung 同鄉

tùhng sih 懂事

Wòhng Daaih Sin 黃大仙

wúigún 會館

yám chàh 飲茶

yām hei 陰氣

yām ngáahn 陰眼

yàn yùhn sehk 姻緣石

yāt gun douh 一貫道

yāt, yih, sàam, hùng luhk dāng
一二三紅綠燈

yíh chān kahp chān 以親及親

yúh 語

yùh nàahn 盂蘭

yùhn hei 元氣

CONTRIBUTORS

Kingsley Bolton is a lecturer in Linguistics at the Hong Kong University.

Selina Ching Chan is a lecturer in anthropology at the National University of Singapore.

Eliza Chan recently completed her M. Phil. in anthropology at The Chinese University of Hong Kong.

Christina, Cheng Miiu-bing, recently completed her Ph.D. in comparative literature at Hong Kong University.

Cheng Sea Ling recently completed her M. Phil. in anthropology at Hong Kong University.

Grant Evans is Reader in anthropology at Hong Kong University.

Gregory Eliyu Guldin is a Professor of anthropology at the Pacific Lutheran University, S.A.

Christopher Hutton is a Lecturer in linguistics at Hong Kong University.

Graeme Lang is a Senior Lecturer in sociology at City University of Hong Kong.

Rosanna Lilley is a Post-doctoral Fellow in anthropology at Macquarie University, Australia.

Diana Martin is currently working for the Hong Kong Federation of Youth Groups.

Philip Robertson works in the Centre for Media Resources at Hong Kong University.

Janet Lee Scott is a lecturer in anthropology at the Hong Kong Baptist University.

Maria Tam is a lecturer in anthropology at The Chinese University of Hong Kong.